THE
ENCYCLOPEDIA OF
GARDENING

THE ENCYCLOPEDIA OF GARDENING

General Editor Stanley Russell

BOOK CLUB ASSOCIATES
LONDON

CONTENTS

General Editor Stanley Russell

Contributors:

Kenneth A Beckett
Ann Bonar
Janet Browne
Oliver Dawson
William 'Jock' Davidson
Roger DuBern
Ray Edwards
Donald Farthing
Xenia Field
H G Witham Fogg
Claire Glasspoole
Geoff Hamilton
Jack Harkness
Roy Hay
Bill Heritage
George Hyde
Peter McHoy
Frances Perry
David Squire
Tony Venison

This edition published 1981 by
Book Club Associates
By arrangement with Octopus Books Limited
59 Grosvenor Street
London W1

© 1981 Octopus Books Limited

ISBN 0 7064 1098 X

Produced by
Mandarin Publishers Limited
22a Westlands Road,
Quarry Bay, Hong Kong

Printed in Hong Kong

Introduction

Conventionally, an encyclopedia works its way alphabetically through the mass of information it has to impart. This book takes a more original approach: for ease of reference, many chapters contain alphabetical lists, but the chapters are arranged in the logical sequence of events associated with making and maintaining a garden.

Gardening is not, in itself, an alphabetical subject. It is a composite, made up of many facets, each with an absorbing interest. It is highly technical, but in many ways very simple, and anyone can join in. The learner can quickly become an expert, yet the expert is always finding something new to learn. That is one of its many fascinations.

If you wish to start a garden, the logical approach is to work out a skeleton programme and decide what you want in the way of style, plants and equipment. With these basics settled, the outline ideas can be developed and the overall plan sub-divided so that there is a clearer idea of the layout and the types of plants required: grass, shrubs, flower borders, perhaps a pool, fruit, vegetables, and so on. Finally, comes the 'nuts and bolts' operation, choosing the plants.

This is precisely the plan on which this book has been devised. But do not imagine, if you have an established garden, that the first section is not for you. Every garden may be changed in part every year, not only to maintain its freshness and air of surprise but, equally important, to reduce the risk of weak and diseased plants that is the price sometimes paid for growing certain plants continually in the same place. There is information in this book to satisfy the most earnest gardener seeking change and knowledge.

Gardening is an enjoyable and fascinating hobby, and one which creates its own camaraderie. Most gardening is done in the open, and for preference on dry and fairly warm days. And immense pleasure can be derived from gardening in a greenhouse which, with a little heat, can provide colour the year round, plus a greater choice of plants. And all within a congenial atmosphere.

A patio, town or roof garden can produce enormous dividends, yet entail little of the day-to-day maintenance associated with conventional gardening. Even a windowbox can offer a vista of colour. And where is the household that can resist the charm of a few houseplants?

But although it is so rewarding, gardening does impose its disciplines. The greatest expert has to perform the same duties as the tyro, and must do so at certain set times; near the end of the book will be found a comprehensive list of the main tasks for each of the 12 months — but remember that the timings of any operation can only be approximate. Climate, soil and local conditions govern the exact timing, and seasons can vary by a fortnight or more in different parts of the country and from one year to another.

In addition, at the end there is a glossary translating over 350 technical definitions, together with a comprehensive index.

Every one of the contributors to this book is an acknowledged expert, with many years of practical experience, and known throughout the gardening world. This book must therefore rank as one of the most authoritative of its kind.

Section One

Planning and Maintenance

The first essential in starting a garden, whether beginning from builder's rubble or reorganizing what was left by the previous occupier, is to decide what you want to do with it. Unless you are very lucky in acquiring one that has been well maintained, and is to your liking, you are almost certain to want to make changes.

This opening section, therefore, deals with the spadework necessary for conceiving ideas and, as it were, getting them off the ground. It presents a logical, easy-to-follow sequence. First we show you how to plan, both in your mind and on paper: the simple facets of design and using (or discarding) existing amenities.

The theoretical approach settled, we then embark on the practical aspect: how to turn ideas into realities.

You will need tools, so there is an adequate list of implements and their purposes. No garden needs every tool on the market; our selective list will help you to choose those most appropriate to your needs.

The next step is to decide on the *kind* of garden you want. Shall it be purely a social amenity (and perhaps even include the luxury touches of lighting and moving water in the form of a pond or fountain), a leisure area affording the delights of colour and perfume with a minimum of effort on your part, or do you want a workhorse of a garden, earning its keep by providing the family with vegetables and fruit?

Whatever you decide to have, there are basic conditions common to all types of garden, and which you must fulfil if you are to derive the greatest enjoyment — and, in turn, to be certain that your work reaps its due reward.

The lists of musts and must-nots can be frightening, but aided by the specially selective chapters in this section, dealing with one situation at a time, you will find that your task of establishing your garden is much easier than it may appear at first.

We explain how to reduce the strain on heart, lungs and muscles with our chapter on labour saving; this will help you to deal with the fundamentals of gardening life: design, easily-operated tools and other equipment, and the chemical aids (whether for protection, production or destruction) that modern science can offer.

We show you how to take care of your greatest asset, your soil, by improving it and maintaining it to get the greatest productivity from it. And we explain how to deal with weeds, pests and diseases (but please absorb our cautionary note that some weeds have their uses, and many insects are wholly beneficial).

Having thus set you on the road to an established garden, the section ends logically by showing how to prolong the usefulness of your plants by discussing the various methods of propagation (to increase and maintain stocks) and pruning (to ensure that they are always, in every sense, in good shape).

From this solid base you will be able to branch out into the way in which you want the garden to reflect your own personality and requirements, and there is an abundant harvest of ideas in the section on special garden features, beginning on page 58.

Planning and design

Attractive gardens do not just grow — they are planned. They are the result of a careful analysis of the site, the problems and the assets that even the most ordinary garden undoubtedly possesses. Whether you have a garden of several acres in the country, or a town house with little more than a backyard, a beautiful garden can be created by thoughtful design and the wise use of plants to suit soil and site.

Whether starting from scratch where the builders left off, or taking over an existing garden, look at it with the long-term in mind. If patience is short, there are ways of quickly achieving impact and colour (see The Impatient Gardener, pages 60 – 63); but it is no substitute for an overall plan.

The urge to make a start with planting or construction must be constrained. A garden is as permanent as the home it surrounds, so it makes no sense to lay it out hurriedly. And planning can be just as exciting as doing the job; usually it's a lot less effort!

Assessing the garden

Before spade is put to soil, or pen to paper, spend time quietly *assessing what you have* — in terms of space, surroundings, and any existing planting. If you can take advantage of any natural assets you will save both time and money, and the garden may look more natural into the bargain.

Take a long look at your plot and decide exactly what is worth preserving. Make full use of the beauty and grace of trees. But unless there are restrictions on their removal (check with your landlord or local council) be on your guard against keeping trees that are growing too near the house, denying it light and perhaps threatening the foundations. Dispense with trees that interfere with a desirable view, and those that are ugly by reason of their habit or age. Other valuable features to cherish may include a wall of warm brick, a stone outcrop, a stream, or a bank that would welcome a rock garden.

A pleasing distant view should be treasured, and if possible enhanced, perhaps by planting trees or groups of shrubs to frame it.

Listing requirements
Only rarely are well-designed gardens planned in the head. Write down a list of features and functions you expect from your garden.

Set out the features that are important to you, such as a patio, terrace, rock garden, pool, play area, or pergola. Then list the buildings or utility features you need to incorporate — such as a shed, greenhouse, summerhouse, storage tank or bunker, compost bin, or dustbin.

A second list should contain broad planting categories that interest you — lawns, trees, shrubs, herbaceous border, roses, fruit or vegetables, for instance.

Don't get carried away. If you try to introduce too many elements the garden will look 'bitty'.

Even a tiny front garden benefits from suitable small trees and shrubs. The flowering cherry is Prunus Triloba, with a flowering currant in front

Practical considerations

There are some features that must be incorporated into the design even though they may not be attractive in their own right. Washing lines, garden sheds and sand-pits fall into this category. None of these need spoil a garden, but they do need thought at the planning stage.

Washing lines are an inevitable requirement, and custom usually demands at least one unsightly post, often stuck in a hole in the lawn. Such a site also means wet feet in winter. A far better choice is a radial drier, which occupies little space, can be slotted into concrete or paving near the house, and is easily removed after use.

Garden sheds may take up valuable space in a small garden, but are essential for storing tools and doing a little potting, unless there is room in the garage.

If possible it is best to place the shed in part of a specially designed utility area, which can also include the compost heap, bonfire site, and storage ground for things like stakes, pots, and bales of peat. Fencing off such an area only draws attention to it, so try to screen it naturally with shrubs, a group of bush fruits, or a weeping tree.

A greenhouse may not be a priority in a new garden, but no enthusiastic gardener is going to be without one for long. So, even if a greenhouse is no more than a pipe-dream, plan a site for it. This should be in an open position (or against a southerly wall for a lean-to), and away from the shade of trees or buildings, but not far from the house. This makes it easy (and cheaper) to connect up the main services — electricity will almost certainly be needed, and perhaps gas.

A greenhouse filled with plants and flowers is also an attractive sight, and there is no reason to try to hide it — especially as any screening inevitably robs it of some light.

Children make their own demands on a garden (see The Children's Garden, pages 84 – 85). Even if a play area can be incorporated near enough to the house for supervision, it's too much to expect children to keep out of the rest of the garden. So until they reach a responsible age, it's wise to provide a hard-wearing lawn that will stand up to games, to avoid using easily damaged plants close to it, and to fix a swing where it won't matter if a bare patch is created.

If the garden is large enough, a 'wild area' will give great enjoyment, especially if there are a few trees to climb and a dense shrubbery in which secret camps can be made.

Making the plan

Decide on your priorities first, then decide how much space you can afford to allow for each. Bear in mind that you must try to arrange them into a satisfying whole, taking into account proportion and balance. Do not allow any one feature to dominate, and match the 'weight' of one part with another, so that the garden will not look lop-sided. If you can 'hide' a section of garden, arranging a jutting peninsula of shrubs, or a group or ornamental trees, you will add interest and form to the garden.

Draw the plan on a sheet of plain paper, sketching the plot roughly to scale, and indicating north and south. Then outline your chosen features as general shapes. Things are unlikely to work out right first time, but with a little juggling and trial and error, you will be able to lay the foundations of a sound plan.

The detailed plan is drawn only after all the options have been explored (see page 16).

Right: planning and designing starts with a sketch outlining only the key features, reflecting the main priorities. This is one person's idea of how to deal with a long, narrow garden. The further developed, final plan appears on page 18 Below: use tall plants to soften the hard lines of a house, and to create pockets of interest

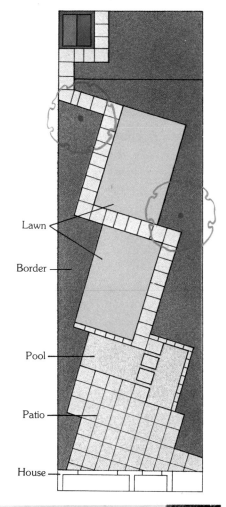

Lawn ◁

Border ——

Pool ——

Patio ——

House ——

The professional touch

There are certain techniques of planning that can be applied to lift your garden out of the ordinary. The first of these is to apply an axis — an invisible line but one that you should draw in on your sketch — to which main features are related.

Ideally, the axis should lead the eye to a compelling focal point — perhaps a distant view, a specimen tree, a statue or sundial, or a summerhouse. To run the axis parallel with the side boundaries, especially if the plot is narrow, only emphasizes its rigid rectangular shape. So experiment, trying an axis at varying angles.

Many excellent gardens have been designed on the theme of a geometrical shape — a circle, rectangle or hexagon. These may assume a severe formality which does not always suit the feel of the neighbourhood, but carefully handled can be very effective.

If an informal garden is the aim, the amateur is more likely to succeed with gentle (but not fussy) curves. These have a softening effect, harmonizing with the loose, flowing habit of most plants.

Don't regard straight lines as taboo. They can create a telling contrast in the most informal garden. And a rectangular shape is undoubtedly the best for a vegetable plot, where crops are grown in straight rows.

Making the most of slopes
Make full use of rises and falls in the ground — these can add much to the attraction of your design. A steep incline may have to be terraced, with retaining walls, to simplify cultivation and maintenance. Lesser slopes can be grassed, planted with groups of shrubs, or used happily as the site for a rock garden, with perhaps a running water feature.

A flat site should be given greater interest by creating changes of level. A long, narrow lawn, for instance, gains extra charm if the far half is either built up or lowered by as little as 15cm (6in), using a shallow paved step.

The soil excavated when a pool is dug can conveniently be used to form a neighbouring rock garden, roughly equal in height to the depth of the pool. Alternatively, if the end of the garden leads on to open ground, the excavated soil could be used to form a bank along the boundary, giving the impression that the garden extends into the open land beyond.

The function of paths
Paths must be sited with care, with strict attention to their purpose. If this is purely one of access — as from gate to front door, or rear door to kitchen garden — a direct path, with an all-weather surface,

is normally best. Curves are not only irritating when you are in a hurry (or your visitor is), but also invite short cuts across the lawn.

If, however, a path is meant for strolling and admiring the garden, slow curves are perfectly acceptable. There may even be a sharp bend, designed to intrigue. Paths can occupy a lot of space — growing space — so keep them to a minimum, especially if your plot is a small one.

Grass paths, provided the traffic is not too heavy and the turf is well-drained, are beautiful if well kept, but should never be narrow. Nor should any 'strolling' path, but a service path can be as

Paths can be both functional and decorative, as demonstrated by this fine example of crazy-paving in a traditional country garden. The slight twist towards the house adds interest and avoids the monotony of straight lines. Suitable edging plants also soften the hard edges

narrow as will permit the easy passage of a wheelbarrow.

The role of the lawn
Most gardens are built around the central feature of a lawn, and there are good reasons for this. A lawn creates a sense of space; it allows the eye to travel to distant features; its texture is pleasant to walk and sit upon; its fresh green is the perfect foil for surrounding plants; its smoothness allows the shadows of trees to

pattern it; and it is a perennially bright living carpet.

Although a level surface is essential for ball games, very gentle undulations can be attractive, but avoid small humps and hollows, which prevent even mowing. Whether you should turf or sow your lawn is a matter of personal priorities (see page 64).

Alternatives to a lawn

Not every garden, particularly if small or enclosed, is suited to a lawn, which needs sun and a free flow of air. The alternative is an artificial surface of some kind, which may be natural stone (most feasible if there is a quarry locally), reconstituted stone (of which good paving slabs are made), concrete (which can be attractive if tastefully handled), pebbles, gravel, or stone chippings.

Some of these materials can be used happily in association with each other: stone flags with chippings, or concrete relieved with pebbles, for example. An artificial surface has the advantage of being usable in all weathers — provided, of course, that concrete or paving set in mortar is slightly sloped to give efficient drainage (that is about 5cm in 3m or 2in in 10ft).

A hard surface also provides good standing for containers of any kind — tubs, urns, vases, troughs and pots which, planted up with colourful or graceful subjects, soften the severity of the floor (see pages 90–91). Although town gardens, in particular, lend themselves to the idea of container gardening, it can be used with effect anywhere, and in particular in an area adjoining the house.

The charm of water

Water adds life and charm to any garden, however small. Still water reflects the sky and surrounding planting, moving water offers sparkle and music. Ornamental fish are an unfailing source of interest, and a pool will soon attract a variety of wildlife — birds, dragonflies, frogs, and aquatic insects.

Plastic or rubberized liners make pool-building a simple matter (see page 27), but digging out the soil is still hard work! Submersible electric pumps efficiently circulate the water for fountain or waterfall (see page 81). Water-loving plants around the margin complete a delightful picture (see pages 172–73).

Remember, however, that a pool has dangers for very young children, who can drown in a mere few centimetres (inches) of water. Take no chances.

Above right: a good example of how bricks and plants can harmonize if planned with thought. Notice how even a tiny formal pool can add interest
Right: Setting rectangular paving slabs at a very slight angle softens an otherwise hard edge

The importance of aspect

Aspect has a marked effect on growing conditions, and must be taken into account when planning. It will also need to be considered when choosing a site for a greenhouse or a sitting-out area.

Ideally a patio should be an extension of the house — a place for outdoor living, with a door or doors opening on to it from the main living-room. Should it face south, the area will receive sun for most of the day. If the aspect is easterly, there will be little afternoon and no evening sun, while a westerly aspect means none till well on in the day. A northerly site will receive low sun only around mid-summer, in early morning or late evening.

When the aspect is unfavourable, it may still be useful to have a small paved area linked directly with the house, but the main leisure area should be sited elsewhere — though for convenience it should always be as near to the house as possible. Privacy may not be so easily secured as with an area adjoining the house, but suitable screening and planting can overcome the problem. A south-facing terrace or patio can become very hot in summer, but before you start planting shade trees, recall that there are many more weeks when the full warmth of the sun is welcome. Large sun umbrellas are a better solution.

Aspect also affects the positioning of flower beds, borders, and food plots. In shady areas suitable plants will have to be chosen, and if a colourful summer border is required, an open, sunny site must be found.

Where one side of the garden is much shaded, perhaps by a boundary wall or fence, the space would be better occupied by a path, with a narrow border along the boundary for climbers, and spring bulbs at their feet.

Some plants are tolerant of shade — a few even prefer it — and many of these are indicated in the plant selection guide in the last section of this book.

The use of 'island' beds cut into the lawn, or circumscribed by a path, takes plants away from the shade of fences, and makes it easier for the gardener to look after them.

A shady spot on the lawn is a blissful place in summer, and few will regret planting a tree to provide it. In a small garden, the tree should be of limited spread and height or it will become too dominant. It should also be chosen not only for its shade value, but for the beauty of its form, foliage, or blossom.

This colourful open-plan front garden proves that even a restricted space need not be dull or unimaginative. Roses are always popular, and have the added merit of being fairly child-proof in this road-side situation

The modern front garden

The design of a modern front garden is nearly always governed by the need for access to the front door and garage. Larger properties approached by a drive require car turning space. In all cases ample room should be allowed to reach the front door without having to pick one's way along an uneven or overgrown path. There should also be room to manoeuvre a car, and to work on it if necessary.

However strong the attraction of an open-plan front garden, a boundary fence or wall may be thought necessary or desirable. In rural areas an old-fashioned white picket fence can look charming. In urban districts a wall or close-boarded fence (see page 30) may be the best choice.

A front garden should be kept simple — an unfussy lawn (paving may be preferable if the garden is tiny), a border with a sweeping curve or cleanly cut flower beds, not too small, and an ornamental tree or two planted near the road, but not hiding the house. A front garden should offer a welcome, and what better finishing touch than flower-filled tubs by the door, a hanging basket, or a climber-clad porch?

Hedges

Hedges or boundary fences and walls will need careful thought. Often there are restrictions in the deeds of the property concerning boundary hedges, and usually you are responsible for only *part* of your boundary, so a chat with a neighbour may be necessary (and is a courtesy anyway) before uprooting existing hedges.

New gardeners often feel it their duty to enclose their plots with fences or hedges. They can, however, be an unnecessary undertaking. Although we all enjoy a measure of privacy, this can usually be satisfied by screening that part of the garden near the house, rather than the whole length of it. Omitting a fence or hedge can make a dramatic difference to the apparent size of a garden. It may be worth discussing with your neighbour the possibility of grubbing out a straggling dividing hedge to plant a variety of attractive shrubs along the common

boundary. If these are arranged in groups instead of a row, the result will be a vista of each other's garden you can both enjoy.

Few people need privacy in their front gardens, which, in any case, are more in the nature of show places to welcome visitors and attract the admiration of passers-by. A series of open-plan gardens frequently presents a far more pleasant prospect than a collection of hedged-in plots — a fact that has not escaped the designers of modern housing estates.

Fences and hedges are sometimes essential to keep animals either in or out of the garden. Fencing is increasingly expensive, and a living screen is not only cheaper but usually more attractive, though as a defence against predators it may have to be reinforced with wire-netting in the early stages.

In exposed areas, hedges offer more than privacy — they provide an essential windbreak. Solid walls or fences can make matters worse by creating turbulence, and the aim should be to filter the wind, using a screen of trees or shrubs, a hedge, or Italian walling.

Hedges conventional and unconventional. The traditional beech (top) contrasts with the spectacular display of Azalea 'Roshomon'

Some Dependable Hedges

For foliage

Name	Description	Planting distance	Annual rate of growth	Best height
Arundinaria japonica (Bamboo)	Willow-like evergreen foliage; forms a dense screen of bamboo canes	1–1.2m (3–4ft)	Rapid	2.4–3m (8–10ft)
Carpinus betulus (Hornbeam)	A strong grower with deep green leaves. Better than Beech for heavy soil	45cm (1½ft)	30cm (1ft)	1.8–2.4m (6–8ft)
× Chamaecyparis lawsoniana (Lawson cypress)	Evergreen conifer; one of the best for hedges. 'Green Hedger' is a good choice. There are also gold forms	60cm (2ft)	30cm (1ft)	2.4m (8ft)
Crataegus monogyna (Quickthorn or May)	Medium green foliage, berries in autumn on untrimmed plants. Forms an impenetrable hedge. Cut back to 10cm (4in) after planting	30cm (1ft)	30cm (1ft)	1.8–2.1m (6–7ft)
× Cupressocyparis leylandii (Leyland cypress)	Evergreen conifer with deep green foliage. Very fast growing. Best grown as a screen	90cm (3ft)	45cm (1½ft)	4.5m (15ft)
Fagus sylvatica (Beech)	Fresh green leaves in spring, turning brown and remaining on plant through winter	45cm (1½ft)	25cm (9in)	1.8–2.4m (6–8ft)
Ilex aquifolium (Holly)	Well-known as a shrub or tree. Evergreen. Female plants will berry if not clipped hard	60cm (2ft)	25cm (9in)	1.5m (5ft)
Ligustrum ovalifolium (Privet)	A well-known and widely-planted hedge. Stands up to adverse conditions. There is a less vigorous golden form	30cm* (1ft)*	30cm (1ft)	1.2–1.8m (4–6ft)
Lonicera nitida (Chinese honeysuckle)	Small leaves, sometimes mistaken for Box. Evergreen	45cm* (1½ft)*	30cm (1ft)	1.2–1.5m (4–5ft)
Prunus laurocerasus (Laurel)	A strong-growing evergreen with dark green glossy leaves. Needs to be trimmed with secateurs	90cm (3ft)	30cm (1ft)	2.4m (8ft)
Taxus baccata (Yew)	Dark green conifer. Evergreen. One of the finest hedges	45cm (1½ft)	30cm (1ft)	1.5–1.8m (5–6ft)

*= plant a double row

For flowers

Name	Description	Planting distance	Annual rate of growth	Best height
Berberis × stenophylla	Loose habit, dark green leaves; cascades of orange flowers in spring	60cm (2ft)	30cm (1ft)	2.1–3m (7–10ft)
Escallonia	Mid-green small evergreen leaves. Does well by the sea. Flowers pink or red	45cm (1½ft)	30cm (1ft)	1.2–1.5m (4–5ft)
Forsythia ovata	Profusion of yellow flowers in spring. Should be pruned immediately after flowering	60cm (2ft)	45cm (1½ft)	1.2–1.5m (4–6ft)
Lavandula spica (Lavender)	Silvery-grey leaves and blue flower spikes	40cm (1¼ft)	15cm (6in)	1–1.2m (3–4ft)
Prunus cerasifera 'Nigra' (Cherry plum)	Deep purple leaves; small pink flowers. Cut back to 30cm (1ft) after planting	60cm (2ft)	45cm (1½ft)	1.8–2.7m (6–9ft)
Pyracantha coccinea (Firethorn)	White flowers in early summer, brilliant red berries in autumn. Evergreen	60cm (2ft)	45cm (1½ft)	1.2–1.8m (4–6ft)

The final plan

Once you have settled the design in a broad way, you should produce a detailed plan. Don't expect to succeed at the first attempt. Start by drawing in your plot, plus any part of the house affected, to scale on a sheet of graph paper, using the side of a large square to represent a foot, yard or metre. Mark in existing features, such as garage, shed or fence, and any trees you intend to retain.

If you wish to plot the boundaries and key points with absolute accuracy (you may feel that pacing out the distances is sufficient), you can do it by the method known as triangulation. Measure the distance between two selected points (A and B) on one boundary, and the distances between these and another point (C) on the opposite boundary. On your plan, applying your chosen scale, measure off and plot A and B. Then with compass arms scaled to distances A–C and B–C, draw arcs; the intersection of these arcs will fix point C. Features within the boundaries, such as trees, can be pinpointed in the same way.

Marking boundaries or key features

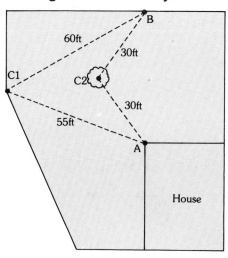

Now you can pin or tape a piece of tracing paper over your master sheet and start placing and fitting together your desired features. But don't finalize your plan before physically checking out the major aspects. Go out on the site and push in canes at the key points, and along the outlines of beds, borders, paths, and so on. A length of hose is useful for trying out the curves of a lawn.

Next make the 'window test'. You can usually get a very good semi-plan view of your proposed garden from an upstairs window and this is particularly useful in assessing the proportions and balance of your plan. Then view the plot and your trial stakes from the downstairs window or windows you use most. This will help you to site accurately trees or other screening material you need to hide an unwanted view or to make sure that an attractive distant view is unimpaired.

When you are happy with every aspect, complete your detailed plan. Only then can you begin the construction of your garden with confidence.

Left: to mark difficult boundaries or key features within a plan, simply select two convenient points, such as the corner of the house or garden, or a measured point along a straight boundary. Call these A and B, then measure the distance between these and the object you wish to mark (say, C1). Set a compass to the scale distance and draw arcs on your plan from both A and B. Where the two intersect will be the desired point on the boundary. C2 shows the same technique used to pinpoint a tree

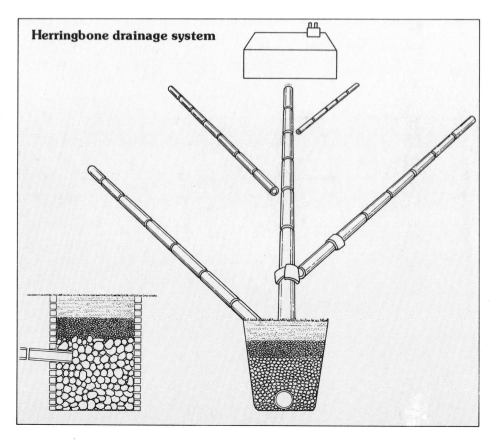

Above: land drains should be laid on a slight fall to a soakaway at a low point away from the house. Feeder drains can be laid, herringbone-fashion, to drain water from as large an area as possible. The soakaway should be at least 1.2m (4ft) deep, with 90cm (3ft) of coarse rubble at the bottom, topped with gravel then turf, if kept
Top right: a spirit-level should be used to ensure an even fall towards the soakaway, and feeder pipes should be cut at an angle to make a good join with the main drain
Right: to prevent soil blocking the drain, cover with a tile before replacing the topsoil, taking care not to dislodge the tile in the process
Below right: always keep the soakaway clear
Below: to level the ground, drive pegs into the soil at intervals, and use a straight-edge and spirit-level to bring the pegs to an even height

Putting the plan into action

After the hours of planning comes the physical effort of putting it all into action. Approach the job methodically, and don't rush it.

Clear the site by collecting rubble into heaps for use in forming foundations for a terrace or paths. If trees and stumps have to be removed, make use of mechanical aids. Powered saws and winches can be hired.

Prepare the soil thoroughly. After clearing the ground of scrub and coarse vegetation using a scythe and mattock (see page 20), large areas are best turned over initially with a powered cultivator (see page 20). Smaller areas can be dug over by hand, after first stripping off the top 5cm (2in) of weeds and grass.

Double-dig the areas that will become beds, borders and the vegetable plot. Incorporate compost or manure.

Drainage is important. If in doubt, take out holes 30cm (1ft) deep at various points after a period of heavy rain. If water is encountered, or enters the holes within a few hours, a drainage system will be required (see opposite).

Levelling should be done methodically. First remove the fertile top-soil and stack it on one side. Then move the sub-soil to the required levels before replacing the top-soil. Accurate levelling cannot be done by eye: a number of pegs, a mallet, a long straight-edged board and a builder's spirit-level are necessary.

Terraces and paths must be marked out and the valuable top-soil removed for use elsewhere. Make a foundation of rubble and sub-soil. Paving slabs are best laid on 5cm (2in) of sand and then four blobs of mortar (five parts sand, one part cement), tamped down and levelled with a spirit-level.

Lawns need careful site preparation. Once drained (if necessary) and levelled, make sure there is a minimum of 15cm (6in) of good top-soil, preferably 20cm (8in). A firm surface for turfing or sowing is assured only by 'treading', shuffling across the site with the weight on the heels. Repeat in two or three different directions before raking smooth.

Beds and borders should be raised slightly. Mound beds in the centre and build up borders slightly towards the back. This not only displays the plants to best advantage but also helps drainage. Keep a 12–15cm (5–6in) channel between soil and lawn.

17

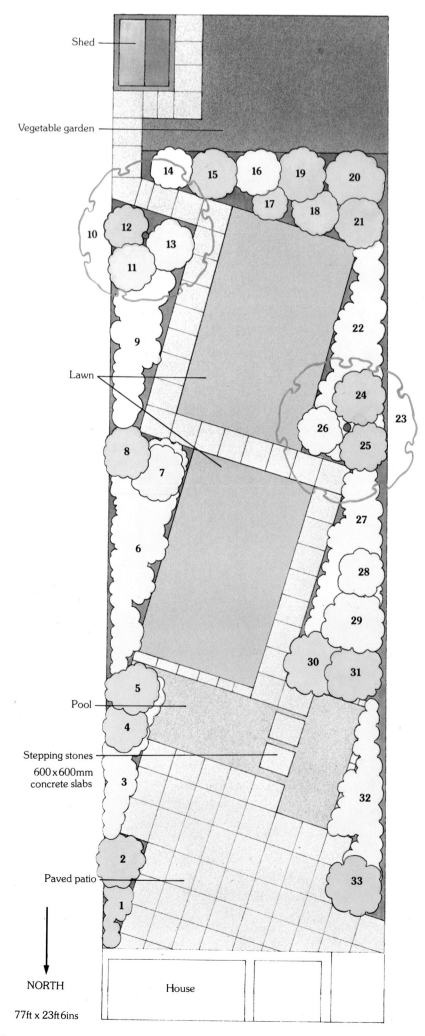

Shed

Vegetable garden

Lawn

Pool

Stepping stones
600 x 600mm
concrete slabs

Paved patio

NORTH

House

77ft x 23ft 6ins

Plan A

This plan shows a finished planting scheme for the outline on page 11. It is an imaginative design for a long, narrow garden 7m×23.5m (23ft×77ft) setting the lawns and accompanying borders at an angle to the boundary fence to give an illusion of greater width. The clever use of a formal pool with stepping stones as a link is another interesting feature

Key to plants:

1. Herbs (rosemary*, sage, mint, chives, etc)
2. *Chamaecyparis pisifera* 'Boulevard'*
3. Hybrid tea or floribunda roses
4. *Rhododendron yakushimanum*
5. *Rhododendron* 'Elizabeth'*
6. Spring bulbs followed by bedding plants
7. *Hydrangea macrophylla* 'Blue Wave' (lacecap type)
8. *Eucalyptus gunnii** (prune back each spring)
9. Border perennials
10. *Robinia pseudoacacia* 'Frisia'
11. *Cytisus × praecox*
12. *Elaeagnus pungens* 'Maculata'*
13. *Weigela* 'Bristol Ruby'
14. *Kolkwitzia amabilis* 'Pink Cloud'
15. *Viburnum tinus**
16. *Philadelphus* 'Belle Etoile'
17. *Ruta graveolens* 'Jackman's Blue'* (in a group)
18. *Berberis darwinii**
19. *Chamaecyparis lawsoniana* 'Green Pillar'*
20. *C. 1.* 'Lanei'*
21. *C. 1.* 'Columnaris'*
22. Border plants
23. *Malus floribunda*
24. *Senecio greyi**
25. *Camellia* 'Donation'*
26. *Hydrangea macrophylla* 'Altona' (hortensia type)
27. Spring bulbs followed by summer bedding
28. *Fuchsia* 'Mrs Popple' (not dependably hardy)
29. *Forsythia* 'Lynwood'
30. *Yucca filamentosa**
31. *Choisya ternata*
32. Waterside plants
33. *Fatsia japonica** (may suffer damage in a severe winter in cold districts)

NOTE: If the soil is alkaline, grow the rhododendrons (4 and 5) and the camellia (25) in tubs of lime-free soil. * Denotes an evergreen

Plan C

Wedge-shaped gardens can be among the most difficult to design well, and the skill comes in creating a tasteful combination of curves and straight lines. The narrow edge of a wedge is frequently unsuitable for planting, but this area can often be used for a garden shed or summerhouse

Key to plants:

1. Yellow roses (suitable cultivars include 'Allgold', 'Arthur Bell', 'Chinatown' and 'Grandpa Dickson'
2. *Rosa* 'Canary Bird' (shrub rose)
3. *Juniperus × media* 'Pfitzerana Aurea'*
4. *Chamaecyparis lawsoniana* 'Elwoodii'*
5. *Picea pungens* 'Moerheimii'*
6. Border perennials
7. *Chimonanthus praecox*
8. *Caryopteris × clandonensis*
9. *Potentilla arbuscula* 'Beesii'
10. *Chamaecyparis lawsoniana* 'Stewartii'*
11. *Euonymus fortunei* 'Silver Queen'*
12. Border perennials (see 6 for suggestions)
13. *Spartium junceum*
14. *Forsythia suspensa*
15. *Laburnum × watereri* 'Vossii'
16. *Fremontodendron* 'Californian Glory'* (in cold districts, substitute *Viburnum × burkwoodii**)
17. Spring bulbs followed by summer bedding
18. *Malus* 'Golden Hornet'
19. *Euonymus fortunei* 'Emerald 'n Gold'*

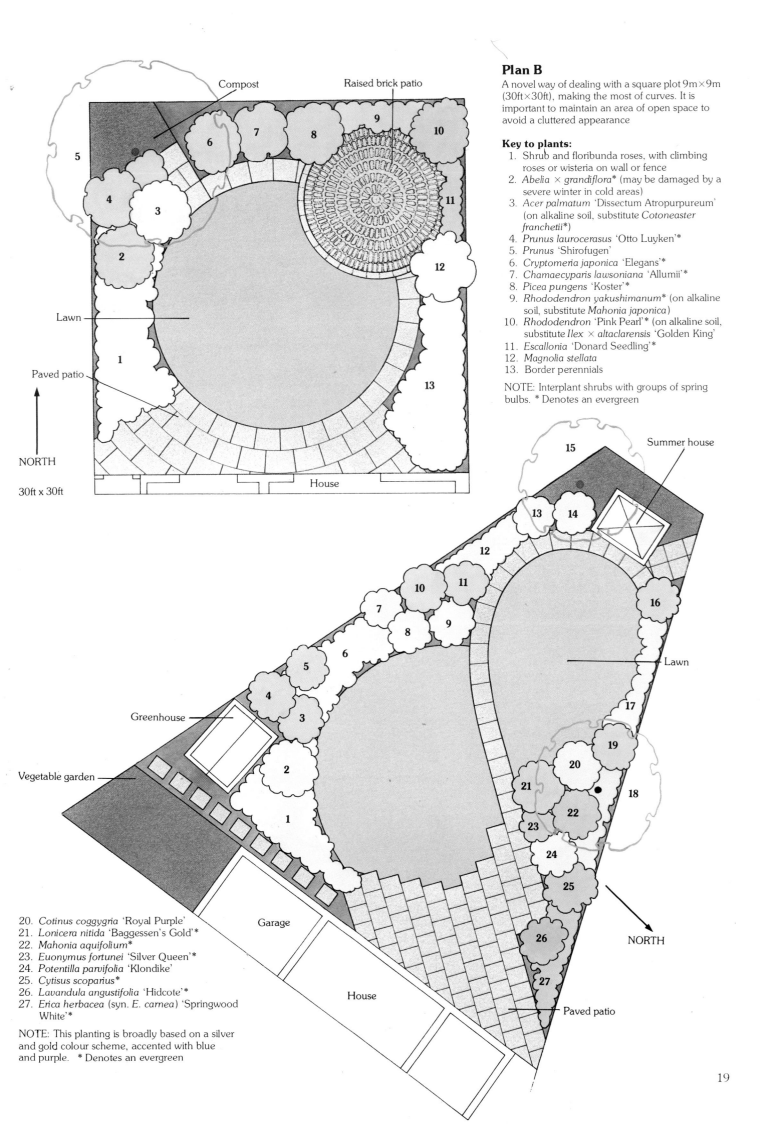

Compost

Raised brick patio

5

6 7 8 9 10

4 3 11

2 12

Lawn

1 13

Paved patio

↑ NORTH

30ft x 30ft

House

Plan B

A novel way of dealing with a square plot 9m×9m (30ft×30ft), making the most of curves. It is important to maintain an area of open space to avoid a cluttered appearance

Key to plants:

1. Shrub and floribunda roses, with climbing roses or wisteria on wall or fence
2. *Abelia* × *grandiflora** (may be damaged by a severe winter in cold areas)
3. *Acer palmatum* 'Dissectum Atropurpureum' (on alkaline soil, substitute *Cotoneaster franchetii**)
4. *Prunus laurocerasus* 'Otto Luyken'*
5. *Prunus* 'Shirofugen'
6. *Cryptomeria japonica* 'Elegans'*
7. *Chamaecyparis lawsoniana* 'Allumii'*
8. *Picea pungens* 'Koster'*
9. *Rhododendron yakushimanum** (on alkaline soil, substitute *Mahonia japonica*)
10. *Rhododendron* 'Pink Pearl'* (on alkaline soil, substitute *Ilex* × *altaclarensis* 'Golden King'
11. *Escallonia* 'Donard Seedling'*
12. *Magnolia stellata*
13. Border perennials

NOTE: Interplant shrubs with groups of spring bulbs. * Denotes an evergreen

15 Summer house

13 14

12 16

10 11

7

8 9 Lawn

6

5 17

4

3 19

Greenhouse 20

2 21 18

Vegetable garden 22

1 23

24

25

Garage 26

27

House

NORTH →

Paved patio

20. *Cotinus coggygria* 'Royal Purple'
21. *Lonicera nitida* 'Baggessen's Gold'*
22. *Mahonia aquifolium**
23. *Euonymus fortunei* 'Silver Queen'*
24. *Potentilla parvifolia* 'Klondike'
25. *Cytisus scoparius**
26. *Lavandula angustifolia* 'Hidcote'*
27. *Erica herbacea* (syn. *E. carnea*) 'Springwood White'*

NOTE: This planting is broadly based on a silver and gold colour scheme, accented with blue and purple. * Denotes an evergreen

19

Tools and equipment

In gardening, as any other field, the right tool makes a job much easier. Better results are obtained with less effort, and valuable time is saved so that you can spend more time enjoying the fruits of your labours.

For the elderly or handicapped the right choice of tool can make the difference between a task being achievable or impossible. Particularly useful are such devices as a hinged spade, which takes the lifting action out of digging, and long-handled tools that obviate bending.

Do not be put off by the variety of equipment listed here, for many of the tools are helpful rather than essential. In fact surprisingly few tools are needed to maintain an established garden.

Tools are not expensive considering the life you can expect from them, but they should be looked after. Wooden handles and metal blades are both harmed by exposure to damp, so storage in a dry shed or garage is essential. It is equally important to clean tools after use. A wipe with an oily rag, kept handy for the purpose, will prevent rusting, and it does not take a moment.

Clearing and cultivating tools

Some of the tools in this section are only required for clearing a neglected site, but others are the real basics of gardening — fork, spade, hoe and rake. Spend as much as you can afford on these tools. With reasonable care they will last for many years whereas cheap tools soon deteriorate however well you care for them, and may be clumsy to use.

Clearing tools
Certain tools are needed for the initial work of clearing uncultivated ground and for constructional work when making a new garden. In particular, a mattock is ideal for stripping off grass and weeds and cutting through small roots.

Right: a garden line is essential for straight rows, and a brightly coloured twine is easier to see. For long rows it is most convenient to make the drill with a corner of a draw-hoe
Far right: for short rows it is often easier to remove the drills with a suitable stick, which can also be used as a measuring stick for spacing large or pelleted seeds

A grass-hook or a miniature scythe is handy for clearing rough growth, especially on banks and around ditches. It is, however, of only limited use in an established garden.

Cultivating tools
As these include the most essential tools in the garden, it is important to try out the 'feel' of them before buying. Weight and size must suit your stature.

Spades come in a surprising number of forms, but choose one with a foot tread, and a blade no larger than about 29cm×19cm (11½in×7½in). Stainless steel reduces friction but plain steel is satisfactory if the blade is kept clean and greased to prevent rusting. Polypropylene handles are particularly long-lasting.

Forks can have the tine dimensions a little larger than for spades, otherwise most of the same comments apply. General-purpose forks have square-section tines.

Rakes are essential for soil-levelling and seedbed preparation. Choose one with about twelve teeth and a light handle.

Hoes come in various designs. A swan-necked draw hoe is best for heavy weed growth, a Dutch hoe for surface weeding between plants, and an onion hoe for close hoeing between small plants. Patent hoes are excellent alternatives to the Dutch hoe.

Hand cultivators are particularly useful on heavy soil. There are several sorts, usually with three or five curved, pointed tines that are effective for breaking compacted or lumpy soil.

Motor cultivators may be warranted where a large area of vegetables is cultivated. These machines are invaluable when developing a new plot but are of only limited use in an established ornamental garden.

In many cases, especially for initial cultivation in a new garden, the answer is to hire a machine.

Most cultivators are petrol-driven but there are one or two mains-electric machines. These tend to be small and some lack the power to dig really hard, uncultivated ground.

Machines with petrol engines are of three types, identified principally by the position of the rotors.

Those with rear-mounted tines, covered by a hood, chop the soil finely and, having power-driven wheels, are the least tiring to use.

Cultivators with rotors mounted under the engine are cheaper but require more effort. They do not have power-driven wheels. The rotors draw the machine forwards while simultaneously digging the soil. The slower the forward progress — controlled by the user — the deeper the blades dig.

Machines with front-mounted rotors work on similar lines, but tend to be best used for routine work in the kitchen garden.

Before buying, arrange a demonstration in your own garden, preferably of two or three types. To get such a demonstration you will have to deal with a specialist garden machinery centre.

Planting tools

Although these may appear to be minor tools, items like a trowel will probably be used as much as a spade, so buy good ones. Stainless steel is expensive, but a delight to work with.

Trowels are essential for many planting jobs. The type with a long, pointed blade will probably be found most satisfactory.

Hand forks are less vital, but useful for weeding and for loosening soil around plants. They can often be bought as part of a matching set with a trowel.

Dibbers, preferably sharp-pointed and steel-tipped, are particularly useful in the vegetable garden for planting onion sets, leeks, cabbages and so on.

Garden lines are most helpful in the vegetable garden. A reel-mounted type is easy to manage. To accompany it, buy a 2m (6ft) planed batten, and paint marks at 15cm (6in) intervals, as a guide to sowing and planting.

Pruning and shaping tools

Pruning tools often receive a great deal of punishment, and for that reason the blades should be protected from abuse.

Secateurs or pruners are essential in every garden. Some work on the anvil principle, with a single cutting blade; others have a scissors action. Both are equally effective. Avoid buying secateurs that are too small, as over-straining is the commonest cause of damage. Always clean and oil after use.

Lopping shears, or two-handed pruners, are ideal for cutting through branches up to about 2cm (¾in) thick. However, like the long-arm pruners with handles up to 2m (6ft) or more long, their expense may not be justified in the

smaller garden unless pruning happens to be a major task.

Pruning saws are something of a luxury unless there are old trees needing drastic attention.

Pruning knives are often preferred to secateurs by experienced gardeners, but unless you can handle one with confidence it is best to keep to secateurs for basic pruning.

Hand shears can be tiring to use, and it really does pay to buy a good quality pair that's light to handle.

Mechanical hedge trimmers are the most labour-saving of garden machines after lawnmowers. They will cut just as effectively as hand shears and in a fraction of the time.

There is a wide choice of power sources. Mains-electric trimmers are popular for garden use. For greater safety, some manufacturers offer 110v models for use with a transformer. There are also 12v models, powered by a car battery or generator, and yet others which

have a rechargeable battery built into the handle. Having no cable, the latter are particularly convenient, but cutting time between charges is limited.

Trimmers driven by miniature petrol engines can be bought for cutting substantial hedges that are not near a mains supply.

Many garden-size trimmers have reciprocating blades about 30cm (1ft) long. This is adequate for small hedges, but blades up to 80cm (2⅔ft) long are available for longer stretches.

Avoid buying a heavier trimmer than you need, or one that is ill-balanced. Either can prove very tiring, especially when reaching across the top of a broad hedge.

When using a cable-supplied trimmer, pass the cable over your shoulder so that it hangs behind your body. Follow the manufacturer's safety instructions.

Garden tools are expensive but will last for many years if looked after. Clean them thoroughly after use (wiping over with an oily rag if necessary), and hang them up tidily. A few nails or hooks will keep the majority of tools off the floor, where they can be damaged or cause injury. Garden chemicals must always be stored on a high shelf.

Lawn care tools

Lawns are probably the most labour-intensive part of the average garden, and the area where mechanical aids can bring the greatest benefit. As many gardeners are confused by the sheer variety of machines for cutting grass, you must first be clear about your needs.

Do you need a lawnmower, a long-grass cutter, or a machine that will do for both? For a lawn, how particular are you about quality of cut and the finished appearance? Do you want a powered mower, and, if so, will petrol or electricity suit you best?

Hand mowers

These provide the simplest solution if you have a small, level lawn. Lowest-priced models are the sidewheel types which will cut unsightly 'bents', or wiry grass stems, that a roller mower passes over. They also cut slightly longer grass. Roller mowers cut the grass more evenly, however, and leave alternate light and dark bands. Both models have blades of the cylinder type.

Powered lawnmowers

The blades may be driven by petrol, mains electricity, or batteries, and many models are self-propelled. Petrol-powered mowers can be used anywhere as they do not have a trailing cable and there is no battery to maintain; but there is a greater chance of mechanical trouble and they are usually noisier than electric mowers.

Mains electric mowers start at the touch of a switch and need the minimum of maintenance. A convenient power point is needed, however, and the trailing cable can be a nuisance if there are beds and borders in the way.

Battery mowers have no trailing cable and start just as easily as mains type, but a power point is needed for recharging — preferably in the garage or storage shed. Battery replacement is necessary every few years.

Cylinder mowers have a multi-bladed cutting cylinder that shears the grass against a fixed bottom blade. Mowers of this type give the finest cut, and are driven by a roller that leaves a banded finish. Width of cut is 30–60cm (12–24in). Some of the bigger mowers can be fitted with a trailing seat.

Rotary mowers have a different action. From two to four small blades revolve at high speed on a horizontal disc or cutter-bar. Really close cutting entails the risk of 'scalping' any slight bumps in the lawn surface, but the performance of many machines is in other respects fairly close to that of cylinder models.

Rotary mowers, which are powered by petrol engines or mains electricity, cut grass that would be too long for a cylinder mower, and are easier to adjust. Some are self-propelled, others have to be pushed. A grass-box is standard on many machines, though not on some of the small mains-electric types. Some have rear rollers for a banded finish.

Air-cushion rotary mowers are supported by a strong, downward-directed current of air, like a hovercraft. Having no wheels or rollers, they glide across the grass at the mere touch of the handles. They are surprisingly effective on long grass as well as on lawns, and can be used on uneven ground with little risk of damage to the turf.

Most air-cushion mowers do not have grass-boxes, so the finely minced mowings are left on the surface. They do not leave a banded finish. There are petrol and mains-electric models.

Heavy-duty rotary grass cutters are available that are capable of tackling the longest grass and weeds, and are useful for orchards, paddocks and similar grass. They work on the same principle as rotary lawnmowers, and many machines might be described as dual-purpose. In this case, there is often the option of a grass box or a deflector plate.

Miniature tractor-type mowers with an integral rotary grass cutter are now sold by several manufacturers. Though relatively expensive, they save time and effort where there is a large area of grass that requires regular cutting.

Mower maintenance

Every cylinder mower incorporates some simple means of adjusting the moving blades in relation to the fixed blades. Regular attention is essential for good cutting, so check the method for your mower in the handbook. Do not confuse this with the separate adjustment for height of cut.

Sharpening is needed every year or so. Put this in hand during the winter as you may have to wait for a while in the spring. Rotary cutters can be sharpened with a broad file or, in some cases, by turning the angle of the circular or triangular blades.

Drain the sump of a petrol mower each spring and fill with fresh oil. Lubricate oiling points regularly, not forgetting

Top left: a spring-tined lawn rake is a basic lawn-care tool, being useful for removing fallen leaves as well as raking up moss in the spring
Top right: the besom is used to sweep up fallen leaves or to brush in a topdressing
Above left: untidy edges can mar a lawn, yet they are easily kept neat by the use of a half-moon edging iron and a straightedge
Above right: long-handled edging shears enable the edges to be kept trim without backache

control cables and levers, and store mowers in a dry shed during the winter after cleaning and greasing.

Check electric cables each spring for signs of damage or perishing. Check plug connections.

Employ a professional if any faults occur. Keep batteries topped up; recharge after mowing, and once a month during the winter.

Wipe rollers and blades clean after use, and lubricate regularly at the points recommended by the manufacturer.

Ancillary lawn care tools

Only a few tools are needed to keep a lawn in good condition, but those listed below will make the various jobs easier. In some cases, however, ordinary garden tools can be used instead.

Edging irons, or half-moon cutters, are used for cutting a new lawn edge, or for straightening an old one. They are much better than a spade, which will leave a scalloped edge.

Edging shears with long handles save bending, and the blades are set at just the right angle for easy cutting. Another form of long-handled shear has the blades set horizontally for cutting grass in corners and around trees.

Mechanical edgers may be hand operated or powered. Hand-operated types are simply pushed along the lawn edge to trim overhanging grass. Powered trimmers, mostly electric, have a shielded high-speed blade that serves the same purpose, but more efficiently.

Lawn rakes of the wire type are invaluable for clearing leaves, removing moss, dead grass and other debris, and for loosening a matted surface. Plastic rakes remove loose material but lack the scratching effect.

Leaf sweepers with a rear collecting bag save much time in the autumn on lawns surrounded by trees. They are also useful for sweeping drives and for collecting mowings.

Distributors simplify sowing lawn seed and ensure accurate distribution of fertilizer on established lawns. Output is adjustable for different materials and rates of application.

Aerators are particularly important for good lawn care. Compacted lawns benefit from regular spiking, preferably when the surface is soft after rain. Some types remove a core of soil, others split the ground. A fork can be used instead (taking care not to lever the turf into ridges), but a rotary spiker saves time and effort. Some sorts can be fitted to mowers, while others have wheels and a handle.

Rollers are less used nowadays than formerly, but will level a lawn disturbed by frost, and are useful when preparing an area for seeding or turfing. It is often possible to borrow one for these occasional needs.

Other tools and aids

There are many tools gardeners tend to manage without for years, then once purchased wonder how they coped before. Wheelbarrows, compost bins, and incinerators are examples. They are not essentials but, once the basic tools have been purchased, are well worth acquiring.

Wheelbarrows are almost essential for carrying soil, paving slabs, concrete and so on. The conventional single-wheel design is still popular, but sturdy construction is the thing to look for. A substantial barrow, preferably with a pneumatic tyre, is invaluable when making a new garden.

A lighter barrow is satisfactory for carrying mowings, prunings and similar light loads on a firm surface. In this case you might consider buying a lightweight two-wheel barrow into which rubbish can be swept when the front is tipped to the ground.

Sieves are handy if you prepare your own compost for seed-sowing and potting. Shape is unimportant; a 6mm (¼in) mesh is suitable for most purposes.

Compost bins are especially useful in small gardens, where home-made containers may look unsightly. A proprietary bin, complete with lid and finished in green, is unobtrusive. Sliding panels allow easy removal of compost and it also has ventilator holes.

Incinerators purpose-made from sheet metal or wire ensure a good draught for efficient burning and keep the bonfire within bounds. Wire-mesh containers that fold can be stored under cover to prevent rusting.

Hose and reel can make watering less of a tiresome chore. A 12mm (½in) plastic hose, preferably stored on a reel, is essential in any garden too large to be watered with a can. Patent couplings, tap connectors and nozzles are easily fitted without tools. Some hose reels are mounted on wheels; others are designed for attaching to the wall of a shed or garage.

Sprinklers avoid the need for you to be tied to the end of the hose. Oscillating types spread water over a rectangular area; fixed and rotating sprinklers cover a circle. Perforated hoses, or lay-flat tubing for attaching to the supply hose, are ideal for row crops.

Watering-cans are needed for pot plants and containers and for the many occasions when it is not worth unreeling a hose. One with a gallon (4.5 litre) capacity and a long spout is best for greenhouse work. Outdoors, a can twice this size is preferable. Most are now made of plastic, which may split if used roughly.

Sprayers are needed in practically every garden to apply insecticides and fungicides. Where fruit is grown it is convenient to have two — a small one, holding a pint or two (1 litre), for treating individual plants; and a larger one, holding at least a gallon (4.5 litres), for major applications of tar-oil wash and lime-sulphur.

Some sprayers need continual pumping; others, first pressurized by pumping, give a continuous output.

The simplest types of syringe are recharged by inserting the nozzle in the spray liquid after each stroke. More sophisticated types draw the liquid through a tube placed in the bucket and eject the spray at each forward and backward movement of the plunger.

Below: large-capacity compression sprayers greatly ease spraying in a large garden, and for fruit trees an extension lance is essential
Right: the traditional wheelbarrow has many modern rivals. This ball-wheeled model is easy to push even over rough land. Some of the modern plastic materials are extremely tough
Below right: modern compost-makers are efficient and comparatively unobtrusive. By protecting the compost from heavy rain, and producing conditions conducive to decomposition, the time taken to turn garden waste into valuable compost is short, and because they are tidier they do not need to be banished to the furthermost corner of the garden
Far right: timber greenhouses are usually of traditional design, but some of the metal-framed models have explored new design concepts

Cloches, frames and greenhouses

Gardening takes on a new dimension when there is some means of protecting plants from the elements (see Gardening Under Glass, pages 94–99). A row of cloches enables crops to be grown a few weeks earlier in the season, just when they are most appreciated. A frame has similar uses, and is invaluable for striking cuttings and hardening-off tender plants. With a greenhouse, there is no end to the interesting and rewarding plants that can be grown, both in and out of season, whatever extremes of weather occur.

Cloches

These are primarily for the food grower. Their main uses are to provide sheltered conditions for growing early crops, including strawberries, for protecting early sowings of half-hardy plants such as runner beans, for protecting tender plants such as melons, and for providing instant and portable cover at any time of

year for plants which are in need of extra protection.

Most cloches are now made of plastic — either individually of semi-rigid plastic, sometimes with a wire support, or in the form of a continuous tunnel of sheet polythene supported on wire hoops. The latter are inexpensive, and are satisfactory for most purposes.

Avoid cloches that are too narrow or low. Crops soon outgrow them and their small volume provides less protection from fluctuations in temperature.

Frames

Though they can be used like cloches for protecting early crops, and during the summer for growing melons and cucumbers, frames have other uses.

During the spring, they provide an ideal site for pots and boxes of half-hardy seedlings that need night protection from drops in temperature during the hardening-off stage (see page 95). During the summer, a shaded frame will provide the right conditions for striking a whole range of cuttings or for sheltering pot plants that are being grown on outdoors during the summer.

By using electric soil-warming cables, a frame can become a frost-proof winter shelter or a sort of miniature greenhouse where out-of-season crops can be grown or early plants raised.

There are many designs, some in red cedar and others made of aluminium or galvanized steel. For winter use, one with solid sides is best. For summer crops, glass sides are equally satisfactory.

Greenhouses

With a heated greenhouse, gardening becomes a year-long hobby rather than one concentrated on the warmer months. But even without heat, or with just a modest amount during the spring, the extra interest provided by a greenhouse is truly remarkable.

There are several designs, most available in either cedar wood or aluminium (see page 94). Both are satisfactory, timber houses perhaps looking less obtrusive in some garden surroundings but aluminium houses being completely maintenance-free and somewhat quicker to glaze.

It comes down to personal taste. The vital point is to choose a convenient spot in the garden that receives plenty of light during the shorter days of winter and early spring.

Shape is not all that critical, either. If you have a sunny wall, a lean-to may be the most convenient. In free-standing designs, the main choice is between those with vertical sides and others with sloping sides. The latter are especially suitable for growing border crops. Either sort can be fitted with side panels or have the glass extending to ground level.

When buying, bear in mind the additional cost of staging along at least one side, heating, and other equipment (see pages 96 – 97).

Also, remember to allow for a power supply (professionally installed) if you plan to have electric heating or other electrical aids.

Construction

A garden without at least one of the features described in this chapter is likely to lack that special something that a well-constructed garden possesses. Yet to have a landscape contractor construct them for you can be expensive . . . and is usually much less satisfying than having done the work yourself.

All the garden features described here are within the ability of most gardeners, and by following the concise instructions it should be possible to achieve a professional finish to these important aspects of good garden design and construction.

Building a patio

Patios have become very fashionable (see page 88), and although a lot of heavy work is involved in making one, the skills are well within the scope of the average gardener.

Levelling the site is the first step, and the area should be marked out with timber pegs. The top-soil is then removed and the area roughly levelled.

For accurate levelling a series of pegs should be inserted over the entire area, the tops of which should be 6.5– 7.5cm (2½– 3in) below the finished surface level of the patio. Remember, however, that the finished surface level should be about 15cm (6in) below the damp-proof course of the house. Use a length of straight timber and a spirit-level between one peg and the next to get them at the right level across the width of the patio. From front to back, a small block of wood should be placed under one end of the straight-edge to give a slight fall away from the house of about 2.5cm in 3m (1in in 10ft).

Laying the foundation provides a chance to use up any old bricks around the garden. Ram down the soil and bang in pieces of brick, rubble or stone if soft areas are encountered. Spread a layer of rammed hardcore over the area and bind the surface of this with ballast (a

Above, right: a pool does not have to be large to be effective, and clever use of plants will soften the rectangular shape of a formal pool. The bed around this pool is particularly effective
Right: greater design skill is called for when space is at a premium, yet even here it has been possible to introduce water and raised beds

mixture of sand and gravel, sold by builders' merchants) to bring the level up to the top of the pegs. Thickness of hardcore should range from 10cm (4in) on soft clay soil, to 5cm (2in) on a sandy soil. No hardcore should be necessary on a firm, gravelly soil.

Positioning the slabs is a matter of laying them on a level bed of moist sand, although a longer-lasting result will be achieved by bedding the slabs in a mortar mix consisting of one part cement to five parts sand (by volume). The mortar mix should be dry enough to support the weight of the slabs, but not so dry that they cannot be tapped down level.

Spread the mortar in a layer about 2.5cm (1in) thick, and carefully lay each slab in place so that it is level with its neighbour, with a space of about 10mm (⅜in) between slabs. To save mortar, large slabs can be bedded on five spots of mortar; one at each corner and one in the centre.

To cut a slab, place it on a level bed of sand. Tap a line with a heavy hammer and bolster (a wide steel chisel) until a vee-nick is visible. The nick should go right around the slab. Continue to tap along the line, gradually increasing the weight of blows on the bolster until the slab splits along the line.

When the bedding mortar has set, all that remains is to fill the joints between the slabs with a nearly dry version of the bedding mortar, pressing it into the joints and brushing off any surplus.

Garden pools

The charm of water in a garden is well recognized (see page 80), and wherever there is the space and a suitable setting, a pool is a valuable asset. Don't, however, be tempted to squeeze in a pool that is too tiny for healthy plant and fish life. The minimum satisfactory surface area is 3.5sq m (40sq ft), while a sensible depth is 60cm (2ft). A depth of 75cm (2½ft) should be considered the maximum, 40cm (1¼ft) the minimum. The sides should ideally slope out at about 20 degrees to the vertical, and around the edge there should be a shelf about 25cm (10in) below water level, on which marginal water plants can be grown.

The choice of material
The choice is quite wide — from concrete to rubber. Few concrete pools are made nowadays; they are difficult to construct, need reinforcing, and frequently leak. The choice for most people will lie between a rigid preformed shape and a flexible liner.

Flexible liners give plenty of scope for natural contours, but rectangles call for complicated and not always successful

pleating; and the acute curves found in many preformed pools are not possible.

Flexible pool liners are able to absorb soil movement without cracking. The cheapest are ordinary polythene liners, which can be expected to last for a season or two. Black is the best colour, and it does not deteriorate so rapidly in sunlight. In increasing order of price there are PVC laminated liners with a life from two to six years, nylon reinforced laminated liners with a life in excess of ten years, and butyl rubber liners, which are the best type, with a life in excess of 50 years. The latter is about six times the price of polythene.

Rigid plastic pools are limited to the manufactured shapes, but installation is simply a matter of digging a hole as if burying a tank to the rim. The glass-fibre types are very strong, and there is no need to be too fussy over installation, but the cheaper thin plastic rigid pools need to be carefully supported in a hole lined with well-packed coarse sand.

Making a pool
To make a pool with a flexible liner, mark the outline shape with pegs, then use a spirit-level and straight-edge across the tops of them to ensure a uniform level.

Remove any turf, and dig out the pool to a depth of 25cm (10in), then make sure the surround is level by checking

that each peg protrudes an equal amount above the surface of the soil.

Dig out the central part of the pool to a depth of 60cm (2ft), or whatever has been planned, leaving a shelf at least 25cm (10in) wide, 25cm (10in) below the surface, for marginal plants (see pages 81, 172–73). Try not to disturb soil that is not to be removed.

Remove any large, protruding stones, then scatter sand in the base and on the marginal shelf to cushion the liner from any jagged edges. Pad the sides of the hole with layers of folded polythene.

Drape the liner over the hole and weight the corners, then start to fill the pool with water. Ease off the weights as the liner is gently stretched and taken into the hole.

When the pool is full, trim off surplus liner to leave 10–15cm (4–6in) around the edge, and hide this overlap with paving stones bedded on a mortar mix of one part cement to three parts sand (by volume).

Soil taken from the pool can be used to form a waterfall and rock garden (see page 78). The waterfall pools can be made from a number of rigid plastic mouldings arranged one above the other like steps, or from a flexible pool liner draped over the excavated soil to form a watercourse. Pools are formed by building dams of stones with mortar laid on the liner. The waterfall is fed by a small electric pump (see page 81).

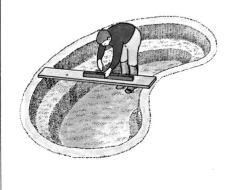

Making a flexible liner pool

Flexible pool liners make pond construction very easy, but it is best to keep to gentle, flowing curves. Carefully excavate the site, leaving a shelf for marginal plants. To ensure the edge of the pool is level all round, use a straight-edge and spirit-level (left). Failure to do this can result in too much liner showing on one side. If the soil is stony, line the excavation with a layer of sand, then lay the sheet in the hole. Place a few heavy stones around the edge to hold the sheet in place (below left) and allow the weight of water to mould the sheet to the contours. When filled, edge with paving stones (below)

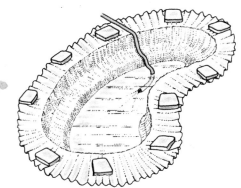

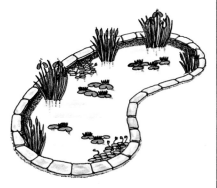

Paths

Paths can be functional or decorative, but in either case they must be well laid if they are to last long and enhance the garden. All except grass paths will require a good foundation, although this is less essential with largely decorative 'stepping stone' paths set in a lawn.

Concrete paths

A concrete path will only be strong if it has a firm base. Well compacted, solid ground or a 5cm (2in) layer of compacted rubble on soft ground is essential. If the path is intended to lie flush with the surrounding ground level, you will have to excavate the site to the combined depth of the concrete and any hardcore foundation.

Mark the line of the path with string lines pulled taut between stakes. Arrange formwork for the concrete, using timber boards set on edge and braced by stakes driven well into the ground. Form curves by making a series of saw cuts about halfway into the boards until they can be bent to the required shape.

The boards used for the formwork should be the same depth as the concrete, 5–7.5cm (2–3in) being adequate for a path. One side of the formwork should be set about 12mm (½in) lower than the other (on a path 1m wide) so that rainwater will drain away. Clear weeds and other vegetation before concreting.

A concrete mix of one part cement to five parts of ballast is needed for a good path. It can be mixed by hand or in a hired concrete mixer. If a large volume is required, and there is no difficulty with access, it may be worth having pre-mixed concrete delivered; this saves a lot of time and effort.

Pour a small batch of concrete into the formwork and spread it out with a shovel or a rake until it is slightly proud. Place a board across the formwork and make two passes with it, the first with a chopping motion, the second with a sawing motion to level it off. Proceed to the next batch.

Every 2.4m (8ft), place a thin board (slightly less deep than the formwork) across the path, and concrete over it. This will allow for any future expansion and prevent the path cracking.

If a textured, non-slip, finish is required, allow the concrete to harden for a while, then draw a stiffish broom across it at right angles. This will leave a slightly rippled finish.

In hot weather, protect the fresh concrete from drying quickly by allowing it to harden for a while and then placing sheets of polythene over it. Place weights on the edges of the sheets to prevent them flapping up in the wind.

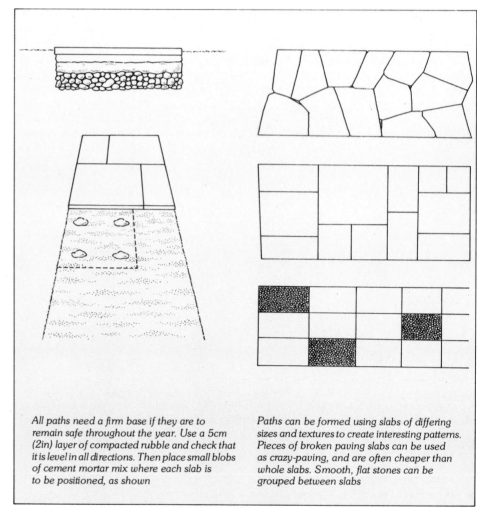

All paths need a firm base if they are to remain safe throughout the year. Use a 5cm (2in) layer of compacted rubble and check that it is level in all directions. Then place small blobs of cement mortar mix where each slab is to be positioned, as shown

Paths can be formed using slabs of differing sizes and textures to create interesting patterns. Pieces of broken paving slabs can be used as crazy-paving, and are often cheaper than whole slabs. Smooth, flat stones can be grouped between slabs

Concrete paving blocks

A concrete block path is a little different. The blocks are available in various colours and shapes and are laid mostly to a herringbone, stretcher or parquet bond.

Plain rectangular blocks are usually 20cm × 10cm (8in × 4in) and are about 6.5cm (2½in) thick. The blocks should be laid on a bed of sharp sand. Solid edge supports (preferably concrete) are needed alongside the path. Sand can be brushed into the joints to complete the job. Special blocks are available for edges to avoid having to make cuts.

Cold macadam paths

A cold macadam path must be laid on a well-compacted base. A black, treacle-like bonding agent is spread over concrete or loose surfaces. After 20 minutes, the macadam is poured from bags and spread evenly using the back of a rake. A roller is necessary to compact the surface, but it must be kept wet to avoid picking up the macadam.

Crazy-paving

If you have a cheap supply of broken paving slabs, preferably in a neutral colour, and a suitable setting, a crazy-paving path can be most effective. The technique of laying is similar to that for rectangular paving slabs (see page 27), but it is wise to lay the pieces out in approximate positions first. Start with the large pieces, and fill in with the smaller ones.

Unless you intend to grow plants between the paving, fill the spaces between the pieces with mortar, otherwise weeds will be a problem.

Bricks

Bricks laid on edge can give a mellow look to a garden, but such paths are only feasible if a supply of free or very cheap hard bricks is available. Lay in the same way as concrete paving slabs (see this page).

Gravel

Although only really suitable for a drive, gravel should not be overlooked. Weeds are no longer a problem with the advent of modern persistent weedkillers.

A firm base is essential, and a depth of 7.5cm (3in) of gravel is not too much. Rake it smooth, and roll it firm.

As with other materials, a slight camber will help in periods of heavy rain.

Stepping-stone paths

Although rectangular paving slabs can be used, the round or irregularly shaped kinds look better. Most attractive of all are wooden rings cut from trees. If wood is used, make sure it is a durable timber such as elm (fairly easily obtained at the moment as a result of the widespread dutch elm disease).

Stepping-stones of any kind set into a lawn should be set on a firm base of sand or shingle, with the surface of the 'stone' slightly lower than the lawn, so that the mower clears it.

Grass paths

Only use grass paths where they are not likely to receive constant wear — and remember that they are not pleasant to walk upon in wet weather.

Where they can be used they look very natural, provided they are mown regularly. Keep them reasonably wide, use a strong-growing grass mixture (see page 65), and consider the use of metal edging strips to keep a neat, firm edge.

Arbours and pergolas

Both these garden features add considerable interest to a garden: they provide an opportunity to grow some attractive climbing plants, and offer a shady retreat on hot summer days.

Arbours can be formed by using trellis panels. Three pieces are arranged in a U-formation, with a fourth section forming the roof.

Timber or plastic trellis sections can be screwed to a wall using zinc-plated wood screws fixed into plastic wall plugs. Make the holes for the wall plugs using a

masonry drill to suit the plug size. To hold the trellis about 2.5cm (1in) from the wall, use pieces of wood, cotton reels, or short pieces of copper pipe as spacers.

Pergolas are formed by building a series of linked arches in a line. Some fencing manufacturers sell pergola kits that use square sawn timber uprights, but rustic poles also look effective. Erect them in the same way as fence posts (see page 30). If preferred, the uprights may be brick or stone pillars. The cross-pieces and linking sections can be in matching timber or poles, joined to the uprights with half-lapped joints and held with galvanized nails.

Right: brick paths can be very attractive if arranged symmetrically, but must be laid carefully as uneven bricks can be a danger
Below: an example of how paving stones can become an integral part of the planting scheme. They also provide easy access to the beds
Below right: careful planting can offset the regular lines of paving slabs. Here a soft carpet of Sagina glabra 'Aurea' *creeps over the edge*

Fences

Fences have two functions: they can be used to provide privacy and security, or to define a boundary line. The type chosen depends on the job that the fence has to do.

Choosing a fence

If privacy is required, then a timber fence of panels 1.8m (6ft) high fixed between posts is the answer. This is one of the most popular fences for back gardens.

The panels can be of narrow overlapping boards (arranged either vertically or horizontally) or of interwoven strips. Panels from 60cm to 1.5m (2–5ft) are also available.

This type of fence has the advantage of being much easier to install than feather-edge boards fixed to arris rails located in posts, generally at 1.8m (6ft) intervals.

Posts can be either timber or concrete, and what the latter may lose in appearance it gains in durability.

Where height is required without a totally solid appearance a panel fence can be topped with trellis panels, which come in matching lengths. Heights are from 30cm to 1.8m (1–6ft), so it is even possible to erect a complete fence of trellis.

Another popular timber fence is the paling type. The pales are fixed to the horizontal rails and can be spaced at a suitable distance to keep animals out (or in!), as you wish.

For economy, wired chestnut palings sold in rolls are good value. These are usually fixed to round chestnut posts.

Another attractive fence for the right rural setting is the picket type, which can look very charming.

Chain-link fencing — either galvanized or plastic-coated — fixed to timber or precast concrete posts is another low-cost fence. Though robust when properly fixed, they are not attractive and should ideally be screened by a hedge.

Ranch-style fences — wide boards, spaced apart and fixed horizontally between posts — can be of timber or plastic. The latter has the advantage of being rot-proof.

Erecting a fence

It is essential to treat timber posts with a good preservative, and this is worth doing even if the posts are supplied pre-treated. The posts are the cornerstone of the fence, yet without protection they will rot in a couple of years.

Stand each post in a bucket of preservative for a few hours before use.

A recent innovation is a form of steel legs which are inserted in the ground, and into which the posts are fitted.

The easiest way to dig the post holes is to use a tool called a post-hole borer. Resembling a large corkscrew, this is driven into the ground using a clockwise-anti-clockwise movement until the required depth is reached. Waste earth is lifted out as boring proceeds. The holes should not be less than 45cm (1½ft) deep for a low fence, at least 60cm (2ft) for a high one.

To position the holes accurately, use a string line, stretched taut between stakes, to denote the line of the fence. A batten the same length as a section of fence is used to mark out the positions of the posts within the line.

Place the first post in its hole and pack stones and rubble around its base to

An attractive fence enhances a garden, whether forming a pleasing background to a border, or marking the boundaries of a front garden. Here can be seen some of the wide range of fences that are available:

1. Feather-board fencing has strips of wood, usually 10–15cm (4–6in) wide, nailed in the upright position on to lateral members, with each vertical strip overlapping its neighbour. This very strong fencing can be bought in heights from 1–1.8m (3½–6ft)

2. A woven fence provides complete privacy and a background that is very complementary to plants. Woven fencing, the height of which can be from 1–1.8m (3½–6ft), is bought in panels, secured to firm upright posts

keep it upright. Check for a true vertical using a 90cm (3ft) spirit-level. Secure one end of the first panel to the post using 5–6.5cm (2–2½in) aluminium alloy nails, dependent on whether thin or thick timbers are being fixed. Three nails (top, middle, bottom) are sufficient on either side of each end of the panel (twelve nails per panel). If a helper is available, let him support the fixed post while the next one is inserted and plumbed upright in its hole and stabilized with rubble. If help is not at hand, use temporary struts fixed to the posts as support.

Check that the post tops are at the same level. To do this lay the spirit-level on a long straight-edge spanning the post tops. Make any adjustments to the second post before nailing the panel to it. Ensure the bottom of the panel is clear of the ground. Follow this procedure to erect the whole fence.

Fill the post holes with alternate layers of a dryish concrete mix (one part cement to eight parts sand and gravel mix) and rubble. Finish with concrete. Timber struts should be nailed to each post to ensure the fence remains rigid while the concrete sets.

Timber capping pieces nailed to the tops of the posts can be used to reduce the chance of them rotting. Alternatively, saw them to a single or double bevel.

A close-boarded fence is erected in much the same way. Posts are plumbed upright and the arris rails inset into the preformed holes in the posts, where they can be secured with aluminium alloy nails. The vertical boards are then nailed to the arris rails with edges overlapping slightly.

Close-board fences should always have a 15cm (6in) deep gravel board fixed between the posts and ground to prevent the main boards from rotting.

Erecting a shed

Nearly all sheds are supplied in prefabricated sections ready to bolt together on a firm, level base. A good base is essential, even when a floor is supplied; thick concrete is ideal, but paving slabs can be used if placed on a layer of sand over rammed soil.

Excavate the soil to take 5cm (2in) of hardcore, over which 7.5cm (3in) of concrete should be laid. The concrete should be retained in a temporary timber formwork, but check that it is square by ensuring the diagonals are equal. The top of the formwork should be levelled, using a spirit-level.

A suitable concrete mix for the base is one part cement, two-and-a-half parts concreting sand, and four parts coarse aggregate, all by volume.

Keep the timber floor off the base by using 7.5cm×5cm (3in×2in) wood bearers which have been pressure-treated with wood preservative (you can buy pressure treated wood from a good fencing contractor).

Lay the bearers on strips of bitumen damp-proof course, then lay the floor over the bearers. The bearers allow air circulation under the floor, but they also create a haven for rodents, so seal the open ends with small-mesh wire-netting.

Sheds without floors are erected directly onto the concrete base, with strips of damp-proof course under the sides. In exposed areas, the shed can be secured using rag bolts set into the concrete.

3. Palisade fencing topped with an extension trellis provides space on which to grow many climbing plants that would otherwise not find a suitable position in the garden. Such fences must be securely erected, as a large area of fencing and plants is very susceptible to battering by strong winds
4. Ranch-style fencing forms a sturdy screen, and can be bought in panels for securing to firm upright posts
5. Picket fencing looks particularly charming in a rural setting and is often used as a low type of fencing for front gardens

Garden walls

Walls take longer to construct than it takes to plant a hedge, and it will almost certainly be more expensive. Both problems are, however, offset by the ease of maintenance afterwards. And in many situations a wall is more practical, and even more aesthetically pleasing, than a living screen.

A wall planted with suitable subjects can combine the best of both worlds.

Brick wall

A low brick wall is certainly within the scope of the beginner. For best appearance use facing bricks, not 'commons'.

Start by sketching out the proposed design on paper, working to accurate dimensions. The standard size for a brick is 22.5cm long, 6.5cm high and 11.2cm deep (about 9in × 2½in × 4½in). This is their nominal size, and it includes a 10mm (⅜in) allowance for mortar joints. Design your wall to nominal dimensions.

It's difficult to be precise on foundations required, but as a guide a 40cm (15in) wide strip should be excavated for a wall up to 60cm (2ft) high. Dig until firm ground is found. Where stability is in doubt, lay a bed of well-compacted hardcore. Allow for a 7.5cm (3in) layer of concrete (one part cement: two-and-a-half parts sharp sand: four parts aggregate) with one brick to be below ground level. If the wall is to be over 1.2m (4ft) high, lay a 10cm (4in) layer of concrete with two bricks below ground level.

Mark out the wall line with two string lines pulled taut and tied to stakes. Use a mortar mix of one part of cement to five parts of builders' sand. The mortar should be buttery (not too dry, nor too wet); it should retain its shape when spread from the trowel. A few drops of washing-up liquid will improve the mortar's workability, but don't mix up more than you can use in an hour — less on a hot day. Always keep wet concrete well away from drains.

Trowel enough mortar along the foundation to bed a couple of bricks. Lay the first brick frog (indentation) upwards, and check it for level using a spirit-level, making sure it is also aligned with the string lines. Trowel mortar on to the mating face of the next brick and lay this ensuring that the joint is 10mm (⅜in) thick. Place a spirit-level across both bricks; tap down the second brick to level using the handle of the trowel.

Subsequent courses should be laid to a string line secured with pins. Having completed the first course, build up the ends of the wall for three or four courses in stepped formation before finishing each course. To check that the vertical joints are being kept uniform, use a

Above: gateways and arches always create the desire to explore a garden, and add interest
Left: dry stone walls provide growing space for a variety of rock plants, many of which thrive in such well-drained conditions

Crinkle-crankle walls are an unusual feature, and have the additional benefit of providing sheltered bays for wall shrubs

Screen blocks make a decorative, see-through wall, that is quick to build. Blocks can be used alone or to add interest to more traditional brick walls

batten which is marked off in 6.5cm (2½in) increments.

Where half bricks are needed they must be cut. Lay the brick (frog down) on a flat, solid surface and mark the cut line in pencil. Chip the brick at both ends of the marked line using a club hammer and bolster chisel (see page 27). Place the bolster on the line, tilted towards the waste side, and cut through with a sharp blow from the hammer.

Point the joints between the bricks before the mortar hardens. Joints can either be left flush with the bricks, shaped downwards and outwards using a pointing trowel, or rounded off with an implement such as an old bucket handle.

Screen block walls

These are made of precast concrete blocks. Various patterns are available. The blocks are 30cm square × 10cm thick (1ft sq × 4in). This is the nominal size which includes a 10mm (⅜in) allowance for joints. Provide firm concrete foundations, using a mixture of one part cement to five parts 20mm (¾in) ballast. For the mortar use one part cement to six parts sand, plus plasticizer.

Foundations should be a minimum of 20cm (8in) deep, including bricks or rubble where needed.

At each end of the wall, pilaster blocks are used. These are reinforced with metal rods and infill concrete (one part cement to three of ballast), which should be fluid enough to sink down into the pilasters.

Loose-lay the blocks between the pilasters to ensure they fit (don't forget to allow for joints). Then lay the blocks as for brickwork except that you should work from both ends to the middle. Check each block for level, and again build up the corners before completing successive courses.

Finish with pilaster caps and coping slabs on the top course. Use a piece of hardwood with a rounded edge to point the joints.

Dry stone walls

Imitation stone blocks for walling can be used to achieve the informality of a dry stone wall. The buff-coloured blocks are 52.5cm × 15cm × 10cm (21in × 6in × 4in) full size; half blocks are 26.2cm × 15cm × 10cm (10¼in × 6in × 4in). Coping slabs are used to complete the wall.

The blocks should be laid on firm foundations using a half-block to start alternate courses. Use a mortar mix of one part of cement to four parts soft sand. Joints should be about 6mm (¼in) thick. Lay the blocks frog (depression) upwards. If the wall is to be higher than four courses, allow 48 hours for the mortar to harden before you begin laying the fifth and subsequent courses.

Dry stone walling blocks are also available for dry laying, that is, without mortar. These are sold as 600mm × 200mm × 70mm (24in × 8in × 2¾in) blocks, and two are joined together when delivered; they must be separated using a wide bolster chisel and club hammer. Preformed vee-shape rebates make this a simple task. On splitting, the limestone aggregate edges are revealed, and these should be left exposed as the wall is built. Cut the return ends in the same way.

A gravel or ballast foundation is adequate for a low wall, but a concrete foundation is needed for a wall over 60cm (2ft) high if it is intended to retain earth. Here, 12mm (½in) joints should be left between blocks.

Erecting a greenhouse

Before erecting a greenhouse, check with your local authority or landlord whether permission is required. There may be regulations if it is to be sited close to the house.

Timber greenhouses usually have prefabricated wall and roof sections, like sheds. Many are supplied with precast concrete base plinths, which are simply placed on levelled soil and to which the walls are anchored. If these are not used, the greenhouse must be set on a single course of bricks on a concrete strip foundation (see page 31).

Most aluminium greenhouses are supplied in packs of separate components which bolt together according to the manufacturer's instructions. The walls can be erected on an aluminium strip or precast concrete base laid on level ground.

The glass is usually bedded on a flexible glazing strip and is held securely in the aluminium sections using stainless-steel clips.

The luxury touch

Gardeners by nature are preoccupied with the down-to-earth. Whatever flight of fancy their horticultural ambitions inspire, their feet remain firmly planted on the ground. Their concern is always with the basic realities and they are, perhaps, more likely than most people to concentrate on necessities and scorn frivolous non-essentials. But gardeners are human too and should not deny themselves the pleasurable enjoyment of indulgence in the occasional touch of luxury.

Somewhere to relax

High on the list of items that have absolutely no functional value in the growing and tending of plants, but which enormously increase the gardener's pleasure in his garden, is a really comfortable vantage point from which he can view the results of his labours.

It might be nothing more ambitious than a picture window to frame the garden panorama, or it could be a custom-built garden room. Here, cosily ensconced in front of his favourite view, with his gardening library and other creature comforts at his elbow, the owner can extend his gardening range with the tender plants that will luxuriate — as he does — in the constant warmth.

An indoor pond
In the relaxing haven of a garden room, where it is always summer, what could be more appropriate or more pleasant-sounding than an indoor pool with a splashing waterfall or fountain?

Attractive though the idea is, however, do not attempt to duplicate indoors the sort of pond you have outdoors. Pond plants are sun-worshippers and do not flourish in moderate levels of indoor lighting. Also, large fish make a lot of waste which, with the accumulation of rotting material from unthrifty plants, calls for pond-cleaning operations that are just not acceptable indoors.

It is best to treat the indoor pool on the lines of a large aquarium, or to settle for the effect of clear water without fish or plants.

An aquarium pool should have the plants set in gravel instead of soil, and only small fish should be chosen. In

temperatures between 16° and 24°C (60° and 75°F), colourful Guppies will thrive prodigiously. Above all, maintain water clarity and hygiene by installing an aquarium-type power filter.

A clear-water pool has no plants or fish at all, but is treated periodically with algicides and chlorine, rather like a swimming-pool. The water, incapable of supporting life, remains clear and sparkling.

This type of pool looks attractive surrounded with decorative houseplants, which will enjoy the humidifying effect while you enjoy the pleasant splash and murmur of water without the need for frequent cleaning-out chores.

A room outdoors

It may be that a room which is part of the house and inevitably involved in its activities will not always provide the ideal retreat. To enjoy the luxury of solitary detachment from everyday affairs, a summerhouse may be the answer.

True luxury in this sphere is exemplified by the gazebo, an elegant circular or hexagonal open-sided structure.

The screened garden room, the oriental tea-house and the trellis-roofed pavilion are variations on the same theme. Such a structure will add a touch of luxury to any garden but should, of course, be added to the garden only after due attention has been paid to planning and building regulations.

Living outdoors

When the gardener can spare a moment to indulge the simple pleasure of putting his feet up he can wallow in the luxury of garden furniture, as relaxing as his favourite armchair indoors.

Garden furniture

For relaxation, there is probably nothing better than a swing-back reclining chair that raises the level of the feet above the head. And for dozing a summer afternoon away, nothing has yet been invented to beat a tautly-strung hammock. If you don't have any trees to string it between there's one that comes with its own supports.

Barbecues

To make the most of summer days it's great fun to eat in the garden, and now it's not even necessary to incorporate a barbecue pit in the design of the patio. You just wheel out the mobile barbecue trolley and light up. Delightfully simple,

Above left: grace and elegance are encapsulated in this patio, demonstrating the role of attractive garden furniture in adding a touch of luxury
Left: a change of level and attractive brickwork ensures that a patio looks planned

Underwater lighting adds a real touch of luxury. Purpose-designed lamps are perfectly safe to use

particularly since bottled gas can be used as an alternative fuel to charcoal.

Garden lights

Modern garden lighting equipment makes it possible, at the touch of a switch, to enjoy the ultimate luxury — the fascinatingly different garden after dark. Different because, instead of one light source flooding everything, a number of light sources can be used to illuminate selected features. They can be made to throw their light from different levels, at different angles. Floodlights can be used to illuminate whole areas, such as the patio or rose border, and spotlights to pick out selected features such as an isolated tree or piece of statuary.

Backlighting produces a dramatic effect, while sidelighting or front lighting also adds interest.

In addition to all this there is the possibility of colour. The scope is unlimited and the effect is a garden enchantingly — almost unbelievably — different from the garden in daylight.

Types of lighting

Outdoor lighting falls into several categories, and all have their place in the garden.

Decorative strings of coloured lights — in effect an outsize outdoor version of Christmas tree lights — give the patio a festive air on special occasions.

Marker lights are really to indicate that the illuminated object is there; porch lights beside doors, lanterns on gateposts and light bollards marking drives and paths, fall into this category. Such lamps

generally employ ordinary bayonet-cap light bulbs of 25 or 40 watts, though some may take 60 watts. It is important not to use a stronger bulb than the maximum indicated by the manufacturer.

Illuminating lamps need to be a good deal more powerful. A popular type for floodlighting or spotlighting consists of a 100 or 150 watt PAR 38 lamp screwed into a moulded synthetic rubber lampholder provided with a silicone-rubber watersealing gasket. They should always be concealed and shielded so that they illuminate the chosen subject without shining directly into the eyes.

Lighting ponds

Moving water is the most spectacularly rewarding of all garden features when illuminated after dark. By far the best effects come from submerged lamps, but they must, of course, be of a type made specifically for that purpose.

Water is best lit from below and behind. A lamp shining up *behind* a waterfall turns it into a rippling sheet of molten coloured glass.

Two lamps of different colours directed up into the spray pattern of a fountain from just below the surface produce a firework display of sparkling droplets. To ensure that the scintillating display of mixed colours stands out against a totally black backcloth, the background must not be illuminated. Do not on any account kill the whole effect by bathing the pool area with a floodlight from the nearest tree.

The most effective positions for all forms of garden lighting will not be discovered without some experimenting, and all the equipment must, of course, be made to the relevant safety standards for its purpose. Installation and connection are best entrusted to the hands of a qualified professional.

Any unusual container with character can be used to give an air of individuality to a garden

Labour saving

An early question many gardeners ask themselves when planning or reassessing a garden is whether it should be designed with maintenance in mind, whether it should save time or physical effort — or both.

Busy working people may have plenty of energy, but not much time to spare for the garden. And older folk may have plenty of time, but are not as able or as strong as they used to be. By careful planning and a few wise purchases, much can be done to help.

Tools to make the job easier

The right tool always makes a job less arduous, but some are particularly labour-saving. Powered equipment in particular can be an asset to anyone short of time or muscle power (see Tools and Equipment, pages 20–25).

Powered tools
The first powered machinery most gardeners buy is a lawnmower. This obviously saves a tremendous amount of effort.

The wisdom of buying a machine that catches the clippings cannot be emphasized too strongly. Except in very hot weather, it is desirable to collect the clippings, but remember that one-third of the time spent mowing a lawn is taken up with emptying the grass-box or catcher. To cut down the emptying time, buy a mower with a wide cut. If you had in mind one with a 30cm (12in) width, consider a 35cm (14in) instead.

If there is a total area upwards of 250sq m (300sq yd) of soil to be cultivated, it is worth considering the purchase of a powered cultivator, while if you have more than 30m (100ft) of hedge, say 2m (6ft) high, an electric hedge trimmer is justified.

Other labour-saving equipment
There are many non-powered labour-saving tools and pieces of equipment that can be used. For example, there is a two-handed pruner like a secateur but with two 35cm (14in) handles; these make pruning very easy, and there's the additional benefit with roses that your hands are now nowhere near the thorns.

Much time is spent in moving materials from one part of the garden to another — compost, weeds, leaves, hedge trimmings, grass mowings, and so on. One of the large squares of canvas or thick plastic with ropes at the corners is an excellent time and labour saver. You can spread it on the lawn and throw your light rubbish on to it, lift it, sling it over your shoulder and carry it to the rubbish heap.

With a single-wheeled two-handled barrow you are still half carrying the load, but with the modern two-wheeled trucks with a pram handle all the weight is taken by the wheels.

A labour-saving way to dig over a piece of ground if you do not have a motorized cultivator but find the lifting difficult is to use a hinge-operated spade. This transfers the weight from your arms and back to a special bracket attached to the spade.

The length of handle on tools such as hoes, rakes and yard-brooms is very important. If you have to bend unnecessarily, it will put a strain on your back. The top of the handle should be level with your ear when the tool is standing on the ground. A shorter partner can hold the tool lower down.

Coping with weeds

Weed control probably takes up as much time, or more, than lawn mowing or any other gardening chore. One of the simplest methods of control is hoeing, and if done while the weeds are still small they will not have to be raked up and carted off to the compost heap. There are other ways to tackle the problem, however, ranging from chemicals to weed-smothering plants.

Chemical control
Modern chemical weedkillers (see page 42) have proved a great boon to the gardener. There is now a type to suit almost every situation: selective weedkillers to kill weeds in grass, or grass among broad-leaved plants; total weedkillers that will persist in the soil for a year; or even one that is harmless to plant growth almost within hours.

Mulching
Much can be done to control weeds by mulching with a good layer of peat, sawdust, pulverized bark, garden compost, half-decayed leaves, spent hops, mushroom compost, or even straw. Do not, however, mulch around strawberry plants until the soil has warmed (about the end of April), otherwise growth may be retarded.

Always be sure that the ground is wet before applying the mulch, then moisten the mulch itself.

Ground-cover plants
Weeds can also be smothered by planting strong, low-growing plants that will carpet the soil. By careful selection of such ground-cover plants (see page 62) much weeding can be saved, and of course they will add considerably to the horticultural interest of the garden.

Top: electric lawn edgers become more appreciated with advancing age. They enable trim, straight edges to be achieved with minimum effort

Above: the 'donkey', a large canvas or plastic square with rope handles at the corners, is invaluable for moving materials such as compost, weeds, leaves or grass mowings from one part of the garden to another — it is capacious and very light

Ground-cover plants take a year or two before they are fully effective, but do not need much maintenance once they are established.

Watering

Watering can take up a great deal of time in dry spells. Hauling lengths of hose about the garden is a time-consuming and dirty job. There are various 'through feed' hose reels available. These are connected to the main supply and one just pulls off enough of the hose-pipe to reach the area to be watered, winding it back when the watering has been done.

Even better is the installation of a 'ring main' of plastic hose around the garden. Plastic sockets are installed at various points, into which a plug with a short length of hose is inserted to take water to a sprinkler. With several of these sockets around the garden one only needs about 5m (15ft) of movable hose, and the sprinkler which can be picked up in one hand.

Design considerations

It may be that some reconstruction of the garden could save a lot of time and labour. Steep grass banks, for instance, are a nuisance because they are not easily mown, and it might be possible to cut them back and by moving some soil make the slope less steep. Or it might be a good idea to build a dry stone retaining wall (see page 35) in which rock plants could be grown, eliminating the mowing chore at the same time. If the difference in levels is more than about 1m (3ft) it might be wise to build the wall in two levels, with a border 30cm (1ft) wide, about 60cm (2ft) above ground level, and a further wall and border behind.

Sometimes there are awkward steps to be negotiated in a garden with barrow or mower. It is often possible to make a gently sloping ramp where these implements may easily be pushed.

For those who find stooping or kneeling difficult there is much to be said for raised beds, which may be constructed of brick, stone or even paving slabs set edgewise.

Many plants that enjoy acid soil can be grown happily in a raised bed consisting of peat blocks and filled with a suitable acid soil mixture. Shade-loving plants may be inserted into the peat walls on one side of the raised bed, sun-lovers the other side.

Labour-saving tips

● To minimize lawn edge trimming lay a 30cm (1ft) wide strip of paving between borders and the lawn. This will also help to bring an air of informality to a border

of hardy flowers because one can allow front row plants to flop on to the paving without damage to the turf.

● If the borders or beds are flanked by turf, grow stocky upright plants in the front of the border. These will not flop on to the lawn and cause bare patches. There are many to choose from, such as dwarf asters (*Callistephus chinensis*) and antirrhinums, African and French marigolds (*Tagetes erecta, T. patula*), *Iberis gibraltarica,* alyssum (*Lobularia maritima,* usually listed as *Alyssum maritimum*), *Begonia semperflorens* and *Coreopsis verticillata.*

● Keep all cutting tools sharp. Also keep a sharp edge on hoes, using a file. A sharp hoe slips through the soil so much more easily than a blunt one. If you can afford stainless-steel tools always choose these as they are so easy to clean. Also look for hoes with a wavy edge as this greatly increases the cutting surface.

● When planting ground-cover plants spread black plastic sheeting over the ground and make holes in it to receive the plants. The plastic should be removed once the plants have grown together and covered the area.

● Replace grass or gravel paths with broken (crazy) or formal paving.

● Plant only bush fruit trees which may be pruned, sprayed or picked without having to climb ladders.

Above: ground cover plants are nature's method of weed control. Here the barren strawberry, waldsteinia, is being used to good effect

Below: mulching with peat or compost not only keeps down weeds but benefits the plants by conserving moisture in the soil

Soil care

Soil is often taken for granted, yet it has a most profound effect on the plants we grow, and largely determines the range of subjects that can be grown successfully. Soil provides more than anchorage: for the vast majority of plants it is the reservoir of nutrients and water on which they have to draw for their growth. It is also host to a great number of micro-organisms — some beneficial to the plants, others harmful.

One of the most important components of soil is humus, the decomposed remains of plants and other organic material. This brown or black organic substance is beneficial to both sand and clay soils; it helps to create larger particles in a clay soil, improving structure, and acts as a reservoir of nutrients and moisture on sandy soil.

Increasing the humus content is the key to improving most soils.

Double digging

Double digging is useful for breaking up uncultivated soil and the technique is simple. First remove a trench one spit wide and deep, and place the soil on one side. Fork over the bottom spit, incorporating manure or compost whenever possible, then invert the next top spit over this. Continue in this manner until the entire plot has been dug, then fill in the last trench with soil removed from the first

Improving your soil

All soils can be improved by good cultivation and the systematic addition of suitable manures and fertilizers.

Improving a sandy soil
Although sandy soils are delightfully easy to work, they are hungry and have little in the way of food reserves. And because they have little moisture-retaining capacity, irrigation is always a problem.

The application of liberal quantities of organic material is the best solution. Work plenty of compost, peat or spent hops into the top spit, but concentrate it in a small area of the garden if the amount is limited; it is better to achieve a significant improvement in one area than to spread the compost so thinly that no real benefit is achieved.

Improving a clay soil
Although double-digging is a chore, its benefits make the exercise worth while on a clay soil. Drainage is improved, and it enables compost or manure to be worked into the bottom spit.

Regular applications of compost, peat or manure over many years will steadily increase the humus content, and lead to a gradual improvement in structure.

Liming is a traditional method of improving a clay soil, and hydrated lime can be applied at 275g per sq m (8oz per sq yd) if the ground is not already alkaline. Never apply lime without determining whether the soil needs it.

The pH scale

Soils can be acid or alkaline, and nature has adapted certain plants to thrive in one extreme or the other. Rhododendrons are a typical example of plants adapted to acid conditions, while dianthus revel in alkaline soils. The degree of alkalinity or acidity is measured on a pH scale, which extends from zero at the acid end to 14 at the alkaline end; these extremes are never encountered in general horticulture, and few soils fall below 5 or are higher than 8. Chemically, 7 is neutral, but 6.5 is considered neutral in gardening terms, for that is the level at which most plants thrive.

Adjusting the pH
To make soil more acid, use aluminium sulphate or sulphate of ammonia at 70g per sq m (2oz per sq yd). Sulphate of ammonia is also a nitrogenous fertilizer, and over-use can affect the balance of growth.

To achieve a similar effect with organic material, use about 1.5kg (3lb) of peat or 7kg (15lb) of garden compost.

Acid soils can be made more alkaline by adding chalk or lime. To increase the pH by about one step on the scale, use about 300g of limestone or 200g of hydrated lime per sq m (9oz and 6oz per sq yd respectively).

Manures and fertilizers

Although plant nutrition is a complex subject, and many minor elements play a crucial role, the gardener is concerned primarily with three major foods: nitrogen, phosphorus and potassium. These can be applied as powders or liquid feeds, but should not be used to the exclusion of bulky manures or compost.

Nitrogen
This element is needed for healthy leaf growth, and can be particularly beneficial for leafy crops such as cabbages.

Sulphate of ammonia is widely used; it is quick-acting and comparatively inexpensive. Its continued use can make soils more acid.

Fertilizers and lime should never be applied indiscriminately. A simple soil testing kit enables deficiencies to be diagnosed accurately by mixing a soil sample with an indicator fluid and comparing the colour reaction against a special chart provided

Nitrate of soda is suitable for most crops, and is particularly useful on clay soils. It is quick-acting and useful when a late fertilizer dressing is required.

Nitro-chalk is a granular product, easy to apply by hand. It is especially useful on land deficient in lime. Its rapid action makes it suitable as an autumn growth booster.

Organic nitrogenous fertilizers include dried blood, hoof and horn, and shoddy (wool waste). The fertilizer content in these varies, and sometimes the nitrogen is released slowly (which can be advantageous).

Phosphates
Phosphorus is associated mainly with root redevelopment, and is especially useful for rootcrops such as turnips. It acts as a counterbalance to nitrogen.

Superphosphate is widely used. It tends to be available to plants over a long period.

Basic slag can be used as a slow-acting fertilizer, and is normally applied in autumn or winter for the following season. It contains a little lime, and is useful on heavy soils.

Bonemeal is a popular organic phosphatic fertilizer. It is slow-acting, and contains a small amount of nitrogen.

A fertilizer distributor is particularly useful for large areas of lawn, but on rough ground it is often necessary to apply by hand

Potash
Potash helps the formation of fruit and storage material in tubers such as potatoes and bulbs such as onions. It also counteracts soft growth and helps to create sturdy plants.

Sulphate of potash is usually used, particularly early in the year.

Wood ash is the main organic source of potash, but it must be kept perfectly dry until used.

Mixed fertilizers
For most purposes, a ready-mixed and balanced fertilizer is best. National Growmore is adequate for most purposes but for particular crops, such as lawns, pot plants, tomatoes and chrysanthemums, there are many special fertilizers. Foliar feeding often brings rapid results, but it is important to buy a suitable formulation.

Bulky organic manures
The value of farmyard manure is legendary, yet garden compost is often as good. The value in these materials lies more in the bulky fibrous and humus-forming material they contain than in the nutrient value. Almost any soil will benefit from well-rotted manure or compost.

Farmyard manure is excellent, but it is not worth paying high prices; if it is not available at the right price locally, use alternative materials.

Garden compost can be made by anyone, although it is unlikely that the average household can ever generate enough to meet all needs. A compost heap need not be an untidy, smelly mess; there are many compost bins that are pleasant to look at and efficient in operation.

Spent hops are sometimes available, and these are excellent — clean and pleasant to handle, and adding water-retaining bulk to the soil while decomposing.

Mushroom compost is another source of bulky organic manure. It normally contains farmyard manure, and plenty of straw. Do not use it on limy soil, or where lime-hating plants are grown, as it contains limestone.

Green manuring involves growing a quick-maturing crop such as mustard, rape or annual lupins, then digging this in before it flowers. It increases the organic content of the soil, but is only feasible in open areas of ground such as a vegetable plot.

Weeds

One definition of a weed is: 'a plant growing wild in the cultivated garden'. But many would say this is an exact definition of our cultivated plants. Another, perhaps better, definition is: 'a plant growing where it is not required'. Both descriptions would cover bluebells Scilla non-scripta (syn. *Endymion*) in some gardens and Peruvian lilies (*Alstroemeria*) in others.

One would prefer to grow the plants of one's choice in a garden, however beautiful invaders such as bindweed may be; and ground elder and couch grass are certainly *persona non grata* now, despite the medicinal qualities for which they were originally grown.

The ability of weeds to spread is an obvious problem, and their increasing presence means that they will absorb more mineral nutrients and moisture, fill space, and take light that would otherwise be available to the plants we wish to grow. Weeds also act as a reservoir of pests and diseases, and nothing looks more neglected than a garden in which the weeds have taken over.

Making use of weeds

There are two sides to every story, and weeds are not totally harmful. The soil surface beneath a leafy cover of weed growth is more moist than bare soil; it acts as a kind of mulch and more water is retained than where the soil is clear of weeds. The skilful gardener can, therefore, allow the weeds to grow, especially the annual kinds, until just before they begin to flower, and then dig or hoe them in to act as a green manure (see page 39). If that isn't convenient they can provide green material for the compost heap.

It is essential, however, to remove weeds before they flower. 'One year's seed is seven years' weed' is a countryman's saying that has been proved scientifically. One chickweed plant, allowed to grow unchecked, is capable of being the sponsor of 15,000 million offspring in one season, so eradication is desirable.

Weeds also have the useful habit of producing roots that penetrate to varying levels in the soil and tap reserves of nutrients which cultivated plants might not reach, or need. If they are then dug up complete, and removed to the compost heap, the rotting material from this will provide a source of major and minor elements, and cut down further on the need to buy artificial fertilizers. Docks in particular have long tap roots, with an ability to store much food; horsetails absorb silica in such quantities that the top growth was once used for scouring pots and pans.

Do not forget that many weeds (native plants) were once used as herbs, and many still have a variety of uses to the gardener or cook, as well as to the doctor, the artist and the perfumer. Nettles can be cooked and eaten like spinach; dandelion roots may be ground up and used as a coffee substitute. Young thistle leaves can be used as a mulch round plants to ward off slugs, and the young fronds of bracken are a very good source of potassium. So don't be in too much of a hurry to destroy your weeds; you can make them work for you, instead of against you.

There are, of course, places where weeds are simply not wanted at all: paths, paved, tiled and bricked areas, hard tennis courts, drives and so on. Among soft fruit, perennial weeds can strangle the plants and reduce a crop to a few berries, and on lawns the cover,

stinging nettle

ground elder

creeping thistle

groundsel

clover

chickweed

pearlwort

black medick

Oxalis corymbosa

although green, can rapidly become a mixture of daisies, speedwells and moss — very pretty but hardly a lawn.

Types of weeds

Although weeds can be a nuisance, various methods of removal and prevention are possible, both natural and chemical.

In order to clear the picture a little, however, it helps to remember that weeds can be classified into two groups, each with different methods of reproduction and increase. Once you can recognize how the weed propagates itself, its name does not matter very much, but you will know where it needs to be attacked, and how to do it.

Annuals

Groundsel, chickweed and shepherd's purse are examples of annual weeds. These germinate in spring, grow large enough to flower, set seed, and die in one growing season. The weed may take the whole of a growing season to do this, from spring to autumn, or it may be an 'ephemeral', completing its cycle in a few weeks, and producing three or four generations in a growing season.

With such weeds it is easy to understand why they spread so rapidly, especially as some of the seed may remain viable for several years. So the very least you should do to these is destroy them before they flower.

Biennial weeds are similar, but do not usually flower until the second season; fortunately there are very few of them.

Perennials

These weeds have herbaceous or woody crowns capable of surviving the winter, and live for several years. They usually produce seed, sometimes in large quantities, but mainly colonize the soil with creeping roots, underground stems, or runners which root at the leaf joints or which produce plantlets.

The roots or underground stems take a great deal of hard work in removal, whether by hand or digging, as anyone will know who has had to dig out a nest of couch grass roots or a tangle of ground elder. They break off easily, and any piece of root, however small, can root of its own accord and establish another centre of infection. Horsetails are particularly irksome as their 'roots' (underground stems) may delve down a considerable distance, and breaking them only stimulates the dormant buds lower down on the remaining root to sprout.

A small group within this perennial section has a long and tenacious taproot, which is easily broken, the remaining piece being capable of producing new top growth; dandelions will ensure their survival in this way, and add insult to injury by producing lots of seed.

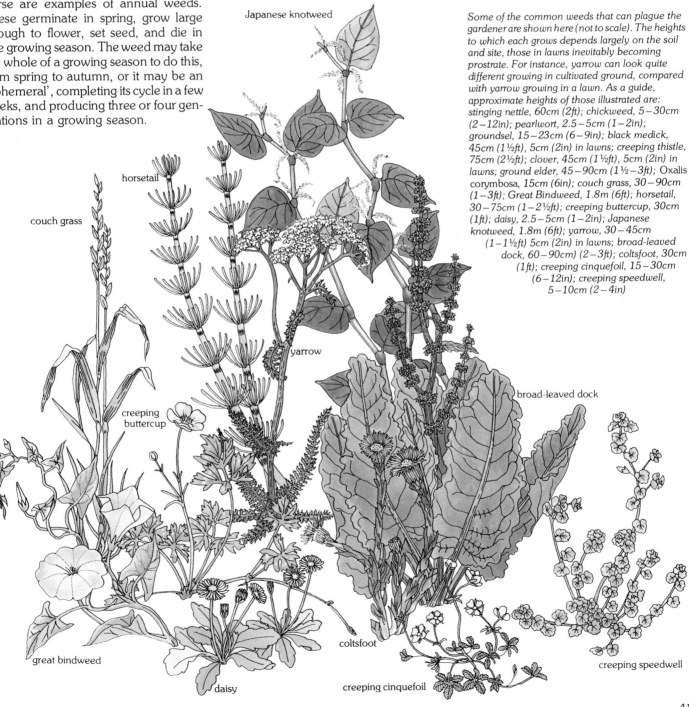

Some of the common weeds that can plague the gardener are shown here (not to scale). The heights to which each grows depends largely on the soil and site, those in lawns inevitably becoming prostrate. For instance, yarrow can look quite different growing in cultivated ground, compared with yarrow growing in a lawn. As a guide, approximate heights of those illustrated are: stinging nettle, 60cm (2ft); chickweed, 5–30cm (2–12in); pearlwort, 2.5–5cm (1–2in); groundsel, 15–23cm (6–9in); black medick, 45cm (1½ft), 5cm (2in) in lawns; creeping thistle, 75cm (2½ft); clover, 45cm (1½ft), 5cm (2in) in lawns; ground elder, 45–90cm (1½–3ft); Oxalis corymbosa, 15cm (6in); couch grass, 30–90cm (1–3ft); Great Bindweed, 1.8m (6ft); horsetail, 30–75cm (1–2½ft); creeping buttercup, 30cm (1ft); daisy, 2.5–5cm (1–2in); Japanese knotweed, 1.8m (6ft); yarrow, 30–45cm (1–1½ft) 5cm (2in) in lawns; broad-leaved dock, 60–90cm) (2–3ft); coltsfoot, 30cm (1ft); creeping cinquefoil, 15–30cm (6–12in); creeping speedwell, 5–10cm (2–4in)

Japanese knotweed

horsetail

couch grass

creeping buttercup

yarrow

broad-leaved dock

great bindweed

daisy

coltsfoot

creeping cinquefoil

creeping speedwell

Weed control

Identifying the weed is the first step to controlling it. Only then is it possible to decide on the most suitable method of eradication.

'Natural' methods

The most obvious non-chemical control is hand removal. A small hand-fork or onion hoe, a cultivator hoe (the kind with three or five prongs which claw through the soil) or Dutch hoe, or a digging fork or spade, all have their uses. It is also possible to buy special tools for removing daisies and dandelions from lawns. Choice depends on whether you are dealing with weed seedlings, rosette-type weeds, creeping weeds or deeply rooted kinds.

If you opt for removing them by hand, it must be thorough to be effective, and the younger and smaller the weeds are when you launch your attack, the easier it will be.

Mulching (see page 40) is an exceedingly good method of control, as it maintains soil moisture and can supply plant food. Materials to use can be garden compost, leafmould, peat or any similar organic material, also plastic sheet (black, or other dark colour), a layer of sand at least 7.5cm (3in) deep on top of organic matter, or even layers of stones and small pebbles.

Grassing weed-infested areas is another technique. The top growth is cleared off, the soil roughly dug and cleared, a coarse grass seed mixture sown, and the resultant sward mown regularly. In time the weed, whether coltsfoot, horsetails, oxalis or whatever, will die out, though it may take from one to several seasons for this to happen.

Chemical control

Chemical control is determined to some extent by the area in which the weeds are growing. One group of chemicals consists of those absorbed through the roots of plants and which therefore have to be applied to the soil and must reach the roots to be effective.

Sodium chlorate is one of these, a much-used weedkiller mixed with water and applied at rates varying from 120–480g per sq m per 4.5 litre (4–16oz per sq yd per gallon) of water, depending on the degree of weed cover and the strength of the weeds. It lasts for at least six months, but has a tendency to creep sideways in the soil, and can be carried down slopes; it will affect all roots to a greater or lesser extent. There is a fire risk with the dry material (including splashes of the solution that have dried), but some manufacturers now include a fire-depressant with their product.

Simazine is a more modern weedkiller, applied in solution to ground free of weeds; it will then keep it clear for twelve months, provided the soil is not disturbed. It can be used round certain established plants at strengths advised by the makers.

Dichlobenil is also a modern root-absorbed chemical, applied dry, to clean ground. At the strength suggested for uncultivated ground, it will keep it clear for a year; around certain cultivated plants, for three to five months. It will kill many weeds and satisfactorily suppress others, and has the advantage that it does not creep sideways. Being an extremely fine powder, great care has to be taken to ensure that it does not drift on to cultivated plants or the soil around them (it has some effect on the leaves also). Don't apply it on a windy day.

Hormone weedkillers can be used where soil application is not possible; these can be sprayed onto the top growth, through which they are absorbed. They include those known as 2,4–D, 2,4,5–T, mecoprop, and dalapon. All except dalapon are effective on broad-leaved weeds; dalapon is specific to couch grass and other grasses (so should never be used on a lawn).

These hormone weedkillers stimulate the plant into overgrowth, especially at the growing points, so that the plant cells eventually collapse and die. The spray must be kept off cultivated plant top growth, but the broad-leaved weedkillers can be used on lawns, as they hardly damage the lawn grass.

Other chemicals having their action through the top growth are paraquat and diquat, which destroy the green colour-

Weeds and their control

Name	Main method of spread	Control, natural	Control, chemical	Remarks
Bindweed (Calystegia sepium)	Roots	Dig out roots, grass down	2, 4-D+2, 4, 5-T (just before flowering best); dichlobenil	Destroy lifted roots
Black medick (Medicago lupulina)	Seed	Hand-fork, remove before flowering	2, 4-D+2, 4, 5-T; morfamquat	Rake lawn before mowing
Buttercup, creeping (Ranunculus repens)	Runners with plantlets	Dig out; mulch heavily and completely	2, 4-D, glyphosate; sodium chlorate on uncultivated ground	Improve drainage of soil
Chickweed (Stellaria media)	Seed	Hoe out seedlings, dig in before flowering	Paraquat	Treat before flowering
Cinquefoil (Potentilla reptans)	Runners with plantlets	Dig out roots completely	Sodium chlorate or dichlobenil on vacant ground; 2, 4-D+2, 4, 5-T (more than once)	Rootstock brittle and breaks easily
Clover, white (Trifolium repens)	Creeping stems rooting at joints	Reduce alkalinity of soil, improve strength of grass	2, 4-D+2, 4, 5-T; mecoprop; glyphosate; sodium chlorate on vacant ground	Apply lawnsand to clover in lawns in spring
Coltsfoot (Tussilago farfara)	Creeping underground stems	Grass down; remove flowers before seeding; dig thoroughly	Sodium chlorate or dichlobenil on vacant ground	Improve soil drainage and nutrition
Couch grass (Agropyron repens)	Rhizomes	Dig repeatedly and thoroughly	Dalapon; glyphosate; sodium chlorate on vacant ground	Destroy rhizomes
Daisy (Bellis perennis)	Runners with plantlets	Remove with two-pronged hand fork	2, 4-D; simazine or dichlobenil at low concentrations and in selected situations	Use grass-box when mowing
Dock (Rumex obtusifolius)	Seed	Remove flower spikes before seeding; dig out roots completely	2, 4-D; glyphosate; dichlobenil on vacant ground	Dig out early in spring
Ground elder (Aegopodium podagraria)	Rhizomes	Mulch heavily and completely; dig thoroughly	Glyphosate; sodium chlorate or dichlobenil on vacant ground	Destroy the brittle rhizomes
Groundsel (Senecio vulgaris)	Seed	Hoe out seedlings, hand-fork young plants, destroy before flowering	Paraquat	

Name	Main method of spread	Control, natural	Control, chemical	Remarks
Horsetail (Equisetum spp.)	Deeply-penetrating rhizomes	Grass down; dig and remove top growth repeatedly	Severely suppressed by dichlobenil and glyphosate	Destroy rhizomes, improve drainage
Japanese knotweed (Polygonum cuspidatum)	Rhizomes	Remove top growth repeatedly; dig and saw out rhizomes	Sodium chlorate at greatest concentration on vacant ground; 2, 4-D+2, 4, 5-T repeated; glyphosate	
Nettle (Urtica dioica, U. urens)	Roots, seed	Dig, grass down; encourage cinnabar moth caterpillars	Paraquat to seedlings; 2, 4-D + .2, 4, 5-T; sodium chlorate, simazine or dichlobenil on vacant ground	Cook top growth as spinach
Oxalis corymbosa	Bulbils	Grass down; hand-weed thoroughly	Dichlobenil or glyphosate, following manufacturer's instructions	Destroy all parts of plant
Pearlwort (Sagina procumbens)	Creeping stems root at joints, seed	Hand-fork	Mecoprop; lawnsand; paraquat (but not on lawns)	Improve strength of lawn grasses
Speedwell (Veronica filiformis)	Creeping stems root at joints	Hoe seedlings; hand-fork; mulch heavily	Paraquat; simazine; morfamquat	Improve soil drainage; mow with box attached
Thistle; creeping (Cirsium arvense)	Creeping roots	Dig thoroughly; grass down	Glyphosate or 2, 4-D, more than one application; sodium chlorate or dichlobenil on vacant ground	Destroy roots
Yarrow (Achillea millefolium)	Creeping stems root at joints	Dig, or cut through stems in a criss-cross and remove; repeat if necessary	2, 4-D+2, 4, 5-T, more than one application	Rake lawn before mowing

NOTE: In many instances weedkillers other than those mentioned for a specific weed can also be used, but the chemicals recommended are among the most suitable for the situation in which the weed is likely to be found, For instance, sodium chlorate and simazine will kill chickweed and groundsel anywhere, but these are unsuitable for use between vegetables or flowers, which is where these weeds are most likely to be a nuisance.

Some of the herbicides are suitable for use only in certain situations — 2, 4-D is perfectly safe to use on lawns to kill daisies, but simazine would kill the grass too; on drives or non-grass paths, however, simazine is the best choice as it will kill a wider range of weeds.

Use this chart as a guide, but check the label carefully before purchasing any herbicide, use strictly according to given instructions and keep well out of reach of children.

Top: marking the strips with string and using a spreader bar attachment for the watering-can ensures even application of weedkillers
Above: particular care should be taken when applying a weedkiller near the edge of flower beds. Use a board to prevent damage from drift

ing matter (chlorophyll) in plants, but which are inactivated in the soil. These are most useful on annual and small weeds; they are applied in solution, and work best in sunlight and warm temperatures. Glyphosate is a recent introduction, and also acts through the leaves without affecting the soil. It is claimed to control such difficult weeds as couch grass and ground elder, as well as annuals.

Ioxynil and morfamquat are two more sprayed onto the leaves and stems, and both are recommended for controlling weed seedlings on newly sown lawns. Morfamquat has also been found to be effective against such small-leaved, difficult weeds on lawns as speedwell and black medick (also known as suckling clover).

By careful choice, the cost of material, the amount of time and the degree of labour can all be cut down considerably. Once you know what type of weed you are dealing with, and the methods of control available, you can eliminate weeds and go a long way towards a garden which looks after itself.

Using herbicides
Herbicides work — but many are not just *weed* killers. Applied in the wrong place, or at the wrong strength, they will kill desirable plants too. Always apply carefully, avoiding drift of either powders or sprays. Dribble bars are very effective, and can be used in conjunction with a suitable piece of board to shield beds.

Keep a watering-can just for weedkillers, and be careful where cans are rinsed out.

When using any garden chemical, *always* read the directions before using, and *always* apply as the manufacturer directs. Always keep them out of the reach of children and pets, and *never* put them in unlabelled containers.

Chemical names can be confusing, but all the names used in this book are the common chemical names. This is because the same active chemical may be sold by several manufacturers under different trade names. You will always find the common chemical name listed, however, if you read the label carefully. And if you buy from a good garden shop with trained staff they will be able to sell you the correct chemical if you ask for the names mentioned in this book.

Gardener's friends and foes

Insects are the most numerous of land animals, both in regard to species and as individuals. More than 20,000 kinds are found in Britain alone, and of these a considerable number live in gardens. So not surprisingly they are regarded with suspicion by many gardeners. Some are harmful, of course, but most do no harm at all, while a few are actually beneficial.

Besides the large number of true insects that inhabit our gardens, there are other creatures which we often loosely associate with them. These include spiders, which prey on small flies, centipedes that hunt slugs and other pests, and the harmful millipedes. Slugs and woodlice are other examples of garden pests that are not insects.

A true insect has three pairs of legs, and characteristically either one or two pairs of wings. Many pass through four distinct stages in their life cycle before they are mature. As far as the gardener is concerned, the larval stage is usually the most significant, for it is then that most feeding takes place. Insect larvae are known by various names, such as maggots, grubs, or caterpillars, and they feed mainly on vegetation. Some larvae reach maturity in a few days, while in others the period can be as long as two years.

The insect population of gardens is naturally varied, and is governed by both size and location. The type of soil is also influential; ants, for example, are usually common in sandy areas. And if weeds are allowed to grow unchecked they will attract more insects of various kinds (see page 40); wild plants such as campions (*Silene*) and docks (*Rumex*) are often badly infested with aphids.

Beneficial insects

Before waging war on insects you find in the garden, it is as well to know how the beneficial kinds may be recognized. One does not want to harm bumblebees, for instance, as they visit the blossoms in the fruit garden, and in doing so carry pollen from flower to flower and so ensure a good crop. Honey bees perform the same useful service. Wasps are not so popular, but they do kill large numbers of harmful larvae.

Beetles are also unpopular in a general way, but of the nearly 4,000 species

inhabiting Britain, some are definitely useful. The principal ones are described below.

Violet ground beetles are often unearthed by the spade. These lively beetles do not harm plants but prey on other insects, so should be allowed to go free. Their larvae, which live in the soil, are also useful.

Ladybirds are recognized by most people as friends of the gardener. They help by preying on aphids, and their larvae also consume countless numbers of these sap-sucking pests. Ladybird larvae are mainly bluish in colour, with black

Top: Queen bumblebee in spring
Above left: larva of ladybird
Above: larva of green lacewing

and yellow markings. They can be seen in summer on the foliage of plants and trees. The ladybird population is subject to considerable variation in numbers from year to year. Vast hordes were seen in the hot summer of 1976, and this was partly due to immigration, but they were far less common the following year.

Green lacewings or lacewing flies are equally useful, because of their destruction of aphids. There are several species of these very delicate-looking insects.

Above: a red admiral on Buddleia davidii, more popularly known as the 'butterfly bush'
Left: the female ichneumon wasp lays her eggs in caterpillars, which are eventually killed

Harmful insects

We are confronted with a depressingly large variety of harmful insects. Some of these are conspicuous, but with others only the symptoms of the attack are evident. The key to control is to act at the first signs.

Aphids are perhaps the best known pests. In addition to weakening plants by sucking their sap, they also secrete a sticky liquid known as honey-dew. This is unsightly on foliage, and it attracts ants.

Aphids increase in numbers at an alarming rate, for the females can give birth to living young without first associating with the males. They also pair in the conventional way and lay fertile eggs which overwinter.

There are many kinds of aphids (commonly known as greenfly and blackfly), some having a marked preference for a particular type of plant.

Cockchafers or May-bugs are very destructive to foliage, and their fleshy, pale larvae live underground and feed on roots.

Wireworms are tough-skinned, long, thin, yellow-brown larvae of the click beetles or skipjacks. They are often found in old grassland and in newly-cultivated ground. They can do much damage to the roots of cultivated plants.

Weevils are beetles of modest size, and are easily recognized by the beak-like projection from the head. Some eat holes in leaves, and these are not easily controlled. The notorious vine weevil often attacks rhododendron leaves, and its whitish larva feeds on the roots of some houseplants.

Cabbage root fly maggots are very destructive. The adult fly looks like a small housefly, and the maggot-like larvae feed on roots of young cabbage.

Narcissus flies and bulb flies also originate from pale-looking maggots, which tunnel into the bulbs of daffodils and related plants.

Leatherjackets are the larvae of crane-flies or daddy-long-legs. They feed on plant roots and can be especially troublesome on lawns.

Moths Numerous different moths are found in gardens, and although many are casual visitors, and do no harm, others are pests because their caterpillars are voracious feeders. The so-called cutworms, which can be so destructive to seedlings and other young plants in

Ichneumons, or ichneumon wasps, are more subtle in behaviour. The females inject eggs into living caterpillars and other larvae. The larvae from these eggs feed inside their hosts and eventually kill them.

Among the more familiar of the ichneumons are the small *Apanteles* species that victimize the caterpillars of cabbage white butterflies. A single caterpillar can contain upwards of 20 of the larvae, which, on becoming fully grown, leave their victim and spin a small, oblong, silken cocoon in which to pupate. The cocoons are often seen on garden walls and fences, and they should be left to produce more of their useful kind.

Neutral insects

Apart from the various beneficial insects described, a number of species found in gardens might be termed 'neutrals', because although they do little good they are not harmful. Many of these are attractive in the garden, especially the brightly coloured butterflies such as the handsome red admiral, the peacock and the small tortoiseshell. The caterpillars of all three live on nettles and never harm garden plants. The only harmful butterflies found in Britain are the cabbage whites. Their caterpillars eat plants of the cabbage family and also nasturtiums. Many of the other caterpillars found eating plants belong to moths.

The true flies of the order *Diptera* include more than 5,000 species, and some are serious pests. A few are useful because their larvae are parasitic, like those of the ichneumons. Garden ponds are sometimes visited by dragonflies, and several of the larger ones have a wing span of 10cm (4in). They are certainly imposing, and some people call them 'horse-stingers', but they do not sting and are harmless. They prey on gnats and other small flies, and their larvae are aquatic.

45

spring, are not really worms, but the caterpillars of various night-moths, including those of the large yellow underwing. They feed after dark, and can be hunted down with the help of a torch. The long-winged ghost swift moth is also a root-feeder in the caterpillar stage, and it can be a troublesome pest.

Several moths appear in late autumn and winter, and the wingless females lay their many eggs on the twigs of different trees. The caterpillars hatch out in early spring, and are of the 'looper' type. They arch the body into a loop when walking, and feed on most woodland and orchard trees. The species include the hated winter moth and the mottled umber. Because the females of these moths are wingless they have to climb the trees on foot, so they can be trapped by fixing sticky bands on the tree trunks. Another unpopular looping caterpillar is the offspring of the magpie moth, or currant moth. This has creamy-white wings liberally spotted with black and yellow. The caterpillars feed on the leaves of currants and gooseberries in early summer. These caterpillars should not be confused with the larvae of gooseberry sawflies which also feed on gooseberries. If neglected the larvae may strip all the leaves from a bush.

Other caterpillars often found in gardens are those of the grey and black peppered moth. They are very twig-like in appearance, and can sometimes be seen on roses in late summer, but they are not usually common enough to be very harmful. A smaller, but far more destructive, caterpillar belongs to the codling moth which lives inside apples and to a lesser extent in pears. It destroys much of the pulp, and on becoming fully grown tunnels through the skin of the fruit to find a place in which to spin its tough silken cocoon, and change into a pupa. The codling moth appears in spring, and can be controlled by spraying immediately after a blossom-fall. The cocoons are often attached to bark, and can be removed by scrubbing the trunks with a stiff brush.

Pests and their control

Pest	Description	Crops affected	Control
Ants (Formicidae)	Immediately recognizable, but there are many species. Can be a nuisance, and encourage aphids	Most plants infested with aphids; ripe fruit	Gamma-HCH; pirimiphos-methyl; pyrethrum; trichlorphon
Aphids (greenfly, blackfly) (Aphididae)	Tiny insects, usually found in clusters; some are winged, some not. May be green, black or grey, depending on type	A wide range of plants, indoors and out, including vegetables	Dimethoate (systemic); gamma-HCH and menazon; fenitrothion; formothion (systemic); malathion; oxydemeton-methyl aerosol; pyrethrum and resmethrin; rotenone; rotenone and quassia
Cabbage root fly maggot (Erioischia brassicae)	Small white grubs that eat the roots of brassica crops. The plants are severely checked. Wilting and a blue cast to the leaves are symptoms	Brassicas such as cabbages, cauliflowers, broccoli, Brussels sprouts, radishes and turnips	Bromophos; mercurous chloride
Capsid bugs (Capsidae)	Whitish or greenish insects, rather like largish aphids. There are several types. Plants become weakened and leaves are distorted	Many ornamental plants and fruit such as gooseberries and currants	Fenitrothion
Carrot fly maggot (Psila rosae)	Small white maggots in roots. Leaves of affected plants often turn bronze	Carrots, celery, parsley and parsnips	Bromophos
Caterpillars (Lepidoptera)	Well-known to all gardeners. Many different kinds, most belonging to moths	Brassica crops affected by cabbage white butterfly caterpillars (Pieris brassicae); many crops, including gooseberries, by moth caterpillars	Bacillus thuringiensis Berliner (biological control); carbaryl, rotenone; rotenone and quassia
Cockchafer (Melolontha melolontha)	A large beetle about 2.5cm (1in) long, with black head and thorax and reddish-brown wing cases. Eats leaves; grubs eat roots	Ornamental trees and shrubs, soft fruit, potatoes and herbaceous plants	Bromophos (for grubs)
Codling moth (Laspuiresia pomonella)	The small white caterpillar eats its way into apples. Not to be confused with the apple sawfly (Hoplocampa testudinea), which usually attacks about a month earlier in May or June and generally causes the fruit to drop	Apples	Fenitrothion.
Cuckoo spit (frog hoppers) (Cercopidae)	Resemble tiny pale yellow grasshoppers. Jump if disturbed. Greenish-yellow larvae protect themselves with a covering of froth	Many garden plants, especially in herbaceous border	Malathion
Earwig (Dermaptera)	Well-known pests, with distinctive forceps, those of the male being rounded like callipers, those of the female straight	Many, but dahlias and chrysanthemums are especially vulnerable	Gamma-HCH; pirimiphos-methyl
Leaf hoppers (Cicadellidae)	Pale yellow insects resembling aphids and capsid bugs. Cause white mottling of leaves	Many plants, outdoors and in. Roses attract one species	Pyrethrum and resmethrin
Leaf miners (various Lepidoptera and Diptera)	White 'tunnels' in the leaves are a tell-tale sign of these small larvae	Chrysanthemums, holly, and certain other ornamentals, and celery	Malathion.
Leatherjackets (Tipula)	The larvae of crane-flies. Resemble dark grey or black caterpillars, but have no legs	Grasses, herbaceous plants and vegetables. Worst on old pasture or newly-cultivated land	Gamma-HCH; methiocarb
Mealy bugs (Pseudococcus)	Troublesome greenhouse pests. The small whitish insects protect themselves with a waxy substance	Greenhouse plants and houseplants	Malathion

Pest	Description	Crops affected	Control
Onion fly maggot (Delia antiqua)	Small white maggots attack onion bulbs at or just below soil level. Foliage droops	Onions, leeks, shallots	Bromophos; mercurous chloride
Raspberry beetle (Byturus tomentosus)	Small yellow-brown or grey beetle, eats buds and flowers. White grub hatches in the raspberry fruit	Raspberries, loganberries and blackberries	Fenitrothion; rotenone; malathion
Red spiders (Arachnida: Acari)	Actually mites, not spiders; tiny and brownish-red. Can just be seen with naked eye. Under a magnifying glass can be seen to have eight legs. Affected leaves become mottled and bronzed. Worst in greenhouses	Greenhouse crops such as perpetual carnations, houseplants; outdoors may sometimes be found on apples and strawberries	Formothion (systemic); malathion; pirimiphos-methyl; rotenone
Sawflies (Tenthredinidae)	Larvae of several fly-like insects resemble caterpillars. The white maggot of the apple sawfly (*Hoplocampa testudinea*) tunnels into young apples; other species eat the leaves of plants such as roses or gooseberries	Apples, roses, gooseberries, plums, and other plants, depending on species	Fenitrothion; rotenone
Scale insects (Coccidae)	Small sucking insects, covered by a scale. The scale is about 3mm (⅛in) long, the colour varying from brown to grey or black, depending on species	Houseplants and greenhouse plants; or fruit trees, aucubas, yew (*Taxus*) and beech (*Fagus*), among others, in the open	Malathion
Slugs and snails (Mollusca: Stylomma tophora)	There are various species of these well-known pests. The type that live below ground are more difficult to control	Almost all crops, but seedlings are most vulnerable	Metaldehyde; methiocarb.
Thrips (Thysanoptera)	Small, narrow insects, from pale yellow to black in colour. Flower buds often badly affected	A wide range of plants, outdoors and indoors	Gamma-HCH; malathion; pyrethrum and resmethrin; rotenone; rotenone and quassia
Turnip flea beetles (Phyllotreta)	Small black beetles that make small round holes in brassica crop leaves, especially seedlings. The beetles jump when disturbed	Turnips, cabbages, broccoli, Brussels sprouts, and allied crops	Gamma-HCH; rotenone; carbaryl
Weevils (Curculionidae)	Beetles with an elongated snout. There are many species, the vine weevil (*Otiorhynchus sulcatus*) grub attacks vine roots, bulbs, corms and tubers, and other roots. The adult beetles eat the leaves	Besides crops mentioned, some favour roses, some apples, others peas and beans	Carbaryl
Whiteflies (Aleyrodidae)	Tiny white flying insects, sometimes rising when disturbed, to form a white cloud	Tomatoes in greenhouses, cabbage family outdoors, ornamental house and greenhouse plants	Bioresmethrin aerosol (for greenhouses); dimethoate (systemic); malathon
Wireworms (Elateridae)	Larvae of click beetles, yellow-brown and hard-skinned. Segmented body; up to 2.5m (1in) long	Roots of many plants	Bromophos; gamma-HCH; diazinon
Woodlice (Crustacea: Oniscoidea)	Grey, hard-coated creatures, some of which roll themselves into a ball when disturbed. Often found under stones or rotting wood. May damage seedlings, and can be a problem in a greenhouse, but not serious outdoors	Live mainly on decaying material, but seedlings may be eaten	Gamma-HCH; methiocarb; pirimiphos-methyl; carbaryl
Woolly aphis (Eriosoma lanigerum)	Most obvious indication of this pest is the cotton-wool-like excretion with which it surrounds itself	Apple trees	Malathion; dimethoate (systemic)

Top: distinctive evidence of the rose sawfly
Above centre: the caterpillar of the magpie or currant moth is a pest of the fruit garden, feeding on the leaves of currants and gooseberries
Above: the mature magpie or currant moth
Opposite page: black aphids (blackfly) are very widespread and a serious pest in the garden

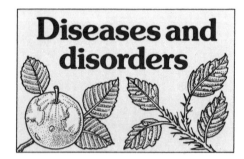

Diseases and disorders

In addition to the numerous harmful insects and other small animals that damage plants, many diseases are also destructive in the garden and greenhouse. Some are familiar, others more obscure, though no less damaging on that account. The effect of some can be devastating, as in the case of the Dutch elm disease, which has killed so many fine elms. The spores of this fungus are carried from tree to tree by small beetles, with dire results.

Most of the diseases in our gardens are caused by fungi, although viruses are also responsible for heavy crop losses. Both viral and bacterial diseases are difficult to control, and usually the only solution is to burn infected material. The array of effective fungicides, however, makes the control of fungus diseases a less drastic affair.

Fungus diseases

Most fungus diseases we are concerned with in the garden in no way resemble the toadstool-shaped kinds with conspicuous fruiting bodies. The majority are invisible to the naked eye, and it is the symptoms that we recognize.

Powdery mildew is an unsightly and weakening disease frequently seen on roses. If allowed to progress, the pale, powdery coating will soon cover twigs, foliage and even flowers during the summer. There are other species of powdery mildew, and these can be seen on a wide range of trees and other plants. The leaves of apple and oak are common victims, as are gooseberries and blackcurrants. The twigs of the last two may become distorted, and should be removed if this happens, otherwise the disease may persist the following year.

Black-spot is another unsightly disease found on roses, although a form also occurs on sycamore. The characteristic black spots, which are the first sign of the disease, are very disfiguring. It is more prevalent in the clean atmosphere of country areas than in towns, where the pollution seems to act as a natural fungicide.

Coral-spot is another disease with a descriptive name. It produces numerous

reddish or deep orange spots on dead twigs. Unfortunately it often spreads from these to living twigs, and can be very destructive to old red currant bushes, although gooseberries and apples are among the other plants attacked.

Honey fungus is even less welcome. This large honey-coloured fungus grows on old tree stumps, and spreads from these by means of black, underground root-like rhizomorphs, known as 'bootlaces'. The problem lies in the fact that it is likely to spread from dead stumps to

Above: Coral spot is a distinctive fungus disease that may be found on several fruit bushes, including red currants and gooseberries
Left: powdery mildew is particularly troublesome on roses, although some cultivars show resistance

living roots of trees and even to any herbaceous plants growing nearby.

Rust is a disfiguring disease, and there are species that affect plants such as hollyhocks, antirrhinums, mint and broad beans. The characteristic sign is the spread of numerous orange and brown pustules on the under surface of the leaves. The disease may eventually kill the plants, and should always be treated quickly. Fortunately there are rust-resistant antirrhinums that can be planted on ground known to contain the spores.

Peach leaf curl is common on peach trees and some related species such as nectarines, almonds and other *Prunus* species. The symptoms are twisted and contorted leaves with red swollen areas; these are conspicuous and unsightly.

Club-root is not visible until the plants are uprooted, although the problem is manifest in the unhealthy and stunted growth made by the plant. Cruciferous plants are affected, and it is often worst on badly-drained acid soils. Affected

plants develop large gall-like swellings on the roots, and when these rot in the ground spores are released and the ground is contaminated for more than a decade. Even crop rotation is of limited value because the spores remain viable for such a long time. With suitable treatment it may be possible to grow brassica crops, but it is best to avoid the disease if your garden is not already affected, by raising all your own brassica plants.

Apple canker is a secondary infection that usually enters through an existing wound, although it can also be spread by aphids. It is a serious disease of apples but also affects some other trees, including pear and beech. First signs are small depressions in the bark, often near a leaf scar. The area affected becomes larger and more oval, and soon the tissue in the centre dies and flakes off to leave a ragged wound surrounded by cracked bark.

Potato blight is a serious potato disease. Brown or black patches appear on the leaves, particularly on the edges, and soon the leaves turn yellow or brown. In moist weather a whitish mould may be seen on the undersides of the brown patches. The disease can also affect the tubers.

Tulip fire and **narcissus fire** cause unsightly brown patches or streaks on the foliage, and damaged leaves look almost scorched. Even the flower petals may be affected with spots.

Bacterial diseases

Bacterial diseases are far less common in plants than in animals, which is fortunate as they are not readily controlled by normal garden chemicals. Strict garden hygiene is the best solution, burning all diseased tissue. As the bacteria may be carried on seeds, never save seed from affected plants.

The two bacterial diseases most likely to be encountered are potato blackleg and soft rot.

Potato blackleg may reveal its presence any time from mid-June onwards. The plants turn a greenish-yellow and become stunted and unhealthy in appearance. If the stems are pulled up they will be seen to be black and rotten. If a stem is cut across, brown or black spots may be seen. Affected tubers will rot in store, and probably spread the disease to other tubers.

Above left: the honey fungus (Armillaria mellea) often grows on dead tree stumps, but can spread to living roots with serious results. Rhododendrons and privets are among plants affected
Left: peach leaf curl is a particularly disfiguring disease that affects Prunus species

49

Soft rot may be caused by various fungi or bacteria. The bacterial kind usually affects carrots, parsnips and other root vegetables. The soft tissue usually disintegrates and becomes soft and slimy. Stored roots are often most affected. Celery heart rot is caused by the same organism.

Virus diseases

Viruses are particularly troublesome because they are so difficult to control. Once a group of plants has become infected it is usually best to burn them and start again.

A typical symptom is a yellowing and mottling of the leaves, sometimes with distortion. The plant looks sickly, and the yield of food crops is significantly reduced. Sometimes, however, the mottling is considered attractive in ornamental subjects; the variegated abutilons are an example.

In fruit and vegetables, however, virus-affected plants must be destroyed immediately. Always buy certified virus-free stock whenever possible, and keep the plants free by controlling the aphids and other sap-sucking insects that transmit the diseases.

Tomato spotted wilt virus causes the young top leaves to brown or bronze, and sometimes concentric rings appear. The whole plant appears to stop growing, and the leaves tend to curl downwards, with thickened veins. This is an especially unwelcome disease as it also affects many other plants, such as winter cherries (*Solanum capsicastrum*), gloxinias (*Sinningia*), dahlias and arum lilies (*Zantedeschia aethiopica*).

Potato leaf roll causes potato leaves to roll upwards, beginning with the lower leaves. The plant becomes stunted, and the crop is reduced. The tubers of affected plants must never be replanted.

Strawberry yellow edge, which causes the young leaves to be dwarfed with yellowish spots on wrinkled leaves, is a serious virus disease. It is best to burn the plants and start again.

Mosaic viruses cause a yellow mottling of the leaves, sometimes accompanied by distortion. Many ornamental plants may be affected, as well as soft fruit such as raspberries and vegetables such as lettuce. It may be possible to buy virus-free lettuce seed from one of the specialist suppliers.

Physiological disorders

Not all unhealthy plants are suffering from pests or diseases. Sometimes a physiological disorder is responsible. Lack of water may cause leaves to wilt and drop; cold draughts may make them turn yellow and fall; chemicals in aerosols can cause spots to appear on the leaves of houseplants; blossom end rot of tomatoes is primarily due to irregular watering.

If there is not an obvious culprit, question the cultural procedure or the environment. Remember also that a deficiency of certain nutrients can cause symptoms resembling diseases. A manganese deficiency, for example, can cause a yellowing of the leaves that could resemble a virus disease.

Using chemicals

The chemicals mentioned in this book are safe if used in accordance with the manufacturers' instructions. But always follow them to the letter.

Sensible spraying and dusting will help in the fight against pests and diseases — but apply chemicals safely and sensibly. Remember:
● Read the label carefully — all of it!
● Certain chemicals may damage particular groups of plants (see labels).
● Mixing stronger solutions will not increase the potency but may damage the plants.
● Do not spray in strong sunshine as this may damage the plants.
● Always dispose of unused spray solutions safely (flush down the WC or outside sink drain, or pour over the soil).
● Insecticides and fungicides are usually most effective if applied as soon as possible after the problem has been diagnosed. Fungus diseases may be particularly difficult to eradicate once the infection has become established (a systemic fungicide may be the best control in this situation).
● Use dusts when the morning dew is still on the leaves — powder will adhere more readily.
● Cover the undersides of the leaves as well as the topsides and shoots when applying sprays.

Consider the other creatures too. Some insecticides will also kill beneficial insects, although primicarb is harmless to lacewings, ladybirds and bees. It is best to spray in the morning or late afternoon when bees are least active.

Even 'natural' chemicals such as pyrethrum may be toxic to fish, so be particularly careful to check the label before applying a garden chemical within close proximity to a pond.

Diseases and their control

Disease	Symptoms	Control
American Gooseberry Mildew	Stems, leaves and berries covered with fungus growth, white at first then dark brown. Shoots stunted. Sometimes affects currants	Benomyl. Cut off affected shoots in August and burn
Apple and Pear Scab	Black round spots or blotches on the fruit, and black or brownish-green blotches on the leaves. Worst in wet seasons	Bupirimate and triforine (systemic) — use for apple only; captan; thiophanate-methyl (systemic); zineb
Black-spot	See text	Bupirimate and triforine (systemic); captan; copper compound; dichlofluanid; thiophanate-methyl (systemic); thiram; zineb
Botrytis	Decay of soft plant tissue, followed by a fluffy grey mould. Affects many crops, including lettuce, strawberries and tomatoes	Captan; copper compound; dichlofluanid; TCNB (tecnazene) smoke (for greenhouses); thiophate-methyl (systemic); thiram
Celery Leaf Spot	Leaves develop brown spots with tiny black dots	Copper compound. The disease can be spread by seed; treated seed is sometimes available
Chocolate Spot	Chocolate-coloured spots on leaves, rapidly increasing in size. Affects mainly broad beans	Copper compound. Improve drainage
Club Root	See text	Calomel dust. Liming helps
Coral Spot	See text	Cut off affected shoots below last affected leaves
Damping-off	Seedlings decay at or near soil level, the seedlings toppling over	Cheshunt compound; copper compound
Downy Mildew	Mealy-looking or furry growth on leaves and stems. Leaves sometimes die from the tips and shrivel	Copper compound; thiophanate-methyl (systemic); thiram; zineb
Canker	See text	Copper compound. Cut out areas affected with a sharp knife as soon as noticed; then paint wound with a wound dressing
Honey Fungus	See text	Dig up old stumps; treat soil with formalin
Narcissus Fire	See text	Dig up and burn severely affected plants. Treat with thiram
Peach Leaf Curl	See text	Copper compound; zineb
Potato Blight	See text. Also affects tomatoes	Copper compound; zineb
Powdery Mildew	See text	Bupirimate and triforine (systemic); dinocap; thiophanate-methyl (systemic); thiram
Raspberry Cane Spot	Young canes develop small circular spots in May or June. These become elliptical and the centres become whitish-grey	Benomyl; copper compound; dichlofluanid
Rust (carnation, chrysanthemum, rose)	See text	Copper compound; oxycarboxin; thiram; zineb
Tomato Leaf Mould	Yellow blotches appear on upper surface of leaves, with velvety brown or purple mould growth at the back	Thiophanate-methyl (systemic); zineb
Tulip Fire	See text	Dig up and burn seriously affected plants. Dust with thiram

Above left: Magnesium deficiency, shown here in potatoes. Mineral deficiencies usually affect several plants of the same crop
Far left: virus disease in a potato plant. In the case of virus diseases, individual plants are usually affected initially. Dig up and burn
Centre left: the leaf yellowing in these strawberry plants is caused by potash deficiency.
Left: lime-induced iron deficiency (chlorosis) shows as yellowing between veins. Correct by using a chelated iron, sold as Sequestene

Propagation

Propagating one's own plants not only saves money, it also generates a tremendous sense of satisfaction. The sight of a box of newly germinated seedlings, or of a mass of healthy white roots on a cutting, is always gratifying. It's an experience to thrill the beginner, but even the most seasoned gardener experiences a similar feeling — for there are always the more difficult species to offer a challenge.

Expensive equipment and a greenhouse are not necessary, though they may help with difficult species. Most will require nothing more than good compost and a warm windowledge; indeed some plants are so easy to propagate that the constant supply of offspring can be an embarrassment.

Raising plants from seed

The miracle of germination holds a fascination for most gardeners, and the promise in a packet of seeds needs only a little moisture, light and warmth to be unleashed (although sometimes a little shock treatment is required to break dormancy).

By following the methods described in this chapter, no difficulty should be experienced with the vast majority of subjects likely to be grown in the garden or home.

Seeds are still inexpensive if you calculate the cost per potential plant, so paying a few pence more for the best strains makes sense. But remember, even if you purchase seeds in hermetically sealed packets they begin ageing the moment the packet is opened, so do not attempt to save some for future sowing.

Compost
Good compost is essential for satisfactory germination and healthy seedlings. Avoid ordinary garden soil, and buy either John Innes Seed Compost (which can be made by anyone, but is mixed to a special formula and is loam-based), or one of the proprietary peat-based seedling composts (most of these are also suitable for growing the plants on).

Soil outdoors is more difficult to control, but peat worked into the top few centimetres (inches) of the seedbed will improve both sand and clay soils. Do not attempt to sow until a fine crumbly structure has been created.

Seed-sowing tips and techniques
A heated propagator (see page 96) will get the plants away to an early start, although it is not essential and really only gains a few weeks on the growing season. If you have a greenhouse, it may be possible to make a small frame within the main structure, or partition a section, so that warmth and humidity can be increased.

Pelleted seeds should be used whenever possible if you find thin sowing difficult. The amount of light, food and water seedlings receive in the first few weeks can be crucial. Thickly-sown, overcrowded seedlings are a major cause of failure. The seeds' size governs the depth of sowing.

Darkness helps the germination of most seeds, but some require light, so read the packet carefully and do not cover too deeply or keep in a dark place if light is advised. If you are not having success with a particular kind of seed, try sowing less deeply and keep in a light place.

Pre-chilling is sometimes necessary for seeds of alpine and herbaceous plants, as well as many shrubs. A satisfactory way with most seeds that need this cold period to break their dormancy is to place them between damp blotting paper and leave them in the refrigerator for about a week.

Nicking hard-coated seeds, such as morning glory (*Ipomoea*) and certain sweet peas (*Lathyrus odoratus*), with a sharp knife enables moisture to penetrate more readily. Soaking overnight before sowing also helps.

1. Seeds should always be sown in carefully prepared boxes or pots of sterilized compost. After placing crocks over the drainage holes, place a generous quantity of compost in the box and firm using the palms and fingers to bed it well down

2. For the final levelling and firming, use a flat piece of wood with a suitable handle. Ensure that the wood is large enough to cover most of the width of the box, as this helps to avoid unevenness and produce a level surface for sowing

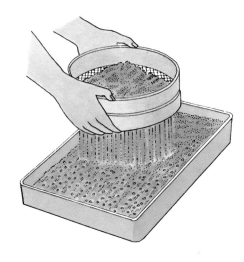

3. Most seeds should be covered with a thin layer of sifted compost, the amount of covering depending on the size of the seed. Very fine seed may not need covering at all

4. Although the boxes can be watered with a fine-rosed watering-can, even gentle force can sometimes wash out the seeds, so it is better to stand the box in a bowl of water after sowing

Sowing indoors

Most seeds can be germinated satisfactorily in the home — the problem comes afterwards, when the seedlings will soon become drawn and sickly unless good all-round light is available. Seed-raising in the home is likely to be restricted by the amount of light windowledge space available for the pricked-out seedlings.

In a greenhouse, the problem is usually one of heat, and here the restraint is holding back until sufficient warmth is available for the seedlings to grow away without check.

Sowing should not be done in a rush. To assist the drainage of loam-based compost, and to prevent compost of any kind being washed through large drainage holes, broken pots or coarse gravel should be placed at the bottom of the seed box or pot.

Whether plastic or clay containers are used, they should be clean; plastic containers have the advantage of being light and easily cleaned, but wooden trays are perfectly adequate and will last for years if treated with a suitable non-toxic preservative.

Fill the container almost to the top, then gently firm down the compost with the bottom of a clean pot, or use an improvised soil firmer.

Moisten the compost before sowing, so that small seeds are not washed out before they have a chance to germinate.

Where seed is of a size that can be handled easily, space them out to eliminate the pricking-out stage. Most fine seeds can be distributed fairly evenly by gently tapping the packet, but in the case of dust-like seeds such as begonias and lobelias, the job will be easier if the seed is mixed with a little dry sand and sprinkled from the fingers and thumb.

If the seeds have to be covered (study the seed packet), do it evenly. A fine-mesh sieve is useful.

Gently firm the covering to make a level finish (even fine seeds that do not need covering may benefit from being pressed into the compost). If the containers are not to be placed in a propagating case, cover with a sheet of clear glass or plastic, then shade with a piece of paper until most of the seeds show signs of germination. Turn the glass daily to avoid excessive condensation.

Pricking-off should start as soon as the seedlings can be handled by the leaves, but first moisten the compost to ease the task of removing them without damage. Space the plants in new boxes or pots of compost, sufficiently far apart to prevent them becoming drawn and overcrowded by planting-out time.

Hardening-off is a crucial stage, and should always be done gradually. The best method is to use cold-frames, but if these are not available it is a case of standing the plants outside during mild weather and bringing them in at night or during cold or windy weather.

Sowing outdoors

Seedbed preparation must be done thoroughly. Remove all weeds, and incorporate a little general fertilizer a few weeks before sowing. Break the soil down into a fine tilth, and incorporate peat if necessary.

Sowing is best done in drills taken out with a draw hoe, using a garden line to ensure straight rows. Do not sow too deeply (check with the seed packet), and be sure to water the ground well after sowing, taking care not to wash away the seeds.

Annuals are often sown broadcast, but weeding and thinning may be easier if sown in drills within irregularly shaped patches. Unless you know what the seedlings look like, weeding an area sown broadcast can be difficult until the plants are established.

Thinning should always be done early, and in two stages. Thin first to half the final distance, to allow for losses, then eventually to the correct spacing.

Thinning is a tiresome task, and thin sowing makes the job much easier. It also tends to produce better plants.

Transplanting may be necessary for biennials (see pages 140–49) and perennials (see Hardy Border Plants, pages 150–159), which usually spend a period in a nursery bed set aside for them to mature in size. Transplant with as little root disturbance as possible, and always try to do it when the soil is moist.

5. Large seeds, or those that resent transplanting after germination, can be sown individually in pots. Sow two or three to a pot, then thin out to the strongest seedlings if more than one germinates. This method is often used when sowing in peat pots

6. Reasonably large seeds can be spaced over a seed tray by holding a few in the palm of the hand and tapping it gently with the fingers of the other hand. Very fine seed is best mixed with a little sand, and sprinkled carefully between the fingers

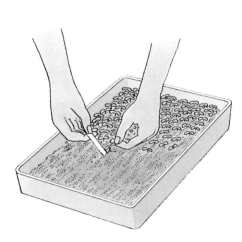

7. When the seedlings are large enough to handle, they should be pricked off (transplanted) into another box. Lift only by the seed leaves and support with a suitable stick

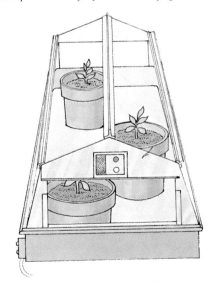

8. Seeds usually germinate most successfully in a warm, humid atmosphere. This is best provided by a propagator, preferably electrically heated, but even an unheated propagator can be useful

Raising plants vegetatively

Many plants are best raised vegetatively — either because they are not available as seed (seeds of some types will not breed true), or simply because it is the most efficient way of raising new stock.

Most vegetative propagation is from cuttings of shoots or roots, but layering is very successful with certain shrubs, and a few are 'live-bearers' producing miniature ready-made plants that only need detaching from the parent.

Propagation aids

A sharp pruning knife, or even a craft knife for softwood cuttings, is basic equipment. Hormone rooting powder is well worth using — difficult subjects benefit greatly while even easy plants root more readily. Buy one with a combined fungicide.

A propagator (see page 96) will provide the right degree of humidity, but a polythene bag will often suffice (provided it is not allowed to touch the cuttings and is reversed daily to prevent too much condensation).

Most useful if you take a lot of cuttings, and have a greenhouse, is a mist unit (see page 97) in which both heat and moisture are automatically controlled.

Cuttings

Shoot cuttings are very popular, and usually very easy to root.

The first batch of cuttings is normally taken from fresh new shoots made early in the year, and these are known as 'softwood' cuttings. Shrubs and pot plants, as well as many rock and herbaceous subjects, are easily raised in this way, including delphiniums, violas, coleus, impatiens, the popular tradescantias, and fuchsias.

Shoots about 7.5–10cm (3–4in) long are ideal. Trim them off cleanly just below a convenient leaf joint with a sharp knife. Remove the lower leaves and insert the shoots into moist well-drained compost or perlite. Rooting compound is not normally necessary for these cuttings, but they should be rooted in the moist warm conditions of a propagator, or covered with a clear polythene bag in a warm, shady place indoors.

From July until autumn is the ideal time to take halfripe cuttings of many shrubs like conifers, roses (*Rosa* spp) and clematis. Sideshoots should be chosen, but at this time the lower part of the stems will be hardening and less pliable. Remove the whole sideshoot, complete with a sliver (heel) of the older wood from which it originates, and dip the base in a rooting compound. Greenhouse shrubs will need to be rooted in a warm, moist frame, but hardy shrubs will form

excellent roots if dibbled into the bed soil of a cold-frame.

A slightly different method is often used for clematis. Instead of severing the stem directly under a leaf joint, cut halfway between the joints. Then trim the top to just above the leaves, and insert the stem sections into pots and place in a warm frame.

Fully ripened ('hardwood') shoots take longer to root. Hardwood cuttings are commonly used for soft fruits like gooseberries, black currants and red currants; often the late summer or autumn prunings furnish suitable material.

Hardwood cuttings usually need to be about the width of a pencil and about 23–30cm (9–12in) long. It is best to use a hormone rooting powder, and insert the cuttings into a cold-frame or the open ground any time from late summer into winter.

Leaf cuttings tend to be more difficult and not so many subjects are suitable. But it is an exciting way to raise new plants. The decorative *Begonia rex* has large colourful leaves that, when laid flat on moist compost and sliced across the veins, will produce plantlets (it may be necessary to peg the leaf down to keep it in contact with the moist compost). And the popular African violet (*Saintpaulia ionantha*) will root if the leaf stalk is inserted into perlite or a peat-sand mixture. Trim the leaf stalk off about 2.5cm (1in) under the blade and push it down at a slight angle so the leaf just touches the compost.

Another type of leaf cutting can be taken from camellias or rubber plants (*Ficus elastica*). With these a leaf is taken complete with one dormant bud on a sliver of old stem.

Another type of leaf cutting is used for two popular houseplants, mother-in-law's tongue (*Sansevieria trifasciata*), and cape primroses (*Streptocarpus*). The leaves are cut cross-wise into 5–7.5cm (2–3in) sections, and the lower cut pushed into the compost. Each section, if kept warm and moist, will produce one or more plantlets from the base; these can be gently detached and potted separately.

Root cuttings. In certain cases, roots can also be used for making cuttings. The hardy herbaceous gypsophila (*G. paniculata*), oriental poppy (*Papaver orientale*) and drumstick primula (*Primula denticulata*) are typical; the latter produces numerous plantlets if the crown is deftly cut off at ground level.

For most kinds, cut the severed roots into 2.5–5cm (1–2in) sections; make a sloping cut on the lower part, but a straight one across the top. The pieces should be inserted vertically into pots of

How to take a cutting (starting from the top):
Stage One: using a sharp knife, cut the shoot to be propagated from the plant
Stage Two: trim just below where the leaves join the stem. Remove the lower leaves
Stage Three: carefully dip the base of the cutting in a hormone rooting powder
Stage Four: use a dibber to make a hole. Insert the cutting and firm the compost well around it

compost and rooted in a cold-frame any time from February until spring.

Phlox roots can be treated in a similar way, but in this case the roots are best laid horizontally on compost in a pan or seed tray and covered with about 2.5cm (1in) of soil.

Layering
Certain woody plants are very reluctant to root from cuttings, many dehydrating very quickly after the shoots are severed from the plant. Layering is often the solution.

Ground layering is the most common form of layering. A low-slung branch of the tree or shrub is pulled down and pegged into the soil, and a peat-soil mulch used to conserve moisture. This method is also ideal for climbing shrubs, including clematis.

In all cases it pays to strip the leaves away where the stem is pegged under the soil, and a sloping cut should be made up into the stem, to encourage root formation. The application of a hormone rooting compound to the wound may encourage roots to form more rapidly.

Aerial layering is used for a few plants, such as the Swiss cheese plant (*Monstera deliciosa*) and rubber plant. It is particularly suitable for tidying up plants that drop their leaves.

Choose a firm, one-year-old stem and make an upward cut into it just under a leaf joint, no more than halfway through, then wedge the wound open with a small wad of moist moss. Apply rooting powder, then wrap more damp moss around the outside of the stem and cover with black polythene.

Once roots have formed, the stem can be cut off below the layer which can then be potted separately.

Tip layers are easiest of all, on plants where these are possible. Blackberries and loganberries are examples. The arching stems are pegged down by their tips, and are severed once rooted.

'Live-bearers'
Some plants, such as the strawberry and mother of thousands (*Saxifraga stolonifera*), naturally produce numerous runners, the tips of which produce plantlets that root where they touch the soil.

Other plants, such as certain bryophyllums, and the cool-house fern *Asplenium bulbiferum*, form tiny plantlets or bulbils on the foliage, many of which produce roots and fall off to start a colony round the mother plant. This character is also displayed by some begonia species and the pick-a-back plant (*Tolmiea menziesii*).

Many plants, such as Begonia rex, can be increased by leaf cuttings. Nick the veins on the underside, using a sharp knife or razor-blade. Nick each vein several times

The leaf is then laid on the surface of moist compost and pegged down with small pieces of bent wire. Roots will form from the nicked surfaces. When large enough, the small plants can be potted

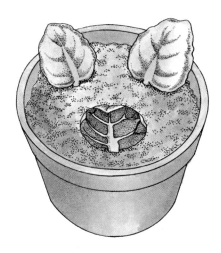

Many plants can be increased by taking leaf-petiole cuttings (cuttings with the leaf-stalk attached). The leaf stalks are inserted into the compost, which is then firmed around them

Some plants can be layered. A small V-shape hole is made in the surface of the soil, and the partly severed stem pegged into it. It often takes several months for roots to form

Plants that produce runners or low and long shoots can be increased by pegging the tips into small pots of soil or compost. They can be severed later and planted elsewhere. Strawberries are normally propagated in this manner, also blackberries (in this case it is known as tip-layering; with strawberries the runner goes on to produce more plantlets)

Pruning

Sensible pruning benefits both plant and gardener, but injudicious pruning can be disastrous. If a forsythia hedge is pruned at the wrong time, for instance, the result the following spring can be plenty of leaves but no flowers.

Many trees and shrubs will grow happily for years without pruning, but in many cases pruning leads to more prolific flowering and a better shape. Shaping is seen at its best in topiary, which is quite feasible for small gardens.

Pruning also provides an opportunity to remove dead or diseased wood, so it also contributes to the general health of garden plants.

Good tools obviously help (see Tools and Equipment, pages 20–25), and they should be sharp.

When to prune

Dead wood should be removed as soon as it is noticed, at any time of the year; the same applies to diseased shoots. For general shaping and to improve cropping, however, the time should be chosen carefully.

Deciduous shrubs or trees are usually pruned in the dormant season, particularly if a large amount of wood is to be removed. This reduces the risk of infection and does not subject the plants to a severe check to growth. But there are exceptions; silver leaf disease, which affects plums and other *Prunus* species, is less likely to become established if pruning is done when the plant is in full growth, preferably before mid-July.

Where flower and fruit buds are to be encouraged in preference to rampant growth, summer pruning is also desirable. This applies particularly to fruit trees of restricted form, such as cordons or espaliers.

Shrubs that flower on wood produced in the previous season are usually cut back after flowering; this allows time for replacement shoots to grow and mature for next season's flowers.

Shrubs that produce flowers on new growth are best pruned early in the year, to encourage a flush of vigorous shoots. The butterfly bush (*Buddleia davidii*) is an example of a shrub that responds to this treatment; to delay pruning may mean all the potential flowering shoots for the current year are removed.

As very early hard cutting back may encourage growth during periods of frost, it is wise to head back the shoots by half in the autumn or winter, and then complete the job when the first sign of growth appears in March. In this way any early shoots damaged by cold can be replaced by others formed lower down the stems after the second pruning.

How to prune

Always start by cutting out dead or diseased wood, cutting back into sound areas of the branch.

Where it is necessary to remove an entire heavy branch, it is best to make an undercut before working down from the upper part of the bough, as this will prevent the bark being torn. The weight of the branch sometimes causes the saw to bind when undercutting, in which case first cut off the branch about 30cm (1ft) from the main branch or trunk.

Once the branch has been removed, clean up any rough edges on the wound, using a sharp knife, then apply a bitumen wound dressing paint, making sure the whole area is thoroughly covered.

Even on smaller shoots or twigs, it is unwise to leave short snags that may die back eventually. Using secateurs, cut just above a suitably-placed bud, ideally sloping down away from the bud slightly. If using a pruning knife, make the cut upwards towards the tip of the bud.

If you are trying to encourage the plant to fill in the centre, cut back to an inward-facing bud, but if the plant is overcrowded or a weeping habit is required, choose an outward-facing bud.

Special cases

Roses often generate controversy when it comes to pruning, and this aspect is discussed with the cultivation of roses (see pages 76–77).

Fruit trees are often complex in pruning requirements, particularly if trained as cordons, espaliers or fans. For that reason pruning is discussed under the relevant fruit.

Clematis often cause difficulties — mainly because one has to decide on the type of clematis being dealt with, and there are different methods of pruning. There are three main groups:

The small-flowered species normally only need light pruning, sufficient to prevent shoots becoming overcrowded and to maintain a good shape.

Dead or unproductive stems can be removed at any time, although late-flowering species can be cut back hard in spring to encourage a new flush of vigorous growth if the plant has become totally overgrown and tangled. Early-flowering species, such as *C. montana*,

Pruning *Buddleia davidii*

Pruning *wisteria sinensis*

Summer pruning

Winter pruning

are best pruned just after flowering.

Large-flowered types that flower on the previous year's shoots, and normally flower in May and June, should be trimmed back lightly after flowering. Tangled specimens can be cut back hard in February if you are prepared to lose the first crop of flowers.

Large-flowered types that flower on new wood, such as the Jackmanii range (these normally flower later), can have old stems cut back to within 30–90cm (1–3ft) off the ground; this promotes plenty of flowering shoots at eye level. If this is not done, the plants continue to grow upwards and soon reach tall proportions with large areas of bare stems towards the base. Pruning for this type is best done in February or March.

Opposite page: pruning is an essential element in keeping shrubs and trees in good order. Plants such as Buddleia davidii should have all wood which produces flowers the previous year cut out in February or March to encourage continued flowering. Wisteria sinensis is trimmed back in summer, and during the winter such shortened shoots are further cut to two or three buds from their base

Above: the ancient art of topiary is here seen at Levens Hall in Cumbria, a garden famed for this refined form of pruning

Right: four steps to removing a branch. First, lop the branch about 30cm (1ft) from where it joins the trunk, then cut it off flush with the trunk. The rough edges will need paring (smoothing) with a sharp knife, then completely cover the wound with an anti-fungicidal paint

A Choice of Gardens

With the basic gardening outline and routine settled, you can diversify and apply your thoughts to the type of garden you want. The range of plants available (even allowing for difficulties of soil and situation) is so vast that the choice is almost painfully bewildering. So this section is designed to offer guidance through the labyrinth of garden types.

Naturally, much depends on individual circumstances, so we offer a comprehensive collection of ideas for most situations.

A rising family, from early childhood to late teens, will need a play area, so we present ideas for a children's garden. A small household of middle years will almost certainly mean a combination of activity and leisure — running a kitchen garden and mowing the lawn, and perhaps relaxing watching the fish in the pond. Approaching age will signal a taste for the less active aspects and more comfortable gardening pursuits. One can delight in pottering in the greenhouse, a warm spot on a bright but windy day even in winter.

This does not, of course, preclude under-cover gardening as a special interest at any age. Apart from the obvious merits of a greenhouse, with its facility for producing earlier and better plants (and many that cannot be raised outside) there are the added attractions of purely indoor gardening, where a specially heated and lighted room (or part of one) can provide an increasingly popular form of picturesque plant culture.

But there are many other facets. Although it is generally accepted that a garden may take many years to mature, not all of us want to wait that long, and modern techniques have made it possible to transform a site from bare soil to complete garden almost overnight. Our special chapter for the impatient gardener has a particular sympathy for the owner who wants to short-circuit the normal processes. The entire range is covered, from quick-growing ground-cover plants to rampant climbers; from the set pieces of patios and terraces to the easy mobility of container plants.

Although the most obvious benefits of an 'immediate' garden are realized when starting from scratch, the techniques also offer strong possibilities and incentives when — as occasionally happens — the owner decides he would like a change. Partial transformation can be achieved very quickly.

Nevertheless, most of us will want a settled pattern, and the choice, our heritage of centuries, is wide. A lawn is the focal point of most gardens, but to give the greatest pleasure it must be laid and maintained properly, and we demonstrate how this should be done. Edge it, or break it up with flower beds: again the range is limitless, from a border of annuals or a display of bulbs to the colourful and perfumed panorama of roses and other shrubs providing their seasons of glory and an air of permanence.

The tiny flowers of alpines in a rock garden, the special appeal of pond plants, or a 'natural' garden, designed to attract wondrously-coloured insects, as well as a variety of birds and small animals, all of these give character and distinction.

Nor must we forget the underlying concept of a garden, that it exists for our needs as well as our pleasure. There is still nothing to beat home-grown produce, whether fruit, vegetables, or herbs to give flavour to our meals. As always, the best results follow individual attention and care, and the advice in this section will help you to escape from the straightjacket of packeted and largely anonymous supplies of undefinable taste from the supermarket.

With your gardening strategy thus frameworked, all that remains is to fill the canvas; providing the flesh and bones of the garden. Our final section, beginning on page 122, sets out in clear and easily digested detail the virtues of many hundreds of plants for all purposes.

The impatient gardener

To achieve an instant garden requires the combination of design techniques with the correct choice of hard materials and plant species, and — most importantly — money. Unfortunately many of the techniques used to change a bare patch into an instant paradise can be expensive, but like house furnishing there will be several priorities that the impatient gardener will think worth the expenditure.

Architectural elements

Perhaps the most expensive items, and the most instantaneous features that can be incorporated into a garden, are the 'architectural' elements. These comprise manufactured or easily built features such as paths, walls and pergolas, which make the skeleton of the garden and also reduce the planting area.

Terraces and patios

Impatient gardeners are frequently lazy gardeners and after a few hectic weeks installing the garden will appreciate a terrace or patio on which to sit and plan future improvements (see pages

An excellent example of 'instant' results, demonstrating how a small group of quick-growing plants can blend harmoniously with a variety of paving with pleasing effect

26–27). A terrace can easily be built in a few days, and by using second-hand stone or brick achieves instant maturity.

Whilst building the terrace, incorporate a few carpeting plants in small soil pockets between the paving. Good plants to grow include *Sagina subulata*, a tiny moss-like plant with linear leaves and minute white flowers in summer; the thrift or sea pink (*Armeria maritima*), with dark green, linear leaves and lavender-pink flowers from June to August; *Saxifraga moschata* × Peter Pan, with evergreen rosettes and pink flowers in late spring; or thyme (*Thymus serpyllum*), another evergreen with small, dark green oval leaves and small, purplish spikes of flowers in early summer.

No terrace is complete without a seat, or chairs and a table, and room should be found for a couple of tubs. At first these can be planted up with bedding plants which can later be replaced by specimen shrubs, such as camellias, which can then be moved onto the terrace during their flowering period.

Paths and drives

Paths are usually built as soon as possible for ease of access to all corners of the garden. There is a wide range of materials, and choice will depend on the desired finish and also the quantities of money and skills available (see page 28). For the do-it-yourself gardener, bricks make an attractive, reasonably cheap finish, but to employ a bricklayer will more than double the costs. Paving bricks can be hard baked, or overfired, with colours varying from yellow to reds and oranges. Although usually laid flat in an even or broken-jointed pattern there are other attractive bonds, such as herringbone. In addition to 'regular' bricks, laid flat, there is a range of specially made pavers which are usually smaller, thinner and cheaper than bricks.

Stone paving is attractive, but very expensive. Use it in small quantities, perhaps interspersed with brick, and remember that local sources of second-hand stone may be available as many local authorities sell off old paving slabs. Old York stone is uneven in shape and thickness, faults which have to be rectified when laying. Newly quarried stone is of even size and can easily be given a weathered look by washing with manure water.

Broken stone slabs are cheaper and if used with carpeting plants can form an attractive informal path or patio. Reconstituted stone is also cheaper than the 'real thing' and is available in a range of sizes, shapes and colours.

Stone cobbles may be used to break up areas of stone or brick. They are usually available in a size known as hens' eggs, and can easily be made into an

An instant feature such as this charming statuette can create an impression of permanence among the short-lived colour of annuals

edging to contrast with other types of paving, as infill panels or as a drainage channel to collect surface water run-off. Another material, used in much the same way, is granite setts. These are available in various sizes and can be grey in colour (from Scotland or Cornwall) or pink (imported from Portugal). Half setts can be laid in beautiful fan patterns, but this usually requires an expert paviour.

Loose or compacted gravel are easy surfaces to lay, either as paths or beds; and the simplest of instant gardens in a limited space is to imitate the Japanese style and combine two or three sizes of gravel, a few boulders and two or three evergreen trees. Self-binding gravels include red or yellow Breedon gravel, which make an attractive drive or all-weather play surface for children. Gravels also have the advantage of being one of the cheapest surfacing materials available. Unfortunately they are prone to weed invasion, but a well-prepared bed plus suitable weedkillers (see pages 42–43) or light hoeing will keep that problem in check.

Pergolas

Pergolas (see page 29) are another architectural element which will provide an instant feature in the garden. They look impressive built with pillars of stone, brick or oak, with teak, larch or oak beams (depending on money available); these are also available in kit form. Also easily built or purchased in kit form are a variety of screen walls made from glazed clay units, pierced concrete blocks, honeycomb brick, bamboo or timber lattice. Both screens and pergolas can be softened by a wide variety of climbers.

Containers and ornaments

Stone or terracotta ornaments such as tubs and pots can be used to provide a sense of instant maturity to a new garden and can be filled initially with herbaceous perennials or bedding plants. The African lily (*Agapanthus campanulatus*) will look spectacular in a pot, with bell-shaped blue (or white) flowers produced from June to September. This plant also has unusual strap-shaped leaves and although generally hardy may need some protection in cold areas. Day lilies (*Hemerocallis*) are also attractive in stone pots; many cultivars are available with red, pink, orange or yellow flowers plus arching broad grassy leaves which make this an ideal accent plant.

Although stone pots are traditional, the genuine articles are expensive and there is now available an interesting range of reconstituted stone pots. Most surprising, and effective, are 'stone' urns made from glass-fibre, which have the added advantage of being easy to move. Also spectacular is a 1.2m (4ft) Ali Baba pot which looks like terracotta, but is also made from glass-fibre.

Another range of garden ornaments with a practical use are seats. Available in teak, red cedar, stone, wrought or cast iron, they provide an immediate sense of place in the garden. For maximum impact the impatient gardener could plant one semi-mature tree in the lawn, surround it by a wrought iron seat around the base, and immediately attain a sense of timelessness that could have taken 30 years to achieve.

One impatient gardener's plan
1. existing fence covered by *Hedera canariensis* 'Variegata'
2. garden furniture
3. wooden pergola with scented climbers — roses or honeysuckle *(Lonicera periclymenum)*
4. tub containing *Camellia* 'Donation'
5. neighbour's screen of large cypress
6. sculpture
7. concrete stepping stones
8. *Betula pendula*, heathers, azaleas and juniper
9. play pit
10. *Cupressocyparis leylandii*
11. *Acer saccharum* (advanced nursery stock)
12. *Cupressocyparis leylandii*
13. existing tree
14. apple trees
15. soft fruit bushes
16. *Prunus subhirtella* 'Autumnalis Rosea'
17. shrubs roses and winter flowering evergreens e.g. *Viburnum tinus*
18. *Magnolia* × *soulangiana* 'Rubra'
19. *Sorbus aucuparia*
20. *Salix* × *chrysocoma*, spring bulbs below
21. flowering plants
22. screen plants: *Clematis montana*; *Hedera helix* 'Dentata Variegata'; *Rosa* 'Albéric Barbier'
23. group of *Elaeagnus* × *ebbingei*
24. tool shed
25. existing fence
26. brick on edge trim
27. brick paving over existing concrete path with break-out pockets for climbers and ground cover

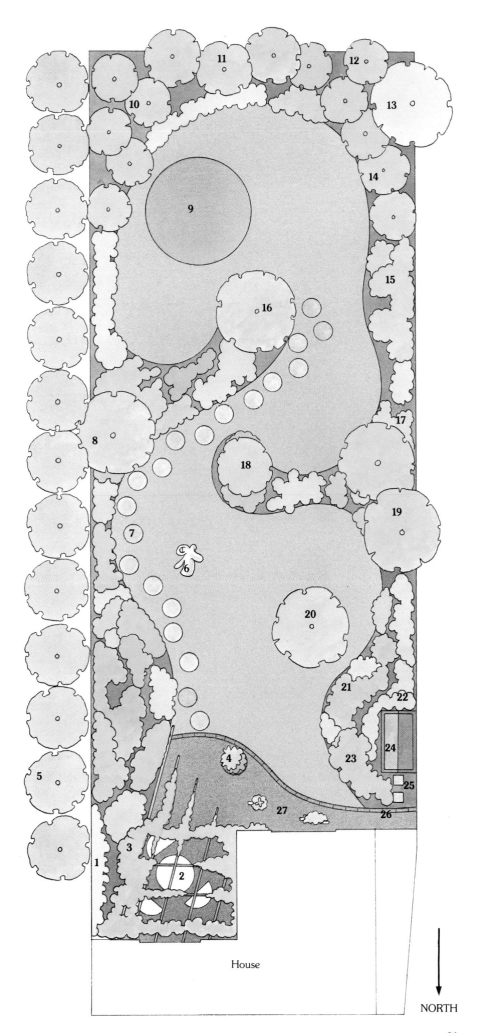

House

NORTH

The plants

Although the architectural elements can give an impression of an established garden, they are not complete until clothed with plants. By careful selection, however, even the trees and shrubs can look established in a surprisingly short time.

Trees

For the impatient gardener, semi-mature trees are an easy solution. Brought in and planted from 8–12m (25–40ft) high they are a perfect, if expensive, instant garden. Many of the more popular trees are available in this large size, such as alder, mountain ash, birch, ash, London plane, oak and lime. However, the cost involved, plus the risk of checking growth, often makes smaller-sized advanced nursery stock of about 5m (17ft) better value for money.

There are other solutions. Certain trees such as willow, sycamore and poplar grow extremely quickly. Even if planted young, say 2m (7ft) high, they will rapidly fill out. Eucalyptus is another good, fast-growing evergreen tree. *Eucalyptus gunnii,* the cidar gum, has unusual glaucous, rounded, bluish leaves when young which become sickle shaped and sage green on older trees.

The weeping willow (*Salix alba* 'Tristis') is another popular, rapidly growing tree (for people with small gardens, frequently too rapid). *Salix* × *chrysocoma* will quickly grow to 18m (60ft), although careful pruning will restrict its development. Young trees can be planted up to 9m (30ft) high and although they prefer a moist soil will tolerate most conditions. One word of warning: willow roots have a tendency to seek out any water and even slightly damaged drains may prove attractive to feeding roots.

Non-weeping willows also grow rapidly. *Salix alba* and its cultivars are spectacular, even in small gardens. 'Chermesina' and 'Vitellina' have bright orange and yellow shoots respectively in winter, which provide an unusual splash of colour. These can be cut back regularly, both to restrict growth and encourage the following year's colourful stems.

Conifers such as the Leyland cypress (× *Cupressocyparis leylandii*) grow rapidly and can be used to form a quick screen or a specimen tree. The Lawson cypress (*Chamaecyparis lawsoniana*) is another fast-grower that will quickly add height to a new planting scheme.

Shrubs

It is well worth planting several of the quick-growing deciduous shrubs which can be interspersed with slower-growing ones. Amongst the most effective, and available from nurseries in a large size, are the mock orange (*Philadelphus coronarius*), dogwood (*Cornus alba sibirica* 'Westonbirt'), golden bell bush (*Forsythia* × *intermedia* 'Spectabilis') and yellow elder (*Sambucus canadensis* 'Aurea'). Good evergreens that are usually available up to 1m (3ft) high include *Berberis* × *stenophylla,* with arching branches covered in golden-yellow flowers in April and May, followed by blue-black berries in August; *Ilex* 'Golden King', a spreading holly with few spines and bright golden leaf margins; and *Elaeagnus* × *ebbingei*, with unusual dark green leaves overlaid with fine white down, silvery on the reverse, plus fragrant white flowers in October and November.

Ground-cover shrubs are of immense value to the impatient gardener for covering large areas of ground by suppressing weeds. For an instant effect plant very thickly and thin or transplant later.

A fast growing shrub is *Cotoneaster salicifolius* 'Autumn Fire', which has evergreen willow-like leaves, and small white flowers in May followed by clusters of red berries in autumn. This succeeds on any soil and will tolerate some shade. The checkerberry (*Gaultheria procumbens*) is best on peaty soils and is noted for its thick, shiny leaves and berries.

Ivies are famous for their rapid growth. The common ivy (*Hedera helix*) is most useful to impatient gardeners, forming a dense evergreen ground cover. The slightly less impatient can try the Irish ivy (*H. h.* 'Hibernica'), which has large, bright green leaves.

Philadelphus coronarius 'Aurea', one of the mock oranges, is a beautiful quick-growing shrub

Also useful as a ground cover is the carpet or Spanish juniper (*Juniperus sabina tamariscifolia*). Available as a substantial plant, this has a dense, prostrate habit with layered branching and feathery foliage that is greyish green when young, developing to bright green when older.

Shrub roses provide a useful collection of plants for the impatient gardener as they are available in a reasonable size

Cornus alba 'Sibirica', the Westonbirt dogwood, a useful plant in winter for its coloured bark

Ivies are especially useful climbers because most are quick-growing, and they are self-clinging

and usually flower in the first year after planting. Amongst those worth a place in a new garden is *Rosa × cantabrigiensis,* an arching specimen with fragrant leaves and creamy-yellow single flowers in May and June followed by small round orange hips.

Rosa moschata 'Penelope', a musk rose, is a sturdy and vigorous plant with semi-double, scented, creamy-pink flowers fading to a paler shade. The coral-pink hips are covered with a grey bloom. *Rosa rugosa* 'Frau Dagmar Has- trup' is a good perpetual-flowering rose. Dark rose flowers with crimson stamens are followed by large, globular crimson hips. This rose has a dense habit and grows to 1m (3ft) high. Although it pref- ers well-drained, light soil and full sun, it will succeed in most locations.

Climbing shrubs can soon give an established feel to a garden, especially if they are quick-growing. One climber guaranteed to please any impatient gar- dener is the Russian vine, (*Fallopia baldschuanica,* better known as *Poly- gonum baldschuanicum*). It can grow up to 4.5m (15ft) in one season, given a deep loamy soil; a deciduous climber with slender twining stems, it is covered with a mass of feathery creamy-pink flowers from July to October.

Other good climbers include *Vitis coignetiae,* a tendril climber with huge leaves turning brilliant scarlet in autumn, and *Hydrangea petiolaris,* a climbing hydrangea that will thrive on a north wall. This has flat heads of white flowers, which cover the plant in June and July.

Bedding plants
For a really instant garden the most impressive results can be obtained by using either half-hardy annuals as bed-

Vitis coignetiae is a bold and vigorous climber to grow for spectacular autumn colour

ding plants, or hardy annuals rapidly grown from seed. These are all best against an evergreen background and can be used between shrubs that are becoming established. Good examples of popular annuals that provide a plethora of flowers are larkspur, clarkia, godetia, calendulas and cornflowers. Buy young bedding plants in May from a nursery or market garden. Look out for *Begonia semperflorens,* Iceland pop- pies, stocks, petunias, African and French marigolds, lobelias, verbenas, zinnias and the spectacular salvias.

Making a start

The impatience of any gardener will, of course, be tempered by the time of year that the garden is first started. A lawn is usually one of the first tasks, and using turf will be the quickest way to establish a lawn (see page 65). If seeding is prefer- red for economic or other reasons, sow in August or September to produce a usable lawn by the following summer.

Planting of bare-rooted trees and shrubs is usually restricted to autumn and spring, although evergreens can be planted in May and September. By choosing container-grown plants, how- ever, a start can be made any time the ground is workable.

Choose well-tried, vigorous species available from a local nursery. As these establish and rapidly change the shape and character of the bare patch, that is perhaps the time to think of a few slower-growing plants which can be added to complete the picture.

Lawns

Lawns are usually the most used but least cared for part of the garden. As much as the vegetable and flower areas they need feeding, watering and weeding, as well as regular mowing.

A good lawn is a combination of suitable grasses to start with and good care afterwards. And to a large extent the use to which it will be put governs the type of lawn that can be expected. A play lawn will naturally be coarse as it must be made up of a mixture of hard-wearing species. On the other hand, a lawn area that is there merely as a foil for the surrounding flower beds, one which is rarely trodden, can be most immaculate if made up of the fine-leaved grasses that respond so well to dedicated care.

Creating a new lawn

A lawn is a permanent feature and preparation should not be hurried. Whether turfing or sowing, a well-prepared site is the first essential. The ground must be cleared completely of rubble.

If the top-soil has been cleared by a bulldozer during construction of the house, it may be necessary to buy in good top-soil to replace it.

Although drainage on most soils is likely to be adequate, on heavy clay it may be necessary to lay land drains. To do this, cut trenches 30–45cm (1–1½ft) deep across the site, following any fall in the land, and lay 7.5cm (3in) diameter pipes end to end so that there is a slight fall from one side to the other, cover with gravel and replace soil. As water will be discharged from the lower end, a deep soakaway must be provided if there is no convenient ditch.

Once these preparations are complete, cover the whole area with a 2.5–5cm (1–2in) layer of well-decayed garden compost, moss peat or well-rotted manure. Also apply a specially formulated lawn fertilizer or a general one such as Growmore, at about 70–100g per sq m (2–3oz per sq yd), and fork it into the top 10–15cm (4–6in) of soil.

After treading the soil thoroughly, rake over the whole area, making it as smooth and level as possible. Try to do this at least a month before sowing, to allow weed seeds to germinate. These can then be killed by hoeing or using a suitable weedkiller.

Seed or turf?
Whether to sow seed or lay turf is always a problem. Seed probably gives the best long-term results and the grasses to be sown can be selected to suit the uses to which the lawn will be put. Turfing produces a sward much quicker, but is about four times more expensive, and it is not usually possible to specify the grasses you want. Most turf has been removed from sites destined for building and may well contain a fair proportion of weeds.

A lawn from seed
Seed mixtures can usually be bought in two distinct qualities: hard-wearing or fine-leaved, although a mixture for

use in shady areas is also available.

For a hard-wearing lawn the main ingredients will be perennial ryegrass (*Lolium perenne*), chewing's fescue (*Festuca rubra commutata*), and crested dog's tail (*Cynosurus cristatus*). The ryegrass spreads by means of questing underground stems and is not recommended for use in a lawn which has no

clear-cut edge, as it can spread into adjacent borders and may be difficult to remove.

For a fine lawn, chewing's fescue is the basic ingredient, with a little brown top bent (*Agrostis tenuis*) added. It is worth paying more for this mixture and buying it from a reputable seedsman. If coarser grasses are included, they will soon dominate the fine ones and the lawn will lose its velvety appearance.

Mixtures for shade usually include the rough-stalked and smooth-stalked meadow grasses (*Poa trivialis* and *P. pratensis* respectively), together with creeping red fescue (*Festuca rubra rubra*).

Sowing is best done in late summer or early autumn, especially in areas where droughts are not infrequent in late spring and early summer. Otherwise late spring is also suitable, but watering is likely to be necessary in dry seasons.

Choose a still day, and mark off a few square metres (yards) with pegs and sow the recommended weight of seed within each. After three or four areas have been

sown you will have a good idea of the rate of cover required. Finally, rake over the ground gently so that most of the seeds are just covered. Protect from birds with sticks and cotton thread (nylon may injure the birds).

A lawn from turf

Laying a lawn with turves is a heavier job, and individual turves must be of the same thickness to get a level lawn. Be prepared to pare off any thick ones or add extra soil beneath those that are too thin.

Mark the outline of the lawn with pegs and string before starting, especially if it is irregular. Lay the first row along one edge of the lawn, then place a plank on these turves and work forward across the area, staggering the joints. If the area is irregular in shape, lay the edges first so that any pieces which have to be cut or patched are in the middle of the lawn.

Water if a dry spell follows, and do not allow anyone to walk on the lawn for the first few weeks. It may need cutting after about a month, although it is best to leave it until spring if laid in the autumn.

Lawn maintenance

Even the best sown lawn, with carefully selected grasses and thorough ground preparation, will degenerate rapidly if regular maintenance is not given sufficient attention.

It is the regular attention a lawn receives that gives it a professional look. The work need not become a chore if the right equipment is used, and the grass not allowed to become too neglected.

Mowing and trimming

This is one task that cannot be neglected. There are many types of mowers (see page 22), and the right choice is dictated by size and type of lawn, cost, and personal preferences. If stripes are required, however, it is essential to choose one with rollers.

Grass-boxes are useful. Normally it is best to remove the clippings (useful for the compost heap or as a mulch, but don't use within six weeks of applying a hormone weedkiller), as clippings left on the surface during damp weather can cause problems such as yellowing of the grass beneath and worm casts, and may encourage disease. The grass-box need not be used in dry summer weather.

Regular mowing is even more important with hand-powered machines, as the physical effort is much less if mown at least once a week.

Keeping a straight edge is important if the lawn is to look neat. Edges can be straightened at the beginning of the season by using a half-moon edger against a straight-edge timber. But resist the temptation to use this tool too often, otherwise the beds will soon become larger and the lawn smaller.

During the growing season, much can be done to improve appearance by using edging shears (see page 23). These avoid the need to bend, and leave a trim edge. There is also a type with the blades set horizontally, for trimming close to a raised edge where it's not possible for the mower to reach.

Electric trimmers are available that are useful for trimming edges and grass beneath shrubs and round the base of trees.

Feeding and weeding

Leaves are the factories of every plant, so it is a source of amazement how the grass plant can continue to thrive with its leaves constantly being pruned back. Survive they do, but like other plants, they need feeding to remain healthy. Hard cutting and no feeding can eventually kill grasses, and their place will be taken by daisies, plantains and other ground-hugging weeds, and by moss.

The most convenient way to deal with feeding and weeding a lawn is to use a combined lawn fertilizer and selective weedkiller. This is easy to apply, and an effective treatment. But do not use a combined lawn conditioner unless your lawn is weedy — an ordinary specially formulated lawn fertilizer is all that's required.

If just a few weeds are present, hand weeding may be sufficient. A daisy grubber is useful for removing daisies, plantains and dandelions.

If moss is a problem, one of the traditional and still very effective treatments is lawn sand (a mixture of sulphate of iron, sulphate of ammonia, and sand), or

To apply fertilizers and weedkillers evenly, stretch string at metre or yard intervals, then space battens at the same distance as you proceed

there are other proprietary moss killers. Selective hormone weedkillers have little or no effect on moss.

Follow the manufacturer's instructions for rates of application for fertilizers and weedkillers.

Aeration and topdressing

The soil beneath a lawn which is in continual use can become very hard and compacted, as can one cut regularly with a mower that has a heavy roller. Action is then required to counteract the effect.

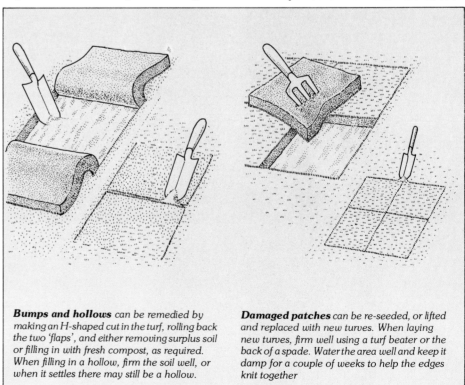

Bumps and hollows *can be remedied by making an H-shaped cut in the turf, rolling back the two 'flaps', and either removing surplus soil or filling in with fresh compost, as required. When filling in a hollow, firm the soil well, or when it settles there may still be a hollow.*

Damaged patches *can be re-seeded, or lifted and replaced with new turves. When laying new turves, firm well using a turf beater or the back of a spade. Water the area well and keep it damp for a couple of weeks to help the edges knit together*

If the soil is naturally light and sandy, it may be sufficient to use a wire lawn rake to loosen the surface, and at the same time remove dead grass and moss.

Heavier soils are best spiked, but this can be done with an ordinary garden fork, pushing it into the ground for 10—15cm (4—6in), provided you are careful not to lift the turf. On heavy clay, however, it is best to use a special hollow-tined aerator. These remove a fine core of soil.

The cores should be swept off the lawn, and a mixture of peat or leafmould and sand (equal parts) brushed into the holes. Apply at about 1kg per sq m(2lb per sq yd), and work it into the surface thoroughly. This should be done in autumn, and is beneficial even if cores are not removed.

Another autumn job is to collect fallen leaves, using a besom broom or lawn rake on a small area, a leaf sweeper on a large lawn.

Watering

It is necessary to water a lawn in its first season while the roots are still shallow. For a long-established lawn, it may never be essential, but is desirable during dry seasons. On light, sandy and freely drained soils it is best begun after about two weeks of dryness, but on heavy soils only begin after about four weeks without rain. Once it is necessary to water, it must be done thoroughly, applying enough to soak the grass roots down to about 15cm (6in). Moistening the surface is of little or no benefit. Sprinklers are best as they produce a fine spray which will not compact the surface. Choose a still day, otherwise coverage may be irregular and spray drift an annoyance to neighbours.

Lawn repairs

Even the best lawns sometimes suffer damage to an edge, wear in a particular spot, or have a bump or a hollow that has resulted from the ground settling after initial laying or sowing. These are not difficult to rectify, and they should be corrected as soon as they are noticed.

Broken edges are easily repaired by removing a section at least 15cm (6in) wide, and reversing the turf so that the damaged edge is on the inside. Be careful to keep the spade flat when removing the slice of turf, and cut the shape first by pressing the spade into the grass against a straight piece of timber.

If necessary, grass seed can be sown in the patch caused by the damaged edge, but only do this if you can match the grass seed. Don't sow a patch on a fine lawn with a coarse grass mixture, or vice versa — it will always show. Usually the edges will soon knit together anyway.

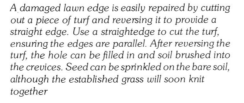

A damaged lawn edge is easily repaired by cutting out a piece of turf and reversing it to provide a straight edge. Use a straightedge to cut the turf, ensuring the edges are parallel. After reversing the turf, the hole can be filled in and soil brushed into the crevices. Seed can be sprinkled on the bare soil, although the established grass will soon knit together

Bumps can be levelled by lifting the turf and taking out sufficient surplus soil before returning the grass. For a small bump it may only be necessary to peel back a small area.

Hollows can also make mowing difficult. Fill any depressions by cutting a straight line through the centre of the depression, then across either end, like the top and bottom of a capital I. Roll back the two freed pieces and put extra soil beneath them.

For very large depressions it is best to remove the turf in strips, fill in with soil, then re-lay the turf. In reverse, the same is true for large lumps. However, providing the site was prepared correctly large bumps and hollows will not occur.

67

The flower garden

The flower garden can be an expression not only of one's growing skills, but also of taste and gardening sense. The form our gardens take, and the plants we choose to grow, all reflect our personal preferences and dislikes. And it is this as much as anything else that makes gardens so interesting, and each one individual no matter how similar the plots.

The kitchen garden is governed by practical matters, but in the flower garden the only considerations are aesthetic (given that soil and site suit the plants). The problem that many gardeners face is an inherited garden — one designed and planted to the taste of the previous owner but probably not what you would choose yourself if you were starting from scratch.

If you are creating a new garden, give careful consideration to the form of the flower garden, merging your interest in particular groups of plants with the need for a pleasing garden as a whole. But even if you are taking over an established garden, much can be done to create the right 'feel', and to provide a 'complete' garden — one that incorporates colour throughout the year, a contrast in shape and form, and flowers for fragrance and for cutting for the home.

Framework plants

Trees, hedges and climbers all give an impression of permanence, and are key plants around which many other garden features can be designed. Evergreens and hedges in particular are an essential part of most gardens, and besides possessing beauty in their own right, provide a natural setting for many of the more colourful subjects.

Hedges and screens
There are many excellent hedging plants (see page 15), some with attractive foliage, others that make ideal informal flowering hedges. Whichever is chosen, it's worth bearing in mind that a hedge provides shelter as well as beauty; careful positioning in an exposed garden can make all the difference when it comes to growing some of the less robust plants. So always consider hedges in relation to the other plants you intend to grow.

Evergreens
Not only do these provide interesting contrasts of foliage texture and colour throughout the year, they also act as a splendid foil for many deciduous shrubs such as hamamelis, *Jasminum nudiflorum*, mahonia, forsythia and daphne, to mention just winter and spring subjects.

As hedges need regular clipping, some such as lonicera and privet quite often, it may be worth considering a less formal type of screen.

Laurels, aucubas and various conifers are obvious candidates, but there are many more. Golden conifers can look particularly effective, and two good ones are *Chamaecyparis lawsoniana* 'Lanei' and *C. l.* 'Lutea'. Among the golden yews, *Taxus baccata* 'Elegantissima' and *T.b.* 'Semperaurea' are both excellent plants.

Although screens of this type make an excellent framework within which to plant the rest of the flower garden, you must have the space to use this treatment. There should be sufficient room to have a border at least 2.4m (8ft) wide around the garden — or at least along one or more sides of the property.

Trees
Unless you have enough ground to form a small arboretum, trees must of necessity be regarded as background or framework plants.

Because trees are so important, they should be chosen carefully and positioned strategically. It is the trees and climbers that will provide the vertical dimension and offer contrast. If there are established trees in the garden, try to make use of them, as nothing gives a greater sense of maturity.

If new trees are being planted, however, it is usually best to settle for those of small stature, and to choose 'multiple merit' subjects. The flowering crabs (*Malus*) should be high on the list: they provide a mass of blossom early in the year, when it is most welcome, and a heavy crop of bright red or yellow berries

A traditional herbaceous border. Although at their best in midsummer, such borders can be planned to provide pockets of colour all through the year

in autumn. Some even have the additional merit of attractive purple foliage to hold attention throughout the summer. Typical of the group is 'Profusion', which has clusters of wine-red flowers up to 4cm (1½in) across, and coppery-crimson young leaves. Autumn produces masses of dark red fruits. For yellow fruits, try 'Golden Hornet', as the small round fruit lasts well into winter.

Another group of trees that must receive consideration are the *Prunus* species. The Japanese cherries are particularly popular, providing masses of blossom in spring. 'Kanzan' is widely planted, and has distinctive stiffly upright-spreading branches and large double pink flowers.

Don't overlook the merits of attractive shape and ornamental foliage. *Catalpa bignonioides* 'Aurea', for instance, has real 'architectural' merit and is a tree of great beauty when in leaf.

Climbers

There are many small gardens where the potential growing space on the walls is greater than the ground area available. This space should never be wasted; climbers not only increase the range of plants that we can grow in our gardens, they also screen what can otherwise be rather bleak walls and fences. Although some, such as wisteria, are planted with the long-term in mind, there are many that will grow rapidly and soon produce a feeling of maturity (see page 63).

In Britain we do not make as much use of 'third dimension' as they do in continental countries. We could make far more use of our walls and fences, poles and pergolas, to grow thereon climbing roses, a wisteria perhaps, honeysuckles (*Lonicera*), cotoneasters, pyracanthas, or even various coloured ivies (*Hedera*). There are dozens of varieties of ivy nowadays, and a very ornamental one is 'Gold Heart', which has green leaves splashed with gold in the centre.

Ivies, Virginia creeper (*Parthenocissus quinquefolia*), and the climbing hydrangea (*Hydrangea petiolaris*) are all self-clinging.

Other excellent plants to grow against a wall include the yellow winter-flowering jasmine (*Jasminum nudiflorum*) and the white summer-flowering *J. officinale*. The latter is very fragrant, but needs a sheltered spot if grown in cold northern gardens.

Clematis in great variety and Japanese quinces (cultivars of *Chaenomeles speciosa* and *C.* × *superba*) are also lovely plants with which to clothe garden walls and pergolas.

Above right: a flowering cherry, Prunus *'Kanzan'*
Right: Catalpa bignonioides *'Aurea', a beautiful tree of much 'architectural' merit*

Flower garden design

Whichever plants we choose to grow, they must be displayed well if they are to look their best. There is no merit in having a choice alpine plant unless it is placed in a position where it can be seen and appreciated; and it doesn't make sense to interplant wallflowers with hyacinths, as they will be lost. Also, why position two fragrant plants together when the perfume can be spread around the garden?

On the other hand, it is the plant associations that can make a garden distinctive. Don't be too rigid in your thinking; break a 'rule' if you think it will work — but be prepared to learn by your mistakes if it doesn't.

Shrub borders

Borders of shrubs are easy to maintain if one uses low-growing plants beneath the shrubs to cover the ground and suppress the weeds. There are many ground-cover plants (see page 63), including ivies (green, silver or gold variegated), bergenia and pulmonaria.

Mixed borders can be most attractive. The shrub border need not be restricted to shrubs and ground-cover plants. Be prepared to make the most of available space by planting lilies between the shrubs, and daffodils and low-growing herbaceous plants such as catmint (*Nepeta*) and dwarf Michaelmas daisies.

The idea of a mixed border may be extended almost indefinitely with a skilful association of herbaceous plants and shrubs. Red hot pokers (*Kniphofia*), lupins, paeonies, rudbeckias, irises, heleniums, erigerons, aquilegias, Japanese anemones (*Anemone* × *hybrida*), and more, associate well with shrubs.

Annuals can be used to brighten up dull patches in a shrub border, or to fill in gaps until newly-planted shrubs become established.

Hardy annuals such as godetia, clarkia, larkspur, nigella, and Shirley poppies (*Papaver rhoeas*), can be used effectively; or half-hardy plants such as antirrhinums, petunias and African and French marigolds (*Tagetes erecta* and *T. patula*) can be bedded out.

Roses

Shrub roses rest happily in a shrub or mixed border, but the Hybrid Tea and Floribunda types (see page 74) are almost always afforded beds of their own. For garden decoration, however, the Floribunda type is best, as they flower almost continuously from July until October.

The problem with rose beds is that they are no objects of beauty from November until the end of June. In large gardens there used to be a separate rose garden where one sat in summer and enjoyed the roses. But in a small garden where the roses are in full view from the sitting-room window all the time, most people like to grow other plants among them.

The fervent rose lover will frown upon this, of course, and not allow any other plant to compete with his beloved roses. But if we have no ambitions about winning prizes at flower shows, we can grow many plants in happy association with our roses. Pansies and violas go well with them; so do dwarf perennials such as aubrieta, *Alyssum saxatile,* arabis and bergenia, and all the early-flowering bulbs like snowdrops (*Galanthus nivalis*), crocuses, muscari, chionodoxas, daffodils and scillas.

Forget-me-nots (*Myosotis*), London pride (*Saxifraga umbrosa*), polyanthus (*Primula polyantha*), primroses (*Primula vulgaris*), lily-of-the-valley (*Convallaria majalis*), honesty (*Lunaria annua*), dwarf campanulas, ajugas, dwarf geraniums such as *G. endressii, Phlox subulata,* intermediate irises, and dianthus, are a few of the flowers we can grow to bring colour to the bed in spring until the roses begin to bloom.

Objectors would say that with these plants growing in the bed it is not possible to feed the roses properly. But by using soluble fertilizers and foliar feeds (see page 39), it is perfectly possible to grow good roses. One must remember, however, to water such beds or borders early and generously in dry spells and to begin watering even as early as May if we run into a period of, say, two weeks with little or no rain.

Herbaceous borders

Herbaceous plants are, of course, the mainstay of any garden. For a long time, the traditional border had to be backed by a wall, fence or hedge — 'to give it

background'. But nowadays we know better and grow our herbaceous plants in free-standing beds.

First, many plants grown in a border against a wall or fence tend to stretch towards the light and become tall and thin, and therefore need staking. Grown in a free-standing bed in the open garden, they will need support only if they are in a very exposed windy position.

Then, if the free-standing bed is not more than about 1.5m (5ft) wide, we can tend it from all sides for staking, tying, hoeing and removing dead flowers without having to trample on the bed.

Also, in a free-standing bed, we can plant those subjects that like a little shade behind taller plants. With a bit of trial and error we can find a spot where each of our plants will be happy.

Anyone who is not in a hurry can fill a garden with perennial hardy herbaceous plants in two years by raising them from seed. If two or three friends club together and buy perhaps two dozen packets of perennial flower seeds, they can raise hundreds of plants to grow between them. There are many to choose from — Lupins, hollyhocks (*Althaea rosea*), coreopsis, gaillardias and delphiniums are just a few.

Left: island beds are a sensible alternative to single-sided herbaceous borders. If a distant focal point can be provided, it gives an added sense of perspective and scale. Although a large tree such as a cedar looks magnificent, the eye can be just as easily attracted by a distant seat or statue
Above left: the Japanese anemone (Anemone × hybrida) is a magnificent border plant for late flowering. Its large blooms are carried on erect stems from August to October, although they sometimes need a few years to settle down
Above centre: graceful Aquilegias are traditional cottage-garden flowers, useful for light shade
Above right: Hosta fortunei 'Albopicta' — a plant in vogue, especially with flower arrangers
Right: seasonal bedding schemes can provide the most spectacular displays, as shown by this fine example of colourful summer bedding

Special use plants

Whatever the design of the flower garden, there are certain groups of plants that can almost always be incorporated into the scheme of things. Bulbs, for instance, have so many uses that it is hard to imagine a garden where some of them would not add interest, while annuals and biennials are often neglected in many established gardens although they can contribute much in the way of colour.

Flowers can be appreciated in the home as well as in the garden, and it seems a pity not to grow suitable kinds for cutting. If they have fragrance, so much the better; and we can find fragrance in all kinds of plants, from bulbs and small alpines to large shrubs.

Bulbs
Although the prices of some bulbs, notably hyacinths and tulips, have risen considerably in recent years, there are still many bulbs that are a worthwhile investment.

Some daffodils are particularly suitable for naturalizing, and these should increase over the years. Some good ones are the trumpet-type 'Rembrandt' (yellow) and 'Mount Hood' (white); small-cupped 'Red Rascal' (yellow and red) and 'Semper Avanti' (white and red); double 'Irene Copeland' (yellow); and Jonquil-type 'Suzy' (red and yellow).

Daffodils grow in nature on the lower slopes of mountains and in spring and early summer receive abundant moisture at the roots. This moisture is the key to success with daffodils, and indeed all the smaller bulbs. They need plenty of water from the time the flowers fade until the foliage begins to die down. Giving the foliage two or three applications of a foliar feed at two-week intervals helps to build up the young offset bulbs to flowering size quickly.

Of the small bulbs, chionodoxas, scillas, crocuses, muscari and winter aconites (*Eranthis hyemalis*) usually increase if cared for properly.

Tulips, on the other hand, do not increase very much, although large-flowered Darwin Hybrid cultivars such as 'Apeldoorn' (vivid scarlet), 'Golden Apeldoorn' (yellow), and 'My Lady' (coral red), may be lifted and replanted to flower again the following year. The cultivars of *Tulipa kaufmanniana* and hybrids of *T. greigii* and *T. fosteriana* often acclimatize themselves and flourish for years in a garden if the conditions suit them.

Tulips grow naturally in the Middle East, where they receive a hot summer baking, so they tend to do best in a light, quick-draining soil.

Cut-flower plants
Many gardeners cannot bring themselves to cut flowers from their beds or borders, and devote a small part of the vegetable plot just for cut flowers. This is an excellent idea, and need not take up very much space. Half a dozen paeonies, a few of the blue *Scabiosa caucasica*

Below left: modern strains of foxgloves (Digitalis purpurea) are a great improvement on the native plants of our woodlands
Below: pansies prefer a moist but well-drained soil in sun or partial shade; removing dead heads extends the flowering period
Far below: Tulipa kaufmanniana, sometimes known as the waterlily tulip. Several cultivars are available, and will thrive if left undisturbed

'Clive Greaves', some pyrethrums and a few early-flowering chrysanthemums, and dahlias, would give a fairly steady supply of flowers from early summer until the coming of the frosts.

Daffodils and tulips give welcome flowers in spring, and for May one can plant wallflowers, to be followed by sweet Williams and Dutch irises in June. Gladioli, too, will provide a supply of cut flowers from August onwards. If gladiolus corms are planted at intervals of ten days from late March until mid-May a succession of flowers will be produced right into autumn.

Annuals also provide plenty of flowers for cutting, and 'everlasting' flowers are always rewarding to grow. There are a surprising number to choose from.

Fragrant plants

Anyone who has planted night scented stock (*Matthiola bicornis*) outside their window and enjoyed the heady fragrance as it wafts through the house on a summer evening, will need no convincing of the merit of planting fragrant plants.

The charts give some idea of the subjects that can be sown or planted in all parts of the garden.

Annuals and biennials

Few people appreciate what wonderful dividends can be realized from the investment of a pound or two in seeds of annuals and biennials.

It is difficult to find any other plants that will transform a bare patch of ground into such a riot of colour in so short a time.

They are of especial use in a newly-constructed garden, but certainly merit inclusion at any time.

Choice is a matter of personal preference, but don't overlook godetia, alyssum (*Lobularia maritima,* but usually listed as *Alyssum maritimum*), clarkia, cosmea, larkspur, linaria, linum or lavatera, among the hardy kinds. In a heated greenhouse one can raise petunias, zinnias, ageratum, verbena, annual rudbeckia, and African and French marigolds, for planting out at the end of May.

In a small well-prepared seedbed one can sow biennials in May or early June. Try pansies and violas, wallflowers, Siberian wallflowers (Erysimum × allionii, usually listed as *Cheiranthus allionii*), sweet Williams, forget-me-nots, foxgloves (*Digitalis purpurea*), double daisies (*Bellis perennis*), and honesty.

Above right: stocks (Matthiola biennis) *are best in double form; it is possible to select double plants at the seedling stage with some strains*
Right: the Sweet William (Dianthus barbatus) *is one of the most popular biennials, combining bright colours with exquisite fragrance*

The rose garden

Roses have been considered worthy of cultivation for many centuries. They were grown for their beauty about 600 BC, when the poetess Sappho named the rose the 'Queen of Flowers', and there is evidence that they were used to provide 'rose scented oil' in Pylos, Greece, about 1400 BC. Today this magnificent plant has a huge following throughout the world, and few gardens look complete without a rose of some kind.

The modern rose has evolved from intricate cross-breeding of three distinct types, which were given to us respectively by the Chinese, the Iranians, and the cradle of Western civilization in western Asia. The results are to be seen in modern gardens in every temperate country in the world, displaying cardinal virtues: a wide colour range, wonderful fragrance, often a long period of bloom, and ease of cultivation.

Rose types

There are roses to suit many situations — from the exhibition bench to the informality of a mixed border, and they vary in size from those suitable for a miniature garden to rampant climbers that will cover a wall.

Most popular, however, are the Hybrid Tea and Floribunda types, for it is among these that the plant breeders have achieved some of their most magnificent results.

Hybrid Tea roses have large, full blooms, carried singly or a few in a head. It is these roses that are most often seen on the show bench.

Floribunda roses have heads of many blooms, the individual flowers usually being smaller and more open than Hybrid Teas; they tend to produce a colourful effect over a long period in the open garden.

Grandiflora and 'Floribunda-Hybrid Tea type' are terms that have been used to describe the increasing number of cultivars with characteristics mid-way between Hybrid Teas and Floribundas. These plants have blooms approaching the size and substance of Hybrid Teas, but in clusters like Floribundas.

It is the merging of various groups, as a result of breeding developments, that has led to efforts to introduce a new classification. At rose shows the new classification is already being used, but for many years gardeners will almost certainly continue using the terms Hybrid Tea (new classification is 'Large') and Floribunda (new classification is 'Cluster').

Climbers and ramblers can add the extra dimension of height to a rose garden, and there are many fine cultivars. Many are climbing versions of normal Hybrid Tea roses, and though beautiful do not flower as prolifically as most of the ramblers. Ramblers tend to branch more from the base, whereas a climber has

Top: hybrid tea rose 'Kathleen Joyce'
Above: hybrid tea rose 'Harry Wheatcroft'
Right: two old garden favourites, frequently found planted against old cottages or walls; 'Paul's Scarlet' (red) and 'Albertine' (pink)

more pronounced lateral branches from the main stem. However, ramblers flower in one great burst of bloom as a rule, whereas some of the climbers flower twice in a season.

Shrub roses are true species or hybrids and cultivars still retaining a shrubby habit. Many of them have attractive leaves and hips as well as beautiful and often fragrant flowers. They are not, however, normally suitable subjects for growing in formal beds arrangements.

Cultivation

Although roses are very easy to grow, a little attention to their basic requirements will be well rewarded with superior blooms and healthier plants.

Soil and sites
Roses should be grown in a well-drained fertile soil, deep enough for the roots to be in top-soil rather than sub-soil, well cultivated and with plenty of humus-forming material incorporated.

As roses do not appreciate excessively acid or alkaline soil, a fairly neutral one is best. Always let the soil settle before planting, so that there are no air pockets.

Choose a suitable site — not too windy, and where sun will be received for at least half the day.

Buying plants
Always buy fresh, strong, healthy, well-rooted plants: the experience of one's neighbours may prove a guide to a source of supply.

Choose reliable cultivars (see pages 136–139), and make sure the plants have abundant roots and a thick main

stem between roots and top growth. The length of the shoots does not matter so much, as long as there are two or three, firmly ripe and reasonably sturdy. Cheap roses are often 'second grade' plants.

Planting

Plant roses firmly, in autumn or spring. Container-grown roses can, however, be planted in early summer.

Always plant with wet roots, if necessary stand them in a bucket of water for an hour or two first. Position the plant upright in the hole, allowing the pliable ends of the roots to lie more or less horizontally on the bottom. Replace the soil gradually, firming it well between the roots. Ensure that the union between roots and stem (which may be recognized by the change in character of the bark) is at ground level and not buried.

Feeding

Roses will benefit from a good rose fertilizer in spring and early summer. Foliar feeding is also possible, and may continue into late summer.

Do not neglect to feed roses: but heavy feeding is only necessary for exhibition blooms.

Pruning

Roses are probably best pruned in spring. Remove damaged wood, including any with brown pith, together with any old wood that has ceased to bear fruitful off-shoots.

What remains should be productive wood that will flower, but remove or shorten all thin shoots to the point where they seem strong enough to bear a flower worth cutting.

Routine care

Help roses to resist insect and disease attacks by prompt application of the appropriate remedy (see pages 46, 51). Most insects are easily dealt with by modern insecticides, but fungi are more difficult — often because the trouble is not spotted soon enough. Fungicides applied promptly will usually control the disease, but after a bad attack of blackspot or rose rust (see page 48) gather and burn fallen leaves.

Remove suckers and weeds completely whenever they are seen, but don't dig deeply between roses and try not to tread on the soil too much.

Trim off the old blooms of cultivars expected to flower again during the season, and keep long shoots of climbers tied to their supports, so that wind cannot damage them.

Above left: 'Eye Paint' is a vigorous floribunda that can be grown as a shrub if pruned lightly
Left: Floribunda 'Escapade' (foreground), with 'Moonmaiden' set against the wall

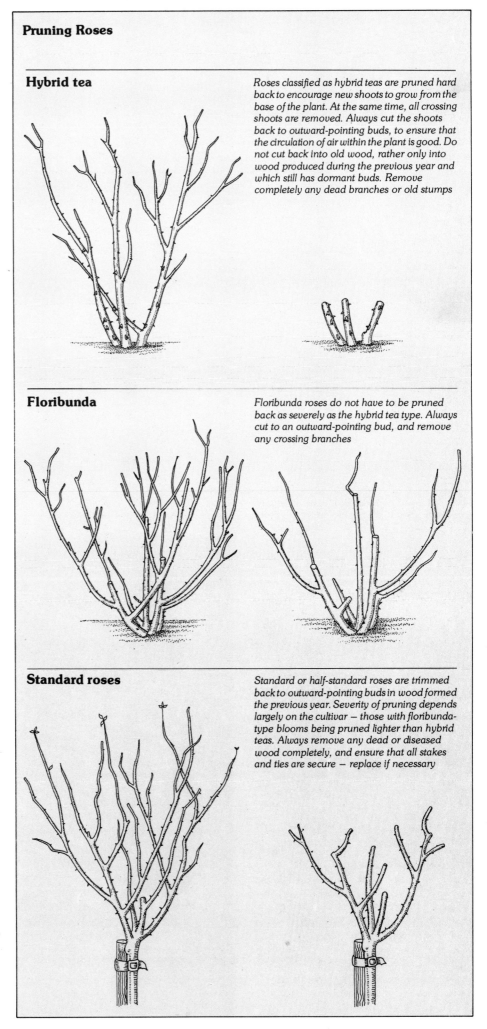

Pruning Roses

Hybrid tea

Roses classified as hybrid teas are pruned hard back to encourage new shoots to grow from the base of the plant. At the same time, all crossing shoots are removed. Always cut the shoots back to outward-pointing buds, to ensure that the circulation of air within the plant is good. Do not cut back into old wood, rather only into wood produced during the previous year and which still has dormant buds. Remove completely any dead branches or old stumps

Floribunda

Floribunda roses do not have to be pruned back as severely as the hybrid tea type. Always cut to an outward-pointing bud, and remove any crossing branches

Standard roses

Standard or half-standard roses are trimmed back to outward-pointing buds in wood formed the previous year. Severity of pruning depends largely on the cultivar — those with floribunda-type blooms being pruned lighter than hybrid teas. Always remove any dead or diseased wood completely, and ensure that all stakes and ties are secure — replace if necessary

The rock garden

Nothing sets off plants better than an environment similar to their natural habitat, but it is not necessary to have a rock garden to grow rock plants. Given plenty of space and suitable rocks this is undoubtedly the ideal, but many people lacking these have to compromise. If you haven't the energy, time or money to make an impressive rock garden, or the garden is too small, don't despair — other options are open, such as dry walls or sink gardens.

Unless you have the right site for a proper rock garden, it may be best to settle for one of the alternatives. Where a suitable spot is available, however, a well-planned rock garden can become a superb feature.

Building a rock garden

The first requirement is a sunny, open site, well clear of overhanging trees. A great asset is a sloping site, for this makes construction easier and the finished result more natural.

Good drainage is also vital, so unless the ground is naturally free-draining, be prepared to excavate the site to at least 30cm (1ft), incorporating plenty of coarse drainage material.

Unless there is a natural slope, it will be necessary to build up a good depth of soil at the back to give height to the garden. Do not underestimate the amount of soil required, and if you intend growing lime-hating alpines, check the pH before you use it (see page 38).

For the soil to pack around the rocks it is best to mix a special compost, and a good one is three parts of loam (well-rotted turves or good garden soil), two parts moss peat, and one-and-a-half parts sharp sand or grit.

Positioning the rocks
Avoid the temptation to make a little rock go a long way by positioning with the maximum exposed surface, regardless of the shape of the stone. Often more should be buried than exposed, with the rock being set well back into the soil, sloping slightly backwards. Try to arrange the 'grain' to follow the same contour in each rock, and set them in tiers with pockets of soil in between.

Rock garden alternatives

Charming little rockeries can be made in old sinks — raised on bricks for easy tending — or suitable plants can be grown between courses of bricks or paving in a dry wall (see page 33). Quite a lot of plants can be grown in a space no bigger than a couple of garden frames. The trick is to go upwards, making a firm foundation and setting each piece of stone securely with soil between, and making the top narrower than the base.

One advantage of this method of growing rock plants is the ability to look after plants like lewisias and rhodohypoxis, which must have sharp drainage. To protect them from winter snow or excessive wet, a frame light or a sheet of polythene can be laid over the top, held clear of the plant.

Another idea is to edge borders and drives with several layers of stone blocks, leaving spaces at intervals for introducing plants, or they can be grown in pockets made in flat crazy-paving. The latter provides an ideal site for carpeting plants such as thyme and aubrieta.

One well-known alpine enthusiast turned his long, narrow suburban garden into a ravine taller than himself. The soil was excavated and thrown up each side of a winding path, rock pockets were then made and filled with good soil, also nooks and crevices, and even a small pool. Here he grew hundreds of rock plants, common and rare, difficult and easy, shade lovers and sun worshippers.

Planting

When planting rock plants, go for small compact specimens rather than large ones, and turn them from their pots carefully, retaining a ball of soil round the roots. Bare-root plants take much longer to establish.

Prevent damp lying near the surface (it can cause the lower leaves of plants like androsaces and cushion saxifrages to rot, and also encourages worms) by top-dressing the soil between such plants with granite chippings, fine shingle or pot shards. Always plant firmly.

Plants for particular situations

Shade lovers are few, but plants like haberleas and ramondas prefer shade, and because they form flat rosettes of foliage are best grown in a vertical position between rocks. Shade lovers for flat positions include the small slipper flowers (*Calceolaria biflora*), the spring-blooming windflower (*Anemone*

One of the main attractions of a rock garden is the ability to grow a large number of different plants in a small area. The result can be striking

nemorosa) in its various forms, the heather-like cassiopes; blue, pink or white anemone-like hepaticas, trilliums, shortias, and most alpine primulas. The majority of these also thrive in sun or partial shade in the colder parts of Britain if they have abundant water during the growing season.

Lime-haters must be avoided if one gardens on chalk, or they must be confined in some form of container with suitable compost. On peaty soils, however, treasures such as the lovely blue-trumpeted autumn gentian (*Gentiana sino-ornata*) can be grown. Others include the twin flower (*Linnaea borealis*), a genus named after the Swedish naturalist Linné, and most heaths and their near relatives the daboecias, cassiopes, rock jasmine (*Androsace carnea*), the dwarf, long-flowering pink-and-white *Rhodohypoxis baurii,* and some irises.

Cultivation

Soils and climate vary so much that it is impossible to lay down hard and fast rules for rock plant cultivation. However, if the soil is gravelly it will require additions of loam and leafmould or peat in the planting pockets. Sandy peats and sands also need loam to give them body, plus some limestone chippings for good drainage (except where lime-hating plants are to be grown).

The rocks, too, have a function beyond holding soil in place and presenting a pleasing appearance; they keep roots cool in summer and retain moisture beneath them in hot, dry summers.

Beyond the right soil and site, little attention is needed apart from tidying the plants after flowering. In the case of strong carpeters like alyssum, perennial candytuft (*Iberis sempervirens*) and aubrieta, it is necessary to cut back old growth to about 15cm (6in) with shears. This will keep the plants compact and encourage strong new shoots to carry the next year's flowers.

Weeds are not likely to be a problem once the plants are growing well, but in the early days it is important to prevent weeds becoming established.

Slugs and snails are the most likely pests, but these are easily controlled with a suitable bait (see page 47).

Feeding is usually confined to a light dressing of bonemeal applied in spring and again in the autumn.

Above right: raised beds enable tiny, mat-forming alpines to be appreciated at close quarters, and a dry stone wall provides a natural niche for many rock plants of cascading habit
Right: these delightful, raised rock beds in a small front garden show what a variety of rock plants can be grown in a small space

The water garden

The cool and tranquil sight of a still pool or the cheering sound of bubbling and cascading water both add an extra dimension to the garden.

Recollections of green, stagnant water and a leaf-covered surface should be dismissed — clear water is only a matter of management, and of careful siting.

A garden pool is not only a feature in its own right, but home for many lovely plants. Besides the deep-water aquatics such as waterlilies and water hawthorn, there are choice plants for the margins and pond surrounds.

Once a pond has been constructed (see page 27) and planted, little further work is required, and it can form a natural and relatively maintenance-free part of the garden. But as with all things, planning and a few sensible precautions can make all the difference.

Siting a pond

Pools, which constitute the most important part of a water garden, need careful siting if they are not to become a perennial source of disappointment. The plants that live in them — waterlilies, marginal aquatics and the like — require abundant sunshine to flower, so avoid shady places near tall buildings or areas with overhanging trees. The latter present a further problem on account of their leaves, since one of the major causes of discoloured water and fish mortality is too much organic material in the water. As this decomposes it releases mineral salts which in turn encourage various forms of algae — or even methane gas in very bad cases.

Site the pool right out in the open; either as a formal feature with a paved or grass surround or as an integral part of a larger feature. It can, for instance, be teamed with a rock garden, perhaps including a stream and waterfall, or be combined with bog plants in an informal setting. Marginal aquatics can be included to disguise the pool edges and to provide extra colour and interest.

Keeping the water clean

Unless the water is clear it loses much of its appeal, and it is difficult to see the fish. All ponds become slightly green or cloudy in spring, mainly because of activity by the small animal occupants, which stirs up the mud. However, this state of affairs usually adjusts itself in a week or two as plant growth becomes stronger. Natural shade, such as that provided by waterlily leaves and underwater vegetation, is the greatest deterrent to algae, which must have light and food in order to thrive. Submerged oxygenators utilize most of the mineral salts released by decaying vegetation, fish excreta and the like, and in the process of growth combine water and carbon dioxide exhaled by the fish. This results in a certain quantity of oxygen being returned to the water, which in turn is utilized by the fish. Thus the two work together and the secret of striking a balance is to have plenty of submerged vegetation, some floating leaves or plants to cast some shade, and the correct types of fish.

There are chemicals which can be added to water to clear algae, but the results tend to be only temporary, and the addition of chemicals changes the nature of the water. This may not matter in a lake or large pond, but can have significance in a small pool. For this reason natural means of keeping down algae are best — pulling out the coarser types with the hands, using a garden rake or twisting a pointed stick in the centre of the mass — and the other kinds by netting and planting more oxygenators and floaters. Some of the latter however — like duckweed — should never be purposely added as they are extremely difficult to eradicate later. If inadvertently introduced, use a hose to drive the offending plants to one corner and then scoop them out with a large net.

Planting and maintenance

Five types of plants are commonly used in water gardens. The deep water ornamentals like waterlilies and water hawthorns have submerged roots but their leaves and flowers float or rise just above the surface. Plant these in baskets of heavy, fibre-free loam with a little added bonemeal, and topdress this with 2.5cm (1in) of clean pea-sized shingle. Gently lower the baskets into the water, prop-

ping them on bricks for a time until new growth appears, then set them at the correct depth for their type and size.

Marginal aquatics have submerged roots but emergent flowers and foliage. These need shallow water of about 5–15cm (2–6in) depth, and a plain loam soil. They may be planted in pond-side pockets or in pots or baskets.

Oxygenators — such as elodea — live entirely submerged and most are almost rootless, so plant these by gently clipping a thin strip of lead round the base of several stems and drop the bunches into the pool.

Floaters are installed in seconds (just place them on the water's surface), but bog plants — such as waterside primulas — require soil that is always moist but never waterlogged. They also need richer compost, so incorporate some leafmould, peat or garden compost.

Maintenance consists of cutting back dead foliage in autumn; dredging out fallen leaves; keeping the pool full of water at all times and dividing plants and clearing out occasionally. All planting operations are best carried out in spring.

Stocking with fish

Fish are the only essential animals required. They are necessary to keep down mosquito larvae and other pests; they also bring movement and colour to the pool. Avoid bottom-of-the-pond dwellers such as carp and tench, which continually stir up mud, and also avoid pugnacious kinds like sunfish and sticklebacks. The best kinds for small pools are goldfish and golden orfe.

Contrary to common belief, water snails and other creatures are not necessary and indeed may become a nuisance by eating or disfiguring the plants.

Accessories

Most specialist water garden stockists offer a varied range of accessories to help make the water garden more attractive or easier to manage. They include water-lily baskets (plastic, with holes round the sides), fountains and simulated streams, cascades and waterfalls, and pumps to keep these moving and to recycle the water. Other pumps will empty the pool when necessary, and there are heaters to prevent the water freezing in winter. Thermometers, hand nets and various ornaments are also available.

Above left: Nymphaea 'Rose Arey' is one of the fragrant waterlilies, suitable for a water depth of about 30cm (1ft)
Left: two charming plants for the waterside — Caltha palustris 'Plena' (yellow) and Leucojum vernum (white)
Above right: aquatic grasses and sedges look particularly effective in a formal pool
Right: marginal plants can be planted in pots placed on a shallow ledge

The naturalist's garden

Because of the growing interest in natural history, many people have made natural gardens in the hope of encouraging birds and other animals to establish homes there, but the results vary considerably. Someone living in a town naturally has less chance of success, even if a reasonable area is available, than a person living in the country with fields and woodland near at hand. With careful planning, however, it should be possible to create a haven for many of the attractive creatures that grace our gardens.

In planning a natural garden, it is important to decide which particular animals and wild plants you wish to encourage; only then can you set about creating the right environment.

Birds

Small birds such as robins, hedge sparrows and blackbirds are regular tenants of countless gardens, and visiting species usually include starlings, mistle thrushes and collared doves. This is a modest list, and in winter, when natural food is scarce, the bird population is increased by various members of the tit family as well as chaffinches and greenfinches.

If there is a pond, speculating moorhens may be attracted. If it also contains fish, it might catch the keen eye of a heron, but this is more likely to happen in early morning. That most brilliant of all our birds, the kingfisher, is another possible visitor if fish are available.

Breeding birds

If low cover is plentiful, and this can include gorse (*Ulex europaeus*), box

Robins are among the friendliest birds. This one has built its nest in a tool cupboard

The bullfinch is a beautiful bird, but can strip buds from fruit trees and cause much damage

(*Buxus*) and some evergreen kinds of berberis, it will provide nesting sites for such birds as linnets and bullfinches. Scrub woodland near at hand, and inside the garden, should attract willow-warblers and some other members of the warbler tribe. These may become established during the summer, though they will leave before autumn.

The domed nest of the willow-warbler will sometimes be built at ground level among low cover.

Nest-boxes are often used by blue-tits and great-tits, but they should be placed at least 1.5m (5ft) above ground, and if there are prowling cats in the area it is a useful precaution to spread pieces of gorse underneath.

Larger nest-boxes, fixed at a greater height, may entice tawny owls or stock doves to make a home there. To avoid disturbance it is wise to use narrow, definite paths, and to avoid trampling carelessly through the covered areas.

Pond-life

A pond not only encourages certain birds, it will support a whole range of wildlife.

Because of the unfortunate decline in frog and toad populations, however, it might be necessary to introduce spawn into the pond. Even then the experiment may not be successful, for these two amphibians are inclined to stick to old haunts — often to their misfortune. The same applies to newts. Water plants that will add to the attraction of a pond include the yellow water iris (*Iris pseudacorus*) and various waterlilies.

Ponds are the haunt of many different insects, including colourful dragonflies and damselflies. The early stages of these two are spent in water, and the nymphs, as they are known, prey on small water creatures. The winged adults pursue gnats and other small flies for food.

That sturdy hunter the great diving beetle also lives in water during its larval stage. The adults fly by night, which accounts for their presence in some garden ponds.

Reptiles and mammals

Many heathy places are tenanted by lizards, slow-worms and snakes, and these are also found in numerous wild gardens, even though they are easily overlooked.

Furry animals such as grey squirrels and rabbits may not be so popular, but if they are present the stoats and weasels might also pay visits.

Hedgehogs are also noted for their nocturnal wanderings, and many visit gardens after dark. They are inclined to be suspicious of human beings, but some are bolder and become tamer if regularly offered scraps, and are particularly fond of milk. Hedgehogs normally hibernate in winter, but if regularly provided with refreshment they may respond even in December or January.

Several smaller furry animals, such as wood mice, voles and shrews, are also mainly nocturnal, so apt to be overlooked even when they are present.

Butterflies and moths

The increased interest in butterflies, and the concern about their decline in many former haunts, has led to their welcome in gardens. The well-known *Buddleia davidii*, often called the butterfly bush, is a favourite for encouraging butterflies, and among wild plants to encourage are fleabane, ragwort, spear thistle and devil's-bit scabious. It should be realized, however, that although butterflies love these plants, fortunately their caterpillars do not eat them.

Three of the more familiar coloured butterflies, the red admiral, peacock and small tortoiseshell, all eat nettles in their caterpillar stages, so it is worth including a patch of nettles in the garden! As the caterpillars of the peacock butterfly also feed on wild hops (*Humulus lupulus*), this climber is worth introducing; it usually does well sprawling over a hedge.

The lively, bright-winged small copper butterfly is fond of fleabane and ragwort

Hedgehogs can be encouraged to take up residence by offering them food or milk

flowers, but the female lays her tiny, button-shaped eggs on sheep's sorrel and some kinds of dock. This species fluctuates, as do most butterflies, from year to year, and it is usually commoner in hot summers. Another attractive small butterfly, that might live in a wild garden, is the common blue. The males are blue in colour, but the females are usually deep brown, with orange spots on the wing borders. The caterpillars of this butterfly feed on birdsfoot trefoil, an attractive low plant with bright yellow flowers shaped like miniature sweet peas. It grows well in sandy soil.

If there are poplars or willows in the garden, there is a good chance that caterpillars of the poplar hawk and puss moths will be found feeding there in

Right: the beautiful peacock butterfly
Below: a red admiral (left) and small tortoiseshell (right) on buddleia flowers

early summer. Both caterpillars grow to 6.5cm (2½in) or so long, but they are not often common enough to be serious pests. The moths of both species emerge in spring, and they fly by night, but can be seen resting by day. Additional attractive moths to look for in wild gardens are the graceful swallowtail, and the brimstone with its sulphur-coloured wings.

The children's garden

Gardens and children are not always complementary: the energy, noise and activity of young members of a family (plus their friends, bikes and pets) can arouse in many an adult a desire to 'banish' them to the bottom of the garden. Younger children will, however, need some supervision so for those families with a large garden there are two options — either a place near the house for watching over smaller children, or one as far away as possible for older children who value independence.

In smaller gardens it is perhaps too hopeful to try to restrict children to one corner, and so the whole garden must be designed to allow children's play without ruining the aesthetic qualities often appreciated by parents.

When the whole garden is to be used by both adults and children there are certain problems. Ball games and greenhouses have a certain attraction, and a ball in the middle of a treasured flower bed will not be appreciated. If you avoid these obvious conflicts it will still be possible to have an attractive and practical garden.

Plants to withstand play

Remember tough shrubs can also be pretty; escallonias, viburnums, olearias, philadelphus, cotoneasters and shrub roses will offer a range of flowers and foliage, whilst shrubs with coloured foliage such as the purple-leaved hazel (*Corylus maxima* 'Purpurea'), the golden elder (*Sambucus nigra* 'Aurea'), or the smoke tree (*Cotinus coggygria*), will provide colourful focal points throughout the summer.

These and many other shrubs can stand quite hard treatment, but with a teenage family it could be advantageous to plant a high proportion of trees. Although obviously spiny trees and shrubs will discourage children, many of these tend to be slow growing. It is far better to accept some degree of accidental damage and plant multi-stemmed trees, such as birch (*Betulus*), alder (*Alnus*) or hornbeam (*Carpinus betulus*), so that even if part of the tree is injured the rest will survive to form an attractive clump.

Constant use of the lawn by children will soon produce bare patches. The fine grasses found in ornamental lawns just can't cope with much activity, so it is advisable to oversow with ryegrass or, if starting from scratch, to use a seed mix containing a large proportion of this grass. An alternative approach, which would also reduce maintenance, is to eliminate part of the lawn and replace it with a hard surface which could be used for games throughout the year.

Design for children

Cycles used in a garden can cause havoc, particularly to the lawn and shrub beds. To reduce their impact build a path in a material that can withstand this sort of treatment, with ramps to take up changes in level and kerbs or low walls, where necessary, to protect fragile plant beds.

In a large garden it may be advantageous to provide one corner especially for children; if sufficient space and activities are provided this may reduce their temptation to run wild in the more precious ornamental areas. And it may be all the better to allow the children to plan their own corner and 'help' lay it out. Depending on the age of the children a sunny, sheltered spot near the house is preferable, although elsewhere the children's area can be screened from draughts by hedges, walls or fences.

A sand pit is usually popular with smaller children and on a domestic scale is relatively easy to keep clean. It should be as large as possible, preferably with an open-jointed brick bottom to allow free drainage. The sides can be brick, concrete or wood. Small swings and slides can be located within the sand area to keep damage caused by falls to a minimum.

To avoid a sand pit becoming a regularly shaped element in an informal garden it can be surrounded by smooth rounded boulders which will also be used for imaginative play. A small-scale, easily constructed alternative design for a sand pit is an old tractor tyre filled with sand. Do remember that regular washing of the sand will reduce health hazards from cats and dogs. Cover it when not in use.

Many people feel children prefer games they invent themselves. Building their own equipment can be fun, and helped by a parent and finding inspiration from an existing tree, older children can build their own fort or tree house from reject materials. Barrels, ladders, wooden planks, ropes and natural changes in level can all be exploited, but because this type of play is often thought to be untidy, such an 'adventure' area is usually best sited some distance from the house.

A garden designed with children in mind should have a play area. Sand is always popular

Plants for children to grow

Most children enjoy growing plants from seed and space should be left for plant beds. The emphasis will be on quickly germinating seeds, often annuals, which produce a lot of growth and flower within a few weeks. Vegetables are sometimes grown, such as mustard and cress, raddish or lettuce. All grow quickly and have the added advantage of being safely edible.

The range of flowers to grow is wide, but an initial selection can be made from those flowers which the small child can play with.

Antirrhinums can provide endless fun for 'nipping' noses, and double daisies (*Bellis perennis* 'Flore-pleno') can be grown to provide material for daisy chains. Foxgloves (*Digitalis purpurea*) make tiny gloves for dolls, and nasturtium (*Tropaeolum majus*) leaves make dolls' hats.

Easy annuals provide a range of flowers throughout the summer. Good kinds to try include mignonette (*Reseda odorata*), with long-lasting spikes of scented yellowish flowers, clarkia with pink, lilac or purple flowers, the multi-coloured candytuft (*Iberis umbellata*), love-in-a-mist (*Nigella damascena*) with its blue spiky flowers, and Chinese lanterns (*Physalis franchetii*) with orange 'balloons'. The last two can be dried,

painted or sprayed to make Christmas decorations.

Amongst other plants which appeal to children are those that change with the time of day or type of weather. The morning glory (*Ipomoea tricolor*) will rapidly grow up a wall and its blue and white flowers open early in the morning and close by mid-afternoon. The Californian poppy (*Eschscholzia californica*) is another example, having brilliant red or orange flowers which open and close during the day. Mesembryanthemums, daisies and thistles are all plants that will not open their flowers in damp or rainy weather.

Gourds are unusual plants that will appeal to children because of their quick growth; they produce a range of strangely coloured and shaped fruit that can be dried and varnished to retain their colour. Loofahs and giant sunflowers can also readily be grown from seed; sow indoors at the end of May and later transfer outside to a sheltered corner.

Although growing annuals can be great fun, children will enjoy planting a tree and watching it grow. Do remember that fully grown trees can take up a great deal of space and may cut out sunlight from house and garden. Smaller trees: birch, whitebeam (*Sorbus aria*), alders, crab apples (*Malus*), or snake-bark maples (*Acer grosseri hersii* and *A. pennsylvanicum*) suit most gardens and grow fast enough for the children to

measure regularly. Where there is space larger trees can be raised from seed; horse chestnut (*Aesculus hippocastanum*) can be grown from conkers; oaks (*Quercus*) will emerge slowly from an acorn, but a young sycamore (*Acer pseudoplatanus*), grown from a winged key, is the most dramatic — up to 1.2m (4ft) a year.

An appreciation of gardening can be fostered at an early age if a child can be allowed to 'help' in the garden – particularly if the flowers are colourful, like rudbeckias (below left). Other suitable plants are the golden sunflowers (below); nasturtiums (below, centre) and bright and easy Californian poppies (far below)

Patios and town gardens

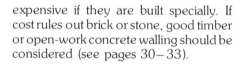

Town dwellers often have to content themselves with little gardening space, but with imagination the most unlikely site can be transformed into a place of beauty with flowers and foliage provided by a surprising range of plants.

Very tiny gardens can be turned into patios, and even in flats gardening can stretch beyond houseplants to window-boxes and hanging baskets, and perhaps the balcony or roof.

The plants and techniques used in confined-space gardening are equally useful outside towns of course, and a patio sitting-out area is often appreciated even in a large garden, while window-boxes and hanging baskets are universally appreciated.

Small town gardens

Everyone seeks something slightly different from a garden, but the chances are the owner of a small garden in a town will want a place for relaxation and perhaps an escape from the world around him.

Privacy

The first need is usually for privacy; the town garden should be a private garden, an enclosure where nobody can overlook you, and where the world can be shut out.

Before erecting new screens, see what use can be made of existing boundaries, and any interesting features. An old pink brick wall would be a gift on such an occasion, but even a dirty town wall has value when painted or whitewashed and planted with something like the mauve-lilac *Solanum crispum* (although this is not hardy except in the south), together with the coral-pink crimson-shaded climbing rose 'Mme Gregoire Staechlin'. A brash, modern brick wall will also be transformed by this treatment.

Climbing plants can be trained to a trellis or wide-meshed netting, in panels fixed against the wall, or by special wall nails with soft attachments that can be bent around the shoot to be supported.

Pear trees or espalier-trained apples planted against walls also make a delightful background to early-flowering herbaceous plants.

Brick walls suit a garden well as a boundary or screen, but can be very expensive if they are built specially. If cost rules out brick or stone, good timber or open-work concrete walling should be considered (see pages 30–33).

Trees

Trees and shrubs afford shelter from wind and noise, and also strengthen the garden's defence from onlookers.

Forest trees should be avoided as a rule, by reason of size, but fastigiate or upright forms take little space and are well suited to most gardens.

Some of the fastigiate trees worth consideration are *Betula pendula* 'Fastigiata' (an erect form of silver birch), *Carpinus betulus* 'Columnaris' (a slow-growing, columnar form of common hornbeam, and useful for a clay soil), *Crataegus monogyna* 'Stricta' (an erect form of common hawthorn), *Quercus robur* 'Fastigiata' (the cypress oak), and *Gingko biloba* 'Fastigiata' (a columnar form of maidenhair tree).

Robinia pseudoacacia 'Frisia', a golden-yellow form of the false acacia, is one of the best trees for a town garden. Its only drawback is brittle branches, and exposed sites must be avoided.

Two weeping trees that are always admired are Young's weeping birch (*Betula pendula* 'Youngii') and the golden-yellow willow *Salix × chrysocoma* (but only plant it where there is sufficient space).

Another favourite tree for a town garden is the Indian bean tree (*Catalpa bignonioides*). The golden form *C. b.* 'Aurea' is the most attractive, but is not so easy to buy.

The Judas tree (*Cercis siliquastrum*) with rosy clusters of pea-shaped flowers borne on the naked branches in May, has great charm. The magnolias are also highly desirable trees or large shrubs; most are deciduous, but *M. grandiflora* is an evergreen with huge cream, sweetly fragrant goblets.

The *Prunus* family provides many decorative forms of cherry, peach, almond and plum, all of which adapt to town conditions.

Conifers can be difficult in town gardens, but there are some dependable kinds. That lightning grower the Leyland cypress (× *Cupressocyparis leylandii*) is one of them. It has an unbeatable record for rapid screening, and makes an excellent, if rather dull, splaying grey-green hedge. But it can be brightened considerably by interplanting with a golden form — 'Castlewellan'.

A pavement garden, with a trough behind to provide height. Spreading plants have been set at the edge of the paving stones to spill over and provide a welcoming splash of colour close by the front door

Windowboxes

All town houses and flats have windows, and that usually means a suitable windowledge. That is valuable growing space, and a priority when it comes to designing a small town garden.

Until fairly recently, windowboxes were as unchanging as the windows; today there are many kinds, from Florentine pottery to plastic, and there should be something to suit all tastes.

Wood is the traditional material, teak, oak, ash, elm, or deal all being used. They are listed in order of durability. The advantage of wood is that the box can be made to fit a particular space.

The prime consideration with any windowbox is safety. Decorative boxes are a delight: safe ones an obligation. Always make sure they are firmly anchored, ideally by securing the box to fixings screwed into the wall or timber frame.

A shallow watertight tray placed underneath the box will catch surplus water and protect the timber beneath.

Compost should not be overlooked in the urge to plant the box with flowers. As ordinary soil seldom brings good results, buy good compost, and place this over a substantial layer of damp peat, with rough drainage material such as stones and pot shards at the bottom of the box.

Watering must never be neglected. Use the watering-can regularly, but be careful not to overwater. The compost should be allowed to become reasonably dry, but never parched.

Feeding is usually most appreciated before the plants come into full bloom, and a liquid fertilizer is the most satisfactory way to feed windowbox plants.

'Geranium' box

Pelargoniums, or 'geraniums' as they are popularly known, are ideal windowbox plants. Upright kinds can be planted at the back of the box, with trailing ivy-leaved kinds tumbling over the front.

A pelargonium specialist will offer many cultivars from which to choose, but some good ones are 'Galilee' (rose-pink), 'Charles Turner' (pink, feathered maroon), and the pick of them all, the superb 'La France' (semi-double lilac with distinctive maroon markings on the upper petals).

A herb box

Ideal for the kitchen window. As a start, try marjoram, lemon thyme, mint, parsley, rosemary and sage (see pages 198–199). Mint and thyme are trespassers and will have to be kept in their place. Plant each of these in individual pots concealed within the box.

Spring box

Plant in three layers. Daffodils at the bottom, golden early double tulips 'Van der Hoef' lightly covered with soil as the second layer, and small bulbs on the top, such as *Iris reticulata,* scillas, and others that do not flower later than April (to avoid interference with summer planting).

Summer box

The choice is legion. Petunias should be high on the list, together with pansies, fuchsias, *Phlox drummondii,* stocks and heliotropes.

Winter box

Use dwarf conifers such as *Juniperus communis* 'Compressa' or *Chamaecyparis lawsoniana* 'Ellwood's Gold', surrounded by variegated ivies.

Shade box

The problem of shade can be overcome by using tuberous-rooted begonias, and ferns. Hostas and London pride (*Saxifraga umbrosa*) are other possibles.

Below left: the yellow-flowered Lysimachia nummularia *is a useful windowbox trailer*
Below: petunias, lobelia and 'geraniums' with ground ivy (Glecoma hederacea *'Variegata')*
Far below: 'Geraniums' (pelargoniums) are indispensable windowbox plants

Terraces and patios

The dictionary has it that the patio is an inner court open to the sky. It is a place for eating, drinking, sitting and, perhaps, thinking and working — outdoors. It is best sited near the house, and when the summer is kind it can be treated as an extra outdoor room.

The patio

Any paved area in the garden can be converted into a patio, or a start can be made from scratch (see page 26). The choice of paving material can be all-important. Old brick paving is warm and friendly, but is almost impossible to come by, and expensive, but modern bricks in dull blue, ochre and purple-brown shades are becoming fashionable.

Real stone paving is perfect in any garden, but generally beyond the budget. On rare occasions, however, second-hand paving stones are to be had from local councils and should be bought if possible. As the slabs often vary in thickness, it may pay to have them laid by a professional.

Precast concrete paving slabs make a very acceptable patio or terrace, and

Above: all the year round, the patio is an ideal site for a wide variety of container-grown plants, and in summer it takes on a new dimension as an extra room outdoors
Left: a minimum-maintenance patio. Trees and shrubs have been planted between the paving, to provide a trouble-free permanent display without the need for replanting or weeding. With this kind of planting choose subjects with year-round interest; evergreens are particularly useful

should certainly be considered if more mellow alternatives are not available.

Gravel is a possibility, but may not appeal to many people; however it can be very effective in the right setting. Patches, squares or strips of gravel, cobbles, or even grass, between paved areas can be effective provided the area is not too large.

Once the floorscope has been settled, the next priority is to screen against wind and draughts, and to hide any eyesores. Walls, of whatever material, should be at least 1.8m (6ft) high; but before going too high, check with your landlord or the deeds of the property, as there may be height restrictions.

Lighting adds an extra dimension (see page 35), and this exciting element should not be overlooked. A spotlight trained on a well-grown tree or shrub will give it fairy-like glamour.

Laying the cable, which should be specially designed for the job, and wiring outdoor lighting, is one of those tasks definitely best left to the professional.

Protection is often desirable. Although a true patio is open to the sky, most people would vote for some kind of protection, at least in part. A wooden frame fitted with a PVC blind is a blessing, but a pergola (see page 29) covered with a wisteria, vine, honeysuckle or rose, to provide some shade, is all that's required in a fine summer.

Barbecues are popular with many eager cooks, and can be the centre of a summer evening party. A metal grid over bricks can be put together quite simply, but many ready-made kinds are available.

Furniture needs to reflect one's own taste, but a table and chairs are basic requirements. A bar, and mattresses to relax on, are extras that provide a luxury touch. A dashing, giant sunshade will give the scene extra colour and continental gaiety.

The courtyard

A courtyard situated at the front of a house or a back-yard are both perfect settings for tubs, baskets and possibly windowboxes.

Dummy windows are not difficult to erect and are excellent for relieving the depression of a blank wall, especially if windowboxes are spilling over with flowers. A decorative seat built into the wall should also be considered, while a series of wire brackets fixed to the bricks, from which flower pots can be hung, is another technique for relieving a dull wall.

The central area could well be used for a flower bed, planted in a formal pattern or confined as a solid block of colour. Nothing is more successful in such a position than pansies or a mixed collection of ivy-leaved 'geraniums' (*Pelargonium peltatum*).

Water is attractive, and a pool is quite easy to construct (see page 27). There is plenty of scope for marginal plants round the edge, and a fountain or water gurgling out of a lion's mouth is always a telling focal point.

Among other attractions, there are old stone sinks for growing miniature plants, old lamp posts, tall terracotta jars, plaques and sundials, all of which add interest. However, some are difficult to obtain, and they can be expensive.

Hanging baskets

Hanging baskets traditionally seen in front porches also brighten courtyards and patios. Half baskets can be hung from walls, or full baskets suspended from beams. But it must be remembered that when large baskets are filled they are heavy to handle.

The basket should be lined with tightly-packed sphagnum moss, followed by a layer of fibrous loam, and filled with a good compost, such as John Innes No. 3, or one of the newer peat-based composts.

Black polythene is an alternative to moss and should not look unsightly once the plants have grown. If moss is used, a saucer should be placed on the layer of moss at the bottom to provide a reservoir of water — life-saving in hot weather.

Planting must be done firmly, and at least 12mm (½in) left between the soil surface and the rim of the basket, to allow for watering. After planting, the basket may be soaked in water, drained off and hung up out of draughts.

Watering can be a problem. Baskets dry out quickly when exposed to sun and wind, and need to be watered daily during the summer. It may be necessary to take the basket down once a week for a good soak; and a syringe with water each evening in hot weather will be appreciated.

Right: a basket of lobelia 'Cascade Mixed'
Below: a combination of troughs and hanging baskets allows scope for growing many flowering plants in a small patio

Suitable plants. Most windowbox plants grow fairly well in baskets, but the fuchsia excels itself, particularly 'Cascade' (single white flushed carmine with a deep carmine corolla).

Saxifraga stolonifera (mother of thousands), the tiny baby's tears (*Helxine solierolii,* now more correctly known as *Soleirolia soleirolii*), and *Campanula isophylla,* all adapt to life in a hanging basket.

Trailers that grow leggy and untidy can be pegged back discreetly into the moss with a paperclip or hairpin.

89

Gardening in tubs and troughs

Windowboxes and hanging baskets have already been discussed, but anyone having a patio or courtyard will probably want to plant up other containers, such as troughs and tubs.

Such containers have the great merit that they can be moved around from season to season, rather like rearranging the furniture in a room, to provide a changing scene in the light of experience and to suit changing moods. Such re-arrangement should, needless to say, be done before planting up, and preferably when the containers are empty.

Tubs are rewarding containers for the paved town garden, for they require little space, and look at home on a verandah, or almost any odd corner. Even the front doorstep will suffice.

Materials

There is a wide range of materials from which to choose, and both personal

Right: select container plants so that some give height and others cascade over the edge of the tub when in full bloom. Flowers planted near the base provide an attractive 'frame'
Below: where the container itself is of special interest, small plants such as pansies should be chosen as they will not detract from its beauty

preferences and price must play a part in the final decision.

There are well-designed tubs in reconstituted stone, glass-fibre and other materials, but wood still has much to commend it. Unlike some other materials it does not heat up excessively in baking sun; nor does it splinter and crack when moisture seeps into cracks and freezes, as can happen with terracotta or earthenware containers. The other great merit of wood is that the container can be made to fit a particular space.

Lovely tubs made from teak or oak can be bought, but the home handyman should be able to make a suitable tub or trough with a little imagination. By treating the timber with a suitable preservative (be sure it is one that doesn't affect plants — and don't use a creosote), a life of many years can be expected.

The return of the converted beer barrel for growing strawberries has aroused a great deal of interest, but the technique need not be confined to strawberries. About six drainage holes should be cut or burnt into the bottom of the barrel and the top removed. The inside should be treated with a horticultural-grade wood preservative, then holes cut in the side of the barrel to take the plants. These should be at least 60cm (2ft) from the base of the barrel. Two tiers should be sufficient for a small barrel, three at most for a large one. The openings should be staggered at each level.

Planting begins with a 15cm (6in) foundation of crocks, followed by a layer of fibrous soil. As the openings are reached, the plants should be packed in with moss to prevent soil being washed away. The top is kept for the larger plants and can be planted effectively with aubrietas or various dianthus.

Water may be applied through a porous tube driven discreetly down into the centre of the barrel. This will ensure moisture reaches the lowest plants.

Size

Always be generous with the depth of any container; the plants will be less likely to dry out and will thrive better. Diameter is not so critical for annuals and small perennials or bulbs, but for permanent shrubs it should be at least 38cm (1¼ft).

Routine care

Soil in containers of all kinds dries out more quickly than the soil in open ground. Never underestimate the amount of watering that may be involved, and only plant as many tubs or other containers as you will be able to keep watered regularly without undue effort.

In hot summer weather, it may be necessary to water every day, and a

---

Some good tub plants

Shrubs

Acer palmatum
(Japanese maple)
A small tree with a round head of attractive foliage, bright green in spring, red in autumn. There are cultivars with purple foliage, some with finely divided leaves.

Azalea
There are both evergreen and deciduous forms. An excellent semi-evergreen is 'Palestrina', a pure white with an olive throat.

Camellia × williamsii 'Donation'
Glossy evergreen foliage and large soft pink flowers resembling open roses.

Chaenomeles
(Japanese quince)
Fine wall shrub, with spring flowers in shades of red, pink or white.

Chamaecyparis lawsoniana
(Lawson Cypress)
Several cultivars make good tub conifers, including C. l. 'Ellwoodii' (blue-grey), C. l. 'Ellwood's Gold' (tinged yellow), and C. l. 'Minima Aurea' (branches edged gold; slow-growing and excellent for a small container).

Elaeagnus pungens 'Maculata'
Variegated evergreen foliage splashed yellow; showy in winter.

Hydrangea macrophylla
Panicles of paper-like pink, blue or white flowers. Blue cultivars turn pink unless grown in an acid compost.

Fuchsia
Well-known patio plants, but too tender to overwinter outdoors except in the South. Take container indoors for winter.

Rhododendron ponticum
Mauve. Standards do well in tubs.

Rosmarinus officinalis
(Rosemary)
Charming sweet-scented, grey-foliaged shrub.

Taxus baccata
(Yew)
A topiary bear of yew, or some other small beast, will give a friendly look to a doorstep.

Other plants

Acanthus mollis
(Bear's breeches)
A perennial with purple and white flowers on stout spikes. Of considerable 'architectural' merit.

Agapanthus 'Headbourne Hybrids'
(African lily)
Fine tub plant, with large heads of blue or white flowers and broad strap-like leaves. Only hardy in favourable districts.

Yucca filamentosa
(Adam's needle)
Creamy-white bells on substantial spikes, and large leaves that impart a tropical air.

---

hosepipe will take much of the physical effort out of the job.

Feeding should not be overlooked. It is wise to feed regularly throughout the growing season, preferably by adding a liquid fertilizer to the watering operation.

Tubs and troughs should also be top-dressed once or twice a year, scraping away the tired surface soil and replacing it with a good loam and leafmould mixture. Two spring dressings may be necessary, allowing a month between applications.

Tubs should be kept on the dry side in winter, as dry roots are less vulnerable to frost than wet ones.

Stone troughs are ideal for a small collection of alpines, but choose slow-growing, compact plants otherwise they soon become overcrowded

A roof garden

A flat roof can easily be converted into a roof garden and will be perfect for a party on a hot summer evening. A few Russian vines (*Polygonum baldschuanicum,* now more correctly *Fallopia baldschuanica*) twining their way round a couple of chimneys will strike the right atmosphere. But for the imaginative planter the scope is much greater.

Structural considerations

Professional advice should be sought before installing heavy containers and decor on the roof. Soil and water, not to mention containers, plants and people, can be very heavy, and an architect, reputable builder or the local authority Building Control Officer should be consulted. And, of course, planning permission sought and obtained.

Raised beds can be built for permanent planting, but in view of the weight this creates it is best to confine planting to tubs, troughs and growing bags where possible.

In the best roof garden I have seen, 23 storeys high and only 2.5m×3.2m (8ft 6in×10ft 6in), lightweight packing cases have been used to form terraces and build up borders and beds on different levels. This has enabled the owner to grow 50 different shrubs, climbers and plants, 24 kinds of vegetables, a collection of herbs and even a few soft fruit bushes!

With roof gardens, high winds can be a trial and considerable tidying up may be necessary after a stormy night, but a windbreak of fine mesh-netting might be erected.

All containers must be very carefully secured using galvanized wire ties. These can be attached to screw eyes fitted in wall plugs in the parapet walls. In all cases, use soil-based composts for planting in preference to lightweight peat-based types.

Small trees need a substantial container, and a brick-built trough, lead tank, or even a wooden crate that holds a generous amount of soil, can be used. Whichever container you finally decide upon, ensure that it has adequate drainage. Also, staking and tying-in of young trees is essential.

The plants

Among trees and shrubs, figs and hebes are worth trying in mild areas. And small apple trees and *Cotoneaster horizontalis* will grow in most places.

It is naturally best to keep to small plants, ground-huggers and creepers.

Nasturtiums will give a magnificent display if sprayed regularly against aphids. Calendulas, petunias, geraniums (upright and trailing), Perilla frutescens 'Nankinensis', lobelia, carnations, cornflowers, primulas, fuchsias, ageratum, dahlias (pom-pon), stocks and silver-leaved foliage plants will all enjoy the sunshine. Small bulbs also thrive, but daffodils and tulips should be chosen for shortness and stoutness of stem.

By careful selection of plants and bulbs, it is possible to provide a long and continuous period of flowers and foliage even in a very small roof garden.

Among the climbers, the Virginia creeper (*Parthenocissus quinquefolia*) is well worth growing — its autumn colour is brilliant. *Clematis montana* and winter jasmine (*Jasminum nudiflorum*), and variegated ivies, should all be found a place.

On the windbreak walls sweet peas would add their brilliant splashes of colour to a luxuriant growth of clematis and variegated ivies.

Vegetables

Although one is unlikely to set out to grow a crop of potatoes on the roof, many vegetables can be grown, especially salad crops. It would be unwise to grow tall crops that need staking, but all the salad crops plus a selection of herbs can be grown most successfully.

Roof gardens can be oases of peace and tranquility. No matter how small the area, only a little imagination is required to make it full of interest, provided the structure is able to take the additional weight. Plants can be used sparingly yet still be most attractive when (opposite page) they complement attractive tiling or when elegant furniture forms the main focal point (below left). The use of indoor pot plants (below) should not be overlooked. Grouping containers is often beneficial on an exposed roof (right) as they afford each other some protection from the wind

Gardening under glass

A greenhouse opens new gardening horizons, and most keen gardeners must at some time think of the very considerable advantages ownership bestows. With a heated greenhouse, gardening becomes a year-long hobby rather than one concentrated on the warmer months. But even without heat, or with just a modest amount during spring, the extra interest provided is remarkable.

If cost or space precludes the possibility of a greenhouse, many of the benefits to the plants are shared by cold-frames and cloches. These are of particular use in the vegetable garden, but they can also greatly increase the range of flowers that can be raised or grown successfully.

Greenhouses

A greenhouse greatly enlarges the scope of one's gardening, saves the costs of buying many kinds of plants, and provides plants for the living-room, as well as enabling one to propagate particular subjects which are costly or in scarce supply, or may not be generally available in plant form. A greenhouse also allows one to work comfortably when outdoor conditions are wintry.

Types of greenhouse

Greenhouses vary greatly in size and shape, and this is the main question to be resolved before you purchase one.

Size is mainly a matter of space, price and growing requirements, and this tends to resolve itself. But remember that the proportion of growing space lost to the central path is much greater in a small greenhouse than in a larger one. In many instances the smaller type also have low eaves and doorway clearance, so bear this in mind if you are tall. You want to spend many pleasant hours in the greenhouse, and this will be impossible if there is insufficient head clearance for comfort.

Shape can be a more difficult question. In days gone by there were just a few conventional shapes from which to choose, but modern materials and designs have changed all that.

Most gardeners, however, will choose one of the conventional types, and the choice usually lies between a ridge or span greenhouse (which is free-standing with a sloping roof and either straight or sloping sides — see page 25) or a lean-to (which uses the wall of a house or shed on one side). There is a compromise between the two that is sometimes seen — a three-quarter span, which has two roof surfaces to catch the sun yet also utilizes an existing wall.

Fairly recently there has been a movement away from these orthodox shapes and there is even an octagonal greenhouse, which is effective because it catches most of the available light.

Whatever kind you consider buying, compare it with the available *growing* space of other types. Also look at the efficiency of the ventilation system. These points can be more important than shape.

Materials

During recent years some prominence has been given to the use of various forms of plastic or polythene as an alternative to glass, but glass is still the best proposition for a greenhouse. It is easier to clean, does not scratch, and will not accumulate as much dirt, which reduces the quality of light transmitted. And, of course, it normally has a long life.

Plastic houses are, however, suitable for providing shelter for various plants, and a polythene lining is of value for the cold or cool greenhouse, preventing the temperature from falling very low at night.

Another important decision is whether the structure should be of wood, metal or concrete. Teak is expensive; Western red cedar durable and cheaper. Painting is unnecessary, but it should then be dressed with linseed oil occasionally. Oak is much in demand, and when used with a steel framework the cost is less.

Metal greenhouses — steel and aluminium alloys — are easy and quick

An amateur's greenhouse, showing how well a group of plants as diverse as polyanthus and alpines can be grown and displayed together

to erect and admit plenty of light because of the smaller framework. However, the larger area of glass can mean greater fluctuation in temperature, and draughts are unavoidable when putty is not used.

Concrete houses are mostly constructed of precast strips, the glass panes being secured to the strips with asbestos from beneath. They do not look as elegant as the other types.

Siting

The siting or placing of a greenhouse is important. The aim should be to provide full sun exposure — not in the shadow of trees, fences or buildings from the east, south or west. On the other hand, avoid positions exposed to strong winds, especially from the north and east.

The traditional alignment is north and south, although some growers prefer east and west because of the improved transmission of light during winter.

Another situation to avoid is one where children are likely to kick balls or throw stones, which would be particularly risky in the case of glass-to-ground structures.

Foundations

Every permanently placed greenhouse must have a proper foundation, and many manufacturers supply a ground plan.

A simple foundation can be made by taking out a trench of the right depth, keeping the sides vertical. Sometimes a wedge of concrete at least 30cm (12in) wide and 13cm (5in) deep is made, and a brickwork footing built on it. If the house has a brickwork base, several courses of bricks should be used. Concrete bricks, including the cavity type, can be employed for footings and walls.

Good surrounds and a proper soakaway for water are other considerations, while a hard approach path should be considered essential.

Garden Frames

Frames (see page 25) should be considered as an annexe to the greenhouse, giving winter protection to plants that will stand a degree or two of frost; accommodating flowering plants out of bloom, or subjects for which the greenhouse would be too warm, except in winter. They are invaluable for early sowings, raising bedding plants and for hardening-off plants raised in early spring. The value of a frame is vastly improved if it can be heated. This can be done inexpensively by making a hot-bed or by using soil-warming cables. A very small paraffin stove can also be effective, especially if the frame is situated in a sheltered south-facing position, unshaded by either trees or buildings.

Above: a lean-to greenhouse with an angled frame designed to capture as much light as possible
Right: the traditional glass barn cloche, ideal for advancing early crops such as lettuce. When considering the design of cloches, always take into account the soil area covered, and the height. These cloches have adequate height at the edges
Below: corrugated rigid plastic tunnel cloches are easier to handle than polythene and longer-lasting, but much more expensive initially

Cloches

The original cloches were bell-shaped but now they are chiefly of a tent or barn-like or tunnel form and can be set together to form long rows for plants. Flat-topped cloches are also available, while several of patent design provide for easy access, watering and ventilation. Various types of plastic are used as glass substitutes, but these are not so easy to fix in a stationary position because they are light.

Cloches begin their usefulness early in the year, for they can be positioned to warm the soil for seed-sowing or planting tender seedlings raised in the greenhouse. They are invaluable, too, for raising bedding plants, pot plants and as cover to harden off plants raised in warmth. They can be used to cover and bring into early flower hardy subjects such as anemones, Christmas roses (*Helleborus niger*), pansies (*Viola × wittrockiana*), polyanthus (*Primula polyantha*) and spring-flowering bulbs. They are also most valuable for covering early vegetables, such as early beans, cauliflowers, lettuces, peas and potatoes, and for sheltering tomatoes.

Greenhouse equipment

Unless you intend to raise only crops that will grow in the border soil without heat, such as lettuces, it is inevitable that one must budget for various accessories — some are almost essential, others are luxuries.

There are many kinds of proprietary staging, and the greenhouse manufacturer can normally supply it as an optional extra, although it is not difficult to make wooden staging.

Some gardeners prefer the appearance of wooden slats, but there is much to be said for staging that can be used to support moist sand. This makes various automatic watering systems feasible.

Heating

After the purchase of the greenhouse, heating is the major cost, and probably the one that will determine the type of plants you attempt to grow.

While the old-fashioned method of using hot water pipes from an outside solid-fuel boiler is efficient, it is not likely to be chosen for the smaller greenhouse today. The choice will usually lie with paraffin or electricity, although natural gas can be an attractive proposition in certain circumstances.

Electricity is undoubtedly the most versatile, but is regrettably very expensive. The advantage of having a power supply in the greenhouse is that so many other pieces of equipment (including lighting) can be operated.

For the main heating, the choice lies between tubular and fan heaters. Tubular heaters have the merit of a fairly even distribution of heat and allow a gap of about 15cm (6in) between the back of the staging and the glass, so that warm air can rise between glass and plants.

Fan heaters can be effective, but unless carefully sited can cause pockets of cold air, especially in the lower half of the structure.

All forms of electrical heating can be controlled by the use of a thermostat, and this is an essential piece of equipment.

Electricity offers an alternative form of heating — undersoil cables. This can prove more economical for raising many plants, but obviously growth will still be controlled to a large extent by air temperature. Soil-warming cables are, however, invaluable for providing extra heat for propagating purposes.

Gas and oil can be used to fire hot-water boilers, or to provide more direct convected heat, but natural gas is normally used only if the greenhouse is very close to, or attached to, the house and supply is no problem. It may be particularly

Top: a mist propagator is a boon to anyone doing a lot of propagating. A section of the greenhouse can be screened off with polythene sheeting to form an enclosed, warm, humid atmosphere in which plants will root more readily
Above: roller blinds, fitted inside, make for easy adjustment. External shading washes are applied in early summer and removed in autumn

attractive if the home is already on a low tariff for central heating. If it is possible to run an additional radiator from the existing central heating system, this may be the most satisfactory solution, but is only feasible in a lean-to or conservatory.

Paraffin heaters are easy to install, and still a favourite for background warmth. They are also economical, but need frequent attention. The wick must always be kept clean, and a blue flame burner should be chosen.

A satisfactory solution could be a combination of paraffin heaters for background heat and soil-warming cables or a propagating case for raising seedlings.

Propagating cases

A simple propagating case merely provides a humid atmosphere in which seedlings can germinate or cuttings root. To make it most effective, however, it should have some form of heating, usually soil-warming cables. An expensive version may have a mist unit to ensure a sufficiently moist atmosphere for the most difficult cuttings.

It is not difficult to make one's own propagator from a suitable box lined with polythene. The thermostatically controlled soil-warming cables are buried in sand, and an air-warming cable used round the side above compost level to increase air temperature slightly. A sheet of glass over the top maintains humidity.

Although a cold greenhouse can be run with the minimum of equipment if it can be attended to during the day, a heated or unattended greenhouse must be suitably equipped. Basic equipment includes a heater (a fan heater and oil heater are illustrated), a ventilating fan, shading blinds, a minimum-maximum thermometer and a heated propagator

Mist units

For difficult cuttings, a mist unit can make all the difference between success and failure. Used with a moisture-sensing device, it emits a fine mist whenever the leaves are likely to become too dry.

Watering devices

The importance that automatic watering assumes must relate to the time you have available to attend to your plants. For anyone who has to leave plants unattended for any length of time, an automatic watering system may be a good investment in the long term.

If the bench is made into a shallow trough, and the plants placed on a bed of sand, kept moist, the plants will probably take all the water they require by capillary action. Alternatively the bench can be lined with polythene and a special capillary mat or blanket placed on it and kept permanently moist by various methods. The two main methods of keeping sand or blanket moist are a reservoir system at one end of the bench, or tubing laid between the plants, with fine holes from which the water dribbles.

Ventilators

Unless there is adequate ventilation, plants will soon suffer. The temperature can soar quickly in sunny weather, and on cool, damp days a lack of ventilation can lead to moist conditions that are ideal for the rapid germination of disease spores.

Automatic ventilators are not difficult to fit, and are efficient and trouble-free in operation. They normally work by the expansion or contraction of a liquid in a cylinder attached to the ventilator.

Most operate a conventional type of window, but some open and close a louvre.

In a greenhouse 2.4m (8ft) long, at least two roof ventilators will be required, and ideally there should be a third ventilator low down in the side or at the end.

Shades

Most gardeners settle for a 'permanent' shading — a white or green wash applied in early summer and removed in autumn.

Roller blinds can be fitted, but they tend to be expensive and still need someone to operate them. This can also be automated, but such equipment must be regarded as a luxury.

Plants to grow

A greenhouse greatly enlarges the scope of one's gardening, but it is important to decide on the warmth you can provide and the type of crops or plants you wish to grow.

For convenience it is usual to break down the temperature ranges for a greenhouse into three groups, depending on the minimum night temperature that can be maintained:

Cold greenhouse: 1°C (34°F)
Cool greenhouse: 7°C (45°F)
Warm greenhouse: 16°C (60°F)

Having settled on the temperature range — which should be maintained even in the most severe weather — it is possible to consider the best plants to grow.

Cold greenhouse

Normally no artificial heat is used, protection being provided by blinds, mats or newspapers if necessary in very cold weather. Double glazing reduces heat loss, but is expensive and cuts down light at a crucial time of year. Lining with polythene may, however, be of benefit provided condensation does not become a problem in consequence.

The limitations of temperature mean that the plants you can have in flower in winter will be confined mainly to those that bloom naturally at that time, and in the early spring months.

Spring-flowering subjects include: *Primula juliae, P. allionii,* auriculas, pansies (*Viola* × *wittrockiana*), violets (*Viola* spp), saxifragas, Kaffir lilies (*Schizostylis coccinea*), and many bulbous subjects such as crocuses (*Crocus* spp), cyclamen, daffodils (*Narcissus* spp), fritillarias, hyacinths (*Hyacinthus*), irises, narcissi and snowdrops (*Galanthus nivalis*).

Showy flowering shrubs in pots include brooms such as *Cytisus kewensis* and *C. praecox,* forsythias, heathers (*Erica carnea,* now more correctly *E. herbacea*), and *Viburnum carlesii.*

Summer-flowering subjects include: annual plants in variety, cannas, carnations (*Dianthus caryophyllus*), pelargoniums, fuchsias, and verbena. Summer-flowering bulbs include hot water plants (*Achimenes* spp), African corn lilies (*Ixia* spp), African harlequin flowers (*Sparaxis* spp), and vallotas.

Summer-flowering shrubs to grow include *Hibiscus syriacus,* fatsias, prickly

heaths (*Pernettya mucronata*), roses (*Rosa* spp) and hydrangeas.

Autumn-flowering subjects include: perpetual carnations (*Dianthus caryophyllus*), eucomis, nerines, yellow star flowers (*Sternbergia lutea*), tritonias, and the Kaffir lilies (*Schizostylis coccinea*). The Chilean bellflower (*Lapageria rosea*) and the passion flower (*Passiflora caerulea*) are good climbers.

Winter-flowering subjects include: Christmas roses (*Helleborus niger*), *Viburnum fragrans* (syn *V. farreri*), winter jasmine (*Jasminum nudiflorum*), and a wide range of bulbs including *Iris reticulata* and *I. danfordiae.*

Below left: Hibiscus rosa-sinensis. *Although this type has single crimson flowers, there are double and semi-double forms in shades of pink, salmon and yellow*
Far below left: a Sinningia speciosa *hybrid. These plants are much better known as gloxinias, and several excellent cultivars are available, mainly in shades of red, pink, purple and white, all variously mottled or marked*
Below: coleus are remarkably easy to grow, and a packet of seed will provide a galaxy of gay colourful forms. Select only those with the best markings to grow on. It is worth propagating the finest plants vegetatively another year

Cool greenhouse

Provided a minimum winter temperature of 7°C (45°F) can be maintained, there is an almost unlimited supply of plants and shrubby subjects available which will ensure the cool greenhouse is always colourful and interesting.

A collection to provide year-round colour should include azaleas (*A. indica*), begonias (both fibrous and tuberous types for flower and *B. rex* for foliage), the slipper flowers (*Calceolaria* spp), cannas, chrysanthemums, cinerarias (*Senecio cruentus*), flame nettles (*Coleus blumei*), cyclamen, heaths (*Erica hiemalis* and *E. gracilis*), fuchsias, *Hydrangea macrophylla*, busy Lizzies (*Impatiens* spp), kalanchoe (particularly *K. carnea, K flammea,* and *K. blossfeldiana*), Chilean bellflower (*Lapageria rosea*), pelargoniums, primulas (*P. obconica, P. malacoides, P. sinensis,* and *P. kewensis*), and the ever-popular African violet (*Saintpaulia ionantha*).

Warm greenhouse

A warm greenhouse, where 16°C (60°F) can be maintained, is suitable for all the plants suggested for the cool house, plus many other beautiful plants.

The flamingo plant (*Anthurium andreanum*) has interesting flowers in shades of pink and red, and often decorative leaves. *Aphelandra squarrosa* also has handsome leaves and flowers.

Cymbidiums are among the easiest orchids to cultivate, and are well worth growing for their lovely flowers from March to May; they like a peaty compost and plenty of moisture during the growing season.

Caladiums and *Cordyline terminalis* (now *C. fruticosa*) are both notable for their coloured foliage.

Crossandras, which come in several colours, can produce spikes of flowers with showy bracts for most of the year, while *Columnea banksii* freely produces its brilliant red flowers on trailing stems throughout summer.

Also noteworthy for simple warm greenhouse culture are *Jacobinia pauciflora,* scarlet and yellow; *Jacaranda ovalifolia,* with fern-like leaves and lavender-blue flowers; *Boronia megastigma,* fragrant foliage; *Hibiscus rosa-sinensis,* rose-red; and *Streptosolen jamesonii,* an evergreen climber with orange-red flowers.

Above right: orchids require special conditions, but the cymbidiums are among the easiest for a warm greenhouse. There are many charming hybrids; this one is 'Bella'. Although many orchid enthusiasts devote a whole greenhouse to their special needs, orchids can be grown in a mixed house with confidence
Right: calceolarias, or slipper flowers, are easy plants for a cool greenhouse, producing colour from May to July from a sowing the previous June

Indoor gardening

Since the term houseplant was coined in 1947 there has been an increasing interest in indoor gardening: no longer is it sufficient to have a lone cyclamen or tradescantia on the kitchen windowsill. We now find that the odd plant or two has become a collection of plants, and the collection has taken on a new dimension as plant rooms, a sort of indoor greenhouse, become more fashionable.

Whatever else one may learn, a good start with indoor gardening is possibly the most important requirement, as initial disappointment can very easily snuff out the flame of interest. Therefore, it is of vital importance to buy sensibly and to buy from a reliable supplier, someone who understands plants and their needs, someone who would never dream of selling a plant knowing that it was an inferior one.

The beginner should bear in mind that the most colourful plants are invariably the most difficult to care for — it is very much better to start with tolerant plants such as tradescantias, grape ivy (*Rhoicissus rhomboidea*), spider plant (*Chlorophytum comosum*), and the less demanding of the philodendrons, such as the sweetheart vine (*P. scandens*). As skills improve, and possibly the environment with better heating, one can progress to the prayer plants (*Maranta*), dracaenas, and more colourful crotons (*Codiaeum variegatum*), but the warning should be given here that almost all of these more difficult plants will present something of a challenge regardless of how skilful the grower of houseplants may become.

Caring for houseplants

Houseplants naturally respond to care, and it is worth taking a little time to understand the basic requirements of the particular plants you buy. At critical times of the year, the same amount of water can be right for one plant but possible death to another; a bright sunny window is fine for a cactus, but not for a fern; an ivy will probably tolerate a cool hall, while the wax flower (*Hoya carnosa*) will demand draught-free warmth if it is to thrive.

If you master a plant's requirements for light, warmth and watering, you are most of the way to growing a good plant.

The tools required for indoor gardening are few, so it pays to buy good ones. A watering-can with a long, narrow spout is vital, while a misting spray will be invaluable for maintaining humidity. A hygrometer can be used to check general humidity

Lighting

While green foliaged plants such as the Swiss cheese plant (*Monstera deliciosa*), philodendrons and rhoicissus will tolerate a less well lit location than variegated plants such as *Hedera canariensis* and dracaenas, it will be found that all plants will require a reasonable amount of light if they are to succeed. However, this does not mean that they should be subjected to direct sunlight streaming through a window pane. The glass will magnify the heat of the sun, and leaves of tough old plants such as the rubber plant (*Ficus elastica* 'Robusta') will suffer scorch marks and irreparable damage. While the light windowsill location is ideal when it is not too sunny, it may well be harmful to the plants in colder weather. In cold weather plants should be taken into the room, where they will be warmer and free from draughts.

The African violet (*Saintpaulia ionantha*) is an excellent example of a plant that does infinitely better when grown in a high-light situation. It will grow better and, perhaps more importantly, adequate light will induce the plant to flower much more freely. More light could well be the answer for a reluctant plant that grows well but is disinclined to produce flowers.

Providing supplementary light is well worth considering. It may only mean placing smaller plants under a table lamp in the evening or, where one is more ambitious, it could well entail fitting specialized lighting that will improve both the appearance of the plant and its performance.

Heating

Trying to grow any form of indoor plant in cold, draughty and inhospitable conditions would be a complete waste of time. Temperatures in the region of 13°C (55°F) are essential, even for the easiest of plants to manage. Where low temperatures prevail it is extremely important to ensure that the soil in the pot is barely moist. Temperatures of 15–21°C (60–70°F) will give best results; although a higher temperature is suitable for some plants, such as crotons, others will become spindly and there will be a higher incidence of red spider mite.

Radical fluctuation in temperature is

also something that one should take particular care to guard against.

Feeding and watering

Every plant you ever purchase will have to be fed fairly soon after placing it on the windowsill, otherwise there will be a slow and inevitable decline.

Established plants should be fed with a balanced houseplant fertilizer, and the most important requirement when feeding is to ensure that the maker's directions are followed. If you have a large collection of plants it will be much more economical to buy larger containers of fertilizer and to dilute accordingly.

Frequently the houseplant grower becomes too enthusiastic when it comes to potting plants on into larger pots or containers — plants growing in containers that are disproportionately large seldom do well. Both plant and pot should look right for one another. Correct and frequent feeding is usually much better for the plant than continually disturbing the roots in order to pot it on.

Although plants grown using hydroponic methods have some of their roots permanently in water, only a very few plants will tolerate constantly moist roots if grown in compost. In fact it is overwatering rather than under-watering that kills the most houseplants. An important requirement of all pot-grown plants is that they must have adequate air around their roots so that they have oxygen to be able to breathe and grow. The healthiest plants are, without question, those that have a vigorous and undamaged root system.

There are, however, some plants, such as the colourful florist's azalea (*A. indica*) that do much better when the roots are kept wet all the time; but this is an exception. The majority prefer to be watered and allowed to dry out a little — some, such as mother-in-law's tongue (*Sansevieria trifasciata*), quite appreciably — before being watered again. Prolonged saturation of the soil ensures that all the air is excluded and an anaerobic condition prevails, which in turn results in rotting of the root system and eventual browning and loss of leaves.

Totally saturated conditions can be alleviated by removing the plant from its pot and standing the root-ball on the inverted pot so that air can get at it and set up a much more rapid drying-out process.

Above right: some of the easiest houseplants include the popular Swiss cheese plant (top), tradescantia (green and silver leaves), the sweetheart vine Philodendron scandens (cascading down on the left), and the prolific chlorophytum or spider plant (standing on floor)
Right: more difficult to grow are the dracaenas (top left), tender ferns (top right), crotons (bottom left), and the hoyas (bottom right)

Hydroponics

In recent years the technique of growing plants in water supplied with balanced nutrients has taken tremendous strides, and we find that an incredible range of plants, many quite delicate, can be grown by this method. Members of the Araceae family, such as philodendrons, scindapsus, nephthytis and aglaonemas, do especially well.

Plants are encouraged to grow on their more succulent water roots and are 'potted' into baked clay granules, which absorb about one-third of their own weight of water. The principal function of the granules is to hold the plant erect in the growing pot, to provide the plant roots with water by capillary action and, most important of all, to ensure that the roots are well aerated.

The 'mechanics' for growing plants in this way may vary, but the principles are similar, and the most successful are those that use an ion exchange fertilizer. This nutrient is bonded to polystyrene granules, and as the pH (see page 38) of the water changes so the nutrient is released to nourish the plant. Only the required amount is released, so there is no danger of overfeeding.

Plant roots are not completely submerged in water, only the bottom 7.5–10cm (3–4in). The level of water in the container is shown on a water level indicator, which makes watering very much simpler than when plants are being reared more conventionally in soil. The water reservoir is filled to the maximum mark on the indicator and allowed to fall to the minimum, and is left at the minimum mark for one week before refilling. Topping up with small amounts of water to maintain the reservoir at maximum prevents aeration of the root system and can be very harmful.

It is of particular importance at any time, but more especially during the winter months, to use tepid water.

Most of the hydroponic units will have cultural instructions provided with the plant, and whatever the type of unit or system it may be geared to, the important requirement is that directions should be followed. Indoors, hydroponic plants will require similar temperature, location and pest control as plants of the same type that may be growing in a more conventional potting mixture.

Perhaps surprisingly, more succulent types of plants such as *Sansevieria trifasciata* 'Laurentii' do surprisingly well provided the water level in the container is allowed to remain on minimum for at least one week before topping up. In fact, although it is seldom recommended, the more succulent plants will go for several weeks in a dry condition without suffering any harm.

Ideally plants should be grown in rooms devoted to their needs, but in the home there usually has to be compromise. As these pictures show, however, a real conservatory atmosphere can be created — whether in a functional area (left), a room devoted to pure relaxation (above), or as an extension to the living area (right)

Plant rooms

Mention has been made of the tremendous strides taken in respect of indoor plants — from homes with a few, often weedy, plants to rooms in some modern homes that almost resemble tropical rain forests. An amazing number of plants can be fitted into the average home — and occasionally what would one time have been considered an essential piece of furniture is dispensed with in preference for a rubber plant or a Swiss cheese plant. Some plants seem to become part of the family and are even given names and referred to as if they were human beings.

There is little doubt that the more plants there are in a particular room the better they are likely to be in respect of growth. The proximity of other plants seems to create a microclimate in the home and they fare better than isolated specimens. It is not surprising, therefore, that there has been greater interest in recent years in the concept of a plant room — somewhere in the house, or in the extension to a house, where one's plants can be concentrated and given the attention they are most likely to enjoy — almost a greenhouse within the walls of the home.

Suitably fitted out, a spare bedroom could well become a much more fascinating place: one that is warm, congenial and a home for the plants and all the other odds and ends that one may accumulate as a result of developing an interest in the care of indoor plants.

Making a plant room
The most important consideration should be adequate light, and this will

almost certainly mean installing lights, in time if not at the outset. Special growing tubes must be used, as these have been designed with plant health as a primary factor. Lights of this kind are constantly being improved, and it is worth enquiring from manufacturers before deciding to purchase. Don't be tempted to depend on ordinary domestic lights — although they are bright, the type of light emitted is not right for plant growth.

It is important when lights are being installed to ensure that the maker's directions are followed, so that plants have sufficient light yet are not so close to the tubes that they are likely to be scorched.

To improve light intensity in the room it is wise to paint walls and ceilings white so that there is as much light reflection as possible.

Adequate heating is also an important need, and one should aim for a constant temperature in the region of 18°C (65°F). Water-filled radiators provide the best form of heating for plants. Open fires and electric fires tend to dry out the atmosphere much too rapidly.

To help maintain a moist atmosphere it is beneficial to place a bowl filled with water on top of the radiator; this will create a slightly damp atmosphere and give the room the right growing feeling. It is a magical quality one cannot go into a shop and purchase: it has to be created.

The prime object of a plant room is to grow as many plants as possible in conditions that are as agreeable as possible. And to achieve one of these ends one can considerably increase the potential of any room by erecting tiered shelving with lighting tubes fitted to the underside of the upper shelves; this ensures that plants at lower levels have their full requirement of ten to twelve hours of light each day.

A growing room will be costly to fit up and run, but in the long term it will be less expensive than a greenhouse in the garden; and on cold winter days it will certainly be much more congenial. Many greenhouse fittings and items of equipment can very easily be used to set up and maintain a plant room.

Displaying plants

No matter how beautiful the plants, an unsuitable container can mar the effect while a quite ordinary plant can look attractive if displayed well in a nice container.

Decorative pots

When purchased, plants will naturally be in a pot, usually plastic or clay, and not all of them are decorative enough to adorn the sitting-room windowsill. The consequence is that we now have an abundance of decorative containers into which plants can be placed — some of these quite hideous, while others do much to improve the appearance of the plant.

When acquiring a decorative pot it is worth remembering that the outer pot should be only slightly larger than the growing pot, otherwise the plant tends to have a lost look.

If pots are placed in decorative outer containers, it is necessary to ensure that excess water does not accumulate in the bottom. Any water in the outer pot should be tipped away, as it will almost inevitably prove to be fatal if the plant is left standing with the lower part of its root system in water for any length of time.

Grouping plants

Besides pots for individual plants there are many excellent larger containers that may be used for accommodating a group of plants. When plants with reasonably compatible requirements in respect of water are grouped together in a well-proportioned container they will be easier to care for, will grow better, and will also provide an important room feature.

Many of these containers are described as self-watering, which means that they have a reservoir in the bottom of the container with an indicator showing maximum and minimum water levels, so making accurate watering a very simple operation. There are many different types of container and various methods of getting the water from the reservoir to the soil as it is required — a broad nylon wick being the most common one. As the soil dries out water is drawn up by capillary action, and it works admirably provided the reservoir is not overfilled. In this latter event the essential gap between water and soil is bridged, with the result that the soil

Above right: even the most attractive plant can be enhanced by the right container. To successfully group a number of containers however, calls for a sense of design and balance if they are not to look untidy or dominate the room

Right: the choice of containers is enormous, from simple shapes in terracotta or cane to Victorian jardinières and modern ceramics

becomes a soggy mess that will quickly put paid to the plants.

Larger containers may also be used for growing groups of hydroponic plants. Here again the growing system varies according to the supplier of the plants and materials, so it is wise to seek advice from the grower or retailer when considering the acquisition of hydroponic plants and planters. The latter have really come into their own in office environments, especially where an open-plan layout is in existence.

With more or less permanent plant groupings indoors it is very much better to confine the group to foliage plants only. Although seasonal plants may be included it will be found that these require frequent replacement, and it is much better to group seasonal plants in a container of their own where they will be much more impressive and can have individual treatment in respect of water and light.

Primroses (*Primula vulgaris*) grouped in a bowl indoors in January introduce a real breath of spring and can be very bright and colourful — but unfortunately they only last for about one month in warm locations. Azaleas, poinsettias (*Euphorbia pulcherrima*), saintpaulias — all can be planted in groups that will be breathtakingly attractive.

This page: plants can play an important part in home decor, especially when a few choice specimens are grouped together, whether on the floor, table, chest or cascading from a high shelf. Do not be afraid to move the plants round occasionally; many will benefit from a change of situation

The kitchen garden

The true gardener will never be able to resist the lure of the kitchen garden. The satisfaction of growing and eating your own produce is unequalled, and although you may not save much money you will rediscover the taste of garden-fresh produce.

Increasing soil fertility

New gardens can be a problem in the early years, but as the seasons go by cultivation becomes easier and fertility increases.

The first essential is to break any hard 'pan' that may exist below the surface; this is a very hard layer created by compaction or many years of cultivation to the same depth by a plough. The solution is deep digging; take the opportunity

A well-maintained vegetable garden can make an attractive feature in its own right. This modest plot shows what a wide range of vegetables can be grown outside the back door

to work in some manure or compost — indeed anything that will help improve soil structure (see pages 38–39).

Digging

Double digging is designed to break up the soil two 'spits' (spade depths) below the surface. It ensures a good, deep root-run, improves drainage and allows soil-improving organic matter to be placed well below the surface.

Once the ground has been worked it will only be necessary to double-dig perhaps a third of the plot each year.

Single digging only breaks up the soil to the depth of the spade, but is adequate for most crops.

If you come across perennial weeds such as docks, nettles or dandelions, dig them out and put them on the bonfire. Annual weeds can be turned into the bottom of the trench to rot down.

Manure and compost

At least half the vegetable plot should be manured every year. Any form of organic matter will improve the soil structure, and although farmyard manure is ideal, spent mushroom compost, peat, spent hops, or well-rotted garden compost, are all good.

The great advantage that compost has over all other forms of organic matter is that it is virtually free, so every gardener should have a compost heap.

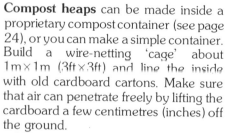

Compost heaps can be made inside a proprietary compost container (see page 24), or you can make a simple container. Build a wire-netting 'cage' about 1m × 1m (3ft × 3ft) and line the inside with old cardboard cartons. Make sure that air can penetrate freely by lifting the cardboard a few centimetres (inches) off the ground.

You can put on anything that will rot down — weeds, waste from harvested vegetables, grass cuttings, leaves etc, and even kitchen waste or screwed-up newspaper. It will all rot down.

Do not put on roots of perennial weeds, anything that is carrying pests or diseases, or anything too thick or woody to rot down quickly.

When you have built up about 23cm (9in) of compost, treat it with a proprietary compost activator before adding the next layer. Once the heap is full, leave it to rot down and start another. The compost will be ready for use when it is a nice crumbly brown, sweet-smelling substance that looks a bit like peat.

Fertilizers

All vegetables will grow better with a little fertilizer. Rather than become involved with the intricacies of 'straight' fertilizers such as sulphate of ammonia or superphosphates, it is more convenient to use a compound fertilizer (see pages 38–39). One of the cheapest and most convenient compound fertilizers is Growmore; and this can be used for all the vegetables described in this chapter. The rate of application varies for different crops.

Lime

Most vegetables prefer a fairly neutral soil, though there are one or two distinct exceptions. It was common practice in the old days to lime every year for certain crops and hope for the best. The modern gardener, however, has realized that this can lead to excesses and do more harm than good. It is very easy to test the soil and make accurate applications (see page 38).

One point to remember is never to apply lime at the same time that manure is applied. This will simply release ammonia and both will be wasted. It is better to manure in autumn and winter and lime in spring.

Sowing

If you dig over the plot in winter, the weather will break it down quite well. Before sowing it must be levelled; start by breaking it down with the back of a fork, and then consolidate the surface. This should never be done when the soil is wet: keep off if you find that the soil sticks to your boots.

Consolidate by treading all over the plot to be sown, with your weight on your heels. Next apply the fertilizer at the recommended rate and rake the soil to a fine tilth, at the same time working in the fertilizer.

Before sowing, stretch a tight garden line across the plot and draw a shallow drill with the corner of a draw hoe.

Sprinkle the seed down the drill as thinly as possible. Thick sowing results in overcrowded and consequently weak seedlings. It also makes thinning more difficult.

After sowing, cover the seed with the soil taken out, and tamp down lightly with the back of the rake.

Thinning

As soon as the seedlings are large enough to handle, they should be thinned to the recommended distances. Some of the thinnings can often be used to transplant another row, but these transplants will mature a little later.

If you intend to replant the thinnings, handle them very carefully by the leaves — not the stems, which are easily bruised — and transplant them before the roots have a chance to dry out.

Some plants, notably the cabbage family and leeks, are best sown in a seed-bed and transplanted. This will save valuable space on the main plot.

Planting

Prepare planting sites in exactly the same way as for sowing, though if cabbages (all of which need firm soil) are to follow another crop, it is not generally necessary to dig. Simply hoe off the weeds and rake the fertilizer into the top.

If plants are to be lifted from a seed-bed, water it well the night before. Plant either with a trowel or a dibber, and firm well. It is important to firm well so that the roots are not left hanging in a pocket of air.

Water well after planting, especially if the soil is dry.

Crop rotation

It is not wise to grow the same crop year after year on the same piece of land. If different crops are moved around the plot in successive years, a build-up of pests and diseases can be avoided. Also, better use is made of valuable organic matter; some plants require manuring for best results, others prefer to grow on ground manured for a previous crop.

The answer is to put the gross feeders like peas, beans, onions and lettuce on freshly manured land, and follow those the next year with root crops that dislike fresh manure.

Crop rotation is an essential part of good soil husbandry and long-term gardening. Perpetually growing the same crop on a plot of soil causes the same elements to be continually taken from the soil by the plants, and the same pests and diseases establish themselves. To avoid this, plots may be divided into three sections, each devoted to growing a different type of crop in a three-year cycle. For example, Plot A would grow leguminous crops such as peas and beans in year one, brassicas such as cabbage and cauliflower in year two, and root crops such as potatoes and carrots in year three. Plot B would grow root crops in year one, leguminous crops in year two and brassicas in year three. Plot C would grow brassicas in year one, root crops in year two and leguminous crops in year three. In the same three year cycle, double dig and manure Plot A in year one, Plot B in year two and Plot C in year three

Plot A

Plot B

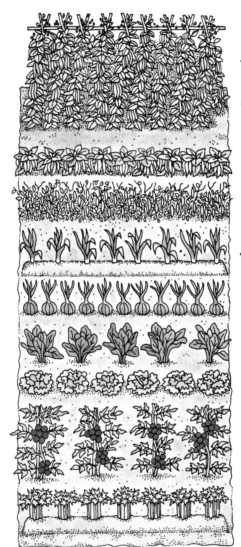

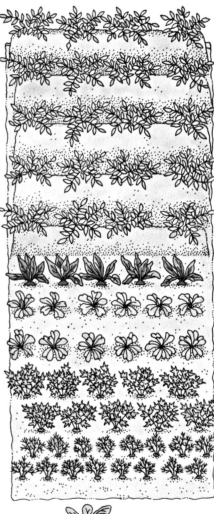

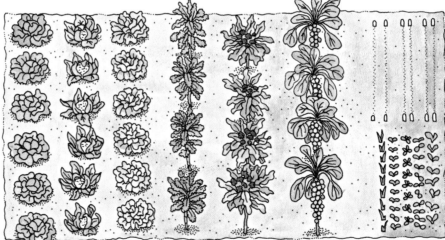

Plot C

How to grow vegetables

The next four pages list most of the popular vegetables, and full cultural instructions are given for each one. Further tips, including soil preferences, will be found on pages 188–97.

All vegetables will benefit from a balanced fertilizer, but the application rates – as with manure and lime – vary for specific crops.

More complete descriptions of pests and diseases mentioned, together with control measures, will be found in the relevant chapters (pages 44–51).

Artichoke, Jerusalem
Plant the tubers in February or March, 15cm (6in) deep and 30cm (1ft) apart.

Jerusalem artichokes do not suffer from any significant problems.

Cut off the tops in August to limit top growth, and lift the tubers as required, from October onwards.

Bean, broad
Sow from February or March until the end of April, placing the seeds 5cm (2in) deep and the same distance apart in a double row 25cm (10in) apart. Allow 60cm (2ft) between each double row. It is also worth sowing in July as a catch-crop, and again in November to stand the winter.

Blackfly is the principal pest, and it is helpful to remove the growing tips as a deterrent once the plants are in full flower.

Pick the pods regularly while they are still fairly young.

Bean, French
Make the first sowing under cloches in March or in the open ground in April or May. Set the seeds 15cm (6in) apart and 5cm (2in) deep in rows 45cm (18in) apart.

Thin to 30cm (1ft) apart and water the soil if it becomes dry. A mulch applied at the thinning stage is usually beneficial. French beans tend to suffer from the same pests and diseases as runner beans.

Pick the pods regularly while still young.

Bean, runner
Early plants can be . raised in the greenhouse from an April sowing, but outdoor sowings should not be made before mid-April under cloches, or May in the open ground. Place canes, poles or strings 25cm (10in) apart in double rows, with 30cm (1ft) between rows and set the seeds up against each support, 5cm (2in) deep. Sow a few extra seeds at the end of the row for possible replacements.

Plant indoor-raised runner beans at

the end of May or early June after thorough hardening-off.

Hoe between the plants regularly and mulch with peat or manure. Keep well watered.

Pinch out the tops when the plants have reached the top of the supports.

Blackfly is the worst pest, but one easily controlled.

Harvest regularly and before the beans have a chance to become long and stringy.

Beetroot
Sow an early globe cultivar under cloches in March, in drills 2.5cm (1in) deep and 20cm (8in) apart, placing two seed clusters every 15cm (6in).

From April to July, globe cultivars can be sown in succession in the open ground. Long-rooted cultivars for storing should be sown in May or June.

Thin to leave the strongest seedlings, and keep the ground between the rows well hoed.

Lift the roots from early sowings while still small. The main crop can be lifted in October and stored. Cut off the leaves near the root and store in boxes of peat.

Above: runner bean 'Prizewinner' is an old favourite, having exceptionally long fleshy pods of good flavour
Below: golden beetroot make a refreshing change from the normal red kinds. Although the colour is unusual, the flavour is equal to that of red cultivars

Beet, spinach
Sow from April to July, in drills 2.5cm (1in) deep and 45cm (1½ft) apart. Thin to 20cm (8in).

Harvest young leaves regularly, always leaving some on the plant to continue growth.

Beet, seakale (Swiss chard)
Sow from April to July, in drills 12mm (½in) deep and 45cm (1½ft) apart. Position two seeds every 38cm (1¼ft), and thin to leave the stronger seedling at each station. Harvest as spinach beet.

Borecole (curly kale)
Sow at the end of April or early in May, planting out 60cm (2ft) apart each way in July or early August.

Very few pests or diseases are troublesome, although club-root and cabbage root fly can be a problem.

Gather young leaves and sideshoots as required.

Broccoli
The term broccoli used to cover both the sprouting type and the heading form, but there has been general agreement that broccoli will now refer only to the sprouting kind — the old 'sprouting broccoli'. The old heading broccolis are now termed 'winter cauliflowers'.

Sow in April on a prepared seed-bed, and plant out in May or June, about 60cm (2ft) apart, with 75cm (2½ft) between rows.

The same pests and diseases that affect cabbages will also attack broccoli. Apart from watching for these it is only necessary to hoe and water.

The first shoots should be ready to cut in February; if the centre shoot is cut first there will be a regular supply of sideshoots.

Brussels sprouts
Sow on a seed-bed in March or April, in drills 12mm (½in) deep and 15cm (6in) apart.

Plant out 60–90cm (2–3ft) apart each way, depending on the vigour of the cultivar, in May or early June.

Hoe and water as necessary and pick off any yellowing leaves in autumn. Stake tall plants on exposed sites. Watch for any of the pests and diseases likely to attack cabbages.

Pick from the bottom of the stem as the sprouts get big enough.

Cabbage
By careful selection of cultivars it is possible to have cabbages maturing at almost any time of year. All types are easy to grow provided the ground is free of club-root.

The main pests are cabbage root fly and the caterpillars of the cabbage white

Cabbage 'Emerald Cross' is an F1 hybrid ballhead cultivar. The uniform, firm, solid heads are ready for cutting in summer and autumn

butterfly. Both can cause heavy losses. Turnip flea beetles can be a problem among seedlings, but are easily controlled (see page 47).

Summer cabbages should be sown 12mm (½in) deep on a prepared seedbed in March or April, in rows 15cm (6in) apart.

Plant 45cm (1½ft) each way in May or June, and keep the ground hoed throughout the season. Water if necessary.

Spring cabbage should be sown 12mm (½in) deep in drills 15cm (6in) apart on a seed-bed in July or August.

Plant 23cm (9in) apart in September or October with 45cm (1½ft) between rows.

Top-dress with nitrate of soda in March applied at 70g per sq m (2oz per sq yard).

Cut every other plant for spring greens, and the remainder when they have hearted.

Winter cabbage should be sown in a seed-bed in May, in drills 12mm (½in) deep and 15cm (6in) apart.

Plant 45cm (1½ft) apart with 60cm (2ft) between rows, in June or July, and cultivate as for summer cabbage.

Savoy cabbage should be sown on a seed-bed in April or May, and planted out in July, leaving 45cm (1½ft) between plants in rows 60cm (2ft) apart.

Remove any dead or decaying leaves as they appear, and cut the heads as required once they have firm hearts.

Calabrese
This crop is very similar to sprouting broccoli, but is ready for late summer and autumn use.

Cultivate and harvest as broccoli.

Cabbage, Chinese
This crop is becoming more widely grown, but it is important not to sow too early otherwise the plants will run to seed prematurely.

Sow during June or July, placing seeds 10cm (4in) apart in rows 30cm (1ft) apart and 12mm (½in) deep.

Thin to 20cm (8in) apart and water copiously. Watch for slugs and caterpillars, which can be a problem. When hearts begin to form, tie the leaves together with raffia.

The heads will be ready to cut nine to ten weeks after sowing.

Capsicums

Plants must be raised in a greenhouse. Sow in pots in March, and transfer to 10cm (4in) pots before hardening off.

Plant in a sunny position in late May or early June. Start the plants under cloches, planting 45cm (1½ft) apart.

Pinch out the growing point when plants are 15cm (6in) high. Keep well watered, and when the fruits start swelling feed with a liquid tomato fertilizer every two weeks.

Start picking in August while the fruits are still green.

Carrot

Sow early varieties in frames or under cloches in early March. Maincrop cultivars are best sown in succession from April to July 12mm (½in) deep in rows 25cm (10in) apart.

Thin to 5cm (2in) apart, and again to 10cm (4in) apart two or three weeks later.

Pull early carrots as required.

Carrot fly larvae, which burrow into the roots, often gain entry after thinning. Do not leave thinnings lying around, and try to do the job in wet weather.

The last sowings can be lifted in September and stored in boxes of peat or sand.

Cauliflower

The term cauliflower now includes the winter hearting kinds that used to be called broccoli. That means cauliflowers can now be harvested practically the year round by careful selection of cultivars, though those maturing from December to March are only suitable for very mild districts.

Sow summer cultivars under glass in January or February, or in a seed-bed outside in April or May. Winter cultivars should be sown in a seed-bed in April or May.

Plant summer cultivars 45cm (1½ft) apart in rows every 60cm (2ft), from March to June. Winter varieties need to be planted 60cm (2ft) each way during June or July.

Pests and diseases are as for summer cabbage.

Cut the curds as they are ready; if they are not needed immediately, break a few leaves over them for protection.

Celeriac

Sow under glass in March and harden off in a garden frame before planting out in May or June. Set them 30cm (1ft) apart in rows 38cm (1¼ft) apart.

Water in dry periods, and cut off sideshoots as they appear. Draw a little soil round the roots in September to blanch them.

Dig the roots in October and store in boxes of peat.

Celery

Deeply cultivated, rich soil is essential. Dig a trench 38cm (1¼ft) wide and 45cm (1½ft) deep and work well-rotted manure or compost into the bottom. Refill the trenches to within 15cm (6in) of the top, leaving the remainder of the soil on either side of the trench.

Sow in a heated greenhouse in March and prick out into boxes. Harden off before planting out in June in double rows with 30cm (1ft) each way between plants.

Water copiously, and feed with a liquid fertilizer every two weeks. Start earthing up when the plants are 30cm (1ft) high. Tie a collar of paper or black polythene round the stems and earth up in three stages with three weeks between each. Protect tops from frost with straw or cloches.

Start harvesting in November. Dig from one end of the row, disturbing the other plants as little as possible.

Celery fly larvae sometimes tunnel through leaves, and will need control. The main disease is celery leaf spot, which can be very disfiguring.

Self-blanching celery needs a well-manured soil but no trenches.

Plant out in June in blocks of short rows, with 23cm (9in) between plants in each direction so that the shade from their leaves helps them to blanch each other.

Start cutting in September or October.

Chicory

Sow both forcing cultivars and open-ground types in June or July, in drills 12mm (½in) deep and 30cm (1ft) apart Thin forcing varieties to 25cm (10in) apart and open-ground types to 38cm (1¼ft). Hoe and water as necessary.

Start digging forcing cultivars in November. Cut off the tops just above the ground and set upright in boxes of compost. Cover the boxes to exclude light and place in slight heat. Check regularly for slugs and caterpillars.

Outdoor cultivars can be cut as soon as they have hearted. Forcing cultivars will form a white 'chicon'. Cut these when they are 15–20cm (6–8in) long.

Courgettes

Treat as marrows, but plant 50cm (1⅔ft) apart.

Start cutting soon after the withered flowers have fallen, when the fruits are about 15–20cm (6–8in) long.

Cucumber

Cucumbers need a deep, rich, freshly manured soil and a sunny site.

Sow in a heated greenhouse in March or April, in peat pots. Alternatively, sow two or three seeds 2.5cm (1in) deep in stations where they are to grow, in May.

Below: celeriac, sometimes known as turnip-rooted celery, has a distinctive celery taste
Below right: kohl rabi 'White Vienna'. A vegetable worth considering as an alternative to turnips. There is also a purple cultivar

Space them 90cm (3ft) apart and thin to leave the strongest plant.

Harden off greenhouse-raised plants and plant out in early June at the same distances.

Hoe and water regularly and if growth seems slow feed them with a general liquid fertilizer. Pinch out the growing point when the plant has seven leaves, to encourage sideshoots.

See marrows for diseases.

Start cutting in July. Cut regularly and do not let the fruits grow too large.

Kohl rabi

A good crop instead of turnips for a hot, dry soil. Even so, the quicker it develops the more tender it will be, so incorporate plenty of organic matter before sowing.

Sow in succession from April to July. Take out drills 38cm (1¼ft) apart and sow 12mm (½in) deep. Thin to 23cm (9in) apart.

Do not allow the swollen stems to become larger than a tennis ball before harvesting.

Leek

Sow in a seed-bed from late February to mid-April, and plant in final positions in June. Drop them into holes made with a dibber, 23cm (9in) apart in rows 38cm (1¼ft) apart. The holes should be deep enough so that only 7.5cm (3in) of the plant protrudes. This deep planting helps to blanch the stems. Water in sufficient water to firm the plant.

Lettuces are indispensable salad crops, and many cultivars are available, for a variety of uses

Lettuce

Start sowing early cultivars in the greenhouse in February. These can be planted outside in April.

Outside, start sowing in early March and continue at two-week intervals until July. Sow in drills 12mm (½in) deep and 30cm (1ft) apart. For early crops outside, sow hardy cultivars in September for overwintering.

Plant greenhouse-raised cultivars in April after hardening-off. They should be set out in rows 30cm (1ft) apart with 25cm (10in) between plants. Throughout the spring and summer, thinnings from outside-sown plants can be used to make another row, maturing slightly later.

Thin seedlings to 25cm (10in) apart as soon as they are large enough to handle. Hoe regularly and water as necessary.

Slugs and greenfly are the most likely pests, but both are easily controlled (see pages 46–47). Grey mould on stems and leaves is a sign of botrytis, while a white powder on the underside of leaves indicates downy mildew; these are the two principal diseases (see page 51).

Marrows and squash

Sow in peat pots under glass in April or May. Alternatively, sow outside in May, setting two seeds in stations 60cm (2ft) apart for bush cultivars and 90cm (3ft) apart for trailing.

Plant at the end of May or June at the distances mentioned.

Water copiously throughout the season, and control slugs and aphids.

White patches on leaves indicate mildew, and this disease is often encouraged by dry soil.

Cut fruits regularly while still young. For storage, allow a few fruits to grow, then when the skin is hard, store in a cool, frost-free place.

Onion

From seed. The first sowing can be made in a heated greenhouse in January, but the main crop is generally sown outside during March or April. Sow 12mm (½in) deep in rows 30cm (1ft) apart.

Plant greenhouse-raised plants in April, 15cm (6in) apart in rows spaced at 30cm (1ft) intervals.

Thin sown onions to 15cm (6in) apart. Weed control is important.

From sets. On heavy soil, grow onions from sets (small bulbs). Trim the dead tops to prevent birds pulling them out, and plant 15cm (6in) apart with 30cm (1ft) between rows.

Japanese onions. For a crop in June or July, sow Japanese onions outside in August. These can be left to overwinter and thinned out in spring.

Pests and diseases are few, but onion

fly larvae sometimes burrow into the bulbs, causing wilting, yellowing and eventual death.

The leaves should start bending over in August. If not, bend them down to help ripening. Lift bulbs in September and dry them on a concrete path. Store in slatted boxes or strings.

Above: marrow 'Green Trailing'. Marrows make large plants, but are rewarding to grow where you can allow space for their development
Below left: onion 'Express Yellow'. The tops are normally bent over towards the end of the growing season to assist ripening of the bulbs

Parsnip

Start sowing in February if soil conditions permit, or up to April if necessary. Set two or three seeds in stations 20cm (8in) apart after taking out drills 2.5cm (1in) deep and 45cm (1½ft) apart.

Harvest the roots as required from October onwards. In the north, lift and store in boxes of peat.

Canker, which shows as cracked orange patches, is the major disease. If troubled by this, use resistant cultivars.

Cracking — when roots split lengthwise. As this condition is usually due to drought, ensure that soil never dries out.

Peas

Sow hardy cultivars in October or November, and others in succession from March to June. Take out a trench a spade's width across and 5cm (2in) deep and place the seeds 5cm (2in) apart in a double row with 10cm (4in) between rows. Provide sticks for support.

Pea moth larvae sometimes burrow into the pods and affect the seeds.

Pick regularly when the pods fill, working from the bottom of the plant.

Potatoes

First sprout or 'chit' the tubers in boxes in a light, cool place, in February.

Plant early cultivars in March 13cm (5in) deep and 30cm (1ft) apart in rows 60cm (2ft) apart. Second earlies and maincrop cultivars should follow in April, planting 13cm (5in) deep and 38cm (1¼ft) apart in rows 75cm (2½ft) apart. Plant either in drills or with a trowel.

When the foliage is 15cm (6in) high earth up by drawing some soil up to the stems. Earth up a second time three weeks later, and water well at this stage by flooding between the rows.

In June, give maincrop cultivars a second application of fertilizer at 135g per sq m (4 oz per sq yd).

Lift earlies as required from June onwards, but leave maincrop cultivars until the haulm has died down, then lift and store in sacks or paper (*not* plastic) bags.

Potatoes are susceptible to several virus diseases, so buy only certified seed, and keep aphids under control as these spread the viruses.

Potato blight is another serious problem, but the severity is often influenced by weather.

Scab causes corky patches on the skins. If this has been a problem in previous years, use plenty of organic matter at planting time and choose resistant cultivars.

Wireworms, cutworms and slugs burrow into tubers, but a soil-pest killer applied before planting should help. If slugs are a problem, use a liquid slug killer regularly.

Radish

Sow in succession from March to July at two-week intervals, in drills 12mm (½in) deep and 15cm (6in) apart.

Salsify and scorzonera

Sow in March or April, 2.5cm (1in) deep in rows 38cm (1¼ft) apart.

Thin to 20cm (8in) apart. Lift the roots as required from October onwards.

Shallots

Plant in February or March 15cm (6in) apart with 30cm (1ft) between rows. Trim the dead tops and plant so that the bulbs just show. Replace any bulbs lifted by birds.

When the leaves start to yellow, lift the bulbs and dry them on a concrete path. Store in slatted boxes.

Spinach

Sow summer cultivars in succession from March to July, 2.5cm (1in) deep in rows 30cm (1ft) apart, and the winter type in August or September.

Thin to 15cm (6in) apart.

Pick young leaves regularly, always leaving some on the plant to grow again.

Spinach, New Zealand

This is a good vegetable for a hot, dry soil.

Soak the seed overnight before sowing in March indoors with heat or outdoors in early May.

Keep picking the largest leaves from each plant and leave the plants to continue cropping over a long period.

Pea 'Petit Pois', a type particularly popular in France. The pods must be picked young, when the peas are exceptionally delicious and tender

Swedes

Sow 12mm (½in) deep in rows 38cm (1¼ft) apart in May or June. Thin to 30cm (1ft) apart.

Lift roots as required throughout the winter.

Sweet corn

A sunny site and a well-manured soil are essential for good results.

Sow in peat pots in the greenhouse in April, or outside in May. Outside, sow two seeds in stations 38cm (1¼ft) apart in rows 60cm (2ft) apart.

Plant in late May or early June in blocks of short rows, at the distances mentioned.

Water regularly and mulch with peat or manure.

When the 'silks' (male flowers) wither, squeeze a seed or two to test ripeness. If the fluid is milky the cob is ripe. If no juice emerges, the cob will be tough. Cut only as needed.

Tomatoes

Tomatoes must be germinated in a heated greenhouse. Sow at the end of March or the beginning of April in boxes or pans of loamless compost. Pot into 10cm (4in) pots and allow plenty of space.

Harden off thoroughly before planting out at the end of May or early June in a warm, sunny situation. Space the plants 45cm (1½ft) apart and stake with a 1.2m (4ft) cane immediately.

Tie the plants to the cane regularly except for bush cultivars, which need no support. These also need no de-shooting, but ordinary cultivars must have sideshoots removed regularly.

When the third truss has formed, pinch out the top one or two leaves above it. Never let the plants go short of water, and start feeding with a liquid tomato fertilizer as soon as the first truss has set fruit. Repeat at two-week intervals.

A mulch of straw or peat under bush cultivars will keep ripening fruit clean.

Aphids sometimes suck the sap of tomato plants, causing stunting and distortion; they also spread virus diseases.

Blight causes dark brown marks on stems and leaves, followed by wilting and eventual death if not treated in time.

Tomatoes are susceptible to several virus diseases, which cause wilting and yellow patches on leaves. There is no cure, so affected plants must be burned.

Turnip

Sow early cultivars 12mm (½in) deep in drills 30cm (1ft) apart, from February to May. For autumn and winter use, sow in June or July. Thin to 15cm (6in) apart.

Flea beetle is a common pest. It makes round holes in leaves.

Fruit

A well-planned fruit garden should be able to provide fresh or stored produce for the family all the year round. Even on a comparatively small plot it is possible to grow a wide range of fruits, particularly if the right rootstock and method of training is chosen for tree fruits.

Unless they are required for purely decorative purposes, there is little point in growing large trees in the kitchen garden. Standard trees on tall stems are difficult to manage, especially at picking time; they also require a lot of room and take much longer to bear fruit. Half-standards and vigorous bush trees have the same disadvantages.

It is wise to grow trees that are trained in an intensive fashion, such as dwarf pyramids, cordons or fans. These will provide as much fruit as their larger counterparts, and they will do so in a much shorter time; they require much less room and the trained shapes can be grown against walls of fences — space that might not otherwise be used. It is also possible to dispense with ladders, long-handled pruners, lance sprayers etcetera that goes with large trees.

Rootstocks

Tree fruits are usually grafted on to another rootstock. This serves to contain tree size in most cases, and also induces earlier cropping.

Apple rootstocks are usually known by a code. The three most common ones for amateurs are:

M9 — the most dwarfing stock and only suitable where the soil is good and fertility will be maintained. Trees on this rootstock need permanent staking.

M26 — the most common rootstock for trained trees. More vigorous than M9, it is suitable for most soils.

MM106 — a semi-dwarfing stock for intensive (trained) trees on poor soils or for bush trees on average soils.

Pear rootstocks are fewer and the two most encountered are:

Quince A — the one generally used in gardens. It makes a tree about 3.6m (12ft) in diameter.

Quince C — has a more dwarfing effect but is generally only used on good soils with a vigorous variety.

Plum rootstocks are less confusing. As Brompton and Myrobalan rootstocks are vigorous and will produce trees too large for the kitchen garden, the best for small gardens is St Julian A. This is semi-dwarfing and is especially suited for fan-trained trees.

The same plum rootstocks are used for gages and damsons.

Training

This is an area that frequently fills the beginner to fruit growing with trepidation. Yet confidence is all that's required, for most systems are based on simple principles.

Although it is mainly tree fruit that is trained in space-saving ways, the same principles can be applied to other fruit, such as gooseberries.

The pruning described below is based on apples, but the method is similar for other fruits.

Dwarf pyramids are upright trees up to 2.1m (7ft) high, with branches growing out in successive tiers to form a pyramidal outline.

After planting, cut the leader back to about 50cm (1⅔ft) from the ground, and shorten any sideshoots longer than 15cm (6in) to four buds.

In the second winter, reduce the leader by about 20cm (8in) and cut back laterals to about 20cm (8in). Then in August or September, cut back laterals to four leaves.

When the tree has reached the required height, cut back the leader and long branches at the top of the tree by half, in May. Subsequently, cut back new growth from these branches to 12mm (½in) each May.

Cordons are single-stemmed trees with fruiting spurs. These should be summer pruned. Cut back laterals to four leaves and any sub-laterals to one leaf, in late July. Any secondary shoots growing in that year from laterals that have been pruned, should be shortened again in September or October to one leaf. As the main leader grows, tie it to the wires.

When the tree has filled its allotted space, free it from the wires and lower it a little to give more space. Finally, when the leader has grown as long as required, cut it back in May. In subsequent years, pruning is the same, though if fruiting spurs become overcrowded they can be thinned out a little.

Fans are popular for stone fruits against walls. The method described below is ideal for peaches and cherries.

If a three-year-old tree is bought, it will already have its main framework of branches. Cut these back in the February after planting, to leave about 60cm (2ft) of last year's wood, cutting back to a cluster of three buds.

This will produce shoots that can be tied in.

When the tree has filled its allotted space, concentrate on pruning for fruit. Allow the end bud on each of the leading

Apple 'Ellison's Orange' trained as an espalier. Branches trained into the horizontal position tend to fruit earlier in the tree's life than those left to grow naturally. Space is used economically, which is useful in a small garden

branches to grow out, and tie it in. Rub out buds that are growing directly towards or away from the wall. Select shoots growing from the top side and the bottom of the main branches, and space these about 10cm (4in) apart, rubbing out others or pinching them back to two leaves. Allow the selected shoots to grow to 45cm (1½ft) and then pinch them back. Tie these shoots in at the end of the summer to produce fruit the next year.

Each year train a new shoot arising from near the base of these laterals to replace them when they are removed after fruiting.

Pollination

Most tree fruits require cross-pollination from another cultivar to set a full crop. Some are self-fertile but most benefit from another *compatible* cultivar in close proximity.

Always choose cultivars with this in mind — compatible kinds are indicated on pages 182–187.

Tree fruit

Although most fruit is undemanding of time once established, a little extra attention can increase yields. And any effort spent in getting the plants off to a good start will be amply repaid. This is especially so with tree fruits.

All tree fruit should be planted in the dormant season between November and March, preferably before Christmas when the soil is warmer. Plant firmly and ensure that the joint between the stem and the rootstock (easily seen as a knobbly growth) is well above the ground.

Avoid sites that are subject to late spring frosts; if your garden is in a hollow where frost collects, flowers are more likely to be damaged in spring. Sometimes frost is trapped by fences, and lifting the fence a little off the ground may allow frost to escape.

Apples

Apples are best grown as cordons, dwarf pyramids or bushes. It is possible to buy these at three or even four years old but they will fruit no sooner than one-year-old (maiden) trees. Maidens are cheaper and provide an opportunity to train the tree from scratch.

Bush trees should be planted 3–4.5m (10–15ft) apart, dwarf pyramids in rows 2.1m (7ft) apart with 1m (3½ft) between trees, and cordons in rows 2.1m (7ft) apart with 75–90cm (2½–3ft) between trees. Bush and dwarf pyramid trees must be supported with a stout stake, while cordons are trained on wires, planting the trees at an angle of about 45 degrees.

After planting, cut bush trees back to a bud about 50–60cm (1⅔–2ft) from the ground.

The next winter, select four of the current season's growths and cut back by half to two-thirds, depending on their vigour (the stronger they have grown, the longer they should be left) and position. In subsequent years, shorten the leading shoots back depending on the growth they have made, and shorten sideshoots to four buds. It may also be necessary in later years to remove any crowded, crossing or damaged branches.

Summer pruning is not generally necessary with bush trees, but if the tree makes a lot of growth each year, it is often an advantage to shorten shoots to about 13cm (5in) in August or September.

Every year, it will pay to mulch the trees with well-rotted manure or com-

Above left: 'Cox's Orange Pippin', justifiably regarded as one of the best dessert apples
Left: peach 'Peregrine', one of the most suitable cultivars for growing outdoors. It has large, juicy fruits of good flavour

post, but do not let it touch the trunk.

In February, apply sulphate of ammonia at 35g per sq m (1oz per sq yd) and sulphate of potash at 20g per sq m (½oz per sq yd).

Every third year also apply superphosphate at 70g per sq m (2oz per sq yd).

Early cultivars should be eaten straight from the tree, but many late apples will store well into the spring. Use immediately any damaged or diseased fruit and place the remainder in perforated polythene bags, and keep them in a cool, frost-free place.

Cherries

Both acid or cooking cherries and sweet cherries are best grown as fans, otherwise they make trees too big for the kitchen garden. Acid cherries will thrive even on north-facing walls, but sweet cherries demand warmer conditions and a deep, fertile soil.

Acid cherries are pruned in the same way as peaches, but sweet cherries are bigger trees so must not be encouraged to grow too much. Do not prune the leading shoot, but when it has filled its space, tie it downwards to limit growth, or cut it out to leave a weaker shoot in its place.

As with peaches, shoots growing towards or away from the wall must be rubbed out. Other shoots should be pinched back to five or six leaves. In the autumn, they should be further shortened to three or four buds.

Manure sweet cherries in spring and apply 20g per sq m (½oz per sq yd) of sulphate of potash. Every second year add 70g per sq m (2oz per sq yd) of superphosphate. Acid cherries should be fed as for plums.

Protect ripening cherries against birds.

Peaches and nectarines

Although peaches can be grown as bushes in the south, it is best to grow fans, especially if you have a south-facing wall. Nectarines *must* be grown against walls as they are less hardy. If you buy a three-year-old tree it will already have its main framework of branches.

Plant in the same way as plums.

Little maintenance is needed, just a good mulch of manure.

For good fruit, thin so that they are spaced at about 23cm (9in) intervals. Thin to single fruits in early June, and about a month later to the final spacing.

Pears

Pears can be grown in the same shapes as apples — bush, dwarf pyramid and cordon. Plant at the same distances as apples.

Pruning is basically the same as for apples, though it can be a little harder as

pears will not make quite so much growth. Summer pruning starts in July.

Feed as for apples.

Early cultivars should be picked when green and hard, while later cultivars should be left on the tree as long as possible. Do not wrap, but place them on shelves or in slatted boxes in a cool, frost-free place.

Plums, gages and damsons

These are generally big trees, so it is probably best to grow fan-trained specimens against a wall or fence.

Fan-trained trees require some skill to produce, so it is probably best to buy one already trained; they are usually two or three years old.

Plant 15–23cm (6–9in) away from the wall, sloping the stem slightly towards it.

In the first spring after planting, little pruning will be necessary, but in the second cut back branches that are to form leaders by about half.

Once established, the leaders should be tied in regularly to the supporting wires to extend the framework. New shoots are also trained in to fill empty

Pear 'Conference', one of the few self-fertile pears, but not really suitable for growing in a restricted form such as cordon or espalier

spaces, perhaps where old wood has been cut out. When growth starts in spring, remove any shoots growing directly away from or towards the wall. Pinch out the tips of other laterals when they have formed six or seven leaves.

When the crop has been picked, these are then shortened back again by about half. At this time, also remove old, dead or diseased wood and anything that is growing too vigorously from the centre of the fan.

Mulch in spring with manure after applying 20g per sq m (½oz per sq yd) of sulphate of ammonia and the same quantity of sulphate of potash. Every second year apply 70g per sq m (2oz per sq yd) of superphosphates.

When the tree is carrying a heavy crop it is important to thin to leave fruits about every 5cm (2in). This is best done in July.

For eating, pick when fully ripe, but for cooking or bottling they should be slightly under-ripe.

Soft fruit

Soft fruit is extremely valuable in the kitchen garden, producing a high yield in a small area.

The biggest problem with all soft fruit is birds, so it is well worth investing in a fruit cage to protect them. The exception here is strawberries which, being low-growing, can easily be protected by laying netting over the plants at fruiting time.

Strawberries are exceptional in one other respect. All other soft fruit is planted in the dormant season between November and March, while strawberries are best planted in August or in spring.

Avoid planting soft fruit on a site prone to late frosts, or on badly drained soil. Incorporate plenty of manure or compost before planting.

Blackberries, loganberries and hybrid berries

These are always grown trained up a fence or wall, or on wires. Loganberries prefer a warmer soil than blackberries, so a south-facing position is ideal.

Plant 3m (10ft) apart, though the less vigorous thornless cultivars can be planted 1.8m (6ft) apart. After planting, cut the old stem back to 23cm (9in) and mulch heavily with manure or compost.

The training wires should be run at 90cm (3ft), 1.2m (4ft) and 1.5m (5ft) from soil level.

After the first year, tie in the shoots so that the older canes are kept separate from the new ones. Cut out the old stems after fruiting and tie in the new ones.

Mulch annually with manure or compost and apply 70g per sq m (2oz per sq yd) of sulphate of ammonia in spring.

Blackcurrants

Plant in rows 1.8m (6ft) apart with 1.2m (4ft) between plants. Ensure they are firmed well and that the crown of the plant is just below soil level. After planting, cut back all the shoots to within 2.5 – 5cm (1 – 2in) of the soil. Mulch with well-rotted manure or compost, or peat.

After fruiting, cut out all fruited wood to within 2.5 – 5cm (1 – 2in) of the soil. This will leave only the current season's wood, which will fruit the following year. Also remove any weak shoots.

Mulch every year with manure and apply a balanced fertilizer at the rate of 100g per sq m (3oz per sq yd) in March.

Gooseberries

These are usually grown on a short stem, in much the same way as redcurrants.

Above right: red currant 'Laxton's No. 1'; this is an early cropper of good flavour.
Right: strawberry 'Red Gauntlet'. It is normal to protect the fruits by laying straw

Plant in rows 1.8m (6ft) apart with 1.2m (4ft) between bushes. Do not plant too deeply.

Prune as redcurrants, but with drooping varieties cut back to an upward-facing bud. The laterals should be pruned back to five or six leaves in July and not shortened to 2.5m (1in) until winter.

Mulch well with manure or compost annually. In spring, apply sulphate of potash at 35g per sq m (1oz per sq yd).

Raspberries

Plant in rows 1.8m (6ft) apart with 38cm (1¼ft) between plants. As raspberries are subject to virus diseases, always plant certified stock.

Before planting, erect the posts and wires used for tying in canes. They should be about 1.5m (5ft) high, with wires 60cm (2ft), 1m (3½ft) and 1.5m (5ft) from the ground. After planting, cut the canes down to about 23cm (9in) from the ground.

After fruiting, cut down those canes that have borne fruit to within 2.5–5cm (1–2in) from the ground. Select the strongest new canes and tie them in to the wires about 30cm (1ft) apart, removing the weaker growths. In the early spring, tip long canes to within 15cm (6in) of the top wire.

Autumn-fruiting varieties should have all canes cut down to within 2.5–5cm (1–2in) of the ground in February.

Apply a heavy mulch of manure or compost annually. Feed with sulphate of potash at 35g per sq m (1oz per sq yd) every March.

Redcurrants and whitecurrants

Unlike blackcurrants, these are grown on a short stem. They should not therefore be planted so deeply. Set them in rows 1.5m (5ft) apart with 1.2m (4ft) between plants.

In winter, cut the main branches of two-year-old bushes back by about half. Subsequently, shorten branches by about half and cut back laterals to about 2.5cm (1in), to form fruiting spurs. When the branches have reached the required height, cut back the year's growth to about 2.5cm (1in). In later years, remove some old wood regularly.

Mulch with well-rotted manure or compost each spring, after applying 70g per sq m (2oz per sq yd) of a high potash fertilizer such as a proprietary tomato feed.

Rhubarb

Plant rhubarb on well-manured ground on an open, sunny site, in February or March. Set the crowns 75–90cm (2–3ft) apart.

Apply a liberal mulch of well-rotted manure or compost each spring after a dressing of a general fertilizer such as Growmore at 135g per sq m (4oz per sq yd).

Do not pull any stems in the first year. In the second and subsequent years, pull stems when they are fully developed but before they become old and stringy, and always leave three or four leaves on the plant in order to avoid loss of vigour.

Strawberries

Strawberries are not gross feeders, so most garden soils are suitable. They will, however, crop better in a sunny position.

Plant only certified stock, as strawberries are subject to virus diseases. For plants to fruit the following year they should be planted in July or August. Planting can be delayed until the spring, but in this case flowers should be removed to build up a strong plant for fruiting the following year. Plant in rows 60cm (2ft) apart with 45cm (1½ft) between plants. It is important to plant so that the crown is above soil level, otherwise rotting may ensue.

The plants are normally set out in beds of four or five rows and left for three

Rhubarb is a trouble-free crop, particularly useful for early forcing. This is 'Victoria'

years. Alternatively, they can be grown in rows in the kitchen garden to crop for a single season.

Keep well watered and weed-free, and as fruits begin to swell mulch underneath with clean straw, black plastic or proprietary strawberry mats. Do not apply the mulch too early.

After fruiting, cut off the leaves to within about 10cm (4in) of the crown, remove any runners and take off the mulch. Lightly fork between plants and apply sulphate of potash at 20g per sq m (½oz per sq yd) between the rows.

Growing under cloches. Early crops can be obtained if plants are covered with cloches, the polythene tunnel type being particularly useful. Plants need a cold period to initiate flowers, so do not cover before January or February.

When plants are in flower, the rows of cloches should be ventilated to allow pollinating insects to enter, and to reduce the temperature.

The herb garden

For a good many years herbs of all kinds were neglected, but during the last 20 years culinary herbs have gradually moved from the back of the stage to the front, and their popularity is still increasing. As an addition to cooking, a herb is no longer required to give an insipid recipe a kick — instead it is expected to supply the final touch which ensures that a dish is highly individual, even though it may not have any flavour of the herb which has been added. A herb can, of course, still supply piquancy to a food: basil added to a tomato salad, for instance, sharpens the tomato flavour and provides its own spiciness.

We should not forget that herbs originally were simply native plants (what we would call weeds nowadays!) which had been found to have medicinal uses. The earliest gardens, or pieces of land attached to a home, would have healing plants growing in them. Since many had to be taken by mouth, those with pleasant flavours were discovered, and eventually added to food. Most of the herbs we grow today are of the culinary kind.

Where to grow herbs

You can grow herbs as part of a herbaceous border, in a bed near the back door for quick dashes by the cook, in containers, or even in a special herb garden. Designs for a herb garden which give the best effect are usually formal, for it must be admitted that herbs tend to be untidy, and they need confining and defining by paving, paths, and edgings, as well as careful staking and trimming. However, they lend themselves very well to this treatment, and a herb garden designed with a cross as the theme, in the shape of a square or a wheel with a sundial or seat in the centre, or as a 'knot' garden, is extremely attractive.

You will find it easier to lay out and plant such a garden if you draw it first on paper, to scale if possible, then lay out the design with string on the site, and put in canes to indicate the position and final height of the plants (see Planning and Design, pages 16–17).

Above right: although it is not always possible to devote a large area solely to herbs, a garden like this can be adapted to a smaller scale
Right: the famous herb garden at Sissinghurst Castle, near Cranbrook, Kent

Growing in containers is a perfectly practicable proposition for many herbs. Most are on the small side, and take kindly to troughs, windowboxes or pots. If you use pots, a 10cm (4in) size is the smallest that will provide a good plant. It is a common mistake to put parsley, chives, or garlic into pots smaller than this, but they never grow strongly. The shrubby kinds can be grown in the large 30cm (12in) pots, or in tubs. Containers can make use of a sunny sheltered place not otherwise accessible to herbs, such as a paved terrace or concrete yard, a balcony or roof, or a windowsill.

Use a good potting compost such as John Innes; if you are growing the smaller annual herbs in containers, loamless composts (with liquid feeding) can be used instead, but these are not really suitable for large or permanent herbs.

The most important cultivation aspect of container growing is the watering. Water occasionally and well, never little and often.

How to grow herbs

Another great advantage that herbs have is the ease with which they can be grown. Some of them, from the Mediterranean region, like sun, others do best with a little shade, and many do not mind a bit of both. The sun-loving kinds prefer a well-drained soil, somewhat short of nutrients; the remainder will grow in any reasonable soil.

Once planted, they can be virtually left alone. They will not need feeding; watering will only be necessary in prolonged, hot drought. In a well-designed herb garden there will be no room for weeds after the early stages.

Staking and tying may be required for some, and removal of flowering stems if seed is not wanted. At the end of summer or in autumn, the summer growth can be cut off, and those that need it given cloche or other protection. Early in spring a light top-dressing of rotted garden compost or leafmould will supply all that is needed to keep the soil structure in good condition, and supply the small amount of plant food that herbs need.

Unlike many plants, herbs do not ail easily; they are not normally subject to endless infections with disease or infestations by pests.

Some of the herbs which die down in winter, such as basil, chives, pot marjoram (*Origanum onites*), mint and tarragon, can be kept going for longer in autumn, and the perennials will sprout earlier in spring, if protected with cloches. July-sown parsley will supply leaves through the winter with cloche protection, lasting until the new season's batch of seedlings is ready for use.

Some herbs will go on through the winter indoors if dug up, early in September, cut down to 5–7.5cm (2–3in) and put into pots of good potting compost. Greenhouse or windowsill protection will then result in fresh growth for the winter.

Propagation

Herbs may be annuals, herbaceous perennials, shrubs or bulbs. The annuals can be hardy or half-hardy, and all are grown from seed sown every year. One or two are biennials, also grown from seed, though the plant will not flower until the second summer after sowing. Seed of nearly all herbs can be sown in spring, from March to the end of May, indoors or outdoors, depending on their hardiness. Some herb seeds germinate better if sown as soon as ripe, generally in August, as their viability (ability to germinate) goes off quickly.

Parsley has a reputation for poor germination, but it will germinate within 14 days if sown in warm soil. Its slow germination when sown in March or April is usually due to the soil temperature being too low; sowing in May for summer and autumn use, or in July for autumn and winter, results in much quicker germination.

The herbaceous perennials can be increased by division in autumn or spring, the latter if your district has bad winters. Examples of herbs that can be propagated by division are balm, chives, garlic, mint, tarragon and thyme. Mint may need holding back, and growing it in a bucket is one solution.

Shrubs can be increased by cuttings taken between June and August, examples being rosemary and sage. Bay can be grown from cuttings, but they are difficult to root — take heel cuttings about 7.5cm (3in) long, insert in compost and provide bottom heat.

The herb garden can be a delightful feature as well as a useful and productive part of the garden. Many herbs have attractive flowers or foliage, and there is usually the bonus of fragrance. In this small plot, clockwise from the top are: a bay tree, rosemary, tarragon, chives, chervil, sage, thyme (lemon and common) parsley, marjoram, angelica, applemint, spearmint. The more prolific herbs, such as mints and thymes can be easily contained if planted in individual pots which can then be sunk into the soil so that the rim is just covered

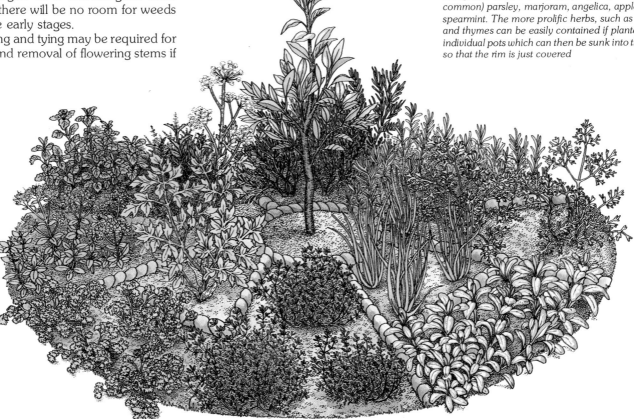

Section Three
A-Z of
Trees, Shrubs and Plants

Having decided what kind of garden you want, and how to achieve it, you now have to make the final and in many ways the most important decisions of all: selecting the plants you propose to use. The theory stage is past; you now have to put your ideas into practice.

By sheer weight of numbers the plants available for selection present a formidable problem. Every catalogue offers a bewildering choice; colour pictures, and sometimes lyrical descriptions of the plants and their attributes, both simplify and complicate the task of choosing.

Yet the overall problem can easily be halved. It is a common mistake to decide that such-and-such a plant will look attractive in a certain position. It may well do so, but only if you have been clever enough to provide the right conditions for it.

So many questions need to be answered. Is the soil right? Is there too much shade, or not enough? Is it likely to be overshadowed by a neighbouring plant, and will there be a colour clash? Where is the right place to site soft fruit? Are the apple trees properly chosen for compatability, so that you have pollinators that will help each other to produce more and better fruit?

Nobody can carry in his head the detailed knowledge required for every plant, but all of us can have the information at our fingertips.

The key to these conditions will be found in the tables and charts that comprise this section, the largest in the book. Here are shown, in easily-read style, the essential details about the cultivation of hundreds of subjects: flowers, shrubs, vegetables, fruit — plants for virtually all situations and seasons, out of doors or in the home.

Sowing, planting, flowering or maturity times are also important items that must be known fairly accurately if your preparations are to be properly rewarded, and all the relevant information will be found in the tables in this section.

Of necessity, the measurements and timings in this book are approximate. Position, soil type and condition, climate and geographical location all influence the growth and prosperity of a plant.

Our measurements are given in both metric and Imperial style, for although at the time of publication metrication is officially observed in almost all weights and measures the old standards are still instinctively used by many people.

Another gradual transformation concerns the classification of roses. Officially, hybrid teas and floribundas are now known respectively as large-flowered and cluster-flowered, which is a much simpler designation, but again it will be many years before the old terms pass out of use. A rose by any other name, indeed!

But whatever names we give, and whatever measurements we use, one universal factor that will remain unaltered is the knowledge that with a little attention to detail anyone can obtain immeasurable joy from owning a garden.

Shrubs and trees

Trees and shrubs form the backbone of a garden, and they are necessary to add height and substance — not to mention their inherent beauty.

No garden is too small for a choice shrub, and even a tiny garden can usually benefit from a carefully selected tree. The key to success is discrimination, and the smaller the garden the more critical this becomes. If space is limited it is better to confine yourself to perhaps one specimen tree or a couple of outstanding shrubs set as lawn specimens, rather than attempt to cram too many into an overcrowded border.

The difference between a tree and a shrub can be subtle. Generally trees are considered to have a clean trunk for some distance, the main growth forming a head, but this is a simplification. Some plants, such as *Acer negundo*, can be grown as a shrub or a tree, depending on the method of training in the early years, while *Cotoneaster × hybridus* 'Pendula' is naturally a carpeting shrub with a spread of up to 1.8m (6ft) and a height of less than 10cm (4in), yet grafted on to a stem of *C. frigidus* it forms a small weeping tree.

Although a few large trees, such as beech, have been included in the following tables, only those trees most likely to be planted in small or medium-sized gardens are mentioned. Some of these will eventually grow into large trees, and a + sign after the height indicates that growth will continue for some time and ultimately be considerably higher. The heights given are those likely to be reached after 20 years in average conditions. But these should be treated with caution, as every garden is different, and there can be significant regional variations; they are most useful as a comparative guide.

There are so many choice trees and shrubs that there is little point in trying to grow one unsuitable for the soil and site. Always check that you can provide the right conditions.

Always prepare the ground well for trees and shrubs. They are permanent garden features and inadequate preparation cannot easily be made good afterwards. Although container-grown specimens can be planted at almost any time of the year, provided the ground is not frozen or waterlogged, the best time to transplant deciduous trees and shrubs is whenever the weather is suitable from September to March, but evergreens are usually planted in September and October or March and April. Exceptions to these general rules are noted in the tables. Wherever the chart does not specify that a tree or shrub is an evergreen, it should be treated as deciduous.

Propagating your own trees is fun, but a long-term exercise. Most shrubs, however, can be propagated easily and many will flower in a year or two, and even make quite respectable bushes in about five years, although there are naturally wide variations between species.

Name	Description	Height/spread*	Flowering period	Soil and site	Remarks	Propagation
Acer grosseri hersii Snake-bark maple	An attractive tree with brilliant autumn colour to the foliage, and eye-catching bark. Young wood is red, older bark has whitish stripes	H:6m+ (20ft+) S:4m+ (12ft+)	May	Plant in well-drained soil in full sun or partial shade	No attention required other than removing damaged or badly-placed branches	Sow seed in pots in a cold-frame in Oct. or outdoors in a sheltered position
A. negundo 'Elegans' (syn. A. n. 'Elegantissimum')	An excellent foliage tree that can also be grown as a large shrub. The maple-like leaves are variegated with bright yellow patches. A similar cultivar with white and green variegation is A. n. 'Variegatum'	H:7.5m+ (25ft+) S:6m+ (20ft+)	March–April	A well-drained soil in sun or partial shade is best	Trim to shape as required, otherwise no other attention is required	The variegated acers must be grafted on to a rootstock of the main species. This can be done in March
Amelanchier canadensis Snowy mespilus	Masses of white flowers appear in spring before the leaves have fully developed. Maroon-purple fruits appear in June, and the foliage is attractive in autumn	H:4m+ (12ft+) S:3m+ (10ft+)	April	Provide a shaded position that is not likely to dry out	No attention is required apart from removing dead or ill-placed branches	Rooted suckers can be removed and planted out from Oct. to March. Low branches can be layered in Sept. Seed can be sown in pots in a cold-frame in Oct.
Araucaria araucana Monkey-puzzle tree	A striking conifer, with branches standing out from the trunk in a distinctive manner. The rigid branches have dark glossy leaves arranged in an overlapping spiral	H:6m+ (20ft+) S:3m+ (10ft+)	—	This tree requires moist but not waterlogged soil	Plant in Oct. or Nov. in very moist soil, otherwise in spring. Plants under 30cm (1ft) transplant best. Stake for first few years	Sow seed in a cold-frame in March, or take cuttings 7.5–10cm (3–4in) long in July
Arbutus unedo Strawberry tree	An attractive evergreen tree with red pitcher-shaped flowers and strawberry-like fruits at the same time. It is a good small-garden tree	H:4.5m (15ft) S:3m (10ft)	Oct.	Provide a neutral soil in a sheltered, sunny position	Plant in Oct. or in March, April or May. Young plants may need protection from cold winds	Take heel cuttings of semi-ripe wood about 7.5–10cm (3–4in) long in July, inserting them in a propagating case in a sand-peat mixture. Seed can be sown in a cold-frame in March
Aucuba japonica	A good shrub for a polluted atmosphere, and for planting in shade. The type has large green leaves, but there is an attractive variegated form, A. j. 'Variegata'. The female plants bear red berries	H:1.8m (6ft) S:1.5m (5ft)	March–April	Any good garden soil is suitable, in a shady or semi-shaded position. Can be planted safely in coastal areas	For a good crop of berries, plant one male to three or four female plants	Take heel cuttings 10–15cm (4–6in) long in Aug. or Sept. Seed can be sown in Sept. or Oct.

Name	Description	Height/spread*	Flowering period	Soil and site	Remarks	Propagation
Azalea	There are two main types of azalea — deciduous and evergreen. Both kinds have colourful flowers at a most useful time of year. The deciduous (leaf-shedding) kinds tend to grow taller than the evergreen ones — about 1.5m (5ft) instead of 90cm (3ft) — and the flowers are usually larger	H:0.9–1.5m (3–5ft) S:0.9–1.5m (3–5ft)	April–June	A moist, acid and peaty soil in semi-shade is essential. Select a position out of wind	Keep the roots moist, and mulch with peat	Azaleas can be increased by seed, cuttings, grafting or layering. Layering is usually the preferable method; choose young shoots that can be pulled down to ground-level and held down by a wire peg. Layer at any time of the year
Bamboo see Pseudosasa japonica and Sinarundinaria nitida						
Barberry see Berberis						
Beech see Fagus sylvatica						
Berberis darwinii Darwin's barberry	A first-class evergreen shrub with small shining green leaves and a mass of bright orange-yellow flowers. Attractive bluish-purple berries appear later	H:2.1m (7ft) S:2.1m (7ft)	April–May	Any good soil suits this plant, in sun or light shade	Plant Sept. and Oct. or March and April. No pruning is required, but old shoots can be cut back to ground level	Take heel cuttings about 10cm (4in) long in Aug. or Sept., setting them in a cold-frame
B. × stenophylla Barberry	An evergreen shrub, ideal as a specimen on its own or as a hedge. It produces cascades of orange-yellow flowers	H:3m (10ft) S:3m (10ft)	May	Ordinary soil in sun or light shade	Plant in Sept. and Oct. or March and April. Pruning consists only of cutting out dead wood and trimming to shape	Take heel cuttings 7.5–10cm (3–4in) long in Aug. or Sept. Insert them in soil in a cold-frame
B. thunbergii Thunberg's barberry	A valuable leaf-shedding shrub, producing bright red fruit and foliage in autumn. Some forms have reddish-purple foliage all summer — B. t. 'Atropurpurea Nana' being a worthwhile hedging plant (this grows to about 45cm/1½ft). Pale yellow flowers appear in spring	H:1.5m (5ft) 1.5m (5ft)	May	Ordinary soil in a sunny position	Little pruning is required other than trimming to shape	Heel cuttings can be taken in Aug. or Sept. They should be about 10cm (4in) long, with a heel
Betula pendula Silver birch	This is a well-known native tree, with a silver bark and graceful habit. The flowers are catkins. Two useful forms for a small garden are B. p. 'Fastigiata' (a slender, upright form of less vigorous habit) and B. p. 'Youngii' (Young's weeping birch), a small weeping tree with a beautiful dome-shaped habit	H:7.5m+ (25ft+) S:3m+ (10ft+)	March–April	This tree will do well even in the poorest soil	No routine attention is required	Sow seed in March, in pots placed in a cold-frame. Both B. p. 'Fastigiata' and B. p. 'Youngii' have to be grafted on to young plants of the main species in March
Boston ivy see Parthenocissus tricuspidata						
Box see Buxus						
Broom see Cytisus						
Buddleia davidii Butterfly bush	The large, tapering flower heads — mainly shades of blue or purple, but sometimes white — are very attractive to butterflies. A good shrub	H:2.1m (7ft) S:2.1m (7ft)	July–Aug.	Provide good soil in full sun. Will tolerate a limy soil	Plant Oct. and Nov. or March and April. To prune, cut back the previous season's growth to within 7.5cm (3in) of old wood	Take heel cuttings of half-ripe wood in July or Aug. Alternatively take hardwood cuttings 23–30cm (9–12in) long in Oct. Root in open ground
Butterfly bush see Buddleia davidii						
Buxus sempervirens Box	A traditional hedging plant with small green leaves, easily trimmed to shape. Also makes a nice free-standing specimen	H:3m+ (10ft+) S:1.8m+ (6ft+)	—	Any good garden soil is suitable, in sun or light shade. Plant variegated forms in good light. Will grow on chalky soil	Clip to shape as required, in spring and late summer. Plant Sept. and Oct. or March and April	Take cuttings 7.5–10cm (3–4in) long in Aug. or Sept., and place in equal parts sand and peat in a cold-frame
Calluna vulgaris Scottish heather (ling)	There are many cultivars of this popular plant, from carpeters of only 5cm (2in) such as 'Golden Carpet' to tall kinds 90cm (3ft) high. Most have olive-green foliage, while others have golden, bronze or silver hues. The flower colours range from white to pinks, purples, and crimson, in double and single forms	H:5–90cm (2–36in) S:7.5–90cm (3–36in)	Aug.–Nov.	These plants are tolerant of salt-laden spray and will even survive moderate atmospheric pollution. Give them a sunny site and lime-free soil	Lightly trim to shape and remove dead heads after flowering season is over	Cuttings can be taken in summer or old plants layered at any time

Shrubs and trees

Name	Description	Height/spread*	Flowering period	Soil and site	Remarks	Propagation
Camellia japonica	An evergreen shrub with beautiful paeony-like flowers, chiefly in shades of red and pink, but also white. There are many cultivars. The plant is not fully hardy	H:1.8m (6ft) S:1.8m (6ft)	March–April	Choose a sheltered position, out of the direct rays of early-morning sun. A peaty, acid soil is essential	Plant in Sept. and Oct. or March and April. Keep young plants moist. Mulch deeply with peat	Take cuttings of half-ripe lateral shoots 7.5–10cm (3–4in) long from June to Aug.
Carpinus betulus Hornbeam	A useful hedging plant, resembling beech, but also effective as a specimen tree. The flowers are hop-like catkins	H:6m+ (20ft+) S:3m+ (10ft+)	March	Any good soil will suit, and they will grow well on chalk or clay. Plant in a sunny or partially shaded position	No pruning is normally required, but if grown as a hedge, clip once a year in July	Sow seed outdoors in Sept. or Oct., transplanting the seedlings the following year
Cassiope lycopodioides	A small evergreen shrub forming a low mat. The tiny, white, bell-like flowers are produced on slender stalks	H:15cm (6in) S:30cm (1ft)	May	Cool, moist conditions and a lime-free soil are essential. Provide peaty soil	Plant from March to May. Mulch deeply with peat	Cuttings of non-flowering shoots can be taken in Aug. or Sept. They should be 4–5cm (1½–2in) long, and placed in a cold-frame
Cercis siliquastrum Judas tree	A distinctive medium-sized tree with clusters of bright purple-rose flowers on slender stalks before most of the leaves appear	H:4.5m (15ft) S:3m (10ft)	April–May	Any good garden soil in full sun is suitable, but provide a sheltered position	Plant in Sept. and Oct. or April and May. Young plants may need protection in their early years	Sow seed in warmth in March, planting seedlings outdoors in June. Set in final position when two years old
Chaenomeles speciosa Flowering quince	A spectacular shrub when trained against a wall. The flowers are chiefly red, pink, or white. The fruits are edible and used in preserves. Good cultivars include 'Cardinalis' (crimson-scarlet), 'Nivalis' (white), 'Phylis Moore' (pink), and 'Simonii' (blood red)	H:1.8m (6ft) S:1.8m (6ft)	March–May	Although this plant will grow on an east or north wall, it does best in a sunny position. Ordinary soil	If grown as a bush, little pruning is required — just trim to shape. If a wall shrub, cut back previous season's growth in May to two or three buds	Take heel cuttings 10cm (4in) long in July or Aug., and insert in a propagating frame
Chamaecyparis lawsoniana Lawson cypress	The species is a large conical conifer with broad fan-like sprays of foliage, but there are many cultivars, ranging from dwarfs suitable for the rock garden to trees of considerable stature. Some have golden or variegated foliage	H:6m+ (20ft+) S:1.8m+ (6ft+)	—	Will thrive on most soils, including those in exposed sites and shady aspect	Plant in Oct. on light soil, but March or April on cold, exposed sites, and heavy ground. Young plants are the easiest to establish. Be sure to allow only the leading shoot to develop on columnar types	Take heel cuttings in January or May

Below: Camellia *'Inspiration'*

Name	Description	Height/ spread*	Flowering period	Soil and site	Remarks	Propagation
Chimonanthus praecox (syn. C. fragrans) Winter sweet	An excellent wall shrub for winter bloom. The yellow, fragrant flowers are borne on bare twigs	H:2.4m (8ft) S:2.4m (8ft)	Dec.–Jan.	An excellent plant for chalk, but will succeed on any well-drained soil	Plant against a south- or west-facing wall in a sheltered position. Plants do not flower well until established for a few years	Layer long shoots in Sept., and remove to their flowering site when well rooted (at least a year). Can also be raised from seed
Cistus Sun rose	An evergreen shrub with flowers that resemble single roses, usually white with blotches, but may be pinkish depending on species	H:0.6–2.4m (2–4ft) S:0.6–2.4m (2–4ft)	June–July	Good plants for hot, dry sites, and will grow happily on chalk. Also wind-tolerant and suitable for coastal areas	These plants resent root disturbance, so plant pot-grown specimens in spring. Keep the plants watered at first. Some species are not very tolerant of severe frosts	Germinate seeds in a temperature of 15°C (60°F) in March, or take half-ripe cuttings in July or Aug. These should be 7.5–10cm (3–4in) long and placed in a propagating case
Clematis (large-flowered hybrids)	There are many cultivars of this popular climber, with flowers in all shades of blue, pink, purple, red and white. Some are attractively striped or shaded. Good cultivars include 'Comtesse de Bouchaud' (pink), 'Ernest Markham' (petunia red), 'The President' (purple-blue), 'Ville de Lyon' (carmine-red), 'Vyvian Pennell' (violet-blue, double), 'Nelly Moser' (pale mauve with carmine bar), 'Hagley Hybrid' (shell-pink), 'Lady Londesborough' (mauve), and 'Jackmanii Superba' (violet-purple)	H:3.5m (12ft)	May–June and Sept.–Oct.	A loamy soil containing lime is preferred. The roots should be in shade, but the top growth in sun	Clematis respond to an annual mulch of well-rotted compost or manure, and plenty of water throughout summer. Cultivars that flower on the previous year's wood should be trimmed back lightly after flowering. Those flowering on current season's growth can be cut back to within 30cm (1ft) of the ground in Feb. or March	Take stem cuttings of half-ripe wood in July, with two buds at the base. The cuttings should be 10–13cm (4–5in) long, and be placed in a frame with a bottom heat of about 15°C (60°F)
C. montana	An extremely vigorous small-flowered clematis, white in the type, pink in some cultivars	H: up to 9m (30ft)	May	As large-flowered type	Immediately after flowering cut out all shoots that have flowered	Stem cuttings, as the large-flowered cultivars
C. tangutica	A vigorous small-flowered species with yellow lantern-like flowers, and decorative silky seed-heads	H:4.5m (15ft)	June–Oct.	As large-flowered type	During Feb. or March, cut back all shoots to a strong pair of buds 90cm (3ft) or less above the ground	Stem cuttings, as the large-flowered cultivars
Corkscrew hazel *see* Corylus avellana 'Contorta'						
Cornelian cherry *see* Cornus mas						
Cornus alba Red-barked dogwood	An attractive shrub with a thicket of stems coloured crimson in winter. 'Wakehurst' is the most colourful form	H:2.4m (8ft) S:2.4m (8ft)	May–June	A rich, moist soil is ideal, in sun or partial shade	Cut back the shoots annually in early April, to within a few inches of the soil	Long stems can be layered in Sept. and severed the following autumn
C. florida 'Rubra' Flowering dogwood	A select shrub with rosy-red bracts when in flower. The plant also has good autumn tints and purplish winter twigs	H:3m (10ft) S:4.5m (15ft)	May	Provide moist, lime-free soil in sun or partial shade	No regular pruning is required	Sow seed in pots in Aug. or Sept. and place in a cold-frame. Germination may be slow
C. kousa Dogwood	An elegant shrub with numerous creamy-white bracts. Sometimes strawberry-like fruits appear	H:3m (10ft) S:3m (10ft)	June	Any good soil will be satisfactory provided it is not chalky. Grow in sun or partial shade	No special treatment is required	Sow seed in Aug. or Sept. in pans in a cold-frame
C. mas Cornelian cherry	A desirable shrub with masses of yellow flowers which appear on bare branches. The flowers are followed by red fruit	H:4.5m (15ft) S:3m (10ft)	Feb.–April	Plant in good, lime-free loam, in sun or partial shade	Plant in autumn in mild areas, in March in cold districts	Sow seed in Aug. or Sept. in a pan in a cold-frame
C. sericea (syn. C. stolonifera) Red osier dogwood	A vigorous but attractive shrub grown for its dark red winter shoots	H:1.8m (6ft) S:1.8m (6ft)	—	A moist soil in sun or partial shade is required	Plant in March or April. Cut back shoots annually in April to within a few inches of the soil	Long stems can be layered in Sept. and severed the following autumn
Corylus avellana 'Contorta' Corkscrew hazel	An eye-catching shrub with zig-zag stems. It is especially interesting in winter while displaying its catkins	H:2.4m (8ft) S:1.8m (6ft)	Feb.	Requires a well-drained site	In the early years the shoots should be cut back by half to form a strong plant	Layer in autumn, or sow seed in Oct. or Nov. in pots in a cold-frame
Cotinus coggygria 'Royal Purple' Smoke plant	This distinctive shrub bears fawn-coloured sprays of flowers that give an impression of rising smoke. The leaves of this cultivar are purple	H:3m (10ft) S:3m (10ft)	June–July	Well-drained soil in full sun produces the best plants	Straggly growths can be shortened in March	Layer long shoots in Sept. or take 10–15cm (4–6in) long cuttings in Aug. or Sept., and root in a cold-frame

Shrubs and trees

Name	Description	Height/spread*	Flowering period	Soil and site	Remarks	Propagation
Cotoneaster conspicuus 'Decorus'	An evergreen shrub suitable for the rock garden or small border, where its prostrate habit is useful. Miniature hawthorn flowers are followed by red berries	H:30cm (1ft) S:60cm (2ft)	May–July	Almost any soil in sun or semi-shade will suit	Plant in Oct. or in March and April. Regular pruning is not required, but if desired trim back in spring	Layer in Oct., or take cuttings 10–15cm (4–6in) long from ripened shoots in Sept., and insert in a cold-frame
C horizontalis Fish-bone cotoneaster	A low-growing shrub for covering banks, or for positioning against a wall. The branches have a herring-bone-like appearance, with small leaves that turn crimson before falling in autumn. Usually covered with red berries	H:60cm (2ft) S:1.8m (6ft)	June	Any good soil in sun or partial shade	A trouble-free plant requiring no special attention other than trimming to shape	Take cuttings of semi-mature shoots in July or Aug. They should be about 10cm (4in) long, and placed in a cold-frame
C. × hybridus 'Pendulus'	An ideal small evergreen weeping tree for the restricted garden. Large red berries are produced in autumn	H:2.4m (8ft) S:1.8m (6ft)	June	A sunny position and any reasonable soil will suit this plant	Plant in Oct. or in March or April	Heel cuttings 7.5–10cm (3–4in) long can be taken in Aug. and set in a cold-frame
Crataegus monogyna 'Pendula' Weeping thorn	An ideal hawthorn for the small garden, with white flowers along graceful, arching branches	H:4.5m (15ft) S:3m (10ft)	May	Will grow on most soils and sites if given an open position	A trouble-free plant	This plant must be budded to a stock of the basic species in spring
× Cupressocyparis leylandii	An extremely fast-growing conifer, either as a specimen or as a hedge. Attractive grey-green foliage	H:12m+ (40ft+) S:4.5m+ (15ft+)	—	Requires a well-drained soil in sun or partial shade	Plant in April or May. Regular pruning not required, but can be trimmed to shape	Take cuttings 7.5m (3in) long from lateral shoots in Sept. or Oct. and insert in a cold-frame
Cytisus battandieri Pineapple broom	A distinctive shrub for a south or west wall. The cone-shaped clusters of yellow flowers are fragrant	H:3m (10ft) S:2.4m (8ft)	July	A well-drained soil in a sunny position is essential. Plant against a sunny wall	The plant is not hardy in in cold districts. Plant in Sept. or Oct., or in April	Sow seeds in pots in a cold-frame in April or May
C. × kewensis	An outstanding shrub of semi-prostrate habit with masses of creamy flowers	H:30cm (1ft) S:1.2m (4ft)	May	A deep, neutral soil, well-drained and in full sun is best	Plant from pots in September or March. Trim back the shoots after flowering	Take cuttings 7.5–10cm (3–4in) long in Aug. or Sept., and insert in a peat-sand mixture in a cold-frame
C. scoparius Broom	A familiar shrub with yellow pea-like flowers. There are cultivars with red, brownish or cream flowers, some bi-coloured	H:1.8m (6ft) S:1.8m (6ft)	May	Best on a slightly acid soil, in full sun	Plant from pots, in Sept. and Oct. or in March and April. After flowering, cut off most of previous season's growth without going into old wood	Sow seed in pots in a cold-frame in April or May
Daboecia cantabrica Irish heath	A heather-like plant with rosy-purple, white, pink or purple bells	H:60cm (2ft) S:60cm (2ft)	May–Oct.	A peaty, acid soil in full sun or partial shade is necessary	Provide sheltered site in exposed areas. Cut off dead flowers in spring	Layers can be taken in March
Daphne mezereum Mezereon	An outstandingly beautiful early-flowering shrub with fragrant purple-red blooms. A white cultivar is also available — D. m. 'Alba'	H:1.2m (4ft) S:90cm (3ft)	Feb.–March	Any good, well-drained soil in sun or partial shade is suitable	Plant in Sept. or March	Take heel cuttings 5–10cm (2–4in) long from non-flowering shoots from July to Sept., or sow seed in a cold-frame in Sept. or Oct.
Deutzia	Easily-grown shrubs with bright flowers, usually in shades of pink or red, on leafy sprays	H:1.2–1.8m (4–6ft) S:1.2–1.8m (4–6ft)	June	Will succeed on any fertile soil, in sun or partial shade. Avoid an exposed aspect	Immediately after flowering, cut flowered shoots to within a few inches of old wood	Take cuttings of semi-ripe lateral shoots in July or Aug., and insert in a cold-frame
Dogwood see Cornus						
Elaeagnus pungens 'Maculata' Wood olive	A variegated evergreen shrub with green leaves attractively splashed deep yellow. The insignificant flowers are fragrant	H:2.4m (8ft) S:2.4m (8ft)	Oct.–Nov.	Will thrive on any fertile soil other than chalk. Plant in sun or semi-shade	A trouble-free plant. Prune to shape as necessary	Cuttings 7.5–10cm (3–4in) long can be taken in Aug. or Sept. Place in a cold-frame
Erica ciliaris Dorset heath	This erica has delightful pitcher-like rich pink flowers (there are cultivars with white or red flowers). Spreading habit. Good cultivars include 'Mrs. C. H. Gill' (clear red), 'Stoborough' (white), and 'Wych' (pink)	H:2.3–45cm (9–18in) S:60cm (2ft)	July–Oct.	The Dorset heath dislikes atmospheric pollution or lime. Provide a sheltered site in full sun	Trim off dead flowers with shears in spring	Layer established plants in March, or take cuttings 12–25mm (½–1in) long in July or Aug. For the cuttings, try to incorporate some soil in which heathers or heaths have been growing
E. cinerea Bell heather	An attractive heather with good colour range — red, pink, mauve, white, purple, and lavender. There are many cultivars from which to choose	H:15–60cm (6–24in) S:30–45cm (1–1½ft)	June–Oct.	An acid soil is desirable, in a sunny position	Remove dead flowers with shears at end of season	As E. ciliaris

Name	Description	Height/ spread*	Flowering period	Soil and site	Remarks	Propagation
E. herbacea (syn. E. carnea) Mountain heath	A valuable winter-flowering dwarf shrub, with many cultivars in all shades of pink and purple, as well as white. Two good ones are 'Springwood White' and 'Vivellii' (vivid carmine)	H:15–30cm (6–12in) S:60cm (2ft)	Dec.–April	Although lime-tolerant, avoid shallow chalky soil. Will tolerate atmospheric pollution. Plant in sun or semi-shade	After flowering, remove dead heads with shears	As E. ciliaris
E. vagans Cornish heath	Spreading bushes producing long sprays of flowers for several months — in shades of cerise, pink, or white	H:30–45cm (1–1½ft) S:1.5m (5ft)	Aug.–Oct.	Will survive on neutral or slightly alkaline soil, but prefers an acid soil	Trim plants with shears to remove dead flowers at end of season	As E. ciliaris
Fagus sylvatica Beech	One of our most attractive native trees; also makes a good hedge, retaining the dead leaves as winter cover. There are several cultivars, including some with weeping habit, upright columnar growth or purple leaves	H:9m+ (30ft+) S:7.5m+ (25ft+)	—	A sunny, open position is best, and a deep well-drained soil ideal	No pruning is required unless grown as a hedge. Trim hedges to shape in July or Aug.	Sow seed outdoors in Oct. and transplant in three years
Fallopia baldschuanicum (syn. Polygonum baldschuanicum) Russian vine	One of the most vigorous climbing shrubs, with masses of white flowers. Ideal for hiding unsightly objects such as garages and sheds	H:6m+ (20ft+)	July–Oct.	Any soil will suit this plant, including chalk	Plant in spring, using pot-grown specimens. The only routine care is trimming to control growth	Heel cuttings 7.5–10cm (3–4in) long can be taken in July or Aug. Use half-ripe wood and insert in a cold-frame
False acacia see Robinia pseudoacacia						
Firethorn see Pyracantha						
Fish-bone cotoneaster see Cotoneaster horizontalis						
Flowering currant see Ribes sanguineum						
Forsythia × intermedia Golden bell bush	One of our most popular spring-flowering shrubs, with long arching sprays of yellow, bell-shaped flowers	H:2.4m (8ft) S:2.4m (8ft)	April–May	Plant in any good soil, in sun or partial shade	Prune immediately after flowering, removing old and damaged wood and shortening vigorous flowered shoots	Take cuttings 25–30cm (10–12in) long in Oct., inserting in the soil outdoors

Below: **Cotinus coggygria** *(smoke bush).* *Below right:* **Elaeagnus pungens** *(wood olive)* 'Maculata'. *Far below right:* **Cytisus × kewensis**

Shrubs and trees

Name	Description	Height/spread*	Flowering period	Soil and site	Remarks	Propagation
Genista hispanica Spanish gorse	A plant related to brooms, covered in late spring with masses of yellow flowers. Forms a compact, prickly mound	H:60cm (2ft) S:1.5m (5ft)	May–June	Will succeed in acid or neutral soil, but is also tolerant of lime. Provide a hot, sunny site	A trouble-free plant requiring no regular attention	Heel cuttings 5–10cm (2–4in) long can be taken in Aug. and placed in a cold-frame
Golden bell bush see Forsythia × intermedia						
Golden rain see Laburnum × vossii						
Hamamelis mollis Witch hazel	Distinctive fragrant yellow flowers are displayed on bare stems during the dullest winter months	H:2.1m (7ft) S:2.1m (7ft)	Dec.–Feb.	Moist, well-drained loam, with added peat is best, in a sheltered shaded site	Plant in Oct. or Nov. Thin overcrowded branches in April	Layer long branches in April, or place heel cuttings in a cold-frame in Sept.
Heath, Cornish see Erica vagans						
Heath, Dorset see Erica ciliaris						
Heath, Irish see Daboecia cantabrica						
Heath, mountain see Erica herbacea						
Heather, bell see Erica cinerea						
Heather, Scottish see Calluna vulgaris						
Hedera colchica Persian ivy	A vigorous climber with large heart-shaped leaves. More attractive is the yellow and creamy variegated H. c. 'Dentata Variegata'	H:6m (20ft)	Sept.–Oct.	Will thrive in almost any soil or situation. Self-clinging	Trim back stray shoots, to control shape	Take cuttings 7.5–13cm (3–5in) long from tips of shoots in July or Aug.
H. helix Common ivy	Although the common kind is known by most gardeners, there are cultivars with a wide variety of leaf shapes and variegations	H:12m (40ft)	Sept.–Oct.	Suitable for any soil or situation. Self-clinging	Cut out stray shoots, to keep under control	As H. colchica
Helianthemum see Rock garden plants, page 169						
Hibiscus syriacus Tree hollyhock	Large hollyhock-like flowers. There are several cultivars, in shades of blue, pink, purple, white. Good cultivars include 'Hamabo' (pink), and 'Blue Bird' (violet-blue)	H:2.4m (8ft) S:1.5m (5ft)	Aug.–Oct.	A fertile soil is desirable, a position in full sun essential. Shelter from wind	Not dependably hardy. Will need winter protection in cold areas. Trim long shoots after flowering	Take heel cuttings 7.5–10cm (3–4in) long of half-ripe wood in July. Use a propagating case at 15°C (60°F)
Holly see Ilex aquifolium						
Honeysuckle see Lonicera						
Hornbeam see Carpinus betulus						
Hydrangea anomala petiolaris Climbing hydrangea	A vigorous self-clinging climber with heart-shaped leaves and large heads of white flowers	H:9m (30ft)	June	Prefers a moist soil. Ideal for a shady wall (height will be more than stated if growing in a tree, less on a wall)	Plant in Oct. and Nov. or March and April	Take cuttings 7.5–10cm (3–4in) long from vigorous shoots in June or July, and place in a cold-frame
H. paniculata 'Grandiflora'	Large spikes of creamy-white flowers, like a large white lilac. A showy shrub	H:4.0m (12ft) S:3m (10ft)	July–Aug.	Provide a moisture-retentive soil well enriched with organic matter	Plant in Oct. and Nov. or March and April. Each March cut back previous year's flowering shoots by half	Cuttings 10–15cm (4–6in) long can be taken from non-flowering shoots in Aug. or Sept. Use a propagating case
H. petiolaris see H. anomala petiolaris						
Hypericum patulum 'Hidcote'	An impressive shrub with numerous large golden-yellow saucer-shaped flowers. Well worth growing	H:1.5m (5ft) S:1.2m (4ft)	July–Sept.	Will thrive in a well-drained soil, and be happy in full sun or semi-shade	Each March cut back the previous year's growth to within a few inches of old wood	Take heel cuttings 10–13cm (4–5in) long between July and Sept. Insert in a cold-frame
Ilex aquifolium 'Aurea Marginata'	An attractive holly with yellow-margined leaves. Forms a nice hedge or a specimen tree	H:4.5m (15ft) S:2.4m (8ft)	May–June	Will grow on most soils, in sun or shade. Tolerant of atmospheric pollution and coastal planting	Plant in Oct. or March. Specimen trees require no pruning; clip hedges to shape in Aug.	Bud or graft on to stocks of I. aquifolium in Jan. or Feb.
Ivy see Hedera						
Jasminum nudiflorum Winter jasmine	An attractive wall shrub with beautiful small yellow flowers in winter	H:3m (10ft)	Nov.–March	Will grow happily in most soils	After flowering, cut back flowered growths to 5–7.5cm (2–3in) of their base	Root cuttings of semi-ripe wood 7.5–10cm (3–4in) long in a heated frame in Sept.
Jew's mallow see Kerria japonica						
Judas tree see Cercis siliquastrum						

Name	Description	Height/spread*	Flowering period	Soil and site	Remarks	Propagation
Juniperus sabina 'Tamariscifolia' Savin	A low, spreading conifer, forming an attractive carpet of growth	H:90cm (3ft) S:2.4m (8ft)	—	Will grow on most soils, including those containing lime. Happy in full sun or light shade	A trouble-free plant requiring little attention	Take heel cuttings 5–10cm (2–4in) long in Sept. or Oct., and root in a cold-frame
Kerria japonica Jew's mallow	Attractive yellow flowers (double in the cultivar 'Pleniflora') on slender arching green branches	H:1.8m (6ft) S:1.8m (6ft)	April–May	Will grow in any ordinary garden soil; best planted against a wall. Sun or semi-shade	Shoots that have flowered should be cut back to strong growth	Cuttings 10–13cm (4–5in) long can be taken in Aug. or Sept. and rooted in a cold-frame
Laburnum × vossii Golden rain	Spectacular cascades of yellow flowers make this a popular early-flowering tree	H:6m (20ft) S:4.0m (12ft)	May–June	Suitable for almost all soils. Sun or semi-shade. Do not plant near ponds, as the seeds are poisonous	Where small children might play, remove all seed pods. Cut back weak shoots after flowering	Graft on to seedling stock in March
Laurel *see* Prunus laurocerasus						
Lavandula angustifolia 'Hidcote' (syn. L. spica 'Hidcote') Lavender	A good form of this well-known shrub. Purple-blue flowers, contrasting well with the silvery foliage	H:60cm (2ft) S:60cm (2ft)	July–Aug.	Provide a well-drained soil in a sunny position	Trim plants in late summer, removing dead flower heads	Make cuttings 7.5–10cm (3–4in) long from ripe non-flowering shoots in Aug. Root in a cold-frame
Lavender *see* Lavandula angustifolia						
Lawson cypress *see* Chamaecyparis lawsoniana						
Leycesteria formosa Pheasant berry	A distinctive suckering shrub with bottle-green stems. Clusters of pale flowers with conspicuous claret bracts, followed by reddish-purple berries	H:1.8m (6ft) S:1.5m (5ft)	July–Aug.	Will grow on any reasonably fertile soil. Will tolerate coastal planting. Grows best in sun	Cut out old flowered shoots to ground level in March	Sow seed in a frame or open ground, or take cuttings 23cm (9in) long in Oct. Root in the open
Ligustrum ovalifolium Privet	The ubiquitous privet, often used for hedging. Useful for a poor site. The golden form, L. o. 'Aureum', is a beautiful plant as a clipped hedge or specimen on its own	H:3m (10ft) S:3m (10ft)	July	Will grow on most soils, in sun or shade	Clip to shape regularly if grown as a hedge; leave unpruned as a specimen plant	Take cuttings of ripe shoots in Oct. They should be 25cm (12in) long and inserted in open ground
Liquidambar styraciflua Sweet gum	A handsome tree with spectacular autumn colours. It forms a straight-trunked tree with a pyramidal-shaped head	H:6m+ (20ft+) S:3m+ (10ft+)	May	A deep, fertile soil is best — avoid shallow chalky soil. Choose container-grown plants and do not disturb roots. Plant in sun or partial shade	Little attention is required, but remove dead or crossing branches	Sow seed in Oct. in pots placed in a cold-frame. Layer branches in March
Lilac *see* Syringa vulgaris						

Below: Hibiscus syriacus *(tree hollyhock) 'Blue Bird'. Below right:* Lavandula angustifolia *(lavender) 'Hidcote'*

Shrubs and trees

Name	Description	Height/spread*	Flowering period	Soil and site	Remarks	Propagation
Liriodendron tulipifera Tulip tree	A superb large tree. It bears unusually-shaped leaves and greenish-yellow cup-shaped flowers. Leaves turn yellow in autumn	H:7.5m+ (25ft+) S:4.5m+ (15ft+)	May–June	Any fertile soil will suit, in sun or light shade	No routine attention required	Sow seed in Oct. or Nov. in pots placed in a cold-frame
Lonicera japonica 'Aureoreticulata' Japanese honeysuckle	A rampant semi-evergreen climber with small leaves conspicuously reticulated with gold	H:4.5m (15ft)	June–Aug.	Best on a south, east or west-facing wall. Will be happy in most soils	Plant during April or May. Thin out shoots that become overcrowded	Take cuttings 10cm (4in) long in Aug. Root in pots in a cold-frame
L. nitida Shrubby honeysuckle	A small-leaved bushy plant often used for hedges, but can be used as a free-standing specimen — especially the golden cultivar 'Baggessen's Gold'. Evergreen	H:1.5m (5ft) S:1.5m (5ft)	—	Will thrive in any normal garden soil, in sun or shade	No regular pruning required unless grown as a hedge	Cuttings 10cm (4in) long will root readily in open ground. Take in July
L. periclymenum 'Serotina' Late Dutch honeysuckle	A vigorous climber with strongly-scented reddish-purple and yellow flowers	H:4.5m (15ft)	Aug.–Sept.	Best in good loam, in a position of semi-shade	Plant in spring. Trim only to keep in shape	Take cuttings 10cm (4in) long and root in pots in a cold-frame in Aug.
Magnolia × soulangiana	A tree of distinction, bearing large white flowers delicately tinged with purple. The branches are leafless when the first flowers open	H:6m (20ft) S:4.5m (15ft)	April–May	Provide a well-drained loam, ideally neutral or slightly acid, sheltered from cold winds	Plant in March or April. No pruning required other than shaping in the early years.	Heel cuttings 10cm (4in) long can be rooted in a propagating case in July. Use half-ripe shoots
Mahonia Oregon grape	A small evergreen shrub with large holly-shaped leaves, which take on a purple tinge in autumn. Yellow flowers are followed by black berries. *M. bealei* and *M.* 'Charity' are particularly fine forms	H:90cm (3ft) S:90cm (3ft)	Feb.–April	Mahonias will grow in most types of soil, including chalk. Will grow happily in shade	Plant in Sept. and Oct. or April and May	Sow seeds in pots placed in a cold-frame in Sept. or take 7.5–10cm (3–4in) cuttings in July. Can also be layered in spring or autumn
Malus 'Golden Hornet'	One of the best fruiting 'crabs'. Makes a small tree and carries a heavy crop of bright yellow fruit, retained late into the year	H:4.5m (15ft) S:2.4m (8ft)	April	Will tolerate a wide range of soils, including those containing lime. Sun or partial shade	Little routine attention is required. Prune out any straggly branches	Plants are normally budded in July or Aug., or grafted in March
M. 'John Downie'	A superb fruiting crab tree, with bright scarlet, rather conical, fruit. The best kind for crab-apple jelly	H:7.5m (25ft) S:4.5m (15ft)	May	As 'Golden Hornet'	As 'Golden Hornet'	As 'Golden Hornet'
M. × purpurea 'Lemoinei'	Large wine-red flowers in spring and reddish-purple fruits in autumn	H:7.5m (25ft) S:4.5m (15ft)	April–May	As 'Golden Hornet'	As 'Golden Hornet'	As 'Golden Hornet'
Mezereon *see* Daphne mezereum						
Mock orange *see* Philadelphus						
Monkey-puzzle tree *see* Araucaria araucana						
Nyssa sylvatica Tupelo	A tree grown primarily for its handsome, brilliant scarlet, autumn foliage	H:6m+ (20ft+) S:3m+ (10ft+)	June	Requires a lime-free soil in sun or partial shade. Moisture is appreciated	Plant young specimens as they resent root disturbance	Sow seed in Oct., in pots placed in a cold-frame
Oregon grape *see* Mahonia						
Parthenocissus quinquefolia (syn. Vitis hederacea) Virginia creeper	A climber noteworthy for its deeply cut, five-lobed leaves, which turn orange and scarlet in autumn. Self-clinging	H:15m+ (50ft+)	—	These plants prefer a good loam, with unrestricted root-run. Sun or semi-shade	Remove unwanted or straggly growth in late summer	Take cuttings of half-ripe wood, 10–13cm (4–5in) long in Aug. or Sept., and root in a heated propagating frame
P. tricuspidata 'Veitchii' (syn. Ampelopsis veitchii) Boston ivy	Sometimes mistaken for the Virginia creeper, which it resembles	H:7.5m+ (25ft+)	—	As *P. quinquefolia*	As *P. quinquefolia*	As *P. quinquefolia*
Perovskia atriplicifolia Russian sage	A low shrub with grey leaves and feathery spikes of blue flowers. Resembles an herbaceous border plant	H:90cm (3ft) S:60cm (2ft)	Aug.–Sept.	Succeeds in well-drained soil, in full sun	Can be cut back to about 25cm (10in) in March	Heel cuttings 7.5cm (3in) long can be taken in July, inserted in pots in a cold-frame
Pheasant berry *see* Leycesteria formosa						
Philadelphus Mock orange	White-flowered shrubs with a heady fragrance. Easy to grow and trouble-free	H:1.2–2.4m (4–8ft) S:1.2–1.8m (4–6ft)	June–July	Will grow on any soil, even poor chalk, in sun or partial shade	Thin old wood after flowering, but do not cut into young shoots	Take cuttings 10cm (4in) long in July or Aug. Use half-ripe wood and place in a cold-frame
Pineapple broom *see* Cytissus battandieri						

Name	Description	Height/ spread*	Flowering period	Soil and site	Remarks	Propagation
Polygonum baldschuanicum *see* Fallopia baldschuanicum						
Potentilla fruticosa	Forms a dense bush that will flower from spring till autumn. Usually yellow flowers	H:0.3–1.2m (1–4ft) S:0.9–1.2m (3–4ft)	June–Sept.	A well-drained soil in full sun produces the best plants	Trouble-free. Trim to shape if necessary	Heel cuttings 7.5cm (3in) long can be taken from half-ripe wood in Sept. or Oct. Insert in a frame
Privet *see* Ligustrum						
Prunus Japanese cherries	The *Prunus* provide many fine garden trees, the Japanese Cherries being among the best. There are many from which to choose — among them *P. serrulata* 'Erecta', usually listed as 'Amanogawa', an upright 'Lombardy poplar' type of growth with masses of pink flowers; *P. serrulata* 'Purpurascens', known as 'Kanzan', with large showy pink flowers, and coppery-brown young leaves	H:6–7.5m (20–25ft) S:6–7.5m (20–30ft)	April	A well-drained, lime-free soil is best	Plant in Aug., Sept., or March. Grown as a shrub, height will be 3–4.5m (10–15ft). Pruning is not normally necessary, but if large branches have to be cut off it is best done in summer	Plants are grafted in March
P. laurocerasus Common laurel	A fine evergreen shrub, traditionally used as a hedge, but it also makes a nice bush	H:6m (20ft) S:7.5m (25ft)	April	Prefers a deep, well-drained soil. Best to avoid shallow, chalky soil. Sun or shade	No pruning needed, unless grown as a hedge. Trim hedges in spring and Aug.	Root heel cuttings 7.5–10cm (3–4in) long in pots in a cold-frame in Aug. or Sept.
Pseudosasa japonica (syn. Arundinaria japonica) Bamboo	An adaptable and hardy bamboo forming thickets of olive-green canes	H:3–4.5m (10–15ft) S:2.4m (8ft)	—	Will thrive in full sun or partial shade, but requires a moist soil. Prefers shelter	Plant in April or May. Keep young plants moist and protected from cold	Lift and divide an established clump in April or May
Pyracantha Firethorn	A highly desirable shrub to grow against a wall, or on its own. Berries are the outstanding feature, usually orange-red but sometimes yellow. There are several kinds. Evergreen	H:3m (10ft) S:3m (10ft)	May–June	Will grow in any fertile soil, and is tolerant of exposure. Sun or semi-shade	Wall specimens can be lightly trimmed back in July	Take cuttings in July or Aug. They should be 7.5–10cm (3–4in) long, and inserted in a heated propagating case
Pyrus salicifolia 'Pendula' Willow-leaved pear	An eye-catching tree for small gardens, with a dense head of pendulous and arching branches of silver-grey leaves	H:4.5m+ (15ft+) S:4.5m+ (15ft+)	April	Will grow in any fertile soil, and tolerate drought, moisture, and towns	Thin out crowded and crossing branches in spring	Hardwood cuttings can be taken in Sept. and inserted in open soil

Below: Magnolia × soulangiana. *Below right:* Philadelphus *(mock orange)* 'Burfordensis'

Shrubs and trees

Name	Description	Height/spread*	Flowering period	Soil and site	Remarks	Propagation
Quince, flowering see Chaenomeles speciosa						
Rhododendron	A large group of shrubs with hundreds of species and hybrids, most hardy but some requiring protection. Beautiful plants for an acid soil. Flowers in many shades of red, pink, yellow and white, often beautifully marked. Evergreen	Wide range	April–June	An acid, peaty soil is essential. Shade or semi-shade, ideally in woodland	No regular attention other than mulching with peat if necessary	Layers can be made at any time of the year
Rhus typhina Stag's-horn sumach	A distinctive plant to grow as a tree or shrub. Large pinnate leaves take on good autumn colour. Clusters of crimson fruits are very decorative	H:4.5m (15ft) S:4.5m (15ft)	June–July	Requires well-drained soil in full sun	On shrubby plants, old wood can be pruned out at ground level in May. Male and female on separate plants	Take heel cuttings of half-ripe wood in July or Aug. Use a heated propagating frame. Suckers can be removed in Oct. or spring. Layer in March
Ribes sanguineum Flowering currant	Popular spring-flowering shrub with sprays of pinkish flowers. 'Pulborough Scarlet' is a good red, 'King Edward' a deep crimson	H:2.4m (8ft) S:2.1m (7ft)	March–April	Prefers well-drained soil in light shade or sun	Prune, if necessary, immediately after flowering	Hardwood cuttings 25–30cm (10–12in) long can be inserted into open soil in autumn
Robinia pseudoacacia False acacia	A striking tree, grown for its pinnate foliage, resembling the acacia. The most beautiful forms is 'Frisia', with golden-yellow leaves	H:7.5m (25ft) S:3m (10ft)	May–June	A good town tree, given a well-drained soil in sun. Does best in a sheltered position	A trouble-free plant	Suckers can be removed during winter and planted in a nursery bed until large enough to be planted out
Rock rose see Cistus						
Rosa see Roses, page 138						
Russian sage see Perovskia atriplicifolia						
Russian vine see Fallopia baldschuanicum						
Savin see Juniperus sabina 'Tamariscifolia'						
Senecio greyi	A useful grey-foliaged shrub for a small garden. Bushy habit, white-felted leaves, and yellow, daisy-like flowers	H:90cm (3ft) S:90cm (3ft)	July–Aug.	Prefers a well-drained soil in sun or light shade	Remove straggly shoots during the summer months	Cuttings of half-ripe wood, 7.5–10cm (3–4in) long, can be rooted in a cold-frame in Sept. Can also be layered
Silver birch see Betula pendula						
Sinarundinaria nitida (syn. Arundinaria nitida) Bamboo	A beautiful bamboo with purple-flushed canes and narrow leaves. Makes an excellent specimen plant	H:3m (10ft) S:1.2m (4ft)	—	Will grow best in a moist, sheltered position in full sun or partial shade	Plant in April or May. Keep young plants moist and protect from cold winds	Divide an established clump in April or May
Skimmia japonica	A neat evergreen shrub with small white, fragrant, flowers and red berries	H:1.5m (5ft) S:1.5m (5ft)	April–May	Undemanding, but avoid an alkaline soil. Grows well in industrial areas and towns. Grows in shade	No routine work required, but male and female plants are needed for berries	Take heel cuttings 7.5cm (3in) long of half-ripe shoots in Aug. Insert in a cold-frame
Smoke plant see Cotinus coggygria						
Snake-bark maple see Acer grosseri hersii						
Snowball bush see Viburnum opulus 'Sterile'						
Snowberry see Symphoricarpos albus						
Snowy mespilus see Amelanchier canadensis						
Spanish gorse see Genista hispanica						
Spiraea × vanhouttei	Sprays of white flowers are produced on arching stems. An excellent shrub	H:2.4m (8ft) S:2.4m (8ft)	May	Requires a fertile soil in sun or partial shade	A trouble-free plant. Prune only to retain shape	Cuttings of half-ripe shoots, 7.5–13cm (3–5in) long can be taken in Aug.
Stag's-horn sumach see Rhus typhina						
Strawberry tree see Arbutus unedo						
Swamp cypress see Taxodium distichum						
Sweet gum see Liquidambar styraciflua						
Symphoricarpos albus Snowberry	A vigorous suckering shrub with white berries about 12mm (½in) across, lasting well into winter	H:1.8m (6ft) S:2.1m (7ft)	June–Sept.	Will grow in most soils, in sun or shade	Prune hard in March if it becomes untidy	Remove suckers during winter or early spring

Name	Description	Height/spread*	Flowering period	Soil and site	Remarks	Propagation
Syringa vulgaris Lilac	This well-known plant needs no introduction. Colours range from mauve to white. Can be grown as a 'standard' tree	H:4.5m (15ft) S:3m (10ft)	May–June	Most soils will suit, and lime is appreciated. Plant in full sun or partial shade	Remove dead flower heads	Named varieties are budded
Taxodium distichum Swamp cypress	A beautiful deciduous conifer, but only suitable for a large garden. Bright green foliage and eye-catching autumn colour	H:10.5m+ (35ft+) S:4.5m+ (15ft+)	—	Requires a moist site to do well. Sun or partial shade	No routine care required. Plant in April	Seed
Taxus baccata Yew	An evergreen conifer, well-known in churchyards. Makes a fine hedge, and is a good topiary plant	H:3m+ (10ft+) S:3m+ (10ft+)	—	Tolerant of most soils, including chalk, but avoid a damp site. Will grow in sun or shade	Plant in Oct. or April	Take heel cuttings 7.5–10cm (3–4in) long in Sept. or Oct. and insert in a cold-frame
Tree hollyhock see Hibiscus syriacus						
Tulip tree see Liriodendron tulipifera						
Tupelo see Nyssa sylvatica						
Viburnum carlesii	A medium-sized shrub with clusters of white flowers, with a sweet, daphne-like fragrance	H:1.5m (5ft) S:1.5m (5ft)	April–May	Likes a moist but well-drained soil, in sun or partial shade	No regular pruning is required, but remove old stems from crowded bushes in winter	Take heel cuttings 7.5–10cm (3–4in) long in June or July, and root in a propagating frame. Hardwood cuttings of the same size can be taken in Sept. and rooted in a cold-frame. Long shoots can be layered in Sept.
V. farreri (syn. V. fragrans)	A popular winter-flowering shrub, with clusters of delicate pinkish-white fragrant flowers	H:2.7m (9ft) S:2.7m (9ft)	Nov.–Feb.	As V. carlesii	No regular pruning required, but cut out old stems from crowded bushes in winter	As V. carlesii
V. opulus 'Sterile' Snowball bush	A shrub with balls of white flowers, followed by translucent red berries in autumn	H:3m (10ft) S:3m (10ft)	April–May	As V. carlesii	As V. carlesii	As V. carlesii
V. tinus Laurustinus	An evergreen shrub with trusses of white flowers. Can be used as individual plants or as a hedge	H:2.4m (8ft) S:1.8m (6ft)	Nov.–April	Any good garden soil that retains moisture will suit	Plant in Sept. and Oct. or March and April. If grown as a hedge, trim in April	As V. carlesii
Virginia creeper see Parthenocissus quinquefolia						
Vitis coignetiae	One of the most spectacular vines, with leaves about 30cm (12in) across, turning crimson and scarlet in autumn. A most striking climber	H:15m+ (50ft+)	—	Undemanding regarding soil. Sun or semi-shade	No routine care necessary other than trimming to shape if necessary	Heel cuttings 10–13cm (4–5in) long of half-ripe wood can be taken in July or Aug. and placed in a propagator with bottom heat. Insert hardwood cuttings 25–30cm (10–12in) long in open soil in Nov.
Weeping thorn see Crataegus monogyna 'Pendula'						
Weigela florida 'Variegata'	A graceful free-flowering shrub with pink flowers and variegated leaves. A good small-garden shrub	H:2.1m (7ft) S:1.8m (6ft)	May–June	Will grow in any reasonable soil, but does best if it is moist but well-drained	After flowering, cut flowered stems to within a few inches of old wood	Take heel cuttings 7.5–10cm (3–4in) long using half-ripe shoots, in June or July. Insert in a propagating case. Hardwood cuttings can be taken in Oct. and inserted in open soil; they should be 25–30cm (10–12in) long
Willow-leaved pear see Pyrus salicifolia 'Pendula'						
Winter jasmine see Jasminum nudiflorum						
Winter sweet see Chimonanthus praecox						
Witch hazel see Hamamelias móllis						
Wood olive see Elaeagnus pungens						
Yew see Taxus baccata						
Young's weeping birch see Betula pendula 'Youngii'						

* = Heights and spreads are those likely to be reached after 20 years in average conditions, but as each garden is different and there will be wide regional variations, these should only be treated as a comparative guide. Those followed by a + sign will continue to grow significantly more and ultimately be considerably larger

Roses

Roses have for long been one of our most popular garden plants, and the following they have today is as strong as ever. The very popularity of the rose has, however, generated such a wealth of breeding activity over the years that for the beginner the sheer number of cultivars offered to him can be bewildering.

There are many thousands of roses from which to choose, and this is only a small selection — but made on the criteria of superior quality and distinctness. Many of them are already popular roses, but others are included whose beauties still deserve to be better known.

As a result of hybridization, classifications have become more blurred over the years, and it is not always helpful to think in rigid terms when looking for a rose. Choose one that suits your particular purpose — its technical classification is less important than the fact that it meets the particular set of qualities that you are looking for in a rose.

Roses should not only be thought of as subjects for formal beds — there are suitable kinds for shrub borders, to clothe a fence, or to grow as an isolated specimen shrub in a lawn. Even the garden boundary itself provides an ideal site for many kinds, which will make a superb hedge that will be bright as well as functional.

Where roses are required primarily to provide cut flowers, any corner of the garden will be suitable providing that the basic requirements discussed on pages 76 and 77 can be met.

Growing for exhibition is a subject in itself, and although some of the cultivars mentioned in the following pages are of excellent quality, the selection has been made on the grounds of how well they perform as general garden plants.

Although most of the publicity inevitably goes to the hybrid teas and floribundas, don't overlook some of the species or species hybrids, for these have qualities of their own, and there are some delightful roses among them. Generally they are more suited to growing in a shrub or mixed border, or as individual specimen plants, but in that situation will excel most other shrubs.

Fragrance is always desirable, but it is rare to find all the desirable qualities in a single rose in equal measure, and sometimes scent has to be sacrificed for perfection of bloom, or an exceptional colour, but by careful selection of cultivars it should be possible to have a garden full of roses providing exceptional beauty and fragrance.

Health is another factor to consider, as some of the older cultivars are particularly susceptible to mildew. There is a tendency now to breed for disease resistance as well as beauty, and many of those included in the table are exceptionally healthy by nature.

Most roses tend to have a long flowering period. The term remontant is applied to those that have a main flush of bloom in June, but continue less prolifically until winter finally puts a stop to them.

Name	Description	Height/ spread	Flowering period	Special merits	Situation/use	Fragrance
'Albéric Barbier'	*Climber:* Cream, double flowers with small pointed buds that open to produce blooms of medium size. Introduced 1900	H:7.5m (25ft) S:6m (20ft)	June–July	Handsome foliage, vigorous	Good for a north wall	Slight
'Alec's Red'	*HT:* Light crimson, double flowers. Globular buds open to very large blooms low at the centre. Introduced 1970	H:90cm (3ft) S:60cm (2ft)	Remontant	One of the most richly scented roses	Ideal for bedding or cutting	Very good
'Alexander'	*HT:* Luminous vermilion, thinly double, the buds opening wide. Glossy foliage, and very healthy. Introduced 1972	H:1.5m (5ft) S:90cm (3ft)	Remontant	Outstanding colour and useful for flower arranging	Makes a nice hedge. Good for cutting. Useful for bedding	Slight
'Allgold'	*Floribunda:* Bright yellow, semi-double, in well-spaced clusters. Glossy dark leaves. Introduced 1956	H:75cm (2½ft) S:60cm (2ft)	Remontant	Flowers early. Healthy	Bedding	Slight
'Aloha'	*Climber:* Two-tone pink. Fully double, the plump buds opening to fat but not large blooms. Introduced 1949	H:1.5m (5ft) S:1.2m (4ft)	Remontant	Useful for a small wall space	Against walls	Slight
'Ballerina'	*Polyantha:* Pale pink single rose with a white centre. Small flowers in dense mop heads. Introduced 1937	H:1.2m (4ft) S:1m (3½ft)	Remontant	Bright hedging plant	Forms an attractive hedge	Slight
'Blue Moon' (syn. 'Mainzer Fastnacht')	*HT:* Double, lilac-pink blooms. The long buds open to produce a rose of fine, pointed form. Introduced 1964	H:1m (3ft) S:60cm (2ft)	Remontant	Sweet, rich scent, and an unusual colour. Useful for cutting	A bedding rose, but tends to become leggy	Very good
'Canary Bird'	*Xanthina hybrid:* Single, yellow blooms of medium size held close to and along the branches. Introduced 1911	H:1.8m (6ft) S:1.8m (6ft)	May	Musky scent, healthy, ferny leaves	Makes a free-flowering shrub	Good

Name	Description	Height/spread	Flowering period	Special merits	Situation/use	Fragrance
'Compassion'	*Climber:* Pink, shaded apricot; double, fairly large flowers of HT shape. Dark leaves; vigorous. Introduced 1973	H:2.7m (9ft) S:2.1m (7ft)	Remontant	A vigorous climber, but well furnished to the base. Strong, sweet scent	Excellent as a pillar rose, or grown against a wall	Very good
'Crimson Shower'	*Climber:* A good red, holding the colour well. Small double flowers in large heads. Introduced 1951	H:2.4m (8ft) S:3m (10ft)	July–Aug.	Trailing, pendulous growth makes it useful for uses described	Excellent as a pillar rose, or for growing against a fence	Slight
'Danse du Feu' (syn. 'Spectacular')	*Climber:* Fat buds open to reveal double, orange flowers that fade towards purple. Healthy. Introduced 1953	H:2.4m (8ft) S:3m (10ft)	Remontant	Useful where a good climber that is not too rampant is required	Suitable for a wall, fence or pillar	Slight
'Elizabeth Harkness'	*HT:* Large, double flowers, ivory white sometimes touched pink on the petal tips. Introduced 1969	H:1m (3½ft) S:90cm (3ft)	Remontant	Exquisitely graceful style of bloom. Flowers early	A good bedding rose	Fair
'Ena Harkness, Climbing'	*Climber:* Large and elegant, closely whorled, flowers in perfect 'red rose' crimson. Introduced 1954	H:4m (12ft) S:4m (12ft)	June–July	Good flowers on a vigorous but not rampant climber	Grow against a wall or fence	Slight
'Escapade'	*Floribunda:* Large, semi-double rosy-violet flowers with large white eye, many to a cluster. Introduced 1967	H:1.2m (4ft) S:90cm (3ft)	Remontant	A spectacular cut flower	Makes an unusual bedding or hedging rose. Also grown for cutting	Good
'Fragrant Cloud' (syn. 'Duftwolke', 'Nuage Parfumé')	*HT:* Big, pointed, double flowers starting as geranium scarlet but soon turning dull. Introduced 1963	H:75cm (1½ft) S:60cm (2ft)	Remontant	Strong, rich scent	A good bedding rose	Very good
'Frau Dagmar Hartopp' (syn. 'Frau Dagmar Hastrup')	*Rugosa hybrid:* Light, satiny pink, single blooms, fairly large and flat, with stamens showing. Introduced about 1914	H:90cm (3ft) S:90cm (3ft)	Remontant	Particularly fine for hedging	Best grown as a hedge or as a specimen shrub	Fair
'Geranium'	*Moyesii hybrid:* Red, single, flowers with prominent dusty stamens. Lovely hips. Introduced 1938	H:1.8m (6ft) S:1.8m (6ft)	June	Impressive hips	Useful in a shrub border	Slight
'Golden Wings'	*Spinosissima hybrid:* Large, single, creamy-yellow blooms with amber stamens. A prominent shrub. Introduced 1956	H:1.2m (4ft) S:90cm (3ft)	Remontant	Provides a very bright display	Best grown as a specimen plant	Slight
'Grandpa Dickson' (syn. 'Irish Gold')	*HT:* Well-formed light yellow flowers with some red flushes. The large blooms have pointed centres. Introduced 1966	H:90cm (3ft) S:60cm (2ft)	Remontant	Good for bedding	Ideal for bedding, but also fine for cutting	Slight
'Handel'	*Climber:* Fairly large, double, creamy-white flowers, flushed and clearly edged with red. Introduced 1965	H:2.7m (9ft) S:2.4m (8ft)	Remontant	Good for cutting and flower arranging	A good climber for walls or fences	Fair
'Iceberg' (syn. 'Schneewittchen')	*Floribunda:* Large clusters of white flowers with occasional touches of pink. Semi-double. Introduced 1958	H:1.2m (4ft) S:90cm (3ft)	Remontant	Colour, and suitability for cutting and flower arranging	Splendid for bedding, but also for hedging or as a specimen plant	Slight
'Just Joey'	*HT:* Coppery-buff, with light pink; ovoid buds open to large double flowers, with little scent. Introduced 1973	H:75cm (2½ft) S:60cm (2ft)	Remontant	Outstanding colour, with unique tints	A bedding rose, also good for cutting	Slight
'Lady Penzance'	*Eglanteria hybrid:* Small, single shrimp-pink flowers touched yellow. Flowers are fleeting. Introduced 1894	H:1.8m (6ft) S:1.5m (5ft)	June	Sweet briar scent from leaves, spreading far in a damp atmosphere	Shrub border	Flowers poor, foliage very good
'Margaret Merril'	*Floribunda:* Thinly double white flowers with a touch of pink. Impeccable form. Introduced 1977	H:90cm (3ft) S:60cm (2ft)	Remontant	Supremely lovely, spicy scent	Fine for bedding or cutting	Very good
'Marjorie Fair'	*Polyantha:* Very small single red flowers with a white eye carried in large mop heads. Introduced 1977	H:1.3m (4½ft) S:1.2m (4ft)	Remontant	Makes a bright hedge when in bloom	Excellent as a hedge, but also nice as a specimen. Useful for cutting	Slight

Roses

Name	Description	Height/spread	Flowering period	Special merits	Situation/use	Fragrance
'Mermaid'	*Bracteata hybrid:* A climber with light primrose single flowers with amber stamens. Introduced 1918	H:6m (20ft) S:6m (20ft)	Remontant	Large flowers	Wall climber	Slight
'Mme Pierre Oger'	*Bourbon:* Fairly large semi-double rosy-salmon and cream flowers. Prone to blackspot. Introduced 1878	H:1.5m (5ft) S:75cm (2½ft)	Remontant	Sweet damask scent	Shrub border	Very good
'National Trust' (syn. 'Bad Nauheim')	*HT:* Bright blood red double flowers of medium size and svelte conical form. Healthy. Introduced 1970	H:75cm (2½ft) S:60cm (2ft)	Remontant	Brilliance and purity of colour	A colourful rose for bedding or cutting	Slight
'Nevada'	*Spinosissima hybrid:* White, very flat, semi-double flowers packed close together. Tall arching growth. Introduced 1927	H:1.8m (6ft) S:1.8m (6ft)	June (some Sept.)	Overall effect as a tall shrub	Best seen as a specimen shrub	Fair
'Ophelia'	*HT:* The fairly large double flowers are palest pink, with each petal touched yellow at the base. Introduced 1912	H:1m (3½ft) S:75cm (2½ft)	Remontant	Spicy fragrance	Good for bedding or cutting	Very good
'Pascali'	*HT:* Elegant double flowers, white touched cream. The centre petals hold a conical form. Introduced 1963	H:1m (3½ft) S:75cm (2½ft)	Remontant	A fine rose for cutting, with good stems and long-lasting qualities	Excellent for bedding and cutting	Slight
'Peace' (syn. 'Mme A. Meilland')	*HT:* A vigorous plant with large double flowers, light yellow flushed pink. A popular rose. Introduced 1942	H:1.3m (4½ft) S:1m (3½ft)	Remontant	Large flowers, vigorous	Fine for bedding or cutting, and also makes a nice specimen rose	Slight
'Piccadilly'	*HT:* Thinly double large flowers, the inner side of petals scarlet, the outside yellow. Introduced 1960	H:75cm (2½ft) S:60cm (2ft)	Remontant	Attractive flowers, good for cutting	Suitable for bedding and cutting	Slight
'Pink Parfait'	*Floribunda:* Elegant, thinly double blooms in clusters. Light rose-pink with cream. Introduced 1960	H:75cm (2½ft) S:60cm (2ft)	Remontant	Attractive massed in beds, or cut	Best grown in rose beds, or as a cut flower	Slight
'Queen Elizabeth'	*Floribunda:* A vigorous, tall and upright bush with clusters of thinly double, pink blooms. Introduced 1954	H:1.8m (6ft) S:90cm (3ft)	Remontant	Produces an abundant supply of roses for cutting	A first-class rose for hedging, bedding or cutting	Slight
'Rob Roy'	*Floribunda:* Bright deep red, thinly double, long-petalled flowers of medium size. Introduced 1971	H:90cm (3ft) S:60cm (2ft)	Remontant	Outstanding shining red colour	Good for bedding and cutting	Slight
Rosa gallica 'Versicolor' (syn. 'Rosa Mundi')	*Gallica:* A short upright bush, with flat, semi-double flowers. Red blush white, in stripes. Introduced about 1650	H:75cm (2½ft) S:60cm (2ft)	June	Interesting old rose	Best in a shrub border	Fair
R. rubrifolia	*Caninae:* Small single pink flowers, short-lived. Grown for its striking leaves and hips. European wild rose	H:1.8m (6ft) S:90cm (3ft)	June	Grown for its red leaves	Grow in a shrub border	Slight
R. rugosa alba	*Rugosa:* White, fairly large, single flowers showing yellow stamens. Makes a rounded bush. Introduced about 1870	H:1.5m (5ft) S:1.2m (4ft)	Remontant	A good hedging rose	Good as a hedge, but also makes a fine specimen plant	Good
R. virginiana	*Carolinae:* Pink, single flowers of medium size, lit by stamens. Healthy leaves down to ground. Introduced about 1750	H:1.3m (4½ft) S:1.8m (6ft)	June–July	A nice hedging shrub, with attractive flowers and red hips	Excellent as a hedge or specimen plant	Slight
'Roseraie de l'Hay'	*Rugosa hybrid:* Fairly large double flowers of irregular form. Remarkable purple colour. Introduced 1902	H:1.8m (6ft) S:1.2m (4ft)	Remontant	An abundance of healthy foliage make this a good hedging plant	Fine for hedges or grown as a specimen plant	Fair
'Scabrosa'	*Rugosa:* Mauve-red large single flowers, with stamens in brilliant relief. Carnation scent. Introduced about 1950	H:1.5m (5ft) S:1.8m (6ft)	Remontant	Large, spreading habit, thick healthy leaves, and bright hips make this a good hedge rose	Superb for hedging	Very good

Name	Description	Height/spread	Flowering period	Special merits	Situation/use	Fragrance
'Silver Jubilee'	*HT:* Handsome, long-petalled blooms, apricot pink in colour with some cream. Compact habit. Introduced 1978	H:75cm (2½ft) S:60cm (2ft)	Remontant	Pretty colour combination, and good form for cutting	Excellent for bedding or cutting	Slight
'Southampton' (syn. 'Susan Ann')	*Floribunda:* Medium-sized, semi-double, apricot-orange flowers in large clusters. Introduced 1972	H:1.2m (4ft) S:75cm (2ft)	Remontant	The best orange colour	A colourful rose for bedding or hedging	Fair
'Stanwell Perpetual'	*Scotch:* Double blush-coloured blooms of 'old-fashioned' form. Low, open growth, and grey-green leaves. Introduced 1838	H:90cm (3ft) S:90cm (3ft)	Remontant	Good cut flower where an 'old-fashioned' touch is required	Charming for cutting. Grow in shrub border	Good
'Sutter's Gold'	*HT:* Yellow flushed pink. Superbly formed, large, thinly double blooms start early. Introduced 1950	H:1m (3½ft) S:75cm (2½ft)	Remontant	Soapy fragrance and crisp, friendly colouring	Excellent for bedding and cutting	Very good
'The Fairy'	*Wichuraiana hybrid:* Small, double, rose-pink flowers, like neat rosettes, in large clusters. Introduced 1932	H:75cm (2½ft) S:60cm (2ft)	July–Sept.	Charming flowers	A delightful bedding rose, or can be grown as a specimen	Slight
'Wendy Cussons'	*HT:* Bulbous buds open to large double rose-red flowers, that finish as deep pink. Introduced 1959	H:1m (3½ft) S:75cm (2½ft)	Remontant	Attractive colouring and sweet scent	An excellent rose for bedding or cutting	Good
'William III'	*Scotch:* Thinly double, purple flowers, lightening in old blooms. Flowers borne close together. Introduced about 1750	H:60cm (2ft) S:45cm (1½ft)	May	An individual and fascinating rose	Grow in a shrub border	Slight
'Yesterday'	*Polyantha:* Airy sprays of small, semi-double pink to lavender-pink flowers. Introduced 1974	H:1.2m (4ft) S:75cm (2½ft)	Remontant	Makes an unusual hedge, especially in colour change	Apart from use as a hedge, it makes an unusual bedding rose	Good
'Zéphirine Drouhin'	*Bourbon:* A 'thornless rose' with medium-sized, deep pink flowers with short petals. Introduced 1868	H:4m (12ft) S:2.4m (8ft)	Remontant	Popular for its distinctive, pleasantly scented flowers	Can be grown on pillars or against walls	Good

Below: Rosa *'Nevada'*. *Below right: rose 'Peace'*

Annuals and biennials

By their very nature, annuals and biennials have to be prolific flowerers, for it is upon the production of adequate seed each year that their future depends, and many of them are gay, colourful plants in the wild.

The fact that their life span is comparatively short means that plant breeders have been able to achieve a lot of work in a reasonably brief time. This in itself has meant that it has been easy to breed even more spectacular and colourful strains, and many of the annuals that we now grow have very mixed parentage and often bear little resemblance to their wild counterparts.

Not only has it been fairly simple to create new colours and larger flowers, but the very habits of the plants have often been changed drastically. Antirrhinums and asters range in height from 15cm (6in) to 75cm (2½ft) or more, and even the tall and stately sweet pea can now be obtained in a form that grows only 30cm (1ft) high.

All this means a wealth of colour is freely available to brighten every corner of the garden, from a bed devoted to annuals alone, to the odd sprinkling used to fill up what would otherwise be a bare patch among shrubs or herbaceous plants.

The value of hardy annuals to fill in between more permanent plants while they are becoming established should never be underestimated. A newly planted heather bed, for example, can look rather stark for the first season or two, but by choosing a low-growing annual such as *Alyssum* 'Oriental Night' it can be transformed into a spectacular sight: a deep violet-purple carpet between the heathers from July to November, and a superb plant association.

Although this table is headed annuals and biennials, some of the plants included do not strictly fall into those categories (the antirrhinum, already mentioned, is strictly a perennial), and the criterion for inclusion is whether they are usually treated as an annual or biennial. Even some biennials can be sown early under glass and flowered the first year, which is half-hardy annual treatment. Conversely many hardy annuals can be sown in the autumn of one year to flower early the next. The best treatment is given in each specific entry.

If a greenhouse is available the scope is widened considerably because there are so many delightful half-hardy annuals, but even if such facilities are not on hand it is still possible to enjoy these plants. Most of them can be bought as bedding plants in late spring or early summer, although the choice of cultivar is often restricted. If just a few plants are required it may be possible to raise them on a light windowsill, but it will be essential to turn the plants regularly to even the directional influence of the light.

Whether you raise your own plants or buy them, half-hardy annuals must be hardened off thoroughly and carefully — and that means gradually. To be sure of success, don't plant before the risk of frost has passed, always ensure that they have been well hardened, and water regularly until established.

Unless this can be done it is better to grow plants that can be treated as hardy annuals or biennials — the range is large.

Below: **Calendula** *(pot marigold)* **'Rays of Sunshine'**

Name	Description	Height/spread	Flowering period	Soil and site	Remarks	Propagation
African daisy see Dimorphotheca						
African marigold see Tagetes erecta						
Ageratum	*Half-hardy annual:* Heads of tiny powderpuff flowers. Good cultivars include 'Blue Angel' (H:15cm/6in, S:25cm/10in, an F1 hybrid with bright lavender-blue flowers), 'Blue Bouquet' or 'Tall Blue' (H:45cm/1½ft, S:45cm/1½ft, lavender-blue), 'Blue Mink' (H:25cm/10in, S:25cm/10in, large azure-blue flowers), and 'North Sea' (H:15cm/6in, S:20cm/8in, an F1 hybrid with reddish-violet buds and rosy-mauve flowers)	See description	July–Oct.	Best in a moist, sheltered site, otherwise ordinary soil	Remove dead flower heads to prolong flowering. 'Blue Bouquet' is useful for cutting	Sow the seed 3mm (⅛in) deep in warmth from Feb. to April, and plant out 15–23cm (6–9in) apart from May onwards after hardening off
Alyssum see Lobularia						
Anchusa capensis	*Hardy annual:* Long sprays of star-like blooms, resembling giant forget-me-nots. A good cultivar is 'Blue Angel' (H:23cm/9in, S:15cm/6in, brilliant ultramarine colour)	See description	June–Sept.	A deep, fertile and moist soil is required, in full sun	Do not allow the soil to become dry	Sow outdoors, 12mm (½in) deep in March or April
Antirrhinum Snapdragon	*Half-hardy annual:* Too well known to need description. *Tall cultivars* (H:60–75cm/2–2½ft, S:45cm/1½ft) include 'Bright Butterflies' (F1 mixture with trumpet-shaped flowers), 'Madame Butterfly' (an F1 strain with double flowers like miniature azaleas), and 'Tetraploid Mixed' (ruffled and veined flowers in many shades). *Intermediate cultivars* (H:45cm/1½ft, S:30cm/1ft) include 'Coronette' (compact, sturdy plants with eight to ten spikes opening together; an F1 hybrid available as separate colours or as a mixture), and 'Little Darling' (like 'Bright Butterflies' but only 45cm/1½ft high; an F1 strain in mixed colours). *Dwarf cultivars* H:15–30cm/6–12in, S:23cm/9in) include 'Floral Carpet' (H:30cm/1ft, an F1 hybrid in the usual snapdragon colours), and 'Tom Thumb' (23cm/9in, compact plants in various colours)	See description	June–Oct.	Rich, well-drained soil in a sunny position produces the best results	Tall cultivars may require support from twiggy sticks while young	Sow 3mm (⅛in) deep in Feb. or March, under glass. Plant out from late March onwards
Aster, china see Callistephus chinensis						
Begonia semperflorens Bedding begonia	*Half-hardy annual:* These bushy tender perennials are grown as half-hardy annuals for bedding out. They produce a profusion of small flowers in shades of pink, red, and white. The glossy leaves are also attractive. Some have bronze foliage	H:15–23cm (6–9in) S:15–23cm (6–9in)	June–Oct.	Requires a light, well-cultivated soil in full sun or partial shade. The soil must not be allowed to dry out	After flowering the plants should be discarded	Sow very thinly in late winter in a temperature of 20–25°C (68–78°F), to produce plants large enough to bed out in late May
Bellis perennis Daisy	*Biennial:* Large, double, and highly decorative forms of our common daisy. Types include 'Giant-flowered Mixed' (H:15cm/6in, S:18cm/7in, rose, crimson, pink, white), 'Colour Carpet' (H:15cm/6in, S:18cm/7in), 'Pomponette' (H:10cm/4in, S:10cm/4in, miniature button-like flowers in mixed colours)	See description	April–June	Best in a fertile soil in sun or partial shade	Dead-head the plants to prevent them seeding	Sow 6mm (¼in) deep from April to June, either in a cold-frame or outdoors, and move to their flowering positions in Sept. or Oct.
Busy Lizzie see Impatiens						

Annuals and biennials

Name	Description	Height/spread	Flowering period	Soil and site	Remarks	Propagation
Calendula Pot marigold	*Hardy annual:* Bright, rayed flowers in shades of orange or yellow. 'Fiesta Gitana' (H:30cm/1ft, S:30cm/1ft, compact, cream and yellow to deep orange), and 'Pacific Beauty' (H:60cm/2ft, S:45cm/1½ft, shades of apricot, primrose, orange and yellow), are good forms	See description	See propagation	Ordinary garden soil is suitable, in good light. Avoid waterlogged soil	Nip out the terminal shoots to encourage branching, and remove all dead heads	Sow outdoors, 12mm (½in) deep, from March to May for summer blooming, or in Aug. or Sept. for early spring flowering
Californian poppy *see* Eschscholzia						
Callistephus chinensis China aster	*Half-hardy annual:* Normally listed in catalogues under the name aster. *Tall* cultivars (H:60cm/2ft, S:45cm/1½ft) include 'Duchess' (incurved, chrysanthemum-like flowers in various colours), and 'Totem Pole' (long upright stems topped with shaggy, double flowers in various colours). *Medium height* cultivars (H:30–45cm/1–1½ft, S:23–30cm/9–12in) include 'Ostrich Plume' (curled, feathery petals in many colours), 'Pepite Mixed' (bushy, semi-double flowers in scarlet, dark blue, light blue, white), 'Pompon' (compact, button-shaped flowers with quilled petals, various colours). *Dwarf* cultivars (under 30cm/1ft height, 23cm/9in spread) include 'Dwarf Bedding' (mound-shaped plants, mixed colours).	See description	July–Oct.	Well-drained soil in an open, sunny position is best, preferably sheltered from strong, cold winds	Support the young growth of tall cultivars with twiggy sticks. Remove the first flush of dead flowers. The dwarf kinds are used for bedding, the taller type for borders or for cutting	Asters are best grown as half-hardy annuals from sowings made 6mm (¼in) deep during March and April in slight warmth; plant out from mid-May after hardening off. Asters can also be sown directly outdoors from mid-April until June, except in cold or late districts
Campanula medium Canterbury bell	*Biennial:* These attractive plants are well known for their large bell-shaped flowers. The 'cup and saucer' cultivars are available as separate colours or as a mixture of blue, mauve, rose, and white. Double and single-flowered sorts are also offered. These all grow to 75cm (2½ft) with a spread of 45cm (1½ft), but there is a 'Dwarf Bedding' mixture at 45cm (1½ft) high and a spread of 30cm (1ft)	See description	May–July	A fertile, well-drained soil in a sunny position is most suitable	Keep the ground free of weeds during the early stages of growth	Sow 6mm (¼in) deep from April to June, and set the plants 15cm (6in) apart in nursery beds before moving to their flowering positions in Sept. or Oct., 38cm (15in) apart. They will flower the following year
Canterbury bell *see* Campanula medium						
Candytuft *see* Iberis umbellata						
Centaurea cyanus Cornflower	*Hardy annual:* Try 'Blue Diadem' (H:75cm/2½ft, S:30cm/1ft, large, deep blue flowers), or 'Polka Dot' (H:45cm/1½ft, S:30cm/1ft, pink, blue, mauve, crimson, white)	See description	See propagation	Does best in fertile, well-drained soil, in full sun	Support the tall cultivars with twiggy sticks	Sow 12mm (½in) deep where they are to flower. Thin to 30cm (1ft) apart. Sow in spring to flower from June onwards, or in Sept. to flower from May onwards the following year
Cheiranthus × allionii *see* Erysimum × allionii						
C. cheiri Wallflower	*Biennial:* Fragrant spring bedding plants. *Tall* cultivars (H:45cm/1½ft, S:30cm/1ft) include 'Blood Red' (dark velvety crimson), 'Primrose Monarch' (primrose), and 'Ruby Gem' (violet-purple). *Dwarf* cultivars (H:30–38cm/12–15in, S: 20–30cm/8–12in) include 'Fair Lady' (charming mixture of pastel shades), and 'Tom Thumb' wallflowers can be bought as separate colours or mixed. Height is 23cm (9in), spread 20cm (8in)	See description	March–May	Wallflowers appreciate lime in the soil, and require full sun	Protect young plants from cold winds. The 'Tom Thumb' strain is useful for exposed positions	Sow 6mm (¼in) deep in open ground during May or June, and prick out the seedlings to 15cm (6in) apart in nursery rows. Do not allow the soil to dry out. Plant in their final positions as early as possible in autumn

Name	Description	Height/spread	Flowering period	Soil and site	Remarks	Propagation
Chrysanthemum carinatum (syn. C. tricolor) Annual chrysanthemum	*Hardy annual:* Bright, daisy-like flowers, red, yellow or white banded with contrasting colours. Good strains include 'Merry Mixed' (H:60cm/2ft, S:45cm/1½ft), and 'Court Jesters' (H:45cm/1½ft, S:45cm/1½ft)	See description	June–Sept.	Fertile, well-drained soil is best, in a sunny position	Support young growth with twiggy sticks. Nip out the growing tips to encourage bushiness. Good for cutting	Sow outdoors, 6mm (¼in) deep, from March to May, where the plants are to flower
Clarkia unguiculata (syn. C. elegans)	*Hardy annual:* Will be found in seed catalogues under the name *Clarkia elegans.* Long, graceful spikes of double flowers in shades of pink, red, mauve, purple, white	H:38cm (15in) S:30cm (1ft)	July–Sept.	Prefers a light, acid soil, in full sun	Do not feed the plants	Sow thinly where they are to flower, 6mm (¼in) deep, from March to May. Eventually thin to the strongest seedlings, about 30cm (1ft) apart
C. pulchella	Long-stemmed clusters of double or semi-double flowers in shades of carmine, violet, white	H:38cm (15in) S:30cm (1ft)	July–Sept.	As *C. unguiculata*	As *C. unguiculata*	As *C. unguiculata*
Convolvulus tricolor (syn. C. minor)	*Hardy annual:* Gay plants with open bell flowers, available in a mixture of pinks and blues, often with contrasting centre. Height is normally about 38cm (15in), but 'Blue Flash' (deep blue flowers with white and yellow centres) grows only 15cm (6in) high	See description	July–Sept.	Ordinary, well-drained soil is suitable, in a sunny position	Remove the dead flower heads, where possible	Sow 12mm (½in) deep, where the plants are to flower

Cornflower *see* Centaurea cyanus

Name	Description	Height/spread	Flowering period	Soil and site	Remarks	Propagation
Cosmos bipinnatus (syn. Cosmea bipinnatus)	*Half-hardy annual:* Vigorous annuals with fern-like leaves and pink, rose, crimson or white flowers resembling an open, single dahlia. The tall Sensation types grow to about 90cm (3ft); the dwarf Klondyke types reach about 60cm (2ft)	See description	Aug.–Sept.	Will grow happily on poor, light, dry soil, in full sun or semi-shade	Support the plants with twiggy sticks. Remove dead flower heads	Sow in a greenhouse, 6mm (¼in) deep, during March or April. Set out the young plants, 45–60cm (1½–2ft) apart from May onwards, after being hardened off

Below: Callistephus chinensis *(aster)* 'Milady Rose', *a dwarf bedding cultivar. Below right:* Cosmos (Cosmea) bipinnatus 'Gloria'

Annuals and biennials

Name	Description	Height/spread	Flowering period	Soil and site	Remarks	Propagation
Daisy *see* Bellis perennis						
Delphinium consolida Larkspur	*Hardy annual:* Like a small delphinium, in shades of blue, pink and red. Listed in catalogues as larkspur. 'Giant Imperial' types reach 1.2m (4ft), with a spread of 45cm (1½ft), but dwarf forms grow to 45cm (1½ft), with a spread of 30cm (1ft)	See description	June–Aug.	Deep, rich soil in a sunny position suits these well	Support tall cultivars with twiggy sticks	Sow thinly outdoors, 6mm (¼in) deep, from March to May, and again in Sept. for early flowering the following year, in their flowering positions. Thin to the strongest seedlings, about 45cm (1½ft) apart
Dianthus barbatus Sweet William	*Biennial:* Popular 'cottage garden' plants for border decoration or cutting. There are many good mixtures in shades of pink, salmon, crimson, and white. Some separate colours are also available	H:45cm (1½ft) S:23cm (9in)	June–July	Any well-drained soil is suitable, but lime is appreciated. Needs full sun	Splendid plants for cutting, possessing both colour and fragrance	Sow 6mm (¼in) deep outdoors from April to June. Prick off the seedlings to 10cm (4in) apart in nursery rows, and set the plants in position in Sept. or Oct., 23cm (9in) apart
D. chinensis heddewigii	*Half-hardy annual:* Brightly-coloured single or double 'pinks'. 'Baby Doll' (H:20cm/8in; S:15cm/6in) is one of the best singles, in shades of crimson, pink, rose and white. 'Queen of Hearts' (H:30cm/1ft; S:25cm/9in) is an F1 hybrid with brilliant scarlet flowers	See description	June–Sept.	As *D. barbatus*	Very bright and free-flowering	Sow under glass, 3mm (⅛in) deep, from Feb. to April. Plant out 15cm (6in) apart from May onwards
Dimorphotheca African daisy	*Hardy annual:* Shades of apricot, orange, primrose and salmon, bloom over a long period	H:30cm (1ft) S:23cm (9in)	June–Sept.	Will succeed even in poor, dry soil	If possible, remove all dead heads to encourage further flowering	Sow outdoors, 6mm (¼in) deep, from April to June. Thin the seedlings to 30cm (1ft) apart
Echium	*Hardy annual:* Low, rather hairy annual, with loose sprays of blue, mauve, pink or white flowers	H:30cm (1ft) S:30cm (1ft)	June–Oct.	Best suited to a light soil in an open, sunny situation	Easy to grow and long-lasting	Sow outdoors, 6mm (¼in) deep, from March to May. Thin seedlings to about 30cm (1ft) apart
Erysimum × allionii (syn. Cheiranthus × allionii) Siberian wallflower	*Biennial:* Normally listed in catalogues as *Cheiranthus × allionii.* A bright plant, with small, more sparsely arranged wallflower heads. Normally orange, but 'Golden Bedder' is deep yellow	H:23cm (9in) S:23cm (9in)	March–May	Requires a non-acid soil in a sunny situation	Protect young plants from cold winds. Nip out the growing tips in autumn to encourage bushiness	Sow 6mm (¼in) deep in May or June, and transplant in autumn. Alternatively, sow from July to Sept. where the plants are to flower. Space 23cm (9in) apart
Eschscholzia Californian poppy	*Hardy annual:* Brilliantly coloured flowers in shades of orange and scarlet, together with yellow, rose, and white. 'Ballerina' and 'Art Shades' are good semi-double mixes; there are numerous single strains	H:30cm (1ft) S:30cm (1ft)	June–Oct.	Best on poor soil in full sun	Seeds itself easily and self-sown seedlings are likely to occur the following year	Sow outdoors, 6mm (¼in) deep, from March to May

Below: Campanula medium *(Canterbury bell). Below right:* Delphinium consolida *(larkspur)* 'Dwarf Rocket'. *Far below right:* Godetia 'Azalea-flowered'

Name	Description	Height/spread*	Flowering period	Soil and site	Remarks	Propagation
French marigold see Tagetes patula						
Godetia	*Hardy annual:* Gay plants of good habit. 'Dwarf Bedding Mixed' (H:30cm/1ft, S:20cm/8in) is compact, with single flowers of crimson, carmine, rose or salmon, some striped or with a picotee edge. 'Tall Double Mixed' (H:60cm/2ft, S:30cm/1ft) has sprays of double flowers in pink, carmine, crimson or mauve	See description	July–Oct.	Light, moist soil in a sunny position is best for these plants	Do not feed, as it may encourage too much lush growth at the expense of flowers	Sow where the plants are to flower, 6mm (¼in) deep, during March or April. Thin to 30cm (1ft) apart
Gypsophila elegans	*Hardy annual:* Dainty, graceful flowers, splendid for cutting. 'Covent Garden White' is a good strain; 'Carminea' is pink, with smaller flowers	H:60cm (2ft) S:45cm (1½ft)	See propagation	Best in well-drained, alkaline soil in full sun	Support the plants with twiggy sticks	Sow where the plants are to flower, 6mm (¼in) deep, from March to May for summer flowering; sow in Sept. for the following spring
Helianthus annuus Sunflower	*Hardy annual:* Too well known to need description. 'Tall Yellow' (H:2.4m/8ft, S:75–90cm/2½–3ft) produces enormous yellow flowers. 'Sunburst' (H:1.2m/4ft, S:45–60cm/1½–2ft) has medium-sized flowers, varying from primrose to bronze and maroon. 'Dwarf Sungold' and 'Teddy Bear' (H:60cm/2ft, S:30cm/1ft) have double, golden-yellow flowers on compact plants	See description	Aug.–Oct.	Provide well-drained soil in a sunny position	In exposed positions it may be necessary to stake tall cultivars	Sow where the plants are to flower, 12mm (½in) deep, from March to May
Helichrysum Strawflower	*Half-hardy annual:* Papery 'everlasting' flowers. Good strains are 'Monstrosum Double Mixed' (H:75cm/2½ft, S:45cm/1½ft), and the dwarf mixtures 'Sparkle' and 'Bright Bikinis' (both H:30cm/1ft, S:23cm/9in). Colours include crimson, rose, yellow, bronze, white	See description	July–Sept.	Requires a light, well-drained soil in a sunny situation	Remove dead flower heads	Sow 6mm (¼in) deep under glass during March or April. Plant out 30cm (1ft) apart in May, after hardening off
Iberis umbellata Candytuft	*Hardy annual:* Normally listed in catalogues under candytuft. Flattish heads of small but bright flowers completely cover the plant. Most mixtures grow to about 30cm/1ft high, with a similar spread but 'Fairy Mixed' reaches only about 20cm (9in). Colours include pink, lavender, purple, and white	See description	June–Sept.	Ordinary soil is adequate, but provide a sunny site	Remove dead flower heads to extend season	Sow where the plants are to flower, 6mm (¼in) deep, from March to May, thinning to 15cm (6in) apart
Impatiens Busy Lizzie	*Half-hardy annual:* This popular houseplant can also be bedded out if suitable cultivars are chosen. 'Imp' and 'Futura Mixed' are both dependable F1 hybrid mixtures (H:23cm/9in; S:23cm/9in).	See description	June–Oct.	Will grow in any good garden soil, and prefer shade or semi-shade	Particularly useful for difficult shady spots	Sow from Feb. to March in a temperature of 15–20°C (60–68°F). Germination is usually slow. Plant out 23cm (9in) apart from late May onwards
Ipomoea Morning glory	*Half-hardy annual:* A free-flowering climber with large blue flowers. Grow in a greenhouse, sunroom, verandah or sheltered patio	Climber	June–Sept.	Requires a light, rich soil	Remove dead flowers to extend period of flowering	Sow individually in pots. Soak seed for 24 hours, then plant 12mm (½in) deep
Larkspur see Delphinium consolida						
Lathyrus odoratus Sweet pea	*Half-hardy annual:* Well-known and popular plants. Many kinds are available. The Spencer types are the traditional exhibition sorts, but the free-flowering Galaxy or multiflora types, as well as 'hedge' forms such as 'Jet Set' (H:90cm/3ft), are becoming more popular. Even more compact are the 'Little Elf' and 'Bijou' strains	Climbing (see description)	See propagation	Ordinary well-drained soil is adequate for general cultivation, but for exhibition a deep, rich soil is necessary. Position in full sun	Remove dead heads and all seed pods. Stake tall cultivars early	Sow 12mm (½in) deep, from Jan. to March under glass, and plant outdoors during April or May. Alternatively the seed can be sown where the plants are to flower, during April and May for summer flowering, or in Sept. or Oct. for early flowering the following year in mild districts

Annuals and biennials

Name	Description	Height/spread	Flowering period	Soil and site	Remarks	Propagation
Lavatera trimestris Mallow	*Hardy annual:* A showy, long-lasting plant for borders or cutting. 'Silver Cup' (H:60–90cm/2–3ft, S:75cm/2½ft) has trumpet-shaped flowers of bright deep pink; 'Mont Blanc' (H:60/2ft, S:30cm/1ft) has glistening pure white flowers	See description	July–Sept.	Will grow successfully in most garden soils, but avoid excessive richness. Provide a sunny, sheltered position	Seeds itself freely	Sow where the plants are to flower, 12mm (½in) deep from March to May, allowing 60cm (2ft) between plants
Linaria maroccana Toadflax	*Hardy annual:* Tiny snapdragon flowers in a range of pretty colour combinations. 'Fairy Bouquet' includes shades of rose, carmine, orange, yellow, mauve, white	H:23cm (9in) S:15cm (6in)	June–July	Ordinary soil is suitable, but requires a sunny position	Cut plants back after first flush of flower — a second may follow	Sow thinly, where the plants are to flower. Sow from March to May, 3mm (⅛in) deep, and thin to 15cm (6in) apart
Lobelia erinus	*Half-hardy annual:* A neat, free-flowering annual, frequently planted with alyssum. The compact cultivars (H:10–15cm/4–6in, S:15cm/6in) include 'Cambridge Blue' (pale blue), 'Crystal Palace Compacta' (dark blue, bronze foliage), and 'Rosamond' (wine red, white eye). Trailing kinds include 'Blue Cascade', 'Red Cascade' and 'Sapphire'	See description	May–Oct.	Best in rich, moist soil in sun or partial shade	Ensure that the roots do not become dry. Trailing kinds are ideal for windowboxes or hanging baskets	Sow from Jan. to March in a heated greenhouse (15–20°C/60–68°F). Press the seeds slightly into the surface of the compost. Prick off seedlings as small clusters. Plant out 15cm (6in) apart from late May onwards, after hardening off
Lobularia maritima (syn. Alyssum maritimum)	*Hardy annual:* A popular edging plant, almost always listed in catalogues as alyssum. The most widely known cultivar is the white 'Little Dorrit', but there are others with carmine-red ('Wonderland'), violet-pink ('Rosie O'Day') and deep violet-purple ('Oriental Night') flowers	H:10cm (4in) S:20cm (8in)	July–Oct.	Ordinary soil in full sun suits these plants	Trouble-free plants. Easy to grow	Sow 6mm (¼in) deep, where the plants are to flower, from March to June. Thin out to about 20cm (8in) apart

Love-in-a-mist *see* Nigella damascena

Mallow *see* Lavatera trimestris

Name	Description	Height/spread	Flowering period	Soil and site	Remarks	Propagation
Matthiola (annual types)	*Half-hardy annual:* Spikes of fragrant flowers ideal for bedding or cutting. The main types are 'Ten Week' (H:30cm/1ft, S:23cm/9in; shades of red, rose, lavender, purple, primrose, white), 'Beauty of Nice' (H:45cm/1½ft, S:23cm/9in; slightly later than 'Ten Week', useful under glass), 'Giant Perfection' (H:45cm/1½ft, S:23cm/9in; vigorous, branching type in shades of pink, rose, crimson, lavender, blue, white), and 'Column' (H:60cm/2ft, S:30cm/1ft)	See description	July–Aug.	Best in a good soil in full sun or partial shade. Avoid planting on acid soil	Stocks produce double and single flowers on different plants, about 60% being double. With some strains it is possible to select the doubles by the lighter green leaf colour of the seedlings (instructions are usually given on the packet)	Sow 6mm (¼in) deep in a heated greenhouse, from Feb. to April, and plant out 30cm (1ft) apart in May. Alternatively, sow directly outdoors from late April, where the plants are to flower
M. (biennial types)	Brompton stocks flower in May and June outdoors, earlier in a cold greenhouse. The East Lothian type are useful for flowering under glass in early spring	H:30cm (1ft) S:23cm (9in)	May–June	As annual types	In cold districts or on heavy soil, winter the plants in a cold-frame and plant out in March	Sow Brompton stocks 6mm (¼in) deep in a cold-frame or greenhouse during June or July. Prick off into boxes or nursery beds and plant out 30cm (1ft) apart during Sept. or Oct. Sow East Lothian stocks in a greenhouse or cold-frame in July or Aug. and prick off into boxes. Later, transplant into 13cm (5in) pots
M. longipetala bicornis (syn. M. bicornis) Night-scented stock	*Half-hardy annual:* Insignificant mauve flowers that close by day but release a delicious perfume in the evening	H:30cm (1ft) S:23cm (9in)	July–Aug.	As annual types	One of the most powerful evening fragrances	Sow 6mm (¼in) deep from March to May, where they are to flower

Morning glory *see* Ipomoea

Name	Description	Height/spread	Flowering period	Soil and site	Remarks	Propagation
Myosotis Forget-me-not	*Biennial:* Popular spring bedding plants. Among the best cultivars are 'Blue Ball' (H:15cm/6in, S:15cm/6in), 'Royal Blue' (H:30cm/1ft, S:20cm/8in), and 'Ultramarine' (H:15cm/6in, S:15cm/6in)	See description	March–June	Best in a moist soil in partial shade	Keep young plants moist at the roots. Self-seeds easily	Sow 6mm (¼in) deep on a seedbed outdoors, from May to July, and plant in flowering position in autumn
Nasturtium *see* Tropaeolum						
Nemesia strumosa	*Half-hardy annual:* Bright heads of flowers completely covering the plant in full bloom. 'Carnival' is one of the best strains, with colours that include bronze, cerise, crimson, pink, orange, scarlet, and yellow	H:20cm (8in) S:15cm (6in)	June–Aug.	Ordinary soil is satisfactory, in full sun or partial shade	Do not allow the plants to become dry at the roots	Sow 3mm (⅛in) deep, from Feb. to May in a heated greenhouse. Plant out 20cm (8in) apart from late May, after hardening them off
Nicotiana Tobacco plant	*Half-hardy annual:* Tubular flowers carried well above the foliage. Good cultivars include 'Lime Green' (H:75cm/2½ft, S:45cm/1½ft, greenish-yellow), and 'Sensation Mixed' (H:75cm/2½ft, S:45cm/1½ft, mauve, pink, crimson, greenish-yellow, white; remain open all day). The species *N. alata* (syn. *N. affinis* – the name under which it will be found) has clusters of extremely fragrant white flowers (H:90cm/3ft, S:45cm/1½ft)	See description	June–Sept.	Requires a rich, well-drained soil in a warm sunny position	Remove dead flower heads if possible	Sow 3mm (⅛in) deep in a heated greenhouse, from Feb. to April. Set the plants in position from late May onwards
Nigella damascena Love-in-a-mist	*Hardy annual:* Spidery flowers set amid feathery foliage. 'Miss Jekyll' (H:45cm/1½ft, S:30cm/1ft) has cornflower-blue flowers, 'Persian Jewels' (H:38cm/15in, S:30cm/1ft) is a mixture of blue, mauve, pink, purple and rosy-red flowers	See description	June–Aug.	Any well-cultivated soil is suitable, in a position of full sun	Remove dead flower heads to prolong flowering period	Sow 6mm (¼in) deep, where the plants are to flower, from March to May for summer flowering, or in Sept. for spring flowering

Below: **Lavatera trimestris** *(mallow)* **'Silver Cup'**

Annuals and biennials

Name	Description	Height/spread	Flowering period	Soil and site	Remarks	Propagation
Night-scented stock *see* Matthiola longipetala bicornis						
Pansy *see* Viola						
Petunia	*Half-hardy annual:* Invaluable bedding plants, with masses of bright open trumpet flowers. F1 hybrids are Grandiflora cultivars 'Colour Parade' (a blend of self colours and some striped flowers) and 'Razzle Dazzle' (a mixture of striped and variegated blooms); these all have very large flowers, 7.5cm (3in) or more across. The Hybrid Multiflora cultivars have smaller flowers, but are better for bedding, windowboxes or containers. 'Resisto' types are recommended because they quickly recover from rainy weather	H:30–38cm (12–15in) S:30cm (1ft)	July–Sept.	Best in light, well-drained soil in a sheltered position. Plant in full sun	Dead-head regularly	Sow from Feb. to April under glass (15–20°C/60–68°F), just pressing the seed into the compost. Plant out 30cm (1ft) apart from May onwards after hardening off
Phlox drummondii	*Half-hardy annual:* Gay plants with heads of small, phlox flowers. Good strains are 'Beauty Mixed' (H:15cm/6in; S:15cm/6in), blue, violet, pink, salmon, scarlet, white; and 'Twinkle Dwarf Star' (H:18cm/7in; S:15cm/6in), star-shaped flowers in various colours	See description	July–Oct.	Any fertile and well-drained soil is suitable, in full sun	Useful for cutting. Dead-heading extends the flowering period	Sow 6mm (¼in) deep under glass from Feb. to April. Plant out 23cm (9in) apart after hardening off in May and June
Pot marigold *see* Calendula						
Rudbeckia hirta	*Biennial:* Spectacular, free-flowering plants with large, rayed flowers, excellent for garden display or cutting. Good cultivars include 'Marmalade' (H:45cm/1½ft, S:45cm/1½ft, golden-orange), and 'Rustic Dwarfs' (H:60cm/2ft, S:45cm/1½ft, shades of yellow, gold, bronze, and mahogany, with black central cones)	See description	June–Oct.	Well-drained, thoroughly cultivated ground is required, in an open, sunny position	Provide an almost unlimited supply of blooms for cutting	Sow 6mm (¼in) deep, from April to July, and prick off into a nursery bed. Transplant to flowering position in autumn. Can also be sown under glass in Feb. and treated as a half-hardy annual
Salvia splendens	*Half-hardy annual:* Popular, brilliant scarlet bedding plants. Of the many cultivars the old 'Blaze of Fire' is still the most reliable	H:30cm (1ft) S:25cm (10in)	July–Oct.	Any ordinary, well-drained soil is suitable	Pinch out the growing tips to encourage bushiness	Sow 6mm (¼in) deep, in a heated greenhouse (20°C/68°F) from Jan. to March. Plant out from late May onwards

Below: Salvia splendens *'Fusilier Scarlet'. Below right:* Cheiranthus cheiri *(wallflower) 'Orange Bedder'*

Name	Description	Height/spread	Flowering period	Soil and site	Remarks	Propagation
Snapdragon see Antirrhinum						
Stock see Matthiola						
Strawflower see Helichrysum						
Sunflower see Helianthus annuus						
Sweet pea see Lathyrus odoratus						
Sweet William see Dianthus barbatus						
Tagetes erecta African marigold	*Half-hardy annual:* Extremely valuable bedding and border plant, with large, globular, yellow or orange flowers. The 'Climax' kinds are excellent F1 hybrids, but among the ordinary kinds 'Hawaii' is interesting because of its odourless foliage	H:60–90cm (2–3ft) S:30cm (1ft)	June–Oct.	Ordinary soil enriched with compost is ideal. Needs a sunny position	Triploid hybrids are available, which are a cross between the African and French kinds	Sow 6mm (½in) deep in a slightly heated greenhouse from Feb. to April. Plant out in May or June, after hardening off
T. patula French marigold	Superb plants for edging a flower bed. Like small African marigolds, but less full. Among the singles, 'Naughty Marietta' (yellow, boldly splashed with maroon) is popular, while there are many charming doubles, such as 'Bolero' (mahogany red and gold)	H:15–30cm (6–12in) S:15cm (6in)	June–Oct.	As *T. erecta*	Often in flower while still in the seedbox. Very prolific	As *T. erecta*
T. tenuifolia (syn. T. signata)	*Half-hardy annual:* Diminutive marigolds of compact growth and lacy foliage, with masses of small single flowers	H:15–23cm (6–9in) S:20cm (8in)	June–Oct.	As *T. erecta*	This is the plant normally listed under tagetes in seed catalogues. Useful for edgings or for windowboxes	As *T. erecta*
Toadflax see Linaria maroccana						
Tobacco plant see Nicotiana						
Tropaeolum Nasturtium	*Hardy annual:* Well-known annuals, often unjustly neglected. The tall cultivars are fine for covering a trellis or bank, but there are also compact types like the 'Gleam Hybrids' that only reach 30cm (1ft). Colours include shades of salmon, golden-yellow, orange-scarlet, cerise, primrose	See description	June–Sept.	Ideal for hot, dry soils in full sun. Will thrive on poor soil	The bush type also make splendid hanging basket plants	Sow 12mm (½in) deep where the plants are to flower, from April to June. Thin out to 23cm (9in) apart
Viola Pansy and viola	*Biennial:* Both pansies (V. wittrockiana hybrids) and violas (V. cornuta) are best treated as biennials. Violas have smaller flowers than pansies, and a neater, more upright habit of growth. Good pansy cultivars include 'Majestic Giants' (H:20cm/8in, S:20cm/8in, F1 hybrid), and 'Roggli Giant' (H:18cm/7in, S:23cm/9in). Among the violas 'Monarch Mixed' (H:20cm/8in, S:20cm/8in) is a compact strain worth growing, with rounded flowers in self colours, bicolours and picotees	See description	April–July	A moist, rich soil is essential for best results. A position of semi-shade is preferred	Dead-head regularly. The flowering period given is the principal period, but the season can be extended at both ends by varying sowing dates and treatment	Sow 6mm (¼in) deep, in a cold-frame or open ground, during June or July. Prick out into nursery beds, 15cm (6in) apart. Move to flowering position in Sept. or Oct. Can also be sown under glass in March, and planted out in early May, or even sown where they are to flower, in March or early April
Wallflower see Cheiranthus cheiri						
Wallflower, Siberian see Erysimum × allionii						
Zinnia	*Half-hardy annual:* Zinnias resemble small dahlias in flower. Giant-flowered cultivars are the tallest (H:60–75cm/2–2½ft, S:30–45cm/1–1½ft), but there are more compact kinds growing to 45cm (1½ft) with a spread of about 30cm (1ft)	See description	July–Sept.	A fertile soil, and a warm, sunny position are essential for good results	Nip out the growing tips to induce the plants to branch. Only sow outdoors in mild districts	Sow 6mm (¼in) deep during March or April in a heated greenhouse and plant out in late May. Can also be sown directly where they are to flower; this should be done in May when the soil is warm, and the depth increased to 12mm (½in)

Hardy border plants

Herbaceous plants are particularly useful because they combine the special quality of being permanent in nature yet immediate in results.

Although some trees and shrubs are essential in any garden, they inevitably take many years to mature into good specimens, yet the plants in the following table will all produce a respectable display in a comparatively short time, and within a year or two can be at their prime. For this reason they have a unique role to play in establishing any garden.

The term 'hardy border plants' has been used for this table because traditional herbaceous borders are tending to disappear: mixed borders, containing shrubs and herbaceous plants, are recognized as legitimate garden features, while some of the plants included are not strictly herbaceous in the sense that they die down to the ground each year. Pampas grass (*Cortaderia selloana*) and barrenwort (*Epimedium grandiflorum*) are examples of plants that retain their foliage throughout the year, yet they both have a place in a border.

Yet others, included because they are worthy of inclusion in an herbaceous or mixed border if the right conditions can be provided, could equally well be regarded as rock garden or woodland subjects — *Omphalodes cappadocica* is an example of the former, Solomon's seal (*Polygonatum multiflorum*) one of the latter.

The important thing is to use plants to create the right colour and texture to provide the picture you want, rather than be constrained by technical classification. All the plants in this table can be used effectively to create a border that will provide some bloom from December (*Helleborus*) to October (*Sedum spectabile* and Michaelmas daisies, to mention just two).

Whether creating a traditional single-faced herbaceous border, an island bed, or a mixed border, always mark out the ground before planting, allocating space and inserting labels where the plants are to grow. If you plant as you go along, the temptation will be to overlook the overall plan, and to set the plants too closely together because they tend to look lost.

Always try to plant in groups of three or five plants, as this makes a really bold display and will look far better than isolated specimens dotted about the border.

Most hardy border plants are easy to propagate by dividing established clumps, but many herbaceous plants can also be raised from seed; although it is sometimes a matter of waiting a year or two longer for results, seed provides an inexpensive way to raise a lot of plants.

The majority of hardy perennial seeds can be sown outdoors on a prepared seedbed in a sunny or semi-shaded place in late spring or early summer. Sow in shallow drills and thin out early; transplant to a spare piece of ground, spacing them about 23cm (9in) apart. They can be moved to their final positions in September and October or March and April. This is the best time to plant all the subjects in this chapter unless specific instructions are given in the table.

Name	Description	Height/ spread	Flowering period	Soil and site	Remarks	Propagation
Acanthus spinosus Bear's breeches	Distinctive, deeply cut foliage and spectacular bold spikes of mauve-purple flowers	H:1.2m (4ft) S:60cm (2ft)	July–Sept.	Deep, well-drained loam is required, ideally moisture-retentive. A sunny or slightly shaded position is best	Acanthus dislike disturbance, and should be left until congested. Cut flowered stems back to ground level	Root cuttings 7.5cm (3in) long can be taken in Jan. or Feb. Large clumps can be divided between Oct. and April
Achillea	Reliable border plants with attractive, divided foliage, and flat yellow flower heads. Two good cultivars are 'Coronation Gold' (deep yellow; H:0.9–1.2m/3–4ft, S:75–90cm/2½–3ft) and 'Moonshine' (silvery foliage, pale yellow flowers; H:60cm/2ft, S:45cm/1½ft)	See description	June–Aug.	Achilleas are useful for stony, gravelly or chalky soils, in full sun	Trouble-free plants provided they have the right conditions. The flower heads retain their colour for many months when cut and dried	Divide established clumps in Sept. or spring. Keep young plants moist until established
Aconitum × cammarum Monkshood	Sturdy border plants that do not require staking. Spikes of hooded flowers, resembling helmets. Two good clones are 'Blue Sceptre' (blue and white flowers; H:60–75cm/ 2–2½ft, S: 45–60cm/ 1½–2½ft), and 'Bressingham Spire' (violet-blue; H:90cm/3ft, S:60cm/2ft)	See description	July–Aug.	Provide deep, moist soil in partial shade. It is essential the soil does not dry out during the early summer months	Aconitums benefit from a mulch during summer. Cut down plants to soil level in autumn	Divide crowded plants in Oct. or March
African lily *see* Agapanthus						
Agapanthus African lily	Lily-like blue flowers and green strap-shaped leaves — a bold plant commanding attention. *A. campanulatus* is a hardy species with sky blue flowers. 'Headbourne Hybrids' are very dependable and come in various shades of blue	H:90cm (3ft) S:75cm (2½ft)	July–Aug.	A well-drained but rich soil in a sheltered, sunny position is best. In cold areas it is wise to provide a south-facing aspect	In cold areas, cover the roots with straw in winter. Plant in March or April	Divide in April. The 'Headbourne Hybrids' can be raised from seed
Alchemilla mollis Lady's mantle	Numerous sulphur-yellow flowers carried above rounded leaves that are downy to the touch	H:45cm (1½ft) S:30cm (1ft)	June–Aug.	A sunny or partially shaded position is best, with well-drained soil	Support plants in early stages of growth, using twiggy sticks	Divide mature plants any time between Oct. and March, whenever the soil is not frozen

Name	Description	Height/ spread	Flowering period	Soil and site	Remarks	Propagation
Alkanet *see* Anchusa azurea						
Alstroemeria 'Ligtu Hybrids' Peruvian lily	Small lily-like flowers at the tops of stems clothed with stalkless leaves. Colours include pink, scarlet, orange and yellow	H:60–90cm (2–3ft) S:30cm (1ft)	June–Aug.	Fertile, well-drained soil is essential, in a position sheltered from cold winds	Plant in early spring, covering the tubers with about 10cm (4in) of soil. Always plant pot-grown specimens, as root disturbance is resented	Divide established clumps in spring. Replant immediately. Can also be raised from seed
Alum root *see* Heuchera						
Anaphalis triplinervis	A distinctive plant with greyish woolly leaves topped with clusters of white, star-like 'everlasting' flowers	H:30cm (1ft) S:30cm (1ft)	July–Sept.	Well-drained soil is essential, in a sunny position. However, if the soil is dry they will also grow in partial shade	The plants often become untidy in autumn, and can then be cut back	Divide established plants between Oct. and April, whenever the weather allows
Anchusa azurea Alkanet	Brilliant blue flowers on tough, bristly stems. An outstanding cultivar is 'Loddon Royalist' (H:90cm/3ft, S:60cm/2ft), and 'Little John' (H:60cm/2ft, S:45cm/1½ft) is a good dwarf form	See description	May–July	Requires a deep, fertile soil in a sunny position. Heavy soil must be dug deeply and lightened with coarse sand	The plants may benefit from the support of a few twigs. Cut down to soil level in Oct.	Take root cuttings in Jan. or Feb.
Anemone × hybrida Japanese anemone	A magnificent plant for late flowering. Individual blooms are 5cm (2in) across, and they are carried clear of the foliage to provide a bright, long-lasting display. Cultivars include 'Bressingham Glow' (rosy-red), 'September Charm' (pink, gold centre, large flowers), and 'White Queen'	H:45–90cm (1½–3ft) S:30–60cm (1–2ft)	Aug.–Oct.	Fertile, moisture-retentive but well-drained soil in slight shade is preferred	May take a year or two to settle down. Avoid unnecessary disturbance. Cut stems to soil level after flowering	Divide large clumps any time between Oct. and March, whenever the ground is suitable
Anthemis tinctoria Ox-eye chamomile	Easily grown plants with an abundance of daisy-like flowers. Two good forms are 'Mrs. E. C. Buxton' (curry yellow) and 'Grallagh Gold' (deep yellow)	H:75–90cm (2½–3ft) S:45cm (1½ft)	June–Aug.	Ordinary garden soil is suitable, preferably in a sunny position	In exposed areas, staking with twiggy sticks may be necessary	Divide mature plants between Sept. and March, whenever the weather allows
Aquilegia 'Dragonfly' Columbine	Distinctive spurred flowers in a wide range of colours, including cream, yellow, pink, red, crimson and blue	H:45cm (1½ft) S:30cm (1ft)	May–June	Best in well-drained soil in sun or partial shade	After flowering, cut stems down to soil level	Divide between Sept. and March. This and some other strains, including an F1 hybrid mixture, are easily raised from seed sown in early summer
Artemisia lactiflora White mugwort	Plumes of fragrant creamy-white flowers on strong stems make this an impressive plant. The mid-green leaves are deeply divided	H:1.2cm (4ft) S:60cm (2ft)	Aug.–Oct.	Well-drained soil in full sun or partial shade is needed, with plenty of organic material to retain moisture	In autumn, cut the plants down to soil level	Divide established plants any time from Oct. to March, weather permitting
Aruncus dioicus (syn. A. sylvester) Goat's beard	Wide, fern-like leaves and large, ivory-white plumes composed of minute individual flowers. A very conspicuous plant	H:1.2m (4ft) S:90cm (3ft)	June–July	A deep, moisture-retentive soil is needed, in slight shade. A good waterside plant	In autumn, cut the stems down to soil level	Divide established plants in Oct.
Aster novi-belgii Michaelmas daisy	Indispensable border plants, providing a mass of colour at a useful time. Good types include 'Ada Ballard' (mauve-blue, H:90cm/3ft), 'Carnival' (semi-double, cherry red, H:60cm/2ft), 'Dandy' (purple-red, H:30cm/1ft), 'Little Pink Beauty' (semi-double, pink, H:45cm/1½ft), Raspberry Ripple' (double, carmine red, H:75cm/2½ft), 'Royal Velvet' (rich violet-blue, H:60cm/2ft). All have a spread of about 45cm (1½ft)	See description	Sept.–Oct.	Asters prefer a fertile soil and a sunny position. It is essential that the soil does not dry out during the flowering season	The tall cultivars may need twiggy supports. Replace with fresh stock every three years, using new growth from around the edges of mature clumps	Divide established clumps in April or March
Astilbe × arendsii	Fern-like foliage and spikes composed of many small flowers. Cultivars include 'Bressingham Beauty' (clear pink), 'Deutchland' (white), 'Fanal' (dark red)	H:60–90cm (2–3ft) S:45–60cm (1½–2ft)	June–Aug.	Moist soil is essential, in sun or partial shade	Water regularly while in flower if the ground is dry. Cut plants to ground level in Oct.	Lift and divide plants every three years

Hardy border plants

Name	Description	Height/spread	Flowering period	Soil and site	Remarks	Propagation
Astrantia maxima Masterwort	Unusual rose-pink flowers, excellent for cutting. The star-like flowers have narrow, greenish-pink bracts. The lobed leaves are bright green	H:90cm (3ft) S:60cm (2ft)	June–Aug.	Useful plant for shade, but will tolerate sun provided the soil is moist	Staking with twiggy sticks may be necessary in exposed places	Divide established plants from Oct. to March
Balloon flower *see* Platycodon grandiflorum						
Barrenwort *see* Epimedium grandiflorum						
Bear's breeches *see* Acanthus spinosus						
Bell flower *see* Campanula lactiflora						
Beramot *see* Monarda didyma						
Bergenia cordifolia Elephant's ears	Large leaves resembling elephants' ears, and sprays of pink flowers in spring	H:25cm (10in) S:30cm (1ft)	April–May	Useful plants for moist soil in full sun or partial shade	Leave the plants undisturbed unless they have spread excessively. Cut off dead flowers	Divide overcrowded plants in March
Blanket flower *see* Gaillardia						
Bleeding heart *see* Dicentra spectabilis						
Bugbane *see* Cimicifuga racemosa						
Campanula lactiflora Bell flower	Light blue bells 2.5cm (1in) across, carried on tall, leafy stems. Cultivars include 'Loddon Anna' (lilac-pink), 'Alba' (white), and 'Prichard's Variety' (violet-blue)	H:1.2m (4ft) S:90cm (3ft)	June–Aug.	Fertile, well-drained soil is required, in sun or partial shade	Some support may be necessary in their early stages of growth, especially in windy areas	Divide established plants in March or April
C. persicifolia	Beautiful tall spires of blue or white flowers. 'Telham Beauty' is one of the best blues	H:1m (3½ft) S:60cm (2ft)	June–Aug.	As *C. lactiflora*	As *C. lactiflora*	As *C. lactiflora*
Carnation *see* Dianthus caryophyllus						
Catananche caerulea 'Major' Cupid's dart	Blue cornflower-like flowers with a papery texture, carried on wiry stems. Narrow grey-green leaves	H:60cm (2ft) S:45cm (1½ft)	June–Aug.	Does best in a well-drained soil and sunny position	Support young plants with twiggy sticks. Cut off dead flower heads	Take root cuttings in March
Catmint *see* Nepeta						
Centaurea dealbata Knapweed	Thistle-like flowers and jagged grey-green leaves, yet not weed-like in appearance or habit. A fine border plant	H:45cm (1½ft) S:30cm (1ft)	June–Aug.	A fertile, well-drained soil in a sunny position suits these plants	Lift and divide every four years. Young growths may need support	Divide established plants in March
C. macrocephala	Beautiful golden yellow flowers like large cornflowers in shape, on branching stems. Last well when cut	H:1.2m (4ft) S:75cm (2½ft)	June–Aug.	As *C. dealbata*	As *C. dealbata*	As *C. dealbata*
Chalk plant *see* Gypsophila						
Chamomile, ox-eye *see* Anthemis tinctoria						
Chelone oblique	Dense, bushy plant with spikes of deep rose flowers. Stiff stems and deep green pointed leaves	H:60cm (2ft) S:45cm (1½ft)	Aug.–Oct.	Plant in light, well-drained soil, in full sun or partial shade	May need support of small twigs in exposed, windy places	Divide plant from Sept. to March, when weather is suitable
Christmas rose *see* Helleborus niger						
Chrysanthemum maximum Shasta daisy	Well-known plant with large white daisy flowers. 'Esther Read' (double, white) and 'Wirral Supreme' (large double white) are good cultivars	H:90cm (3ft) S:45cm (1½ft)	July–Sept.	Best in well-drained soil in a sunny position	Divide clumps after three years	Divide established plants in spring
Cimicifuga racemosa Bugbane	A distinctive plant with slender spires of creamy-white flowers towering over the foliage	H:1.2m (4ft) S:30cm (1ft)	Aug.–Sept.	Provide a lightly shaded position and good, fertile soil. Shelter is beneficial	In exposed sites the plants will require stakes. Topdress with peat or leafmould in March	Divide established plants from Oct. to March, whenever weather permits
Cinquefoil *see* Potentilla						
Columbine *see* Aquilegia						
Convallaria majalis Lily-of-the-valley	Exquisitely scented white flowers, and pale green foliage	H:15cm (6in) S:7.5cm (3in)	April–May	Grow in partial shade in peaty soil. The plants require ample moisture in spring	Plant crowns in Sept., 10cm (4in) apart and just below surface	Divide crowns in Sept.

Name	Description	Height/spread	Flowering period	Soil and site	Remarks	Propagation
Coreopsis verticillata 'Grandiflora'	An attractive plant with small starry, rich yellow flowers that last for many weeks	H:60cm (2ft) S:30cm (1ft)	July–Sept.	Fertile, well-drained soil is advisable. Not suitable for heavy, sticky soil	Trouble-free plants	Divide established plants in spring
Cortaderia selloana (syn. C. argentea) Pampas grass	An impressive grass with large silvery plumes held on very rigid stems	H:1.5m (5ft) S:90cm (3ft)	Aug.–Oct.	Grows best in fertile, well-drained soil in a sunny, sheltered position	Plant in April. Wear gloves when handling the plant as the leaf edges are sharp	Divide established plants in April
Cranesbill see Geranium sanguineum						
Cupid's dart see Catananche caerulea 'Major'						
Day lily see Hemerocallis						
Delphinium (garden hybrids)	Popular plants that need no introduction. There are many good cultivars, such as 'Ann Page' (semi-double, cornflower blue), 'Black Knight' (dark blue), 'King Arthur' (purple, with white eye) and 'Startling' (deep violet, white eye)	H:1.8m (6ft) S:75–90cm (2½–3ft)	June–Aug.	Best in deep fertile soil in a sunny position. Select a site in a position sheltered from strong winds	Staking is essential. After flowering, cut the stems back to soil level. Protect from slugs	Take cuttings 7.5–10cm (3–4in) long in April. Insert in equal parts peat and sand in a cold-frame. Divide established plants in spring. Some strains, such as 'Pacific Giants' can be raised from seed
Dianthus caryophyllus Carnation	Popular flowers, the type mentioned here being the hardy border carnations. Typical cultivars are 'Cherry Clove' (strongly scented, cherry red), 'Robin Thain' (white flecked crimson), 'Spindrift' (white), and 'Sunray' (yellow)	H:23cm (9in) S:30cm (1ft)	Sept.	Good drainage and a sunny site are both necessary. Appreciate lime in the soil	Support with split bamboo canes or wire hoops. Plant in March or Sept.	Layer the stems in July or Aug.
Dicentra spectabilis Bleeding heart	Drooping cascades of heart-shaped rosy-red flowers with white inner petals. Attractive, fern-like foliage	H:60cm (2ft) S:45cm (1½ft)	May–June	Requires a rich, well-drained soil, with plenty of peat or leafmould. Provide a sheltered position	Trouble-free, self-supporting plants	Divide established plants in spring
Doronicum 'Harpur Crewe' Leopard's-bane	Rayed, daisy-like bright yellow flowers, good for cutting. A particularly useful plant for early flower	H:90cm (3ft) S:60cm (2ft)	April–May	A rich soil in partial shade suits these plants. The soil should not dry out	In exposed places staking may be necessary. Cut down in autumn	Divide established plants in autumn or spring
Echinacea purpurea (syn. Rudbeckia purpurea) Purple cone flower	A distinctive herbaceous plant with large, magenta-purple rayed flowers, having dark centres, drooping petals	H:90cm (3ft) S:75cm (2½ft)	July–Sept.	A fertile, well-drained soil in a sunny position should be provided	Support the plants with twigs. Cut down to soil level in autumn	Divide established plants in autumn or spring
Echinops ritro Globe thistle	Attractive grey-green leaves and steel-blue spherical flower heads borne on upright rigid stems	H:1m (1½ft) S:60cm (2ft)	July–Aug.	Ordinary, well-drained soil is suitable, preferably in full sun	A trouble-free plant requiring no staking	Divide established plants in autumn or spring. Can also be raised from seed

Below: Aquilegia *(columbine)* 'Long-spurred Hybrids'. *Below right:* Dicentra spectabilis *(bleeding heart)*

Hardy border plants

Name	Description	Height/spread	Flowering period	Soil and site	Remarks	Propagation
Elephant's ears see Bergenia cordifolia						
Epimedium grandiflorum Barrenwort	A useful ground-cover plant; practically evergreen foliage with pleasant spring and autumn tints	H:25cm (10in) S:30cm (1ft)	April–May	Best in a light, sandy soil in partial shade	Mulch in spring and ensure the ground does not dry out	Divide established plants in autumn or spring
Eremurus robustus Foxtail lily	A really large border plant with massive spikes of starry pale pink flowers. There are also hybrids that can be raised from seed: these tend to be less full	H:1.8–2.4m (6–8ft) S:1–1.2m (3½–4ft)	May–June	Moist, well-drained loam is ideal, in a sunny, sheltered position	Once established, do not disturb unnecessarily. Mulch in spring	Divide established plants in autumn or spring. Some hybrids can be raised from seed
Erigeron (garden hybrids) Fleabane	Like a low-growing and summer-flowering Michaelmas daisy. Cultivars include 'Amity' (lilac-pink), 'Charity' (clear pink), and 'Darkest of All' (violet-blue)	H:60cm (2ft) S:45cm (1½ft)	June–Aug.	Best in moist, well-drained soil in full sun	Trouble-free plants for the front of the border	Divide established plants in spring or autumn
Eryngium × oliverianum Sea holly	Attractive, jagged-edged leaves. Bright blue teasel-like flower heads. Excellent dried for winter decoration	H:90cm (3ft) S:75cm (2½ft)	June–Aug.	Provide a well-drained soil in full sun	Twiggy sticks may be necessary for support. Cut down to ground level in autumn	Take root cuttings in Feb., inserting in boxes of peat-sand mixture and placing in a cold-frame
Eupatorium purpureum Joe-pye weed	Tall, clustered heads of purple-crimson flowers borne on strong stems. The dull green foliage provides good contrast	H:1.5m (5ft) S:90cm (3ft)	Aug.–Sept.	Ordinary garden soil is suitable, in sun or partial shade	Ensure the soil is kept moist. Cut foliage down to ground in autumn	Divide established clumps in Oct. or March
Euphorbia polychroma Spurge	A gay little plant with bright yellow bracts. The foliage, though individual leaves are small, is dense, and a good ground cover	H:45cm (1½ft) S:45cm (1½ft)	April–May	Requires a sunny, well-drained position	Cut the plant down to soil level in autumn	Take cuttings 7.5cm (3in) long in April, and root in a peat-sand mixture in a cold-frame
Evening primrose see Oenothera						
Flax see Linum narbonense						
Fleabane see Erigeron						
Foxtail lily see Eremurus robustus						
Gaillardia Blanket flower	Large daisy-like flowers, good for cutting or garden display. 'Croftway Yellow' is a bright yellow, growing to 35cm (14in), while 'Mandarin' is an orange-flame that reaches 90cm (3ft). Spread is about 30cm (1ft) for both	See description	June–Aug.	Light, well-drained soil in a sunny position suits these plants	Remove dead heads. Tall kinds may need support	Take cuttings or sow seeds in May or June. Some hybrid strains can be grown from seed
Gay feather see Liatris spicata						
Geranium Cranesbill	A valuable group of plants for the herbaceous border. Of the many kinds, two good ones are 'Johnson's Blue' (cup-shaped, bright blue flowers, H:30cm/1ft, S:30cm/1ft) and 'Russell Prichard' (rich rose flowers, H:30cm/1ft, S:30cm/1ft). Other kinds may grow to 90cm (3ft)	See description	May–Aug.	Best if provided with well-drained soil in sun or partial shade	A trouble-free plant	Divide established plants in autumn or spring
Geum	Bright flowers carried well clear of strawberry-like leaves. The two most popular cultivars are 'Mrs. Bradshaw' (semi-double, crimson) and 'Lady Stratheden' (double, yellow)	H:60cm (2ft) S:45cm (1½ft)	June–Aug.	A rich, moist but well-drained soil is preferred. Plant in sun or partial shade	Mulch with peat or leafmould in spring	Divide established plants in spring. Easily raised from seed sown in spring or summer
Globe flower see Trollius						
Globe thistle see Echinops ritro						
Goat's beard see Aruncus dioicus						
Golden rod see Solidago						
Gypsophila 'Bristol Fairy' Chalk plant	Small, semi-double white flowers are borne in a shimmering mass. There is also a pink form	H:90cm (3ft) S:60cm (2ft)	June–July	Requires a well-drained soil in a sunny position	Support young growth with twiggy sticks	Divide established plants in spring. Some forms can also be raised from seed

Name	Description	Height/spread	Flowering period	Soil and site	Remarks	Propagation
Helenium	Showy border plants with rayed flowers in shades of yellow, orange and red, according to cultivar	H:60–90cm (2–3ft) S:45–60cm (1½–2ft)	July–Aug.	Ordinary garden soil is adequate, preferably in full sun	Support with twiggy sticks, especially in exposed positions	Divide established plants in Oct. or March
Helianthus 'Loddon Gold' Perennial sunflower	A double, golden-yellow perennial sunflower, which puts up a barrage of spectacular flowers high above the foliage	H:1.5m (5ft) S:1m (3½ft)	Aug.–Sept.	Best in well-drained soil in full sun	May require support, especially in exposed places	Divide established plants in Oct. or April
Heliopsis scabra 'Golden Plume'	Spear-shaped leaves and glorious double yellow flowers which are excellent as cut flowers or for garden decoration	H:1.2m (4ft) S:90cm (3ft)	July–Sept.	Ordinary garden soil is suitable, in a sunny position	Cut flowered stems to ground level in autumn	Divide established plants between Oct. and March
Helleborus niger	A popular winter-flowering plant with open white flowers carried on short, branched stems	H:30cm (1ft) S:30cm (1ft)	Dec.–March	Deep, well-drained soil in partial shade is necessary	Do not disturb once established. Keep moist in summer. Blooms can be protected with a cloche	Divide established plants in March or April. Can also be raised from seed sown in late summer in boxes and exposed to winter frosts
H. orientalis Lenten rose	Similar to Christmas rose. Flowers vary from white to purple	H:30cm (1ft) S:30cm (1ft)	Feb.–April	As *H. niger*	As *H. niger*	As *H. niger*
Hemerocallis (garden hybrids) Day lily	A succession of lily-like flowers produced over a long period. There is a wide colour range. Representative cultivars are 'Black Magic' (ruby and purple), 'Buzz Bomb' (velvety-red), 'Fandango' (rich orange)	H:60–90cm (2–3ft) S:45cm (1½ft)	June–Sept.	Provide good garden soil in a sunny or partially shaded position	These plants dislike root disturbance	Divide established plants in Oct. or April
Heuchera Alum root	Slender stems of tiny bell-shaped flowers, carried well clear of neat basal leaves. There are many fine hybrids, mainly in shades of pink or red	H:45cm (1½ft) S:30cm (1ft)	June–Sept.	Requires a well-drained soil in sun or partial shade	Mulch annually. Divide every four years	Lift and divide old plants. Can also be raised from seed
Incarvillea delavayi Trumpet flower	Gloxinia-like rose-carmine flowers 5–7.5cm (2–3in) long and wide, and foliage resembling that of mountain ash	H:60cm (2ft) S:45cm (1½ft)	June–July	Rich, well-drained soil in full sun is required	Set the fleshy crowns just below the surface in March or April. Mulch annually	Established plants can be divided in autumn, but stock is best raised from seed

Below: Helleborus niger. *Below right:* Iris *'Braithwaite', one of the flag or German irises*

Hardy border plants

Name	Description	Height/spread	Flowering period	Soil and site	Remarks	Propagation
Inula magnifica	A very large plant, bearing hoary leaves and sturdy flower stems with bright yellow daisy-like blooms	H:1.8m (6ft) S:90cm (3ft)	July–Aug.	Best in a moisture-retentive soil in full sun	Ensure that the plants do not become dry	Divide established plants in March
Iris (flag or German type)	The well-known flag, or bearded, irises as they are sometimes known, need no introduction. There are now many superb cultivars, examples being 'Berkeley Gold' (rich yellow), 'Braithwaite' (lavender standards, purple falls), 'Jane Phillips' (flax blue), 'Pearly Dawn' (pink), 'The Rocket' (orange-chrome), and 'Violet Symphony' (violet)	H:90cm (3ft) S:45cm (1½ft)	May–June	A well-drained, sunny position is ideal. Lime is appreciated	Plant in late June or early July, with the rhizomes just below the surface (do not bury deeply — the tops should almost be showing). Divide clumps after four years, discard the inner portions and replant the outer fans	Divide old clumps immediately after flowering
Jacob's ladder see Polemonium foliosissimum						
Japanese anemone see Anemone × hybrida						
Joe-pye weed see Eupatorium purpureum						
Knapweed see Centaurea dealbata						
Kniphofia (garden hybrids) (syn. Tritoma) Red hot poker	A familiar flower, with stiff spikes in shades of glowing orange, red or yellow	H:1–1.2m (3½–4ft) S:45cm (1½ft)	June–July	Any good soil in full sun will suit provided it does not become waterlogged	Plant in Sept. or Oct. Mulch in spring	Divide established plants in April
Lady's mantle see Alchemilla mollis						
Lenten rose see Helleborus orientalis						
Leopard's-bane see Doronicum						
Liatris spicata Gay feather	Rigid spikes of rosy-purple flowers opening from the top. An impressive plant and a good cut flower	H:90cm (3ft) S:30cm (1ft)	Aug.–Sept.	Best in well-drained soil in full sun	Remove dead flower heads after blooming	Divide established plants in April. Sow seed in summer
Ligularia dentata (syn. L. clivorum, Senecio clivorum)	'Desdemona' is the one to grow. It has large, vivid orange daisy-like heads and large leaves flushed purple	H:1.2m (4ft) S:90cm (3ft)	July–Sept.	A moist, deeply-cultivated soil is best in full sun	Early growth may require support and protection from winds	Divide established plants in April
Lily-of-the-valley see Convallaria majalis						
Limonium latifolium Sea lavender, statice	Forms a rosette of mid-green leaves and throws up sprays of lavender-blue flowers. Retains colour when cut and dried	H:60cm (2ft) S:45cm (1½ft)	July–Sept.	Enjoys well-drained soil in a sunny position	Plant in March or April. Cut down to soil level in Oct.	Divide established plants in April. Can also be raised from seed
Linum narbonense Flax	Brilliant blue flowers that last for many weeks are carried above narrow, grey-green leaves	H:45cm (1½ft) S:30cm (1ft)	June–Sept.	Ordinary garden soil in full sun produces the best results	Plant March, April or Oct. Cut off dead growth in Nov.	Take cuttings of soft basal shoots in April, rooting in a peat-sand mixture in a cold-frame. Also very easy from seed
Loosestrife, dotted see Lysimachia punctata						
Lupin see Lupinus						
Lupinus (garden hybrids) Lupin	Too well known to need detailed description. Excellent mixtures can be raised from seed, or named cultivars propagated vegetatively	H:60–90cm (2–3ft) S:45–60cm (1½–2ft)	June–July	A light soil in full sun or partial shade is best. Avoid rich soil	Remove dead spikes after flowering	Take cuttings of named cultivars in March or April, and root in a cold-frame. Sow seed in spring or summer
Lychnis chalcedonica Maltese cross	A spectacular plant with heads of brilliant scarlet flowers, shaped like a Maltese Cross. The leaves are mid-green	H:90cm (3ft) S:45cm (1½ft)	June–Aug.	Ordinary garden soil in full sun or partial shade suits these plants	Support young growth with twigs. Mulch with peat or compost in spring	Easily raised from seed, or by division. Cuttings 2.5–5cm (1–2in) long can be taken in April and rooted in a cold-frame
Lysimachia punctata Dotted loosestrife	A well-known border plant with whorls of bright yellow flowers on upright spikes above mid-green leaves	H:90cm (3ft) S:45cm (1½ft)	June–Aug.	A moist soil in full sun or partial shade suits these plants	Cut back to ground level in autumn	Divide established plants in spring or autumn. Can also be raised from seed
Macleaya cordata (syn. Bocconia cordata) Plume poppy	Creamy-white, 12mm (½in) long flowers are carried in sprays above lobed, glaucous leaves	H:1.2m (4ft) S:90cm (3ft)	Aug.–Sept.	Requires a deep soil in a sunny but sheltered position	Support young growth with twiggy sticks	Divide established plants from Oct. to April
Maltese cross see Lychnis chalcedonica						

Name	Description	Height/spread	Flowering period	Soil and site	Remarks	Propagation
Masterwort *see* Astrantia maxima						
Meadow rue *see* Thalictrum dipterocarpum						
Mertensia virginica Virginian cowslip	An unusual plant for the front of a border. Drooping clusters of purple-blue bells. Foliage dies down in July	H:45cm (1½ft) S:30cm (1ft)	April—June	Requires a moist, rich soil, preferably in shade or partial shade	For best results, lift and replant every three or four years	Divide established plants in March or Oct.
Michaelmas daisy *see* Aster novi-belgii						
Monarda didyma Bergamot	Flowers are produced in dense whorls on top of stems standing clear of the foliage. In shades of red, pink, purple and white	H:90cm (3ft) S:60cm (2ft)	July—Sept.	Moist, well-cultivated fertile soil in full sun or partial shade is best	Mulch with compost in spring. Can be invasive	Divide established plants in March or April. Can also be raised from seed
Monkshood *see* Aconitum						
Morina longifolia Whorl flower	An attractive plant forming a rosette of spiny toothed leaves and whorled spikes of white or rose flowers	H:75cm (2½ft) S:45cm (1½ft)	June—Sept.	Best in well-drained soil and a sunny position. Avoid a windy site	In cold winters, protect the roots with a layer of peat or bracken	Sow seed in Sept. or April, in a cold-frame
Mullein *see* Verbascum						
Nepeta Catmint	An excellent plant for the front of an herbaceous border, with attractive grey-green foliage and masses of lavender-blue flowers. There is often confusion over names — N. × faassenii is a plant of about 30cm (1ft) height and spread, but is often sold as N. mussinii. The true N. mussinii is a larger plant reaching 1m (3½ft)	See description	May—Sept.	A well-drained soil in a sunny or partially shaded position is necessary	Cut the plants down to soil level in autumn	Divide established plants in April. Can also be grown from seed
Obedient plant *see* Physostegia virginiana						

Below: Lupinus (lupin), garden hybrids

Hardy border plants

Name	Description	Height/ spread	Flowering period	Soil and site	Remarks	Propagation
Oenothera tetragona 'Highlight' Evening primrose	An erect plant with shiny leaves and masses of wide, bright yellow, saucer-shaped flowers	H:60cm (2ft) S:30cm (1ft)	June–Aug.	Best on light soil in full sun	Water freely in dry weather. Cut to ground in autumn	Divide established plants in April
Omphalodes cappadocica	A low-growing plant useful as a ground cover in shade. Bright blue forget-me-not flowers cover the plants in spring	H:15cm (6in) S:30cm (1ft)	April–May	Peaty, moist soil in a shaded position is essential	Remove faded flowers. Water freely in hot weather	Divide established plants in April
Paeonia (garden hybrids) Peony	Spectacular plants with flowers like large, full, roses. There are many cultivars, in shades of pink and red as well as white	H:75–90cm (2½–3ft) S:60cm (2ft)	June–July	Require a moist, well-drained soil in sun or partial shade. A rich soil is essential	Mulch in spring. Support plants with stakes	Divide established plants in Sept.
Pampas grass *see* Cortaderia selloana						
Papaver orientale Oriental poppy	Exceptionally large blooms, like large open poppies. There are several named cultivars in shades of red, pink and white	H:30–90cm (1–3ft) S:30–60cm (1–2ft)	May–June	Prefer a well-drained soil in full sun	Stake young growth. Remove all dead flowers	Divide established plants in spring. Can be raised from seed
Penstemon barbatus (syn. Chelone barbata)	Tubular red or pink flowers hang from tapering spikes. Lance-shaped mid-green leaves are a useful foil	H:90cm (3ft) S:45cm (1½ft)	June–Sept.	Best in well-drained soil in full sun	Plant in March or April. May need some protection during winter	Take cuttings 7.5cm (3in) long in Sept., and root in a cold-frame. Can also be raised from seed
Peony *see* Paeonia						
Peruvian lily *see* Alstroemeria						
Phlox paniculata (garden hybrids) (syn. P. decussata)	Well-known border plants. Typical cultivars are 'Dorothy Hanbury Forbes' (clear pink), 'Endurance' (salmon-orange), 'Prospero' (pale lilac), 'Toits de Paris' (lavender-blue), and 'White Admiral' (white)	H:90cm (3ft) S:45cm (1½ft)	July–Sept.	A fertile, moisture-retentive soil in sun or partial shade is required for good results	Mulch annually in March or April. Water freely in dry weather on light soils. Stake with twiggy sticks.	Divide established plants in Oct. or April
Physostegia virginiana 'Vivid' Obedient plant	A useful plant for late colour. Rose-lilac tubular flowers are carried on stiff stems. Another common name is obedient plant, because individual flowers tend to remain in the position they are turned	H:60cm (2ft) S:30cm (1ft)	Aug.–Nov.	Grows well in any ordinary soil, in sun or partial shade	Tends to be invasive. Water and mulch in dry weather in summer	Divide established plants in Oct. or April
Platycodon grandiflorus Balloon flower	'Mariesii' is a beautiful plant with glaucous foliage and large, cup-like flowers in shades of blue	H:45cm (1½ft) S:30cm (1ft)	July–Sept.	Best in well-drained soil and full sun	Once established, do not disturb unnecessarily	Divide established plants in April. Very easily raised from seed
Plume poppy *see* Macleaya cordata						
Polemonium foliosissimum Jacob's ladder	A leafy plant with spectacular clusters of mauve-blue flowers produced over a long period	H:75cm (2½ft) S:30cm (1ft)	June–Sept.	Ordinary garden soil in sun or partial shade is suitable	Cut off all dead flowers	Divide established plants from Oct. to April, whenever weather is suitable
Polygonatum multiflorum Solomon's seal	Arching sprays of dangling white bells from leafy stems. The plant usually sold is a hybrid form (sometimes listed as *P. × hybridum*)	H:75cm (2½ft) S:60cm (2ft)	May–June	A useful shade-loving plant that will grow in any well-drained soil	Mulch in spring with peat or well-rotted compost	Divide established plants in Oct. or April
Polygonum affine	An invaluable carpeter, forming a mat of narrow leaves which become coppery in autumn. Small spikes of pink flowers	H:15–25cm (6–10in) S:25cm+ (10in+)	June–Sept.	Best in a rich, moist, fertile soil, in sun or partial shade	Young plants must not be allowed to become dry at the roots	Divide established plants in Oct. or April
Potentilla atrosanguinea Cinquefoil	Not to be confused with the shrubby potentillas, the herbaceous type die down in winter. They are free-flowering, trouble-free plants. 'Gibson's Scarlet' has brilliant single red flowers	H:45cm (1½ft) S:30cm (1ft)	June–Aug.	Ordinary garden soil in full sun is suitable	Mulch in spring, and water well if weather is dry	Divide established plants in Oct. or April
Purple cone flower *see* Echinacea purpurea						
Pyrethrum (garden hybrids)	Large, colourful daisy-like flowers, excellent for cutting. There are many cultivars, in shades of pink, red, white	H:75cm (2½ft) S:45cm (1½ft)	May–July	Best in light, well-drained soil and full sun	Stake with twiggy sticks. Do not let young plants dry out	Divide established plants in April. Can also be raised from seed

Name	Description	Height/spread	Flowering period	Soil and site	Remarks	Propagation
Red hot poker *see* Kniphofia						
Salvia × superba	An attractive plant with branching spires of violet-purple flowers. Makes an effective and bold display	H:90cm (3ft) S:60cm (2ft)	July–Sept.	Will thrive on ordinary well-drained soil in full sun	Mulch with well-rotted compost in spring	Divide established clumps in autumn or spring
Scabiosa caucasia Scabious	'Clive Greaves' has large mauve, 'pincushion' flower heads, useful for cutting. 'Miss Willmott' is white	H:75cm (2½ft) S:45cm (1½ft)	June–Sept.	Rich, well-drained soil in sun or partial shade is necessary for good results	Regular cutting will encourage further flowering	Divide established plants in March or April. Can also be raised from seed
Sea holly *see* Eryngium × oliverianum						
Sea lavender *see* Limonium latifolium						
Sedum spectabile	An excellent plant, providing colour at a useful time. Fleshy leaves are topped with flat heads of long-lasting flowers, in pink or red	H:30–60cm (1–2ft) S:30–45cm (1–1½ft)	Aug.–Oct.	Ordinary, well-drained soil in full sun is suitable	Remove the dead flower heads in spring	Divide established plants in autumn or spring
Shasta daisy *see* Chrysanthemum maximum						
Sidalcea	A first-class plant bearing tall spires of attractive mallow-like pink flowers. The leaves form a neat basal clump. Cultivars include 'Pink Pinnacle' (clear pink), 'Rose Queen' (clear rose), and 'William Smith' (salmon)	H:1.2m (4ft) S:60cm (2ft)	June–Aug.	Ordinary garden soil in full sun is suitable	Cut flowering stems down to 30cm (1ft) immediately after blooming. Staking may be necessary	Divide established plants in spring. Can also be grown from seed
Solidago (dwarf hybrids) Golden rod	Improved forms of the old golden rod. Plumes of golden flowers. Cultivars include 'Cloth of Gold' (deep yellow), and 'Goldenmosa' (golden yellow)	H:45–75cm (1½–2½ft) S:30–60cm (1–2ft)	Aug.–Sept.	Thrives in ordinary garden soil in full sun or partial shade	Support young growth with twiggy sticks	Divide established plants in autumn or early spring. Can also be grown from seed, but use division for named kinds
Solomon's seal *see* Polygonatum multiflorum						
Spurge *see* Euphorbia						
Statice *see* Limonium						
Stokesia laevis 'Blue Star' Stoke's aster	A choice border plant displaying large, lavender-blue cornflower-like flowers in late summer	H:45cm (1½ft) S:30cm (1ft)	July–Sept.	Requires light, well-drained soil in full sun or partial shade	Plant in April. Support with twiggy sticks	Divide old plants in March or April
Sunflower, perennial *see* Helianthus						
Thalictrum dipterocarpum Meadow rue	A handsome plant with large sprays of dainty foliage, and a profusion of lavender, yellow-centred flowers on rather lanky stems. 'Album' has white flowers, and 'Hewitt's Double' has fully double mauve flowers	H:1.2–1.8m (4–6ft) S:60–75cm (2–2½ft)	July–Aug.	A rich, moist soil, in sun or partial shade, is necessary for best results	Stake early, and mulch with peat or well-rotted compost in spring	Divide established plants in spring
Trollius Globe flower	Ideal plants for a moist situation or by the waterside; they have large buttercup-like flowers in yellow	H:45–60cm (1½–2ft) S:45cm (1½ft)	May–June	A moist soil in full sun or partial shade is best	Keep young plants well watered	Divide established plants in autumn or spring. Can be grown from seed, but germination is slow and erratic
Trumpet flower *see* Incarvillea delavayi						
Verbascum × hybridum Mullein	Felted, silvery leaves and tall spires of flowers. Good cultivars are 'Cotswold Queen' (buff, purple, orange shades), 'Gainsborough' (yellow) and 'Pink Domino' (rose)	H:1.2m (4ft) S:60cm (2ft)	June–Aug.	A well-drained site in full sun is necessary for these plants	A trouble-free plant, apart from self-sown seedlings	Root cuttings 7.5 (3in) long can be taken in Feb. and rooted in a cold-frame. Named forms may not come true from seed
Veronica spicata	Plants of neat habit, with tapestry spikes of blue, pink or white flowers	H:38cm (15in) S:30cm (1ft)	July–Sept.	Well-drained but moisture-retentive soil is ideal, in full sun or partial shade	Easy, well-behaved plants to grow towards the front of a border	Divide established plants in March or April
Virginian cowslip *see* Mertensia virginica						
White mugwort *see* Artemesia lactiflora						
Whorl flower *see* Morina longifolia						
Yarrow *see* Achillea						

Bulbs

Bulbs are the most accommodating and diverse of plants, and there is hardly anywhere in a garden that is not suitable for one sort or another. Even in shade under a north wall or under trees, winter aconites, bluebells and snowdrops thrive. And although usually thought of principally as flowering in spring, there is seldom a month when bulbs are not in bloom.

A true bulb is made up of thickened leaves, hopefully with an embryo flower bud inside. Corms, such as crocuses and gladioli, consist of modified stems. Tubers are composed of thickened underground roots, anemones and winter aconites being examples. All three kinds of storage organs are included in the following tables, as all are commonly referred to as bulbs, and are available from bulb merchants.

Almost all plants grown from bulbs, corms and tubers have a resting period when their foliage dies down. Some prefer to be dug up, dried off and stored in net bags or old stockings, in a cool, frost-free, dry and airy place until replanting shortly before growth recommences. This technique suits hyacinths and tulips, other than the small species, and most summer-flowering bulbs that die down in autumn.

Tulips, ideal for spring bedding, can be planted in masses by themselves, or among wallflowers, forget-me-nots, double daisies or polyanthus. As hyacinth bulbs are expensive and their flower heads are easily knocked down by rain, they are more popular in tubs and windowboxes.

After flowering, tulips and hyacinths can be moved to make room for summer bedding plants. The bulbs should be dug up with their leaves intact and replanted into shallow trenches until their top growth dies down and they can be stored.

Bulbs that remain in the ground for several years save work, but their foliage must not be cut off until it turns yellow, generally in late May with crocuses, for example, and early July with daffodils. Siting groups close to edges of lawns, around trees, or on hedge banks, allows most of the grass to be mown. Bulbs particularly suitable for naturalizing in this way include daffodils, chionodoxa, winter aconites and *Fritillaria meleagris*. Bulbs can be planted with a trowel or bulb-planter, which acts rather like an apple corer. If being planted in grass, an H-shaped cut can be made in the turf, slicing under it with a spade and rolling it back in opposite directions from the centre. The bulbs are then planted and the turf replaced. Planting depths in the tables are the depth above the top of the bulb.

Fertilizers should be applied only in moderation. Bulbs will grow in almost any soil, but to keep them flowering, naturalized bulbs need a scattering of bonemeal every winter. Those not set in grass should have a mulch of peat or leafmould.

Name	Description	Height/ spread	Flowering period	Soil and site	Remarks	Propagation
Allium	There are many good species, including *A. aflatunense* (star-shaped pink flowers, useful for flower arrangements; 75cm/2½ft; May, June), *A. flavum* (yellow flowers; 25cm/10in; July and Aug.), *A. giganteum* (lilac star-shaped flower heads, 10cm/4in wide: 90cm/3ft; June), *A. moly* (compact heads of yellow flowers, nice in a shrubbery or naturalized in grass; 25cm/10in; June), and *A. oreophilum* (rose-coloured flowers, and a nice rock garden plant; 25cm/10in; June). All have narrow grass-like leaves	H:15–90cm (6in–3ft) S:23–30cm (9–12in)	April–Aug.	Will grow in most soils, but do best on well-drained sandy ground. Full sun is essential for good results	Plant in Sept. or Oct., three times the depth of the bulb. Dead-head the flowers and remove dead foliage in autumn	Sow seed soon after ripening, or divide clumps in autumn or spring. Do not allow lifted bulbs to dry out; keep moist and replant directly
Amaryllis belladona Belladona lily	Strong stems are topped by three or four large, rosy or salmon-pink trumpet-shaped flowers; the leaves develop later	H:60cm (2ft) S:30cm (1ft)	Sept.	Hardy against a south-facing wall despite its sub-tropical appearance. Requires well-drained soil	Plant in June or July, 15–20cm (6–8in) deep. Stake if necessary. Remove dead heads and cut down stems in autumn. Leave undisturbed	Sow seed in March in a greenhouse, or lift mature clumps in late summer and replant divided pieces
Anemone coronaria Windflower	Excellent cut flowers, and popular florists' plants. De Caen type are the single poppy anemones, and St. Brigid the double and semi-double kind. By sowing in succession and providing protection, can be flowered over a long period	H:23cm (9in) S:10cm (4in)	Feb.–Oct.	A fertile, well-drained but moisture-retentive soil is required. Full sun is best but they will grow in partial shade	Plant 4–5cm (1½–2in) deep in Sept. or Oct.	Divide and replant established clumps between Oct. and March, whenever the weather permits
Angel's tears *see* Narcissus triandus						
Autumn crocus *see* Colchicum autumnale						
Bear grass *see* Camassia leichtlinii						
Belladona lily *see* Amaryllis belladona						
Bluebell *see* Scilla non-scripta						
Bluebell, giant *see* Scilla hispanica						

Name	Description	Height/spread	Flowering period	Soil and site	Remarks	Propagation
Brodiaea laxa *see* Triteleia laxa						
Californian lily *see* Lilium pardalinum						
Camassia leichtlinii Bear grass	One of the best camassias, bearing spires of 4cm (1½in) blue or white flowers. The leaves are long and strap-like	H:90cm (3ft) S:45cm (1½ft)	June–July	Prefers a heavy, moist soil that does not dry out, especially in spring. Sun or semi-shade	Plant in Sept. or Oct., 7.5–10cm (3–4in) deep. Remove dead flower heads	Remove offsets in Sept. and replant them directly
Cape lily *see* Crinum × powellii						
Cardiocrinum giganteum (syn. Lilium giganteum)	Large funnel-shaped flowers, white on the inside with red markings, green on the outside. Fragrant	H:1.8–3m (6–10ft) S:90cm (3ft)	June–Aug.	Requires well-drained fertile soil in light shade	Plant in Oct., 15–20cm (6–8in) deep. Plant dies after flowering, but small bulbs grow from around it and flower after four or five years	After flowering lift the bulbs and plant in a nursery bed for about four years, until they reach flowering size
Chincherinchee *see* Ornithogalum thyrsoides						
Chionodoxa luciliae Glory of the snow	Attractive vivid blue flowers with a beautiful white eye, carried in dainty sprays	H:15cm (6in) S:10cm (4in)	Feb.–March	Ordinary well-drained soil is adequate, in full sun	Plant in autumn, 5–7.5cm (2–3in) deep, in groups	Lift and divide overcrowded groups in Sept. Sow seed in late spring in a cold-frame
Colchicum autumnale Autumn crocus	Small, lavender-coloured blooms in autumn. A white form is *C. a.* 'Album'	H:15cm (6in) S:23cm (9in)	Sept.–Nov.	Plant near the front of a border in well-drained soil. Will be happy in sun or semi-shade	Plant 7.5–10cm (3–4in) deep in Aug. or Sept., in small groups	Divide old clumps in July or Aug., or sow seed in a cold-frame in June
C. byzantinum Meadow saffron	A free-flowering plant with pale lilac-pink crocus-like flowers 10–13cm (4–5in) deep. Attractive planted in grass or beneath tall trees	H:30cm (1ft) S:23cm (9in)	Sept.	As *C. autumnale*	As *C. autumnale*	Divide established clumps in July or Aug.
C. speciosum Meadow saffron	A beautiful autumn-flowering bulb with amethyst-violet flowers. There is also a white form, *C. s.* 'Album'	H:15cm (6in) S:23cm (9in)	Oct.–Nov.	As *C. autumnale*	As *C. autumnale*	As *C. autumnale*
Crinum × powellii Cape lily	Although not a true lily, this impressive plant has rosy-pink or white lily-like flowers on stout stems	H:90cm (3ft) S:45cm (1½ft)	July–Sept.	Requires a rich, well-drained soil, ideally with the protection of a south-facing wall	Plant 25–30cm (10–12in) deep in April or May. Protect young plants from frost and cold winds	Remove offsets in March, pot up and place in a cold-frame
Crocus (large-flowered)	Too well-known to need description. There are many named cultivars, including 'Little Dorrit' (silvery-lilac), 'Queen of the Blues' (lavender-blue), 'Rememberance' (violet-purple with purple base), and 'Yellow Giant' (bright yellow)	H:10cm (4in) S:7.5cm (3in)	March	Will thrive in most soils, but require full sun. Naturalize well in grass	Do not mow grass where bulbs are naturalized until the leaves have died down	Large clumps can be lifted and divided as soon as the foliage has died down
C. chrysanthus	Smaller versions of the more popular large-flowered crocuses, but particularly useful because of their earlier flowering. Good cultivars include 'Blue Pearl' (delicate blue, shading to white), 'E. A. Bowles' (yellow and bronze), and 'Snowbunting' (white)	H:7.5cm (3in) S:5cm (2in)	Feb.	Best in a well-drained soil at the base of a shrub, which will provide some protection for the blooms	Plant the corms 5–7.5cm (2–3in) deep in Sept. or Oct. After flowering allow the foliage to die down naturally	As large-flowered crocuses
C. speciosus	A true autumn crocus (the plants usually called autumn crocuses are colchicums). Lilac-blue flowers with yellow anthers. 'Aitchisonii' bears pale blue flowers, 'Albus' white blooms, and 'Artobir' pale blue flowers	H:13cm (5in) S:10cm (4in)	Sept.–Oct.	As *C. chrysanthus*, but enjoy a sunny position	Plant 5–7.5cm (2–3in) deep in Aug. or Sept. Allow foliage to wither naturally	As large-flowered crocuses
Crown imperial *see* Fritillaria imperialis						
Cyclamen coum (syn. *C. vernum*)	A valuable miniature cyclamen flowering over the winter period. Pink to carmine, also white	H:7.5cm (3in) S:13cm (5in)	Dec.–March	Provide a rich, free-draining soil, shaded from direct sun and protected from cold winds	Plant in Sept. or Oct., setting the corms 4–5cm (1½–2in) deep. Mulch annually with peat in spring	Sow seed in Sept. in pots in a cold-frame
C. purpurascens (syn. *C. europaeum*)	A charming small cyclamen with fragrant vivid crimson flowers. Mid-green marbled leaves	H:10cm (4in) S:13cm (5in)	July–Sept.	As *C. coum*	As *C. coum*	As *C. coum*

Bulbs

Name	Description	Height/spread	Flowering period	Soil and site	Remarks	Propagation
C. hederifolium (syn. C. neapolitanum)	Similar to above. Mauve to pale pink, also white	H:10cm (4in) S:13cm (5in)	Aug.– Nov.	As *C. coum*	As *C. coum*	As *C. coum*
Daffodil *see* Narcissus						
Dog's tooth violet *see* Erythronium dens-canis						
Endymion *see* Scilla						
Eranthis hyemalis Winter aconite	An extremely hardy plant, with distinctive lemon-yellow flowers surrounded by a deep green ruff. A group will form an eye-catching clump	H:10cm (4in) S:7.5cm (3in)	Feb.– March	A well-drained but moisture-retentive soil is best. Plant among shrubs where the flowers will receive some protection	Set the tubers 2.5cm (1in) deep as soon as they are available in early autumn	Divide the tubers from old, established clumps when the plants die down in late summer. Large tubers can be broken up into smaller pieces
Erythronium dens-canis Dog's tooth violet	It is the tubers of this plant that resemble a dog's tooth, not the flowers. The leaves are attractively mottled. Cultivars include 'Snowflake' (white), 'Pink Perfection' (bright shell-pink), and 'Lilac Wonder' (pale purple, blotched brown at the base)	H:15cm (6in) S:10cm (4in)	April– May	Requires a moist soil well enriched with organic matter. A shady, north-facing slope is best	Plant the tubers in late summer, 10– 15cm (4– 6in) deep	Offsets can be removed as the leaves die down, and placed in a nursery bed until large enough to be planted out
Flower of the west wind *see* Zephyranthes candida						
Fritillaria imperialis Crown imperial	Clusters of yellow, bronze or orange flowers like pendent bells are borne atop stout stems, and are crowned with a cluster of green leaves	H:90cm (3ft) S:30cm (1ft)	April	Well-drained fertile soil is essential, in sun or partial shade	Plant the bulbs so that the hollow crowns are on the side and do not collect water. Plant in Sept. Oct. or Nov., 20cm (8in) deep, and surround with coarse sand. Plant as soon as possible after purchase	Divide old clumps after four years, not later than Aug. Offsets can also be grown on in a nursery bed. Seed can be sown in July or Aug. in a cool greenhouse; they will flower after four or five years
F. meleagris Snake head fritillary	Dainty, drooping, bell-shaped blooms on slender stems. Distinctive chequered pattern on the petals. Colours include white, purple and brownish-purple	H:30cm (1ft) S:15cm (6in)	April– May	Does best in moist conditions in a sunny and well-protected border, or in the rock garden	As *F. imperialis* but plant only 10– 15cm (4– 6in) deep	As *F. imperialis*

Below: Crocus *'Little Dorrit'*, *one of the large-flowered crocuses. Below right:* Eranthis hyemalis *(winter aconite)*

Name	Description	Height/ spread	Flowering period	Soil and site	Remarks	Propagation
Galanthus nivalis Snowdrop	Distinctive, nodding white flowers and slightly glaucous strap-shaped leaves. *G. n.* 'Flore-plena' has double flowers. A particularly fine cultivar is 'S. Arnott' (vigorous, flowers 4cm/ 1½in long)	H:10cm (4in) S:10cm (4in)	Jan.–Feb.	Prefers a moisture-retentive soil in slight shade. Attractive planted in small groups in a rock garden	Plant in autumn, preferably before the bulbs have dried out. Plant 7.5cm (3in) deep	Divide established clumps immediately after flowering, before the leaves die down. Ensure that the bulbs do not dry out during transplanting
Galtonia candicans Summer hyacinth	A prolific bulb, producing many stems of 4cm (1½in) long white flowers with pale green basal markings	H:1m (3½ft) S:25cm (10in)	July–Sept.	Will grow in any garden soil that is not too heavy	Plant 15cm (6in) deep in March or April. Divide only when the clumps become congested	Remove offsets in Sept. and replant immediately
Giant bluebell *see* Scilla hispanica						
Gladiolus (hybrids)	These popular plants need no introduction. The large-flowered cultivars have strong spikes 0.6–1.2m (2–4ft) tall. Among the many fine cultivars are 'Deciso' (salmon-pink), 'Flowersong' (yellow), 'Oscar' (glowing red), and 'Spic and Span' (rose-cerise). Butterfly gladioli are small-flowered with waved and fluffy petals, and usually grow to about 90cm (3ft); 'Greenwich' (yellow-green), is an attractive variety. Primulinus hybrids have loosely arranged florets on slender stems, lasting well in water; heights vary from 45–90cm (1½–3ft). The miniature hybrids grow to about the same height as the primulinus kinds, but have smaller flowers	See description	July–Aug.	For best results provide a well-drained soil in a sunny position, and add plenty of well-rotted manure or compost, and a dressing of bonemeal	Plant 10–15cm (4–6in) deep in March or April. Large-flowered kinds will require stakes	Cormlets can be detached and grown on in a nursery bed for several years, until large enough to flower
G. byzantinus	This graceful species bears its dainty purple-red flowers in June, and has the merit of being hardy	H:60cm (2ft) S:15cm (6in)	June	As hybrids	As hybrids	As hybrids
Glory of the snow *see* Chionodoxa luciliae						
Golden-rayed lily *see* Lilium auratum						
Grape hyacinth *see* Muscari armeniacum						
Hyacinthus Hyacinth	Although hyacinths are mainly grown as indoor plants, they are perfectly hardy and are most effective used for spring bedding	H:25cm (10in) S:15cm (6in)	May	A light, well-drained soil suits hyacinths. If planted near the window, preferably in sun, the fragrance can be appreciated	Plant the bulbs 13–15cm (5–6in) deep, 10–13cm (4–5in) apart in autumn. In a windy site the stems can be staked by pushing a split cane into the bulb	Slit the base of the bulb to form a cross, before planting. This will encourage bulblets to form, which can be grown on for several years until flowering size is reached
Ipheion uniflorum (syn. Brodiaea uniflora)	Star-shaped, delicate flowers 4–5cm (1½–2in) wide and fragrant, white to violet-blue. The pale green leaves have a garlic-like odour	H:15cm (6in) S:10cm (4in)	March–May	Requires well-drained soil in sun or partial shade, in a sheltered position	Set the bulbs 2.5–5cm (1–2in) deep during Sept. or Oct. Divide and replant the clumps every three years, in Sept.	Offsets can be removed from lifted bulbs as soon as the foliage dies down
Iris (bulbous-rooted)	These are the irises usually bought in florists, and include the Dutch (flowering in early June), Spanish (flowering in late June) and English (flowering late June and early July). There are several cultivars, blue and yellow being the dominant colours	H:45–60cm (1½–2ft) S:15cm (6in)	June–July	A rich soil in full sun is required for best results. The English type are not so hardy and should be well covered in winter as protection against severe frost	Plant 7.5–10cm (3–4in) deep, 13–15cm (5–6in) apart in autumn	Lift and divide established clumps when they become too large
I. danfordiae	Bright yellow iris flowers with a delicate fragrance	H:13cm (5in) S:7.5cm (3in)	March	For best results, provide a limy soil with plenty of peat or leafmould added	Plant 13cm (5in) deep and about 10cm (4in) apart. Deep planting prevents the bulbs splitting up into non-flowering bulblets	As bulbous-rooted
I. reticulata	Purple-blue iris flowers with golden-yellow marks on lower petals. There are cultivars with other shades of purple and blue. Fragrant	H:10–15cm (4–6in) S:7.5cm (3in)	Feb.–March	As *I. danfordiae*	Plant 7.5cm (3in) deep and 10cm (4in) apart	As bulbous-rooted

Bulbs

Name	Description	Height/spread	Flowering period	Soil and site	Remarks	Propagation
Ixia African corn lily	Bright, cheerful plants with colourful star-shaped flowers borne on spikes — somewhat like frail miniature gladioli	H:45cm (1½ft) S:10cm (4in)	May–June	Any well-drained soil in a sunny, protected position is suitable if protection from severe frost can be provided	Plant the corms 5–7.5cm (2–3in) deep in Oct. or Nov. and cover with straw or bracken	Offsets can be saved when the bulbs are being replanted, and grown on in a nursery bed
Ixiolirion tataricum (syn. I. pallassii)	Clusters of deep blue tubular flowers on stiff but slender stems. A good cut flower	H:30cm (1ft) S:10cm (4in)	June	Provide a sunny, sheltered position and rich, well-drained soil	Plant the bulbs 2.5–4cm (1–1½in) deep in Sept. or Oct.	Replant offsets when lifting old bulbs
Leucojum aestivum Summer snowflake	Nodding, white bell-shaped flowers tipped with green	H:45cm (1½ft) S:13cm (5in)	April–May	Plant in a peaty, moist soil in sun or shade	Plant 2.5–4cm (1–1½in) deep in autumn. Divide oversized clumps in autumn	Divide established clumps in autumn
Lilium auratum Golden-rayed lily	Pure white flowers covered with crimson and brown spots, with a golden band through the centre of each petal. Flowers almost 30cm (1ft) across, and fragrant	H:1.5m (5ft) S:30cm (1ft)	Aug.–Sept.	Requires a lime-free soil, with very good drainage. Will grow in sun or semi-shade but the roots must not be subjected to full sun	Plant between Oct. and March, whenever the weather allows, ideally as soon as possible after bulbs are received. Cover the bulb with two-and-a-half times its own depth of soil. Mulch the plants liberally in summer	Lift, divide and replant the clumps every three or four years, in Oct. or March
L. candidum Madonna lily	A popular lily with fragrant silvery-white flowers	H:1m (3½ft) S:30cm (1ft)	June	Requires a position in full sun, and needs a moist but very free-draining soil. Tolerates lime	Cover bulbs with 5cm (2in) of soil. Plant in Oct., as soon as the bulbs are available	Lift and divide established clumps in Oct.
L. giganteum *see* Cardiocrinum giganteum						
L. henryi	Deep orange flowers spotted with brown	H:1.5m (5ft) S:30cm (1ft)	Aug.–Sept.	Best in well-drained soil in light shade. Tolerant of lime	Plant 20cm (8in) deep in Oct. Mulch liberally during summer	Lift and divide established clumps in autumn
L. Mid Century Group	A group of lilies of outstanding merit. Valuable border plants, but equally happy in wilder parts of the garden. 'Destiny' is a beautiful lemon yellow with tiny brown spots, 'Enchantment' has vivid red flowers with black spots, and 'Prosperity' is a vigorous plant with yellow blooms. The Mid Century Hybrids come in a range of colours. All are good plants	H:90cm (3ft) S:30cm (1ft)	June–July	Require a well-drained soil but must be kept moist. Add liberal amounts of leafmould. Will grow in sun or partial shade	Plant 10cm (4in) deep, 15cm (6in) in light soil. Staking is not normally necessary	As *L. henryi*

Below: Lilium auratum *(golden-rayed lily).* *Below right:* Narcissus *'Spellbinder', one of the trumpet daffodils*

Name	Description	Height/spread	Flowering period	Soil and site	Remarks	Propagation
L. pardalinum Californian lily	The stems carry 12–20 recurving flowers, deep orange-crimson with maroon spots	H:1.5m (5ft) S:30cm (1ft)	July	Grows best in a damp position in partial shade. Avoid lime	Plant 13cm (5in) deep in Oct.	Lift and divide old clumps in Oct.
Madonna lily *see* Lilium candidum						
Meadow saffron *see* Colchicum byzantinum and C. speciosum						
Muscari armeniacum Grape hyacinth	Tightly clustered heads of small fragrant blue flowers; look most effective massed in a group or as an edging	H:20cm (8in) S:10cm (4in)	April–May	A well-drained soil in full sun is best	Plant 7.5cm (3in) deep in clusters in Aug., Sept., or Oct.	Lift and divide existing clumps every three or four years
Narcissus (garden hybrids) Daffodil	Among the trumpet cultivars 'Golden Harvest' (yellow), 'Beersheba' (good white), and 'Spellbinder' (yellow perianth, yellow trumpet fading to almost white inside), are all worth trying. Good large-cupped cultivars include: 'Carlton' (soft yellow perianth, frilled, clear yellow cup) 'Semper Avanti' (creamy perianth, orange cup), 'Flower Record' (white perianth, orange cup with a vivid orange edge). 'Passionale' has a pure soft pink cup against a white perianth. Among the doubles 'White Lion' has creamy white petals interspersed with small coppery ochre petals, 'Tahiti' has a perfect colour combination of yellow and orange-red. The Poeticus group includes the charming 'Actaea' (large white perianth, small yellow 'eye' edged fiery red). The Poetaz group bear clusters of small flowers on one stem; one of the most popular cultivars is 'Cheerfulness' (white perianth, creamy double centre, fragrant)	H:30–56cm (12–22in) S:15–20cm (6–8in)	March–May	Fertile soil in sun or semi-shade suits them best. Moisture is appreciated but the soil must be well drained with no chance of waterlogging	Plant the bulbs in Aug. or Sept., covering with about three times the depth of the bulb. They are often most effective if left undisturbed to form large clumps, but can be lifted after flowering and put into a trench until the foliage dies down, then stored in a dry place for replanting in autumn. An annual dressing of bonemeal each spring before flowering will be beneficial. If naturalized in grass, try to avoid cutting the grass until the foliage has died down	Divide established clumps in early autumn, or separate young bulbs when lifting to store
N. bulbocodium Yellow hoop petticoat	An unusual narcissus for the rock garden. The perianth petals are very small and the trumpet disproportionately large	H:15cm (6in) S:7.5cm (3in)	March–April	Any good garden soil is suitable, in sun or semi-shade. Useful for the rock garden or for naturalizing in fine grass	Plant in autumn, covering each bulb with twice its own depth of soil	Separate the small bulbs from parent bulbs in autumn
N. canaliculatus	A miniature daffodil with small clusters of white and yellow flowers on each stem	H:15cm (6in) S:7.5cm (3in)	April	Any good garden soil is suitable, but a position in full sun is required	As *N. bulbocodium*	As *N. bulbocodium*
N. cyclamineus Cyclamen-flowered narcissus	The true species has strongly reflexed perianth petals, which give rise to its name. The various hybrids look more like conventional, but miniature, daffodils. These include 'February Gold' (yellow with deeper yellow trumpet), 'Peeping Tom' (deep yellow), and 'Tête-à-Tête' (clusters of buttercup-gold flowers)	Species H:15cm (6in) S:7.5cm (3in) Hybrids H:20–30cm (8–12in) S:10cm (4in)	March	Grows best in a moist, peaty soil in sun or semi-shade	As *N. bulbocodium*	As *N. bulbocodium*
N. triandus Angel's tears	Another charming group of miniature daffodils. There are several cultivars, such as 'Albus' (clusters of creamy-white flowers, with globular cup and reflexed petals), and 'April Tears' (clusters of pendent yellow blooms with reflexed petals)	H:15cm (6in) S:7.5cm (3in)	April	As *N. cyclamineus*	As *N. bulbocodium*	As *N. bulbocodium*
Nerine bowdenii	A beautiful late-flowering plant, unfortunately on the borderline of hardiness. Large, spiky pink flowers	H:60cm (2ft) S:15cm (6in)	Sept.–Nov.	Any good garden soil is suitable, in sun or semi-shade. A well-drained border in the shelter of a south or west-facing wall is ideal	Plant in Aug. or April. 10cm (4in) deep. Except in very mild areas, protect with bracken or straw in winter	Large clumps can be divided, taking care not to damage the bulbs

Bulbs

Name	Description	Height/spread	Flowering period	Soil and site	Remarks	Propagation
Ornithogalum nutans	White and pale green star-like flowers borne in loose spikes on erect stems	H:38cm (15in) S:15cm (6in)	April–May	Ordinary, well-drained soil is adequate, in full sun or partial shade	Plant in Oct., setting the bulbs 5–7.5cm (2–3in) deep. Remove dead flower heads	Lift and divide large clumps in Oct. Replant immediately
O. pyramidale	Similar to *O. nutans*, but bears larger, white flowers a month or two later	H:60cm (2ft) S:15cm (6in)	June–July	As *O. nutans*	As *O. nutans*	As *O. nutans*
O. thyrsoides Chincherinchee	Upright stems carry 20–30 white to cream flowers packed on long-lasting spikes. Make excellent cut flowers	H:45cm (1½ft) S:10cm (4in)	May–July	As *O. nutans*	Not hardy. Plant in March or April and lift in Nov.	Plant bulblets formed by mature bulbs
O. umbellatum Star of Bethlehem	Stiff stems support an abundance of white star-shaped flowers. Very good beneath shrubs	H:20cm (8in) S:10cm (4in)	May–June	As *O. nutans*, but will tolerate full shade well	As *O. nutans*	As *O. nutans*
Puschkinia scilloides libanotica Striped squill	Attractive blue, scilla-like flowers with darker blue stripes	H:10cm (4in) S:5cm (2in)	April–May	A gritty soil with plenty of peat added is ideal, in full sun or partial shade	Plant 5cm (2in) deep in Oct. Leave undisturbed for several years, and allow foliage to die down naturally	Large clumps can be lifted and divided in Aug., replanting immediately
Ranunculus asiaticus Turban buttercup	Often called French ranunculus, these plants have a colour range from yellow to red and orange. The beautiful double or semi-double flowers are about 7.5cm (3in) across	H:30cm (1ft) S:15cm (6in)	May–June	Requires a sheltered position in good, humus-rich soil, in full sun or partial shade	Plant from the end of Feb. in a sheltered border. The tubers should be set claws down, 5cm (2in) deep	Lift and divide the tubers in Oct. or March
Scilla hispanica (syn. Endymion hispanicus) Giant bluebell	A large and vigorous bluebell. Cultivars include 'Myosotis' (clear blue), 'White Triumphator' (pure white), 'Excelsior' (deep blue), and 'Queen of the Pinks' (deep pink)	H:30cm (1ft) S:15cm (6in)	April–June	Requires a moist but not waterlogged soil with plenty of organic matter	Plant in autumn, 10–15cm (4–6in) deep. Plant bulbs as soon as they are available, and do not allow them to dry out	Divide large clumps in autumn, spacing out the bulbs
S. non-scripta (syn. Endymion non-scriptus) Bluebell	Apart from the blue version of this native plant, there are also pink and white forms	H:18cm (7in) S:10cm (4in)	April–May	A moist, humus-rich soil in full shade is ideal	Plant the bulbs as soon as they are available, setting them 10–13cm (4–5in) deep. Do not allow the bulbs to dry out if it can be avoided	Lift and divide large clumps in autumn, and replant immediately
S. sibirica Siberian squill	Each bulb produces three or four stems, each bearing two to four brilliant blue bell-shaped flowers	H:15cm (6in) S:10cm (4in)	March	Best in a moist but well-drained soil in partial shade	Plant as soon as the bulbs are available, about Oct. Set them 5–7.5cm (2–3in) deep	Lift large clumps and remove offsets. Replant in a nursery bed, where they can remain for a few years

Below: Galanthus sp. (snowdrop). Below right: Tulipa 'Gudoshnik', one of the Darwin Hydrid tulips

Name	Description	Height/spread	Flowering period	Soil and site	Remarks	Propagation
Siberian squill *see* Scilla sibirica						
Snake head fritillary *see* Fritillaria meleagris						
Snowdrop *see* Galanthus nivalis						
Star of Bethlehem *see* Ornithogalum umbellatum						
Sternbergia lutea Yellow star flower	Yellow crocus-like flowers, produced in autumn. Leaves and flowers appear at the same time	H:10cm (4in) S:7.5cm (3in)	Sept.–Oct.	Requires a sandy soil in full sun	Plant 10cm (4in) deep, and leave undisturbed for several years. Cut off dead flower heads but allow foliage to die naturally	Lift large clumps, divide and replant at once
Striped squill *see* Puschkinia scilloides libanotica						
Summer hyacinth *see* Galtonia candicans						
Summer snowflake *see* Leucojum aestivum						
Triteleia laxa (syn. Brodiaea laxa)	Clusters of bluish-purple tubular flowers 4cm (1½in) across. Makes a nice cut-flower for the home	H:60cm (2ft) S:7.5cm (3in)	July	Needs well-drained soil in the shelter of a south-facing wall	Plant in Sept., in groups, 5–7.5cm (2–3in) deep. Water well after planting	Lift and divide an established clump of corms in Sept.
Tulip *see* Tulipa						
Tulipa (garden hybrids) Tulip	Types include Early Doubles 'Orange Nassau' (orange-brown), 'Peach Blossom' (pink), and 'Mr van der Hoef' (yellow); 30cm (1ft), late April. Triumph tulips include 'Garden Party' (pink with a blaze of white), 'Orange Wonder' (bronze-scarlet with orange sheen), and 'Red Matador' (coral-crimson); 41–50cm (16–20in), end of April. Darwin Hybrids include 'Apeldoorn' (vivid scarlet), 'Gudoshnik' (creamy peach, flecked and flushed cerise-red), and 'Queen Wilhelmina' (orange-scarlet); 50–65cm (20–26in), end of April. Lily-flowered tulips include 'Mariette' (pink), 'Maytime' (purple-violet with white edge), and 'Queen of Sheba' (ruby red with yellow margin); 50–60cm (20–24in). Parrot tulips include 'Fantasy' (pink), and 'Texas Gold' (yellow); 45–55cm (18–22in), April, May	See description	April–May	Any good garden soil that is not acid will suit tulips, though for the bulbs to increase and flower in future years, a sandy soil is advisable	Plant in November, setting the bulbs 15–20cm (6–8in) deep in light soil, 10–15cm (4–6in) deep in heavy soil. Lift and store after flowering unless the soil is sandy, but allow the foliage to die naturally before storing for the summer. Early Double and Early Single tulips are particularly useful for early flowering, or windy places. Triumph tulips are ideal for mass planting, and their sturdy nature makes them useful for exposed areas. Lily-flowered tulips are delightful for cutting, with their gracefully reflexed petals. Darwin Hybrids have the largest flowers of all tulips, and have brilliant colours. Parrot tulips have full, fringed petals, but need protection from strong winds	When the bulbs are lifted, some will have split into three or four smaller bulbs. If these are much smaller they should be planted in a nursery bed for the following year, then set in the flowering positions
T. fosteriana	There are now several excellent hyrids of this species, all have large, brilliant blooms on low, sturdy plants. 'Red Emperor' (also known as 'Madame Lefeber') is bright scarlet with no shading; 'Cantata' is vivid orange-scarlet with a pronounced black centre	H:25–38cm (12–15in) S:15cm (6in)	March–April	As garden hybrids	Plant in Nov., 15cm (6in) deep. Remove dead heads when petals fall	As garden hybrids
T. greigii	A sturdy, dwarf tulip with large and brilliant flowers. The leaves are usually mottled with purple-brown	H:20–30cm (8–12in) S:13cm (5in)	April–May	As garden hybrids	As T. fosteriana	As garden hybrids
Turban buttercup *see* Ranunculus asiaticus						
Windflower *see* Anemone coronaria						
Winter aconite *see* Eranthis hyemalis						
Yellow star flower *see* Sternbergia lutea						
Zephyranthes candida Flower of the west wind	Delicate, pure white, crocus-like flowers are produced in autumn. The leaves are present the entire year. Not fully hardy	H:15cm (6in) S:10cm (4in)	Sept.–Oct.	Requires a well-drained soil in a sheltered position	Plant in Oct., 7.5cm (3in) deep. Mulch with peat in Nov.	Lift and divide large clumps every three or four years

Rock plants

Rock plants as a group are frequently misunderstood. They are sometimes avoided for fear of being difficult, yet most will thrive with very little attention if the drainage is good and the site not shaded; they are occasionally dismissed as being insignificant, yet a sheet of aubrieta in flower can hardly be regarded as anything less than striking, and anyone who takes the trouble to look at the smallest rock plant will find exquisite beauty. Even the claim that a rock garden is attractive only in spring is soon disproved by a glance at the following tables — in which plants can be found to provide bloom from February to November.

Because rock plants are comparatively small, it is possible to amass a good collection even in a small garden, and besides the plants listed in the following tables, there are hundreds of equally charming plants to discover and grow. There are also many small bulbs well suited to planting in a rock garden, and these will be found on pages 160–167.

Although rock plants are seen to best advantage in a well-constructed rock garden, many of them can be grown perfectly satisfactorily in dry stone walls, or between crazy-paving, although for the latter position only the more robust types should be tried. Among those that can be grown successfully between paving stones are armerias (thrift), *Campanula cochleariifolia*, *Saxifraga muscoides*, and *Thymus serpyllum*. Many of the sedums, such as *S. dasyphyllum*, *S. lydium*, *S. spathulifolium*, and *S. spurium*, are also good.

Most rock plants are sold in pots, and many can be planted at any time of the year provided the ground is not frozen. Preferred planting times for particular plants are given in the individual entries. If planted in summer, always water thoroughly until the plants become established.

When planting, always make allowances for the habit of the plant — some are fairly compact in growth, but others, such as thyme, are spreading and will soon cover a substantial area. This may not matter in a pocket planted with bulbs, which can push their way through and look quite attractive, but other subjects can become an entangled mess. The spread dimensions in the tables give some indication of what a mature plant may reach, although there are bound to be wide variations.

Rock plants can be propagated in a variety of ways, but seed, division and cuttings are the most popular. Generally, the seeds need to be sown soon after ripening, and it is best to use a gritty soil mix. Great warmth is not usually necessary, and the seed pans or pots can stand in a cold-frame, or outdoors covered with a pane of glass.

Most cuttings should be made from the soft tips of young non-flowering stems, 12–35mm (½–1½in) long, the lower leaves trimmed off and the shoot inserted into a gritty compost. Keep shaded and moist until rooted.

Some plants can be divided satisfactorily, but make sure that all portions have some roots.

Name	Description	Height/spread	Flowering period	Soil and site	Remarks	Propagation
Aethionema 'Warley Rose'	An indispensable rock plant; low bushy growth and a mass of deep pink flowers on a cushion of dainty leaves	H:15cm (6in) S:30cm (1ft)	April–July	Requires a well-drained lime-free soil in full sun	Plant Sept. to March. Remove dead flower heads	Softwood cuttings of non-flowering wood taken from June to Sept.
Alyssum saxatile Gold dust	A popular plant, covered with masses of golden-yellow flowers, conspicuous from a distance	H:15–20cm (6–8in) S:30cm (1ft)	April–June	Prefers a sandy soil in a sunny situation, but will grow in any soil that is not too heavy	Cut back hard after flowering to retain compact habit	Sow seed in Aug. or take cuttings in July or Aug.
Androsace carnea	Forms a green mat of narrow leaves studded with umbels of pink flowers	H:2.5–5cm (1–2in) S:15cm (6in)	June–July	A humus-rich soil or a mixture of peat and gritty loam is best, in full sun	Plant in March or April. Dress soil around plant with coarse chippings	Sow seed in pots in a cold-frame in Feb. Do not allow the plant to flower the first year
Anemone nemorosa Wood anemone	A woodland plant that can be found a place in the rock garden. The white, open, daisy-like flowers are about 2.5cm (1in) across. There are forms with pinkish or lavender-blue flowers	H:15cm (6in) S:10cm (4in)	March–April	Moist soil and shady conditions are best	Plant in Sept. or Oct.	Divide or cut up roots in July or Aug.
Arabis caucasia (syn. A. albida) White rock cress	A rampant plant forming a carpet of white flowers. Hoary foliage. There are also double-flowered and variegated forms	H:15–23cm (6–9in) S:45cm (1½ft)	April–June	Sandy loam in full sun is preferred	Plant in autumn or spring. Remove dead flower heads. Peg down growth to keep it neat	Divide old plants from Sept. to Dec., or in March. Cuttings can be taken in July
Armeria maritima Thrift	Evergreen cushion plant with grass-like leaves and red, pink or white rounded flower heads	H:15–20cm (6–8in) S:23cm (9in)	May–July	Ordinary but well-drained soil is adequate, in full sun	Remove dead heads regularly	Divide old plants in March, or take small cuttings with some old wood at the base in July or Aug.
Aubrieta Rock cress	One of the most popular rock plants, producing a sheet of colour. There are several named cultivars, and colours include shades of purple, pink and blue	H:7.5–10cm (3–4in) S:45cm (1½ft)	March–June	These plants love sun and prefer a sandy soil. Successful planted in chinks in walls or between paving stones	Cut back closely after flowering to keep growth compact (don't trim wall plants)	Divide old plants between Aug. and Oct. or take cuttings in Aug. or Sept.
Baby's breath *see* Gypsophila repens						
Bitter root *see* Lewisia						

Name	Description	Height/spread	Flowering period	Soil and site	Remarks	Propagation
Burnt candytuft *see* Aethionema						
Calceolaria biflora	Pouch-shaped yellow flowers carried in pairs above a basal rosette of leaves	H:15–30cm (6–12in) S:30–45cm (1–1½ft)	July–Aug.	Well-drained but moisture-retentive soil is required, in full sun or or partial shade	Plant in April or May in a sheltered position. Be prepared to protect with a pane of glass in winter	Sow seed in a cold-frame in Feb.
Campanula carpatica	Superb carpeting plant, having a trailing habit. The large saucer-shaped flowers, from white to deep blue, appear over a long period	H:10–15cm (4–6in) S:30cm (1ft)	June–Sept.	A rich gravelly loam is best, with some lime, and a site in full sun	Remove dead flowers	Divide in April, take softwood cuttings in March or April, or sow seed in Feb.
C. cochleariifolia Fairy thimbles	A dainty plant with nodding flowers in shades from white to blue. Grows freely	H:5cm (2in) S:30cm (1ft)	June–Sept.	A moist but well-drained soil suits this plant. Good for crevices or as an edging to stone paving	Tidy old clumps if they become invasive	Divide in Sept. or March, or take softwood cuttings in April or Sept.
Candytuft (perennial) *see* Iberis sempervirens						
Dianthus deltoides Maiden pink	A pretty plant with white to crimson flowers borne profusely over neat grey-green narrow leaves	H:15cm (6in) S:10cm (4in)	June–July	Requires a sunny, well-drained crevice, and appreciates lime in the soil	Plant firmly in March, Sept. or Oct. Test soil every few years to ensure pH is above 6.5	Easily raised from seed sown in a cold-frame in Feb., or by softwood cuttings taken after flowering
Dryas octopetala Mountain avens	A mat-forming evergreen with rich green oak-like leaves, white beneath, and white flowers like small open roses with yellow centres. Silky white seedheads follow	H:7.5–10cm (3–4in) S:60cm (2ft)	May–June	A gritty loam in full sun is ideal	These plants resent root disturbance, but if left undisturbed will form large clumps	Take cuttings about 7.5cm (3in) long with a heel, in March or July. Place in a closed cold-frame
Erigeron karvinskianus (syn. E. mucronatus)	A charming prostrate plant useful for walls and the sides of paths as well as the rockery. Pink and white daisy-like flowers	H:15–20cm (6–9in) S:23cm (9in)	June–July	A moist but well-drained soil in full sun suits these plants	Dead head the plants to encourage further flowers. May need winter protection	Very easily raised from seed sown in a cold-frame in Feb.
Erinus alpinus	Dainty spikes of crimson, pink or white flowers. An excellent plant for dry walls. Compact plants of tufted habit	H:7.5cm (3in) S:15cm (6in)	April–Aug.	A well-drained soil in full sun is ideal	Seeds itself freely, and although it is not a long-lived plant there are usually plenty of seedlings	Easily raised from seed, scattered in spring where the plants are to flower
Fairy thimbles — *see* Campanula cochleariifolia						
Gentian — *see* Gentiana						
Gentiana sino-ornata Gentian	An ever-popular rock plant with masses of deep blue large trumpet-shaped upward-facing flowers	H:15cm (6in) S:30cm (1ft)	Sept.–Nov.	A moist but well-drained acid soil is essential for success. Will tolerate full sun or semi-shade	Never allow the soil to become too dry — water as necessary throughout summer	Divide large clumps in spring
Gold dust *see* Alyssum saxatile						
Gromwell *see* Lithodora diffusa						
Gypsophila repens Baby's breath	A prolific plant with sprays of white or pink flowers. A good wall plant	H:7.5–15cm (3–6in) S:45cm (1½ft)	May–Sept.	A chalky soil and full sun are ideal for this plant	Young plants from cuttings should be 'stopped' to encourage bushiness	Cuttings can be taken in May or June, or the plants divided in Oct. Can also be raised from seed sown in April
Haberlea ferdinandi-coburgii	Flat rosettes of dark evergreen leaves and pretty lilac flowers resembling streptocarpus	H:10cm (4in) S:23cm (9in)	June–July	Thrives in a peaty or moist but well-drained soil, and is useful for full shade	Haberleas are best planted in crevices where water can run away. May require some winter protection	Leaf cuttings taken in June or July are usually successful, but choose leaves from the centre of the rosette
Helianthemum Rock rose	An excellent plant for quick growth and brilliant colour. Evergreen dwarf shrub producing a multitude of flowers. All colours except blue. Excellent for dry walls and are good space fillers	H:15–20cm (6–8in) S:60cm (2ft)	June–Aug.	Full sun is essential. Ordinary soil is adequate, but a little extra lime is usually appreciated	To keep the plant under control, clip back to size in early July; this will not affect subsequent flowering	Take longish cuttings in June and insert them in a cold-frame
Hepatica nobilis (syn. H. triloba)	A beautiful, partially evergreen, plant with single or double anemone-like flowers in shades of blue, purple, red or white	H:10cm (4in) S:23cm (9in)	Feb.–April	A moist, humus-rich soil is required; lime is appreciated. Although shade is best sun is tolerated	Plant in Sept. or after flowering, incorporating plenty of peat	Divide in Aug. or Sept.
Houseleek *see* Sempervivum						
Iberis sempervirens Perennial candytuft	An evergreen shrublet with masses of snowy-white candytuft-like flowers covering the plant in late spring	H:15–20cm (6–8in) S:45cm (1½ft)	May–June	Ordinary soil in full sun	Dead-head regularly to extend flowering period	Take cuttings with a heel any time from April to Aug. and root in a cold-frame

Rock plants

Name	Description	Height/spread	Flowering period	Soil and site	Remarks	Propagation
Lewisia Bitter root	Showy plants with leaves arranged in rosettes. The garden hybrids are the most suitable and have sprays of flowers in shades of pink or apricot, or white	H:10–13cm (4–5in) S:15–23cm (6–9in)	May–June	Well-drained, lime-free soil is required, in full sun	Plants must be kept free of standing water; protect with glass in winter if necessary, and place a thick layer of chippings round the plant	Seed is best sown as soon as ripe, usually July, but if bought sow in Feb.
Linnaea borealis Twin flower	A fast-creeping evergreen with flesh-pink flowers resembling abelia	H:5cm (2in) S:45cm (1½ft)	May–June	Needs a moist, humus-rich, lime-free soil in partial shade	A trouble-free plant requiring little attention if conditions are right	Peg down runners with small pieces of wire, and pot into a peaty compost when rooted
Lithodora diffusa (syn. Lithospermum diffusum) Gromwell	An evergreen creeping shrub, covered with long-lasting flowers — white in the cultivar 'Album', blue in 'Heavenly Blue' and 'Grace Ward'	H:10cm (4in) S:45cm (1½ft)	May–Aug.	Provide a moist but well-drained lime-free soil in sun or partial shade	Plant in April	Take softwood cuttings in late July or early Aug.
Maiden pink *see* Dianthus deltoides						
Mexican fleabane *see* Erigeron karvinskianus						
Moss campion *see* Silene schafta						
Moss phlox *see* Phlox subulata						
Mountain avens *see* Dryas octopetala						
Navelwort *see* Omphalodes cappadocica						
Pasque flower *see* Pulsatilla vulgaris						
Phlox subulata Moss phlox	A mat-forming, long-lived and free-flowering rock plant of considerable merit. The small, neat leaves are covered with a sheet of bloom, in shades of pink, red, mauve or white. A good non-invasive wall plant	H:10cm (4in) S:30cm (1ft)	April–May	A sandy, gritty loam is best, in a dry, sunny position	Young cuttings should be 'stopped' to encourage bushiness	Take softwood cuttings from June to Sept.
Polygonum vacciniifolium	Vigorous and creeping habit, forming a conspicuous pink mat in autumn, with rose-pink spikes on wiry trailing stems	H:15cm (6in) S:75cm (2½ft)	Aug.–Oct.	Grow in moist, lime-free soil in shade	If a good form is planted it will make a fine, well-behaved plant — but some forms can become invasive if not kept in check	Take cuttings from June to Sept., or divide in March or Sept.
Pulsatilla vulgaris Pasque flower	A beautiful plant with cup-shaped mauve-purple flowers set amid feathery foliage	H:30cm (1ft) S:38cm (15in)	April	Moist conditions in full sun produce the best plants	Plant in Sept.	Can be raised from seed, but to propagate a fine form, take root cuttings (2.5cm/1in long) in July or Aug.

Below: Helianthemum nummularium *'Wisley Pink'*. *Below right:* Pulsatilla vulgaris *(pasque flower)* 'Rubra'

Name	Description	Height/ spread	Flowering period	Soil and site	Remarks	Propagation
Rhodohypoxis baurii	A bulbous plant with narrow tufted leaves and an abundance of pink, red or white six-petalled flowers	H:7.5cm (3in) S:13cm (5in)	June–Aug.	A well-drained, lime-free soil is essential in full sun	Plant in Sept., providing a protected site	Use offsets (bulblets about the size of a sweet pea seed) taken in Aug. or Sept., after flowering
Rock cress *see* Aubrieta						
Rock rose *see* Helianthemum						
Saponaria ocymoides Soapwort	A vigorous, mat-forming pink-flowered trailer ideal for a hot, dry wall or a sunny bank	H:5cm (2in) S:30cm (1ft)	July–Sept.	Suitable for dry soils in full sun	Pinch out the growing tips of young plants to encourage bushiness	Take softwood cuttings from non-flowering shoots, ideally from near the root, in July or Aug.
Saxifraga spp.	This is a large and varied group of rosette-forming plants, many making ideal rock plants. The cushion (Kabschia) type grow only 2.5–5cm (1–2in) high and are studded with pink, white or yellow blooms	H:2.5–45cm (1–18in) S:30–45cm (1–1½ft)	March–June	An open, sunny, well-drained site with plenty of grit suits most kinds. Lime is also appreciated by these plants, especially the Encrusted group. Mossy kinds prefer a cool root-run and partial shade	Generally trouble-free if correct soil and aspect have been provided	Division, cuttings or seed. Treatment depends on species
Sedum spp. Stonecrop	Another large group of fine rock plants. Of the many kinds suitable for the rock garden *S. dasyphyllum* and *S. spathuifolium* are representative. *S. dasyphyllum* forms dense mats of blue-green fleshy oval leaves, the plant reaching only 2.5mm (1in) in height; it has small white flowers in June. *S. spathuifolium* 'Purpureum' reaches 5–10cm (2–4in) and forms mats or low hummocks of spoon-shaped fleshy red-purple leaves, flushed waxy-white when young; golden-yellow flowers are borne in May or June	H:1–30cm (½–12in) S:15–38cm (6–15in)	May–Aug.	Ideal for rocks or dry walls, often with little soil, but require a position in full sun or partial shade	Trouble-free plants	Division is usually the easiest method of propagation, done in March or Sept., but cuttings can be taken of many kinds in July or Aug. Seed is another option
Sempervivum spp. Houseleek	Succulents grown mainly for their attractive leaf rosettes which are sometimes richly coloured or have a 'cobwebbing'. Flowering stems are taller than the heights given. Ideal plants for a hot, dry place	H:5–75cm (2–3in) S:15–30cm (6–12in)	June–July	Will thrive in dry, sandy soil unsuitable for most other plants. A little extra lime may be beneficial	Cobweb types should be protected from excess winter moisture with a pane of glass – otherwise trouble-free	Remove offsets in spring or summer, or sow seed in spring
Shortia galacifolia	Beautiful white flowers fade to rose as they mature, carried over deep green oval leaves that turn almost crimson in autumn	H:15cm (6in) S:30cm (1ft)	April–May	A moist, peaty soil in shade or partial shade is essential for success	Remove dead flower heads	Divide in June, after flowering, or take cuttings in Aug. or Sept.
Silene schafta 'Abbotswood' Moss campion	A carpeting plant with masses of pink flowers. Ideal for planting in crevices	H:15cm (6in) S:30cm (1ft)	Aug.–Sept.	Well-drained light loam suits this plant. Site in full sun	As silenes resent root disturbance, do not move unnecessarily	Take cuttings in July or sow seed in March
Soapwort *see* Saponaria ocymoides						
Stonecrop *see* Sedum						
Thrift *see* Armeria maritima						
Thyme *see* Thymus serpyllum						
Thymus serpyllum Thyme	An aromatic, mat-forming plant of considerable merit. There are various forms, with flowers from pink to red, as well as white, throughout summer	H:2.5cm (1in) S:60cm (2ft)	June–Aug.	Light sandy soil in full sun	Remove dead heads with shears after flowering	Divide in March or take cuttings in May or June
Trillium grandiflorum Wake robin	An interesting plant with the floral parts in threes. Large snow-white flowers	H:20–30cm (8–12in) S:30cm (1ft)	April–May	A moist rich soil with plenty of leafmould is essential. Grow only in full shade	Plant in Aug. or Sept. in groups	Divide in Aug. or sow seed in March
Twinflower *see* Linnaea borealis						
Wake robin *see* Trillium grandiflorum						
White rock cress *see* Arabis caucasia						

Water plants

Although the range of hardy plants for the water garden is not so vast as in many other areas of gardening, there are still many delightful subjects; no matter how large the pond or stream, it is unlikely to be able to accommodate more than a selection of the plants listed in the following table. Apart from the true aquatics, there are many waterside plants, such as marsh marigolds (*Caltha palustris*) and water forget-me-nots (*Myosotis palustris*), that add considerable interest and colour to the margin of a pond or stream. There are, too, many marginal plants that like to stand in shallow water even though the top growth is normally carried well above the surface.

Planting depth can be critical for some plants, and where this is important the optimum depth is given under soil and site in the table. Many water plants are best planted in containers, which can be bought for the purpose; in the case of rampant subjects it helps to keep them in check.

A position in full sun is best for the majority of water plants, but as a pond should be sited away from overshadowing trees this should pose no problem.

Avoid the temptation to plant large or vigorous plants in a small pool — it is usually possible to find subjects to suit any pond, whatever its size. But careful selection is necessary; for example, there are some waterlilies that can be grown in an aquarium, yet others are only suitable for a lake.

The table suggests waterlilies suitable for water depths from 30–90cm (1–3ft), which is well within the range of most garden pools, and no pond is complete without one of these magnificent aquatics.

Apart from the decorative plants mentioned, there are submerged oxygenating plants such as the Canadian pondweed (*Elodea canadensis*), which play an important part in the natural balance of a pond, and should always be included.

Propagation can be specialized. Increasing water plants by division is not difficult, but raising them from seed is a task best left to the experienced.

To increase them by division, the roots of aquatic plants are best lifted in May and cut into pieces. It is essential that each piece should have a growing shoot, and in the case of a waterlily also part of the tuber. If possible the pieces of tuber should also have roots attached, although this is not essential provided several good 'eyes' are present.

Pot the pieces individually in heavy loam, finely screened and with a little added charcoal. Ensure that the pieces are firmly planted, and in the case of waterlily tubers fix them into the soil with pieces of hooked wire to prevent them floating away.

Position the pots in shallow water, then as soon as they grow they can be placed at a greater depth. Try to prevent the new leaves being totally submerged.

Name	Description	Height/ spread	Flowering period	Soil and site	Remarks	Propagation
Acorus calamus 'Variegatus' Variegated sweet flag	Variegated form of the common sweet flag. Chiefly grown for its broad, strap-like leaves, which are striped white	H: 60–90cm (2–3ft) S: 45cm (1½ft)	—	Position at the edge of of the pool in shallow water. Can be set in boxes positioned below the surface	Set the rhizomes just below soil level. Firm roots well into the compost	Divide the rhizomes in spring
Aponogeton distachyus Water hawthorn	An adaptable and decorative aquatic with a free-flowering habit. Vanilla-scented black-and-white flowers during summer	Aquatic	April–Oct.	Not hardy in North. Set in 15–60cm (6in–2ft) of water during spring, in a container of heavy loam	Can be invasive, and may need to be trimmed back. If seedlings are normally a problem remove dead flowers	Plants can be divided in spring or early summer, and can also be raised from seed
Arrowhead see Sagittaria sagittifolia						
Bulrush see Scirpus tabernaemontani						
Butomus umbellatus Flowering rush	A handsome aquatic, with tapering, sedge-like leaves and heads of showy pink flowers	H: 60cm–1.2m (2–4ft) S: 60cm (2ft)	June–Sept.	Set at the side of the pool in shallow water, or plant in a container set on bricks. Thrives in loamy soil	Cut off old growth in early autumn	Divide old plants in spring or early summer
Caltha palustris 'Plena'	Large buttercup-like double yellow flowers are borne on branched stems amid large, almost round, leaves	H: 30cm (1ft) S: 23cm (9in)	April–May	Grows well in shallow water or wet soil at the edge of a pool	Ensure that the plants do not dry out	Divide the roots in March or July
Flowering rush see Butomus umbellatus						
Golden club see Orontium aquaticum						
Hydrocleys commersonii Water poppy	One of the most attractive flowering aquatics, but only suitable outdoors for the most sheltered areas. Yellow, three-petalled flowers stand just above the water	Aquatic	July–Sept.	Plant in a wire basket full of sifted loam. Position it 15–23cm (6–9in) below the surface	Remove dead flowers throughout the season	Divide the tuberous roots in spring, or grow on separated runners
Myosotis palustris Water forget-me-not	The bright blue forget-me-not flowers are always cheering when growing along the margin of a pond	H: 30cm (1ft) S: 23cm (9in)	May–Aug.	Plant along the margin of the pond	A trouble-free plant, but only grow it where it does not matter about self-sown seedlings	Seed can be sown *in situ*, or cuttings taken in spring. Plants can also be divided in spring
Myriophyllum brasiliense (syn. M. proserpinacoides) Water milfoil	Long feathery trails of foliage, turning red at the tips in autumn	H: 15cm (6in) trailing	—	Plant in shallow water at the pond edge	Not dependably hardy, so take cuttings in Sept. and overwinter in a greenhouse or shed until the following May	Take cuttings in Sept., rooting them in pans of sandy loam, and overwinter indoors

Name	Description	Height/ spread	Flowering period	Soil and site	Remarks	Propagation
Nymphaea hybrids Waterlily	Some good cultivars are 'Escarboucle', a rich crimson with star-shaped flowers 20cm (8in) across; 'James Brydon' is an extremely free-flowering cultivar with compact carmine-red flowers; 'Paul Hariot' has flowers that open as apricot-yellow, change to pink, and mature to red	Aquatic	May–Sept.	Plant in a basket containing rich loam. The correct planting depth will depend on the cultivar. 'Escarboucle' — 75–90cm (2½–3ft); 'James Brydon' and 'Paul Hariot' — 45–60cm (1½–2ft)	Remove any dead flowers or foliage. Cut back the growth of rampant cultivars before they become too large	Divide established roots in May or June
N. × laydekeri 'Purpurata'	An easy cultivar to grow, with delightful crimson flowers spotted white	Aquatic	June–Aug.	Plant in baskets containing rich loam, set in 30–45cm (1–1½ft) of water	Remove dead flowers and foliage	Divide in May or June
N. pygmaea 'Alba'	An excellent waterlily for a very small pool. Delicate white flowers	Aquatic	June–Aug.	Set in baskets of rich soil, in a depth of about 30cm (1ft) of water	Remove dead flowers and foliage. Protect in winter	Divide established plants in May or June
Nymphoides peltata Water fringe	Yellow fringed flowers stand several inches above the water	Aquatic	July–Sept.	Provide a light position and plant in shallow water	Generally trouble-free	Propagate by division
Orontium aquaticum Golden club	A member of the arum family, with yellow finger-like flowers	H:30cm (1ft) S:30cm (1ft) (or floating)	May–June	Best grown in a basket in 15–45cm (6–18in) of water	Generally trouble-free	Propagate by division or from seed
Pickerel weed *see* Pontederia cordata						
Pontederia cordata Pickerel weed	Useful for its blue flowers held on spikes above the smooth, glossy, spear-shaped leaves	H:45–60cm (1½–2ft) S:23cm (9in)	June–Oct.	Plant in spring in 7.5–13cm (3–5in) of water, in rich loam	After autumn frosts have cut back the stems, trim them back to water level	Increase by seed or divide established plants in spring
Ranunculus lingua 'Grandiflora' Spearwort	A plant with attractive narrow leaves and branching stems with very large golden buttercup-like flowers	H:60–90cm (2–3ft) S:23cm (9in)	June–Aug.	Likes marshy ground or 2.5–5cm (1–2in) of water	Remove dead foliage at the end of the season	Divide established plants in spring
Reedmace *see* Typha						
Rush *see* Juncus						
Sagittaria sagittifolia Arrowhead	The normal form of this plant can be very invasive, but S. s. 'Japonica' is more restrained. Spikes of large double white flowers resemble stocks; arrow-shaped foliage	H:38cm (15in) S:30cm (1ft)	June–July	Plant the tubers about 2.5cm (1in) deep in good loam or in a basket or box, with about 10cm (4in) of water above	Remove dead foliage and flowers as necessary. The plants will not flower so well if planted too deeply	Divide the tubers, which tend to be produced slowly
Saururus cernuus	This is another choice aquatic, with bright green heart-shaped leaves and fragrant white flowers	H:60cm (2ft) S:30cm (1ft)	June–July	Wet soil or very shallow water is required for this plant	Generally trouble-free	Divide established clumps in spring
Scirpus tabernaemontani 'Zebrinus' Bulrush	A plant with bizarre appearance, with round fat stems alternately barred green and white	H:0.6–1.2m (2–4ft) S:38cm (15in)	June–July	Plant in a group in shallow water, where they can form a colony	Cut out any all-green stems that appear	Divide old plants in spring
Spearwort *see* Ranunculus lingua						
Sweet flag, variegated *see* Acorus calamus						
Typha laxmannii Reedmace	A slender plant with tall, narrow leaves and spikes of bulrush-like flowers	H:0.9–1.2m (3–4ft) S:30cm (1ft)	July–Aug.	Grow in containers in shallow water	Generally trouble-free	Divide old plants
T. minima Dwarf reedmace	This is a diminutive reedmace that grows only 30–45cm (1–1½ft) tall. It is free-flowering and dainty	H:30–45cm (1–1½ft) S:15cm (6in)	May–Sept.	Grow in containers in shallow water	Generally trouble-free	Propagation is by division
Water forget-me-not *see* Myosotis palustris						
Water fringe *see* Nymphoides peltata						
Water hawthorn *see* Aponogeton distachyus						
Waterlily *see* Nymphaea						
Water milfoil *see* Myriophyllum brasiliense						
Water poppy *see* Hydrocleys						

Greenhouse and indoor plants

The point at which a greenhouse plant becomes a houseplant is difficult to define — much depends on the conditions that can be offered in the home, and for how long the plant is expected to last indoors.

A houseplant should ideally be able to spend the whole of its existence in the home, growing actively and healthily. Many other plants can be used, however, if they are treated as expendable after providing a useful period of decoration, or can be exchanged for other plants in a greenhouse where they can recover sufficiently to be used another day.

The decision of what to grow in a greenhouse is less difficult, for almost all plants grown in the home will grow equally well — often better — in a greenhouse, given sufficient warmth.

In these tables plants for both home and greenhouse have been included, and an indication is given of the best location. All those marked as suitable for both situations will benefit from a period in the more natural environment of a greenhouse.

Although most greenhouse plants benefit from good light, many of the green-leaved plants grown in the home are naturally adapted to shady conditions, and every effort should be made to provide the correct light intensity.

The temperatures indicate the minimum winter temperature that should be provided. Some plants will survive lower temperatures than those indicated, but may suffer a severe check to growth. There is no precise temperature at which a tender plant will cease to remain healthy — much depends on other factors such as draughts, humidity and above all soil moisture. Many plants will survive surprisingly low temperatures if the soil is barely moist: it is a combination of wet roots and low temperature that frequently proves fatal.

Equally unsatisfactory for many plants is an excessively warm temperature in winter. Balanced, healthy growth is not produced by warmth alone, and without the accompanying light some houseplants will soon become sickly. Many cacti only flower well if subjected to a cold spell during the winter.

Lack of humidity is also a problem in most homes, and unless it can be provided by regular misting, by humidifiers, or by other means, it is best to avoid those plants indicated as requiring high humidity in the table.

Few of the plants listed require special composts, and most of them will grow happily in either a proprietary peat-based compost, or one based on loam, such as John Innes. Where a particular type has been shown to give better results, however, this has been indicated.

Always bear in mind that plants in pots only have a limited root-run and the nutrients in the compost can soon become exhausted. For that reason most houseplants will benefit from regular feeding during the growing period.

Name	Description	Height/ spread	Temp.	Compost and situation	Remarks	Propagation
Achimenes Hot-water plant	*Greenhouse/house:* Tubular flowers opening out into an open bell; very prolific in bloom, colours including shades of red, pink, purple, yellow or white. July to Sept. is the usual flowering period	H:30–45cm (1–1½ft) S:23–38cm (9–15in)	16°C (61°F)	A loam-based compost is preferred. Shade from direct sunlight	Plant tubers in March or April, 2.5cm (1in) deep, six to eight in a 15cm (6in) pot. Syringe during dry, hot weather. Dry off soil and tubers after flowering; replant following spring	Divide old tubers, before replanting in spring
Adiantum capillus-veneris Maidenhair fern	*Greenhouse/house:* An attractive fern with delicate light green fronds and black stems	H:15–25cm (6–10in) S:15–25cm (6–10in)	7°C (45°F)	Use a peat-based compost, and provide humid conditions in shade	Little attention is required apart from spraying with tepid water	Divide roots in spring, or raise from spores
Aechmea rhodocyanea Urn plant	*Greenhouse/house:* Broad, grey leaves shaped in the form of a watertight urn. Pink bracts and bright blue flowers last for about six months	H:45cm (1½ft) S:38cm (15in)	16°C (61°F)	Provide a peat-based, lime-free compost. Best in good light out of direct sun	Keep central vase topped up with water during summer	Young rosettes that form around the main vase after flowering can be potted up in summer
African violet *see* Saintpaulia ionantha						
Aglaonema	*House:* A fine foliage plant with leaves resembling an aspidistra. 'Silver Queen' has grey-green leaves	H:15–20cm (6–8in) S:30cm (1ft)	16°C (61°F)	Plant in a loam-based compost. Requires a shady position and plenty of moisture and humidity	Keep the compost moist, and feed once a week in summer. Repot in March	Divide mature plants in spring
Aloe variegata Partridge-breasted aloe	*Greenhouse/house:* Stemless, keeled leaves with irregular white banding closely overlap to form a kind of rosette	H:30cm (1ft) S:15–20cm (6–8in)	5°C (41°F)	Loam-based composts are best for this plant. Protect from strong sunlight	Keep away from a windowsill in cold weather. Keep quite dry during winter. Repot in April	Remove offsets in summer
Aluminium plant *see* Pilea cadierei						
Anthurium scherzerianum Flamingo flower	*Greenhouse/house:* Distinctive, palette-shaped scarlet spathes with curled orange-red spadix	H:23–30cm (9–12in) S:30–45cm (1–1½ft)	10°C (50°F)	A peaty compost incorporating sphagnum moss and charcoal is best. Good drainage is essential. Provide shade	During winter, keep the compost only just moist, but water freely in warm weather. High humidity is important	Divide mature plants in March or April. Can also be raised from seed if sufficient warmth can be provided
Aporocactus flagelliformis Rat's tail cactus	*Greenhouse/house:* Trailing cactus with ribbed stems about 12mm (½in) thick, covered with short spines. Red flowers may appear on old stems in March or April	Trailing stems up to 75cm (2½ft)	5°C (41°F)	Does best in a peaty, moisture-retentive soil, but good drainage is essential. Position in full sun	Feed once a fortnight during spring and summer	Take cuttings in April or May, or sow seed in May. If stems are directed over a pot of well-drained soil they will root of their own accord

Name	Description	Height/spread	Temp.	Compost and situation	Remarks	Propagation
Artillery plant *see* Pilea muscosa						
Asclepias curassavica Blood flower	*Greenhouse:* Perennial with orange-red flowers from June to Oct.	H:45—60cm (1½—2ft) S:30—45cm (1—1½ft)	15°C (60°F)	Prefers a light, peaty compost. Best in good light	Makes a long-lasting pot plant	Raise from seed in March Can also be divided in April or Oct.
Asparagus Asparagus fern	*Greenhouse/house:* Not a true fern, but the feathery sprays of needle-like foliage give a fern-like appearance. *A. densiflorus* (syn. *A. sprengeri*) has a bolder, more pendulous habit, while *A. setaceus* (syn. *A. plumosus*) has finer, more upright growth	H:38cm (15in) S:75—90cm (2½—3ft)	7°C (45°F)	Asparagus ferns prefer a loam-based compost. Position in good light but out of direct sun	Keep well watered, especially during summer. Feed once a fortnight during summer	Divide plants in March or April, or sow seed in spring
Aspidistra elatior Cast iron plant	*House:* A traditional houseplant, with green lance-shaped leaves arising from the crown on slender stalks	H:30cm (1ft) S:45cm (1½ft)	1°C (34°F)	Grow in a loam-based compost in a cool, shady position	Keep the soil moist, and avoid using leaf-shining chemicals on the leaves	Divide old plants in spring or summer
Astrophytum myriostigma Bishop's cap cactus	*House:* An attractive cactus that derives its common name from its distinctive mitre shape. Yellow flowers appear from June to August	H:15—20cm (6—8in) S:10—15cm (4—6in)	5°C (41°F)	Best in a sandy soil containing lime. Good light is required	Water freely in summer, sparingly the rest of the year	Sow seed in spring in a temperature of 21°C (70°F)
Barrel cactus *see* Echinocactus grusonii						
Begonia	*Greenhouse/house:* There are three main types of begonias — the tuberous-rooted type are generally deciduous and grown for their large flowers; rhizomatous begonias are usually evergreen and grown for their attractive foliage; fibrous-rooted kinds are evergreen and grown chiefly for their flowers. Among the rhizomatous foliage kinds are *B. boweri* (H:15—25cm/ 6—10in: S:13—23cm/5—9in), *B. manicata* (H:38—45cm/15—18in, S:35—41cm/14—16in), *B. masoniana* (H:25cm/10in, S:30cm/1ft), and *B. rex* (H:30cm/1ft, S:45cm/1½ft)	See description	10—20°C (50—60°F)	Both peat and loam-based composts are suitable, but drainage should be good. Position in partial shade	Tuberous-rooted: Start into growth in March or April at 18°C (64°F). Rhizomatous and fibrous-rooted: Water generously during growing season	*Begonia rex* is normally propagated from leaf cuttings, and the fibrous-rooted kinds such as *B. semperflorens* from seed. Most kinds can be propagated from stem cuttings
Beloperone guttata (syn. Justicia brandegeana) Shrimp plant	*Greenhouse/house:* Distinctively-shaped bracts resembling shrimps; the flowers themselves are fairly inconspicuous. April to Dec. is the main period of flowering	H:60cm (2ft) S:45cm (1½ft)	7°C (45°F)	Use a loam-based compost, and repot in March. During summer keep the plants cool and in some shade	Keep well watered during summer, and feed once a fortnight. If plants become straggly, trim back	Take cuttings 5—7.5cm (2—3in) long in April, and root in a temperature of 18°C (64°F)
Billbergia nutans Queen's tears	*Greenhouse/house:* Clusters of long, drooping flowers in May and June. Rose-pink bracts hold greenish-yellow and purple flowers	H:38—45cm (15—18in) S:38—50cm (15—20in)	7°C (45°F)	Requires a lime-free compost with good drainage. Provide a humid atmosphere and good light out of direct sunlight	Keep well watered, especially during summer	Remove offsets in summer and pot up in a mixture of loam-based compost and sphagnum moss
Bishop's cap cactus *see* Astrophytum myriostigma						
Black-eyed Susan *see* Thunbergia alata						
Blood flower *see* Aslepias curassavica						
Bougainvillea × buttiana	*Greenhouse:* Shrubby, climbing deciduous plant for a large greenhouse. Good cultivars include 'Mrs. Butt' (rose-crimson bracts fading to magenta), 'Brilliant' (coppery-orange bracts becoming cerise-red), and 'Kiltie Campbell' (orange bracts)	Climber to 2.4m (8ft)	7°C (45°F)	Provide a rich loam-based compost. To restrict height to that indicated, plant in pots — grown in the border heights can be considerably more. Provide good light without direct sun	During summer, feed once a week. After flowering reduce water until March, then start into growth. In Feb. shorten main growths by one-third, and spur back all sideshoots	Cuttings of half-ripe shoots can be taken in early summer. They should be 7.5cm (3in) long and rooted in pots of sandy soil placed in a propagator
Calamondin orange *see* Citrus microcarpa						
Canary Island ivy *see* Hedera canariensis						
Cape primrose *see* Streptocarpus						

Greenhouse and indoor plants

Name	Description	Height/ spread	Flowering period	Soil and site	Remarks	Propagation
Cast iron plant *see* Aspidistra elatior						
Cathedral bells *see* Cobaea scandens						
Celosia argentea 'Cristata' Cockscomb	*Greenhouse:* Colourful crested flower heads in scarlet or gold	H:30cm (1ft) S:15cm (6in)	15°C (60°F)	Will grow in any good potting compost. Requires good light	An easily-grown annual, flowering all summer	Raise from seed in March
Ceropegia woodii Hearts entangled	*Greenhouse/house:* A fascinating plant with puffed-out mottled grey, heart-shaped leaves. The flowers, produced in Sept. and Oct. are insignificant, foliage being the main attraction	Trailing to 75cm (2½ft)	10°C (50°F)	Does best in a peat-based compost. Requires good light	Water sparingly, even in summer	Divide old plants, or the calluses on the stems can be removed and rooted
Cereus peruvianus	*Greenhouse/house:* A columnar cactus, bluish-green in colour, with five to eight ribs bearing spiteful barbs	H:60–90cm (2–3ft) S:5–7.5cm (2–3in)	5°C (41°F)	Requires a well-drained, rich, chalky soil, with extra grit or fine gravel. Needs a sunny position	Water well during summer, but keep much drier in winter	Sow seed in April in a temperature of 21°C (70°F). Cuttings 7.5–10cm (3–4in) long can be rooted in a sandy compost
Cherry pie *see* Heliotropium arborescens						
Chlorophytum comosum Spider plant	*Greenhouse/house:* A popular houseplant with cream and green, long, narrow foliage and plantlets at the ends of long stalks	H:25–30cm (10–15in) S:38–45cm (15–18in)	7°C (45°F)	Plant in a loam-based compost. Will grow well in light or shade	Give only a little water during winter but water freely during summer and feed once a fortnight	Peg the plantlets into small pots of compost. Once rooted, sever the stem
Cigar plant *see* Cuphea						
Citrus microcarpa (syn. C. mitis) Calamondin orange	*Greenhouse:* A fascinating miniature orange, the fruits lasting a long time. Small white flowers appear most of the year	H:45cm (1½ft) S:30–38cm (12–15in)	13°C (55°F)	Grow in a loam-based compost, in good light. Can be stood outside in summer	If possible, keep outside during summer. Feed regularly. If leaves turn yellow try watering with an iron chelate (Sequestrene). Do not repot too frequently	Sow seed in spring, or take cuttings 7.5–10cm (3–4in) long in July or Aug. Cuttings should be rooted in a peat and sand mixture in a propagator

Below: Bougainvillea × buttiana *'Kiltie Campbell'*. *Below right:* Adiantum *sp. (maidenhair fern)*. *Far below right:* Dracaena fragrans

Name	Description	Height/ spread	Flowering period	Soil and site	Remarks	Propagation
Cobaea scandens Cathedral bells, cup and saucer vine	*Greenhouse:* Climber with large bell-shaped flowers, from June to Oct., usually purple, sometimes greenish	H:2.4–3.5m (8–12ft) S:1.8–2.4m (6–8ft)	13°C (55°F)	Best in a loam-based mix, or greenhouse border	Best grown in the greenhouse border, but can be rampant	Raise from seed in March
Cockscomb *see* Celosia argentea 'Cristata'						
Codiaeum variegatum pictum Croton	*Greenhouse/house:* An attractive plant with variegated leaves in shades of red, yellow, green, and brown. If grown in a greenhouse border, may reach 1.2–1.8m (4–6ft). There are several cultivars, including 'Disraeli' (mid-green, blotched cream above), 'Reidii' (patterned like a ladder), and 'Carrierei' (yellow and green with a red centre)	H:45–60cm (1½–2ft) S:38–45cm (15–18in)	13°C (55°F)	Best in a loam-based compost, with good drainage. Requires good light, but preferably out of direct sunlight	It is vital to avoid draughts or fluctuations in temperature	Tip cuttings can be taken from March to June, and rooted in a propagator
Creeping fig *see* Ficus pumila						
Croton *see* Codiaeum variegatum pictum						
Crown of thorns *see* Euphorbia milii						
Cryptanthus bivittatus Earth star	*Greenhouse/house:* A bromeliad with wavy leaves about 23cm (9in) long, forming a rosette	H:7.5–13cm (3–5in) S:15–23cm (6–9in)	7°C (45°F)	Requires a compost of open texture but water-retentive, ideally containing peat and sphagnum moss. Best in good light out of direct sun	Water freely during summer, only enough to keep plants alive in winter	Offshoots can be removed in April and potted up
Cup and saucer vine *see* Cobaea scandens						
Cuphea Cigar plant	*Greenhouse:* Flowering evergreen. Red flowers have dark 'ash' ring at end	H:30–38cm (12–15in) S:30–38cm (12–15in)	15°C (60°F)	Grow in a loam-based compost in good light	Carries its interesting flowers from June to Sept.	Sow seed in March, or take cuttings of young shoots in March, April or Aug.
Cyclamen persicum	*Greenhouse/house:* Popular plants, especially at Christmas, although they will flower from Oct. to April. Colours range from white to magenta, and many have frilled edges. The foliage is often attractively mottled or marbled with silver	H:23–30cm (9–12in) S:20–25cm (8–10in)	10°C (50°F)	Will grow well in loam-based or peat composts, in a shady position	Keep the plant cool when in flower, and ensure the compost does not dry out. As the flowers die, pull them away from the base, complete with flower stalk. Corms can be kept from year to year, but must have a resting period after flowering	Propagate from seed, sown in spring or autumn in a temperature of 15°C (60°F)
Dieffenbachia Dumb cane	*Greenhouse/house:* Foliage plants with a poisonous sap that is liable to cause speech impediment if in contact with the mouth. *D. amoena* (H:0.6–1.2m/2–4ft, S:23–30cm/9–12in) has dark green leaves with white and cream marbling along the lateral veins. *D. maculata* (H:45–90cm/1½–3ft, S:23–30cm (9–12in) displays dark green leaves with large cream blotches between the veins	See description	13°C (55°F)	Best in a loam-based compost, but requires good drainage. Needs a draught-free situation out of direct sunlight	Water sparingly during winter, generously in summer. Spray leaves occasionally with tepid water	Take stem cuttings 5–7.5cm (2–3in) long in late spring, rooting them in a propagator
Dracaena	*Greenhouse/house:* There are several good species of this decorative group of plants. *D. deremensis* (H:0.9–1.2m/3–4ft, S:30–38cm/12–15in) bears sword-like leaves, glossy green and with two long, silver stripes. *D. fragrans* (H:45–60cm/1½–2ft, S:30–45cm/1–1½ft) has broad leaves striped gold and green and often up to 90cm (3ft) long. *D. godseffiana* (H:45–60cm/1½–2ft, S:30–45cm/1–1½ft) has thin, wiry stems, and dark green laurel-like leaves spotted with cream	See description	13°C (55°F)	Grow in a loam-based compost, with good drainage. Place in full light, but protect from strong sun	Water freely from April to Sept., but sparingly at other times	Take cuttings of basal shoots 7.5cm (3in) long in March or April, and root in a propagating case

Greenhouse and indoor plants

Name	Description	Height/ spread	Temp.	Compost and situation	Remarks	Propagation
Dumb cane *see* Dieffenbachia						
Earth star *see* Cryptanthus bivittatus						
Echeveria	*Greenhouse/house:* A large group of succulents, mainly producing rosettes of greyish leaves. Bell-like flowers are produced on arching stems in late summer	H:10–15cm (4–6in) S:7.5–13cm (3–5in)	5°C (41°F)	Best in a loam-based compost. Good drainage is essential. Position in good light	Avoid water splashing on the leaves. Be careful not to overwater	Remove side rosettes, or take leaf cuttings
Echinocactus grusonii Barrel cactus	*Greenhouse/house:* A rounded, almost ball-shaped cactus with golden spines. Tubular yellow flowers may be borne in May	H:15cm (6in) S:10cm (4in)	5°C (41°F)	A sandy, well-drained compost should be provided. Requires good light	Keep moist in summer, almost dry in winter	Raise from seed sown in April at 21°C (70°F)
Epiphyllum Orchid cactus	*Greenhouse/house:* An epiphytic cactus with rather ungainly stems, resembling strap-like leaves, but spectacular flowers that may be up to 15cm (6in) across. There are many excellent hybrids. Colours range from red to yellow. White is also found, and some are bi-coloured	H:60–90cm (2–3ft) S:30–45cm (1–1½ft)	5°C (41°F)	Requires a rich compost, preferably loam-based, but it must be well drained. Grows best in semi-shade	Feed during summer and water freely during growing period. Do not overwater in winter. May benefit from being stood outside in summer	Can be raised from seed sown in April in a temperature of 21°C (70°F), but named kinds should be raised from cuttings taken in spring. Allow the cutting to dry off for a few days before inserting in a rooting compost
Euphorbia milii (syn. E. splendens) Crown of thorns	*Greenhouse/house:* A distinctive succulent with spines on its stems, small leaves and flowers with deep crimson bracts	H:30–90cm (1–3ft) S:30–60cm (1–2ft)	13°C (55°F)	Provide a well-drained loam-based compost. Best in good light	Water freely during summer but only enough to keep compost just moist in winter. Feed fortnightly in summer	Take cuttings in July and insert in a propagator
Ficus benjamina Weeping fig	*Greenhouse/house:* Beautiful, elliptical, soft green leaves on pendulous branches. May eventually reach tree-like proportions, and mature leaves are a darker green	H:0.9–1.8m (3–6ft) S:45–75cm (1½–2½ft)	13°C (55°F)	Loam-based or peat composts are suitable. Position in good light but out of direct sunlight	Water freely during summer, only enough to keep compost slightly moist in winter	Cuttings 7.5–10cm (3–4in) long can be taken from April to June, and inserted in a peat-sand mix in a propagator
F. elastica Rubber plant	*Greenhouse/house:* A popular houseplant that requires no introduction. The best green-leafed cultivar is 'Robusta', which has large, shiny green leaves, but there are also variegated kinds such as 'Doescheri' (pale green with broad ivory edges), and 'Schryveriana' (cream patches)	H:0.9–1.8m (3–6ft) S:45–75cm (1½–2½ft)	16°C (61°F)	As *F. benjamina*	As *F. benjamina*	Leggy plants can be air layered, or cuttings taken as *F. benjamina*
F. pumila Creeping fig	*Greenhouse/house:* A small plant of trailing habit with irregular dark green leaves	Trailing	7°C (45°F)	As *F. benjamina*	As *F. benjamina*	As *F. benjamina*

Below: Saintpaulia ionantha *(African violet). Below right:* Zebrina pendula

Name	Description	Height/spread	Temp.	Compost and situation	Remarks	Propagation
F. radicans see F. sagittata						
F. sagittata (syn. F. radicans)	*Greenhouse/house:* Similar to *F. pumila*, but with larger, pointed, oval leaves. The best form is *F. s.* 'Variegata' which has creamy-white edges	Trailing	13°C (55°F)	As *F. benjamina*	As *F. benjamina*	As *F. benjamina*
Fittonia verschaffeltii Snakeskin plant	*Greenhouse/house:* Foliage plant with dark green leaves and attractive carmine veins. *F. v.* 'Argyroneura' has white veins	Prostrate	16°C (61°F)	Best in a peat-based compost, in reasonable light but always out of direct sunlight	A humid atmosphere is essential. Water well during summer, and feed occasionally. Water less in winter	Divide mature plants in summer, or take cuttings in spring or summer and root in a propagator
Flamingo flower see Anthurium scherzerianum						
Grevillea robusta Silk oak	*Greenhouse/house:* Decorative foliage plant, with feathery leaves	H:1–3m (3–10ft) S:30–75cm (1–2½ft)	15°C (60°F)	Grows well in a loam-based compost. Requires good light	Will eventually grow into a tree, but excellent for a living-room while small	Sow seed in March
Hedera Ivy	*Greenhouse/house:* There are some charming small-leaved kinds suitable for the home, such as 'Aureo-variegata' (yellow and green leaves), and 'Conglomerata' (small, wavy-edged leaves). The Canary island ivy, *H. canariensis* is another good houseplant; its heart-shaped leaves are bright green with cream marbling	Climber/trailer	Hardy	Both loam-based and peat composts are suitable. Require semi-shade; keep variegated kinds out of direct sunlight, but all ivies may grow spindly if kept in deep shade	Repot annually. The plants will need canes or some other support to climb up, or they can be allowed to trail	Take cuttings 7.5–10cm (3–4in) long in summer and insert in a peat-sand mixture in a propagator
Hearts entangled see Ceropegia woodii						
Heliotropium arborescens Cherry pie	*Greenhouse:* Fragrant lavender and blue flowers from July to Oct.	H:30–90cm (1–3ft) S:30–45cm (1–1½ft)	15°C (60°F)	Will grow well in any good compost, in pots or the greenhouse border	Water freely from March to Oct., and feed regularly	Sow seed in March, or root cuttings 5–7.5cm (2–3in) long in a propagator in spring or autumn
Hibiscus rosa-sinensis Rose mallow	*Greenhouse:* Flowering plant with large blooms (10–13cm/4–5in across) from June to Sept. Each flower is short-lived but there are plenty of them. Colours include shades of pink, red and orange	H:1.5m (5ft) S:1.2m (4ft)	7°C (45°F)	A loam-based compost suits these plants. Good light is necessary but there should be protection from direct sun	Ventilate well if the temperature exceeds 21°C (70°F). Feed generously from June to Sept.	Take cuttings 7.5–10cm (3–4in) long from May to Aug., rooting them in a propagator
Hot-water plant see Achimenes						
Impatiens wallerana Busy Lizzie	*Greenhouse/house:* A well-known houseplant, with flowers up to 5cm (2in) across, from April to Oct. Colours include orange, white, scarlet and crimson	H:30–60cm (1–2ft) S:30–45cm (1–1½ft)	13°C (55°F)	Best in a loam-based compost, in good light	Avoid widely fluctuating temperatures. Feed during summer. Avoid splashing water on flowers	Cuttings are easily rooted in water or, preferably, equal parts peat and sand. They should be 7.5–10cm (3–4in) long, and taken from April to Sept.
Ipomoea Morning glory	*Greenhouse:* Sky-blue saucer-shaped flowers, short-lived but freely produced, from June to Sept.	H:1.8–3m (6–10ft) S:0.9–1.5m (3–5ft)	10°C (50°F)	Will grow in any good compost, but requires good light	An annual climber, best grown up a trellis	Sow seed in March
Ivy see Hedera						
Justicia brandegeana see Beloperone guttata						
Kalanchoe blossfeldiana	*Greenhouse/house:* A compact plant with clusters of scarlet flowers. The natural flowering period is February to May, but by adjusting the day length commercial growers flower them over a longer period	H:30cm (1ft) S:30cm (1ft)	5°C (41°F)	Provide a loam-based compost, and full light in winter, though partial shade is best in summer	Water well in summer	Sow seed in March in a temperature of 21°C (70°F), or take cuttings in spring or summer
Lithops Living stones	*Greenhouse/house:* These fascinating succulents resemble small pebbles, but in late summer or autumn white or yellow daisy-like flowers appear. There are many species	H:4cm (1½in) S:2.5cm (1in)	5°C (41°F)	Requires a gritty, free-draining compost. Position in full sun	During the resting period, from Oct. to April, lithops should be watered; the rest of the year the compost should be kept just moist, but not wet	Sow seed in April, in a temperature of 21°C (70°F), or divide mature clumps in June
Living stones see Lithops						

Greenhouse and indoor plants

Name	Description	Height/spread	Temp.	Compost and situation	Remarks	Propagation
Lobivia haageana	*Greenhouse/house:* An almost spherical cactus with large spines. Old specimens are likely to flower regularly	H:15cm (6in) S:7.5cm (3in)	2°C (36°F)	Provide a gritty, free-draining compost and a bright position	Withhold water from Oct. to early April. Water moderately at other times	Sow seed in March in a temperature of 21°C (70°F). Offsets can be removed from large plants
Maidenhair fern *see* Adiantum capillus-veneris						
Mammillaria bocasana	*Greenhouse/house:* An easy-to-grow cactus with cream flowers in June. The spherical stems are covered with white spines. There are other good mammillarias	H:15cm (6in) S:13cm (5in)	5°C (41°F)	A loam-based compost with added grit or sharp sand is ideal. Full sun is required	Water freely in summer by standing the pot in water then allowing to drain thoroughly	Propagate from offsets formed around mature plants
Monstera deliciosa Swiss cheese plant	*Greenhouse/house:* A popular plant, with dramatic appearance, the large glossy green leaves being deeply slashed, and sometimes perforated	H:1.2–2.4m (4–8ft) S:1.2–1.8m (4–6ft)	10°C (50°F)	Provide a loam-based compost and a shady position	High humidity is required, and plenty of water during spring and summer. In winter keep the compost just moist. Wipe the leaves with moist cotton-wool to keep them shiny	Cuttings can be taken with one leaf in summer, but this can spoil the appearance of a specimen plant
Mother-in-law's tongue *see* Sansevieria trifasciata						
Opuntia Prickly pear	*Greenhouse/house:* Cactus with many-jointed fleshy pads	H:25–50cm (10–20in) S:15–25cm (6–10in)	10°C (50°F)	Best in a well-drained loam-based compost in full sun	Water extremely sparingly in winter; keep almost dry	Sow seed in March, or insert pieces of stem in a gritty compost after exposing to air for a few days
Orchid cactus *see* Epiphyllum						
Partridge-breasted (aloe) *see* Aloe variegata						
Peperomia argyreia (syn. P. sandersii)	*Greenhouse/house:* Distinctive leaves are thick, smooth, and about 7.5–10cm (3–4in) long, silver-grey with dark green bands along the veins	H:20cm (8in) S:15cm (6in)	13°C (55°F)	These plants prefer a loam-based compost, although good results are also achieved with a peat compost. Position in good light but out of direct sun	Take care not to saturate the compost. Provide a humid atmosphere	Cuttings can be taken from April to Aug., and rooted in a propagator
P. magnoliifolia *see* P. obtusifolia						
P. obtusifolia (syn. P. magnoliifolia)	*Greenhouse/house:* A plant of open habit and glossy green leaves up to 5cm (2in) long. A variegated form, *P. o.* 'Variegata' has green and cream leaves	H:18cm (7in) S:20cm (8in)	10°C (50°)	As *P. argyreia*	As *P. argyreia*	As *P. argyreia*
P. scandens	*Greenhouse/house:* A vigorous climber or trailer with glossy heart-shaped leaves. A variegated form has cream edges	Climbing or trailing	13°C (55°F)	As *P. argyreia*	As *P. argyreia*	As *P. argyreia*
Philodendron scandens Sweetheart plant	*Greenhouse/house:* A vigorous climbing plant with glossy, heart-shaped, dark green leaves. It will easily reach 1.2–1.8m (4–6ft). Other species are available, including non-climbers, and one — *P. bipinnatifidum* — that resembles the Swiss cheese plant *(Monstera deliciosa)* at first glance	Climber	13°C (55°F)	Good results are likely with any good potting compost, and they are ideal for a shady position	The sweetheart plant can be grown up a moss pole, which should be kept moist by spraying regularly with water. High humidity is necessary. Can also be allowed to trail	Take cuttings 10–13cm (4–5in) long in May or June, inserting them in a peat and sand mixture in a propagator
Pilea cadierei Aluminium plant	*Greenhouse/house:* The silvery bands on the rather crinkly green leaves give rise to the common name — the foliage looks as though it has been painted with aluminium paint	H:20cm (8in) S:20cm (8in)	10°C (50°F)	Provide a loam-based compost and a position in good light but out of direct sunlight	Feed regularly during the summer months. To keep the plants bushy, pinch out the growing tips of the leading shoots	Cuttings taken in spring or summer will root easily
P. muscosa Artillery plant	*Greenhouse/house:* Finely divided green foliage. Insignificant flowers discharge pollen forcibly	H:38cm (15in) S:20cm (8in)	13°C (55°F)	As *P. cadierei*	As *P. cadierei*	As *P. cadierei*
Poor man's orchid *see* Schizanthus						
Prickly pear *see* Opuntia						
Queen's tears *see* Billbergia nutans						
Rat's tail cactus *see* Aporocactus flagelliformis						

Name	Description	Height/spread	Temp.	Compost and situation	Remarks	Propagation
Rebutia	*Greenhouse/house:* A group of cacti that are particularly popular because they tend to flower readily, even when young. They are mostly globular in shape, and form clumps. Colours include red, pink, orange, yellow, lilac, violet, and white	H:5–10cm (2–4in) S:5–10cm (2–4in)	5°C (41°F)	Grow well in a loam-based compost with additional grit or sharp sand; a little bonemeal is also beneficial. Provide a position in full light	Keep dry during winter, and only water sparingly in summer	Remove offsets during summer
Rose mallow *see* Hibiscus rosa-sinensis						
Rubber plant *see* Ficus elastica						
Saintpaulia ionantha African violet	*Greenhouse/house:* Extremely popular houseplants, with rounded hairy leaves and clusters of violet-like flowers borne for most of the year. There are many charming cultivars of improved constitution and habit, including: 'Blue Fairy Tale' (deep blue), 'Diana Red' (reddish-purple), 'Grandiflora Pink' (rose-pink), and 'Rhapsody' (semi-double, purplish-blue)	H:7.5–15cm (3–6in) S:7.5–15cm (3–6in)	13°C (55°F)	Saintpaulias prefer a peat-based compost, and a position in good light but not direct sun	Keep moist at all times, but not saturated. Do not allow water to fall on the leaves	Take leaf cuttings from June to Sept., inserting the stem into the compost so that the leaf blade just touches the surface. Root in a propagator
Sansevieria trifasciata Mother-in-law's tongue	*Greenhouse/house:* A distinctive succulent with sword-like leaves arising from compost-level. The long, fleshy leaves are dark green with grey bands, and *S. t.* 'Laurentii' has a golden band round the edge of each leaf. There is another form. *S. t.* 'Hahnii', that is quite different in appearance, forming a low rosette	H:45cm (1½ft) S:15cm (6in)	16°C (61°F)	Any good potting compost is suitable, but drainage must be good. Position in good light	Keep almost dry in winter, but water as normal plants in summer	Divide mature plants in summer. Sections of leaf can also be rooted if inserted into a potting compost
Schizanthus Poor man's orchid	*Greenhouse:* Colourful butterfly-like flowers from July to Sept.	H:30–90cm (1–3ft) S:20–45cm (8–18in)	13°C (55°F)	Will grow well in any good compost. Keep in good light	May need staking. Prick out growing tip to encourage bushiness	Sow seed in March
Shrimp plant *see* Belloperone guttata						
Silk oak *see* Grevillea robusta						
Snakeskin plant *see* Fittonia verschaffeltii						
Spider plant *see* Chlorophytum comosum						
Streptocarpus Cape primrose	*Greenhouse:* Graceful heads of trumpet shaped flowers, mainly in shades of blue. Strap-shaped hairy leaves	H:25–50cm (10–20in) S:15–25cm (6–10in)	15°C (60°F)	Grow well in any good compost. Shade from sun	Blooms continuously from May to Oct.	Sow seed in spring, or take leaf cuttings from May to June
Sweetheart plant *see* Philodendron scandens						
Swiss cheese plant *see* Monstera deliciosa						
Thunbergia alata Black-eyed Susan	*Greenhouse:* A rapid climber having gay orange flowers, with a black eye	H:1.8m (6ft) S:90cm (3ft)	15°C (60°F)	Grows in any good compost. Best in a sunny position	An annual, useful for pillars	Sow seed in March
Tradescantia fluminensis Wandering Jew	*Greenhouse/house:* A well-known and easy-to-grow foliage plant. The leaves are longitudinally striped with silver. A good form is 'Quicksilver'	Trailing	7°C (45°F)	Tradescantias prefer a loam-based compost, but drainage should be good. A well-lit situation is required for compact plants with good colouring	Water well during summer, but keep compost only just moist in winter. Remove any shoots with green leaves that appear	Cuttings taken during summer are easily rooted in a peat-sand mixture
Urn plant *see* Aechmea rhodocyanea						
Wandering Jew *see* Tradescantia fluminensis						
Weeping fig *see* Ficus benjamina						
Zebrina pendula	*Greenhouse/house:* A foliage plant closely resembling *Tradescantia fluminensis*, but with larger and more purple leaves. The upper surface has green and silver stripes, but the underside is a rich purple	Trailing	15°C (60°F)	A loam-based compost is suitable, but drainage must be good. Position in good light	Water sparingly in winter, but freely in summer	Cuttings taken in spring or summer are easily rooted in a peat-sand mixture

Fruit

Contrary to established ideas, you do not need a lot of space to grow a good selection of fruit. At present plums and cherries require considerable space (though even these will be grown on dwarf rootstocks in the near future), but apples and pears can be grown as very small trees on dwarfing rootstocks or as trained specimens against a wall. For apples in particular, there are many space-saving methods of training that are ideally suited to a small garden (see page 114).

Some of the bush fruits such as black currants and gooseberries may seem demanding of space at first impression, but careful selection of cultivars can usually enable at least one or two bushes to be accommodated. The black currant 'Amos Black' makes only a small, compact bush, for instance, whereas 'Boskoop Giant' and 'Wellington XXX' both make large, spreading bushes; the gooseberry 'Langley Gage' has upright but compact growth, while 'Careless' will make a large, spreading bush. Don't overlook the possibility of training a gooseberry as a cordon.

Blackberries and loganberries can be grown against a boundary fence, and again cultivars can be found to suit most needs. If the idea of thorns deters you, then 'Oregon Thornless' is the blackberry for you, and 'LY 654' is a thornless loganberry.

It is, perhaps, the raspberries and strawberries that are the most popular fruits. Many old names are still to be found, but some of the newer kinds have greater disease resistance as well as heavier crops.

Strawberries and raspberries are particularly susceptible to virus diseases, and these will lead to a steady decline in quality and yield. Always try to buy certified virus-free stock.

Rootstocks are important for some of the tree fruits, such as apples and plums, as these have a profound influence on the height and vigour of the tree. The main rootstocks are described in detail on page 114, but if in doubt your nurseryman will always advise you on the most suitable for your purpose. When buying from a garden centre the rootstock may not be indicated, and it is safe to assume that one suitable for a small garden has been used; but if in doubt, ask the staff to check for you.

When buying apples, pears, plums and cherries, the question of pollination has to be considered. In all these fruits some cultivars will not set an adequate crop with their own pollen (in some cases, no crop at all). No amount of careful cultivation, or beehives under every tree, will be of any use unless a cultivar with suitable pollen is nearby.

A suitable pollinator may be available in a neighbouring garden, but unless you know there is one it is always best to plant a cross-pollinator.

Some plums are self-fertile, in which case no other plum need be planted. To simplify choice, all those recommended in the table are self-fertile. In the case of apples and pears a key to the pollination group is given for each entry, and an explanation will be found on the relevant page.

Sweet cherries are particularly complicated in their requirements, and because only a few cultivars are given, some suggested pollinators will be found in individual entries.

Name	Description	Time of use	Pollination group	Special merits	Remarks	Culinary notes
Apples						
'Beauty of Bath'	Small, bright red fruits of good flavour. The flesh is both firm and tender, juicy, but slightly acid	Aug.	A	Decorative in flower. Good flavour	A moderately vigorous cultivar with spreading habit, inclined to bear its fruits on the branch tips	An excellent dessert cultivar. Because it does not keep well it is best eaten straight from the tree
'Blenheim Orange'	A vigorous cultivar producing medium to large fruits, orange in colour and with a slight russet appearance. The flesh is firm, crisp and nutty	Nov.–Jan.	B(X)	Tends to be resistant to mildew	For good crops it is best to plant this with *two* other suitable cultivars	Can be used as a dessert or culinary apple
'Bramley's Seedling'	A large fruit, somewhat flattened and irregular in shape, often with knobs at the top. Its flesh is white and juicy	Nov.–Feb.	B(X)	Considered to be one of the finest culinary cultivars	Forms a large tree and is therefore not suitable for a small garden	Excellent flavour when cooked
'Cox's Orange Pippin'	A famous cultivar, bearing medium-sized fruit with red flushes and some russeting. Has a fine texture, with aromatic flavour	Nov.–Jan.	B	Almost universally popular	Best for frost-free areas. It forms a somewhat upright tree with slender growth	Superb flavour as a dessert apple
'Discovery'	A relatively new cultivar, producing juicy, deep red fruit of good quality	Aug.–Oct.	B	Produces an early crop	Moderately vigorous, and a tree of medium size	A good dessert apple, best eaten straight from the tree
'Egremont Russet'	One of the best russet cultivars, cropping early in its life. Medium-sized fruits with a distinctive nutty flavour	Oct.–Dec.	A	The foliage shows some resistance to disease. Crops well	Forms an upright tree of medium size	A dessert apple with distinctive flavour
'Ellison's Orange'	Distinctive yellowish fruit with much red streaking, and a flavour that is usually appreciated	Sept.–Oct.	B	Flowers tend to be resistant to frost, therefore useful in difficult areas	Growth tends to be upright. Inclined to bear fruit biennially	A dessert apple especially good if eaten soon after being picked
'Grenadier'	Large, irregular, roundish to conical fruits, greenish-yellow in colour. Juicy, acid flesh	Aug.–Oct.	B	Heavy crops, early. Some disease resistance	A moderately vigorous tree	Best used as a cooking apple

Name	Description	Time of use	Pollination group	Special merits	Remarks	Culinary notes
'Idared'	Medium-sized, bright red fruits with juicy flesh	Nov.–March	A	Keeps very well	A small tree producing a prolific crop, but susceptible to mildew	A dual-purpose apple — can be used as a dessert cultivar or for cooking
'James Grieve'	Attractive, medium-sized fruits, oval or irregular in shape, with a red flush overlaying a pale yellow colour	Sept.–Oct.	B	A dependable cultivar, suitable for a small garden	Crops heavily and regularly, but fruit bruises easily	Can be picked and eaten straight from the tree when ripe, when its rich flavour is at its best
'Kent'	A recent cultivar of considerable promise	Dec.–Jan.	B	Produces apples of fine quality, resembling 'Cox's Orange Pippin'	Crops a little later than 'Cox's Orange Pippin', but more heavily	A dessert apple of very good flavour
'Laxton's Fortune'	Medium-sized fruit, often roundish, yellow in colour with red streaks or flushes	Sept.–Oct.	A	Pleasant flavour	Inclined to crop biennially. Spreading, upright shape	A dessert apple with juicy flesh and a slight banana flavour
'Lord Derby'	Large, yellowish-green, rather oblong fruits. A very old apple	Nov.–Dec.	B	Disease resistant. Regular cropper	Robust, vigorous growth; erect habit	The coarse white flesh has a rather acid but good flavour
'Lord Lambourne'	Medium-sized, round, greenish-yellow fruits flushed and streaked crimson	Oct.–Nov.	A	In season just before 'Cox's Orange Pippin' and useful for continuity of supply	Moderately vigorous, and upright habit. A heavy cropper	A dessert apple with crisp, white flesh. Skins tend to be tough
'Merton Knave'	A recent introduction. Bright red, crisp fruits	Aug.–Sept.	B	Resistant to mildew, and fairly resistant to canker	A useful early dessert apple	A dessert apple with sweet flesh
'Suntan'	A new cultivar resembling 'Cox's Orange Pippin'	Nov.–March	C	Considered by some to be more flavoursome than 'Cox's Orange Pippin'	Heavy cropper. Keeps well into March	A dessert apple of excellent quality and flavour

POLLINATION OF APPLES

All apples set a better crop if pollinated by another cultivar.

Because some apples have a different number of chromosomes they are not successful pollinators, although they set a good crop if provided with pollen from another kind. These apples are indicated by 'X' following the letter A, B, or C, representing the three main cross-pollination groupings. Because those cultivars marked 'X' cannot reciprocate with good pollen, the pollinator will in turn need another ordinary cultivar to ensure a good crop on all trees (i.e. a minimum of three trees will be needed).

For all other apples it is sufficient to plant just one other cultivar *from the same group*.

Apricots						
'Hemskerke'	Rather large, conical fruits, pale yellow with red blotches	Early Aug.	—	Hardier than 'Moorpark'	The best for northern areas, where it can be grown against a wall	Excellent flavour. Sweet flesh
'Moorpark'	Large, round fruits, brownish-orange with a brownish-red flush	Late Aug.	—	Particularly fine flavour	Crops regularly. Useful for a small garden	Excellent cooked or uncooked. The flesh is juicy and sweet
Blackberry						
'Bedford Giant'	Very large berries, shining black and sweet	Late July	—	A heavy, reliable cropper	The canes are of medium vigour	Excellent flavour, good to eat cooked or uncooked. Juicy
'Himalaya Giant'	Large, rounded, jet-black berries, sweet when fully ripe	Aug.–Sept.	—	A useful culinary kind	Very vigorous, particularly thorny canes	The fruit, which is of moderate flavour, is best used in pies and tarts. Bottles well
'Oregon Thornless'	Large, succulent fruits and 'parsley-type' leaves	Sept.–Oct.	—	Thornless. Good flavour	Medium vigour. Tends to need plenty of water to swell the berries	Good 'bramble' flavour
Black currants						
'Amos Black'	A late cultivar of compact habit	Aug.	—	Because of its small size, is useful if space is limited	Comparatively light crops. Because it flowers late it can usually be depended on to miss most frosts	Reasonable flavour
'Baldwin'	Medium to large fruit, often rather acid in flavour	Aug.	—	A heavy cropper and dependable	Forms a moderately vigorous, compact bush	An ideal culinary cultivar
'Boskoop Giant'	Large, slightly flattened currants with thin skins. Large bunches	July	—	An early cultivar with sweet fruits	Vigorous, forming a large, spreading bush	Good for bottling
'Laxton's Giant'	Huge fruits. Makes a large bush	July	—	Earliness and flavour make this a valuable cultivar	Somewhat spreading habit. The early flowers are prone to frost damage	Excellent flavour
'Malling Jet'	Long trusses that are easy to pick	Aug.	—	Late, heavy crop	A recent introduction	Reasonable flavour
'Wellington XXX'	Medium to large currants, with thin skins	July–Aug.	—	A mid-season heavy cropper	Vigorous, forming a large, spreading bush	Sweet flesh of good flavour

Fruit

Name	Description	Time of use	Pollination group	Special merits	Remarks	Culinary notes
Cherries						
'Bigarreau Napoleon'	Pale yellow, mottled with dark red. Firm flesh	Late July	See Remarks	Useful for a late crop of sweet cherries	Makes a spreading, moderately vigorous tree. Plant with 'Governor Wood' as a pollinator	A sweet dessert cherry
'Early Rivers'	Very large, deep crimson-black fruits, with reddish-pink flesh	Mid June	See Remarks	A good sweet cherry to grow against a wall	Forms a tall, rather weeping tree. Needs another cultivar to pollinate — such as 'Elton Heart', 'Emperor Frances' or 'Governor Wood'	A dessert cherry, tender and of good flavour
'Governor Wood'	Medium to large, dark red fruits with a pale yellow ground colour. The flesh is pale yellow	Early July	See Remarks	Ideal for areas with a low rainfall. Heavy cropper	Forms a small tree. Needs a different sweet cherry for pollination. Good pollinators are 'Elton Heart' and 'Bigarreau Napoleon'	A sweet, dessert cherry with soft juicy fruits and fine flavour
'Kentish Red'	Medium-sized cherries, shining scarlet, with yellow, pink-tinged, flesh	Early July	—	More suitable than sweet cherries for a small garden	A tree of moderate size. Self-fertile and does not require a pollinator	A useful culinary cherry, acid in flavour
'Morello'	Large, roundish cherries, deep red to black. Flesh is deep crimson	Aug.–Sept.	—	A heavy regular cropper	Moderately vigorous, forming a spreading, rather pendulous tree. Self-fertile, so no pollinator is necessary	A culinary cherry. Juicy but slightly bitter
Damsons						
'Farleigh'	Small, oval fruits, black with a lot of bloom. The flesh is greenish-yellow	Mid Sept.	—	Can be used to make a windbreak for the rest of the fruit garden. Prolific cropper	Rather pyramidal in shape	A good dessert damson of excellent flavour
'Merryweather'	Large, oval black fruits, with thick skins and a little bloom. The firm flesh is greenish-yellow	Sept.–Oct.	—	Grows well in tree or bush form, fruiting when three or four years old	A vigorous cultivar with spreading habit. Heavy crops	Good for bottling or jam

Below: pear *'Doyenne du Comice'*. *Below right:* loganberry. *Far below right:* blackcurrant *'Boskoop Giant'*

Name	Description	Time of use	Pollination group	Special merits	Remarks	Culinary notes
Gooseberries						
'Careless'	Popular cultivar with large, oval, green to creamy-white berries. However, they tend to lose their flavour as they ripen	June–July	—	Heavy cropper. Suitable for eating raw or cooking	Forms a large spreading bush. Drooping growth	Can be eaten raw or cooked. Also good for bottling and jam
'Leveller'	Very large, yellow-green berries	July	—	One of the best flavours for dessert use	Requires a fertile soil to grow well. Spreading growth	Equally fine as a dessert or culinary cultivar. Freezes well
'Whinham's Industry'	Medium to large, dark red berries	July	—	Prolific cropper, yet suitable for a small garden	Vigorous growth on long shoots	Can be used as a dessert or culinary cultivar. Also bottles well
'Whitesmith'	Large, oval, pale yellowish-green berries	June–July	—	A good all-round cultivar	Vigorous growth, forming an upright and spreading bush	Can be used for dessert or culinary purposes. Delicious flavour
Hybrid berries						
Boysenberry	A hybrid berry with large, purplish-black fruits, which are very juicy but acid	July–Aug.	—	An excellent choice for dry soils	Vigorous growth	Suitable for dessert or culinary purposes
Loganberry	Large, oblong fruits, with dark claret-red colour. Initially the berries are acid but sweeten as they ripen	July–Aug.	—	Can be trained against a fence or wall	Strong, vigorous growth. 'LY 59' is a heavy cropper, but 'LY 654' has the advantage of thornless canes	Excellent for cooking or bottling
Nectarines						
'Early Rivers'	Large, greenish-yellow fruits, flushed and streaked with scarlet. The flesh is pale yellow	Late July	—	One of the best early nectarines, suitable for forcing	Can be grown as a fan-trained specimen against a wall	Dessert fruit. Juicy with a rich flavour
'Humboldt'	Large, yellowish-orange fruits with a deep crimson flush. The flesh is golden	Late Aug.	—	One of the best nectarines for flavour	Can be grown as a fan-trained specimen against a wall	Dessert
Peaches						
'Duke of York'	Large fruits, rich crimson in colour. Tender, pale greenish-yellow flesh	Mid July	—	One of the easiest to grow	Can be grown as a small tree or as a wall-trained fan	Dessert. Good flavour
'Peregrine'	The fruits are large and rounded, with smooth, bright crimson skin. The flesh is almost white	Mid Aug.	—	Excellent flavour	As 'Duke of York'	Dessert
Pears						
'Beurre Hardy'	Large, conical fruits, greenish-yellow and covered with patches of russet-bronze. The skin is often flushed faint red. Flesh is white, tender, and juicy	Oct.	L	Excellent flavour	Crops regularly and heavily	Dessert
'Bristol Cross'	Medium-large fruit, clear yellow with a fine golden russet. White, juicy flesh	Sept.–Oct.	L	Good flavour. Considered by some to be of better quality than 'Conference'	A moderately vigorous tree producing a good crop	Dessert
'Conference'	Medium-sized, dark green fruit covered with a brown russet. The flesh is pale yellow	Oct.–Nov.	Self-fertile M	One of the best for flavour. Easy to grow	Vigorous, upright habit. Crops heavily	Dessert. Juicy and Sweet
'Doyenne du Comice'	The fruits are large, oval, pale yellow covered with a fine russet. The flesh is white	Nov.	L	Extremely tender, juicy, and full of flavour	Moderate vigour. Not a heavy cropper	Dessert
'William's Bon Cretien'	An old, well-known pear, with medium to large fruits — golden-yellow with a faint red blush	Sept.	M	Heavy, reliable cropper. Juicy and sweet	Moderate vigour	Dessert
'Winter Nelis'	Small to medium fruits, round and dull green. The colour often changes to yellow, with blackish dots. The flesh is yellowish	Nov.–Jan.	L	One of the best late pears	A moderately vigorous tree	Dessert. Sweet and juicy

POLLINATION OF PEARS

The pollination of pears can be complicated — some have extra chromosomes and cannot successfully be used to pollinate other cultivars; and there are a few kinds that though having the right number of chromosomes are incompatible with certain other cultivars. All those selected for inclusion in this chart, however, are compatible provided they flower at the right time for pollination to occur.

Plant any two cultivars with the same code (M — mid-season, L — late flowering). 'Conference' can be planted successfully on its own, but is also a good pollinator for other pears flowering at the same time.

Fruit

Name	Description	Time of use	Pollination group	Special merits	Remarks	Culinary notes
Plums						
'Czar'	A medium-sized, roundish plum, dull red but becoming blue on the sunny side. There is considerable bloom. Flesh is golden	Early Aug.	Self-fertile	Resists spring frosts. Heavy crop	Moderately vigorous growth. Upright habit	Excellent for cooking
'Denniston's Superb'	Medium-sized, greenish-yellow fruits	Mid Aug.	Self-fertile	Dependable, heavy crops	Moderate vigour. Can be trained as a pyramid or cordon. As a tree it has upright but spreading habit	Dessert plum, juicy and good flavour
'Marjorie's Seedling'	Large, roundish, blue-black fruits, covered with a blue bloom. The flesh is yellow, firm and juicy	Late Sept.	Self-fertile	A useful late cultivar. Good flavour	Forms a large tree of upright habit	A good cooking plum
'Pershore'	Medium-sized, golden-yellow fruits. Firm yellow flesh	Late Aug.	Self-fertile	A popular bottling plum. Crops heavily	Moderately vigorous. Forms a relatively large tree	Poor flavour, but cooks well
'Victoria'	Large, oval, bright red fruits speckled with darker dots. Golden-yellow flesh	Late Aug.	Self-fertile	Very heavy crops, excellent flavour	Vigorous growth, with a spreading and slightly weeping habit	Equally successful as a dessert or culinary plum
Raspberries						
'Glen Clova'	Medium to large fruits of fine flavour	July–Aug.	—	Good quality fruits. Crops over a long period	Heavy cropper. The plants show some resistance to fungus diseases (though mildew can be a problem in some areas).	Dessert or culinary. Freezes well
'Lloyd George'	Darkish red berries. Large	July	—	Heavy crop over a long period	Can be grown as an autumn-fruiting cultivar (mid-Sept. onwards) if the canes are cut down in Feb.	Excellent for jams or desserts. Also freezes well
'Malling Jewel'	Bright red berries, becoming darker as they ripen; conical in outline	July–Aug.	—	A heavy crop of high quality	Vigorous, the canes reaching 1.8–2.4m (6–8ft)	A versatile cultivar, useful as a dessert, but also freezing and bottling well

Below: plum *'Victoria'*. *Below right:* peach *'Peregrine'*

Name	Description	Time of use	Pollination group	Special merits	Remarks	Culinary notes
'Malling Orion'	Medium to large fruits with good flavour	July–Aug.	—	Shows resistance to aphids and mildew	The resistance to aphids should help to keep the plants free from virus diseases	A dessert or culinary raspberry of good flavour
'Malling Promise'	Large, round fruit, of moderate flavour	July	—	Heavy crop. Tends to be tolerant of virus infection	Vigorous, often producing an excess of canes	Dessert or culinary
'Norfolk Giant'	Firm, bright red, conical berries. Medium size	Aug.	—	One of the latest of the summer-fruiting raspberries to ripen, and useful to follow earlier kinds	Vigorous canes. Heavy, regular crops	Ideal for freezing or bottling
'September'	Firm, medium-sized bright red berries of good quality	Sept.–Oct.	—	Useful because of its late cropping	Moderately vigorous. Tends to require regular feeding	Dessert or culinary use
'Zeva'	Large, dark red juicy fruits	Sept.–Oct.	—	An autumn-fruiting cultivar of excellent flavour	Vigorous but dwarf	Equally good as a dessert or culinary cultivar
Red currants 'Earliest of Fourlands'	Firm, clear bright red berries	Early July	—	Ripens early — very soon after 'Laxton's No. 1'	Forms a very large bush of erect habit. Heavy cropper	Dessert and culinary
'Jonkheer van Tets'	A recent cultivar, showing vigour and earliness	Early July	—	Early and prolific	Very vigorous	Dessert and culinary
'Laxton's No. 1'	Large, bright red berries. Long bunches	Early July	—	A dependable early cultivar	Makes a sturdy bush of upright habit	Dessert and culinary
'Red Lake'	Large, bright red berries in long, loose bunches that are easy to pick	Mid July	—	One of the best mid-season cultivars. Heavy cropper	Forms an erect bush with strong growth	Dessert and culinary
'Wilson's Long Bunch'	Medium-sized berries in very long bunches	Late July	—	A late cultivar useful to provide continuity	Growth is often straggly and uneven, and rather spreading	Dessert and culinary
Rhubarb 'Timperley Early'	Thin-stemmed	Jan.–June	—	The best for forcing	Do not harvest until plants become established	Particularly fine as forced sticks
'Champagne'	Deep red stems	Feb.–Aug.	—	Produces a good maincrop yield	As 'Timperley Early'	—
'Victoria'	Long, red, tender stems, produced over a long period	Feb.–Aug.	—	A good cultivar to raise from seed (though it takes some years before stems can be harvested)	As 'Timperley Early'	—
Strawberries 'Baron Solemacher'	A runnerless, alpine cultivar. Bright crimson finger-nail-sized fruits	June–Oct.	—	Long cropping period	Seeds tend to be rather large and woody	Dessert, particularly good for jam-making
'Cambridge Favourite'	Large, rounded, pinkish-red berries	June–July	—	Produces a heavy crop. Easy to grow	Reliable	Dessert, quite good flavour
'Cambridge Rival'	Large, crimson fruits	June	—	Prolific and early	Suitable for forcing	Dessert, good flavour
'Cambridge Vigour'	Attractive, large, glossy, rather conical, scarlet fruits	June	—	Good flavour; ideal for forcing under cloches	Also suitable for growing in pots	Dessert, good but slightly acid flavour
'Gento'	Large, round, crimson berries	July–Oct.	—	Useful to extend the strawberry season	Crops well into autumn if given cloche protection	Dessert, good flavour
'Grandee'	Exceptionally large fruits, scarlet-crimson in colour	June–July	—	Heavy crop of massive berries	Berries tend to be uneven and ridged in shape	Dessert, good flavour
'Redgauntlet'	An old cultivar with large scarlet-crimson berries	June–July	—	A good cultivar for northern areas. Heavy crop	Can be forced successfully in heat	Dessert, fair flavour
'Royal Sovereign'	Large, scarlet berries, rather wedge-shaped	June–July	—	Useful for heavy soils	Tends to be prone to diseases, and does not crop dependably well	Very good flavour
'Talisman'	Medium-sized fruits of excellent quality; deep scarlet; conical outline	June–July	—	Excellent quality and flavour	Needs a fertile soil to succeed, when it is very prolific	Dessert, very good flavour
White currants 'White Versailles'	Large, semi-transparent fruits on long bunches	July	—	The most popular white currant. Prolific	Strong growth	Dessert

Vegetables

Deciding which cultivars of a particular vegetable to grow can be much more of a problem than choosing a flower. You can usually see a flower growing, or look at a picture in a catalogue, and know instinctively if it's one that you want to grow. You either like the look of it or you don't. That's not so with vegetables — a picture of a carrot tells you nothing of its flavour, earliness, or cropping potential.

There can be no 'best buy', for although one person may wish to grow for flavour, another may be more interested in sheer weight of crop, while for the exhibitor neither of these considerations counts as much as perfection of form.

Suitability for freezing is often an important factor, and cultivars that freeze particularly well are indicated in the following table.

Many of the F₁ hybrid vegetables have been bred primarily for commercial growers, where uniformity of crop makes harvesting easier, but these are often superior cultivars for amateur use too. Remember, however, that uniformity of growth is not always desirable when growing for a family — it is often better to have a crop maturing unevenly rather than have a whole row ready at the same time and be faced with waste because you can't eat them quickly enough. If you have a freezer this is less of a problem, but not all crops freeze satisfactorily.

Early crops are always worth more, and usually appreciated the most, and by using cloches and cultivars that are naturally suited to early cropping, the season can be extended. Don't expect heavy yields from early crops, however; forcing cultivars of carrots, for instance, are nearly always very small.

Never be tempted to sow too early, for a crop sown a week or two later when the ground is warm and the environment more hospitable will often overtake those sown earlier that have languished in the ground or received a severe check to growth.

By careful selection of crops and cultivars it is possible to have fresh vegetables to harvest the whole year round, even without the need for out-of-season sowings. Even in the winter and spring months there should always be something to pick; celery from November to January, kale, leeks and Brussels sprouts from November to March, parsnips until January, winter spinach from December to March, and winter cabbage through till April. Spring cabbages take over from April, together with sprouting broccoli. Winter cauliflowers can be cropped in April. Broad beans start cropping in May, with Japanese onions soon following in June.

Full sowing instructions are given on pages 106–113, but always avoid sowing too thickly — if sown correctly germination will be good and then the job of thinning can become a tiresome chore.

Name	Description	Sow	Plant	Special merits	Remarks	Culinary notes
Artichokes, globe						
'Green Ball'	Grown for the fleshy scales that form part of the flower head. The plants reach a height of about 1.5m (5ft)	March–April	Plant out following spring	Epicurean vegetable	Will not produce a useable head until the second year	Before cooking, soak the flower heads in salted water for two hours, and then boil until tender and the fleshy scales can be removed easily
Artichokes, Jerusalem						
'Fuseau'	Purple-skinned tubers; tall, leafy top growth	—	Feb.–March	The smooth skin is easily peeled	Can be used to form a screen in the vegetable plot. Reaches over 1.8m (6ft)	May be lifted and stored, but flavour is retained better if left in ground until required
'Silver Skinned'	A white-skinned cultivar	—	Feb.–March	The most readily-available cultivar	As 'Fuseau'	As 'Fuseau'
Asparagus						
'Connover's Colossal'	A purple-tinged cultivar, with slender tips and plump shoots	April	Plant out following April	An early and productive cultivar	Do not cut until the plants are in their third year. Planting two-year-old roots produces quicker results	Thick, succulent stalks, Freezes well
'Martha Washington'	Similar to 'Connover's Colossal', but with shoots of more outstanding size and quality	April	Plant out following April	Excellent quality and very prolific	As 'Connover's Colossal'. Tends to be resistant to asparagus rust	Fleshy shoots of good quality
Beans, broad						
'Aquadulce'	A hardy cultivar with pods 30–38cm (12–15in) long, containing eight or nine seeds	Nov.	—	Matures very early in the year	Never sow later than the end of January	Not a good cultivar to freeze
'Conqueror' see 'Exhibition Longpod'						
'Dreadnought'	Extra-long pods of excellent quality	Feb.–April	—	Extraordinary size	Good for exhibition	Reasonable flavour. Good for freezing
'Exhibition Longpod' (syn. 'Conqueror')	Pods of good length contain eight or nine beans	Feb.–April	—	A prolific cultivar, useful for an early spring sowing	Suitable for exhibition	Recommended for freezing
'Imperial White Windsor'	A good cropper with pods containing up to eight beans	Feb.–April	—	A quality bean for a late spring sowing	A good all-round cultivar	Good quality. Suitable for freezing
'The Sutton'	A dwarf broad bean little over 30cm (1ft) high. Branches at base to produce several stems bearing 13–15cm (5–6in) long pods	Feb.–April, and Nov.	—	An excellent cultivar to grow where space is limited	A good cultivar to sow in succession over a long period. Sow as a catch crop in July	Excellent flavour. Freezes well

Name	Description	Sow	Plant	Special merits	Remarks	Culinary notes
Beans, French						
'Cordon'	Straight, oval pods about 15cm (6in) long, carried clear of the soil	April–May	—	Completely stringless. High disease resistance, and a heavy cropper	Pods last on the plant in good condition	Freezes well
'Kinghorn Wax'	Round, yellowish pods, slightly curved	April–May	—	Provides a variety of colour	A reliable cultivar, with an unusual appearance	Fleshy pods of good flavour. Freezes well
'Loch Ness'	Straight, round pods on upright plants	April–May	—	Perfectly stringless and an excellent cropper	Distinctive, upright habit of growth, with little branching	Very good flavour, and freezes well
'Masterpiece'	Long, straight pods. An early cultivar	March–May	—	One of the finest forcing cultivars. A heavy cropper	Pick regularly to ensure continuous cropping	Reasonable flavour. Suitable for freezing
'Tendergreen'	Round pods of medium length. An early cultivar	March–May	—	Matures early. Heavy yield	Dwarf and stringless	Good flavour. Ideal for freezing
'The Prince'	Straight, narrow yet fleshy pods. An early cultivar	March–May	—	Exceptionally heavy crops	A good exhibition cultivar	Tender, but pick while young to avoid stringiness. Suitable for freezing
Beans, French (climbing)						
'Blue Lake White Seeded'	Small, round, stringless pods, similar to ordinary French beans, but on climbing plants	April–May	May–June	Easy to pick. Stringless	Treat as runner beans	Very attractive when cooked whole. Very good flavour. Freezes well
Beans, runner						
'Best of All' see 'Streamline'						
'Enorma'	This is an improved strain of 'Prizewinner'. Long, slender pods, smooth and rich green in colour	April–May	May–June	One of the finest exhibition cultivars	Some pods exceed 50cm (20in)	Superb flavour. Excellent for freezing
'Prizewinner'	Medium-length pods, 38–45cm (15–18in) long	April–May	May–June	Heavy crop of fine-textured pods	A dependable kind for general use	Moderate flavour. Suitable for freezing
'Scarlet Emperor'	Long and spectacular pods, borne on very heavy cropping plants	April–May	May–June	An excellent exhibition cultivar	A good cultivar for general garden use. Can be grown as a ground bean	Moderate quality
'Streamline' (syn. 'Best of All')	Long, smooth-skinned pods. An old but popular cultivar	April–May	May–June	An all-round cultivar for general use. Yields a heavy crop	Robust constitution and dependable	Good flavour
Beetroot						
'Avonearly'	Normal round beet in appearance	March–July	—	Bolt-resistant, and ideal for early sowing	Sow under cloches for an early crop. It is the most bolt-resistant cultivar available	Ideal for use as 'baby beet'. Can be frozen
'Boltardy'	Deep, blood-red globes with a fine texture	March–July	—	Exhibits a high resistance to bolting	Suitable for sowing earlier than most cultivars	Good appearance, with an absence of 'rings'
'Cheltenham Green Top'	A long cultivar, with a hard shoulder	May–June	—	The best cultivar for normal storage	Do not sow before May or after June for storage purposes	Good quality
'Cylindra' (previously known as 'Housewives' Choice')	Cylindrical roots, about 15cm (6in) long and 5cm (2in) across	April–June	—	Provides an interesting variation in shape	Of equal quality to the globe type	An ideal size and shape for slicing
'Detroit Little Ball'	Blood-red, ball-shaped roots, which are small and smooth-skinned	April–July	—	A quick-growing cultivar which matures rapidly	Can be sown late for use in Sept. and Oct.	Ideal for bottling, and suitable for freezing
'Housewives' Choice' see 'Cylindra'						
Beet, spinach						
'Perpetual Spinach'	Succulent, spinach-like leaves	March–July	—	Especially useful on dry soil, where ordinary spinach is likely to run to seed	If young leaves are taken from the outside, cropping will continue for a long period	Not of such fine flavour as ordinary spinach
Beet, seakale (Swiss chard)						
'Rhubarb Chard'	Long, bright red leaf-stalks	April–July	—	Provides an abundant crop of leaves, even in dry weather	Decorative enough for a place in the flower garden	Flavour is not as good as the 'Silver' cultivar
'Silver'	A foliage beet with white midribs and fresh green leaf blades	April–July	—	As 'Ruby Chard'	The roots are not edible	The fleshy leaf-stems and mid-ribs are cooked like seakale — the green portion is cut away before cooking

Vegetables

Name	Description	Sow	Plant	Special merits	Remarks	Culinary notes
Borecole (curly kale)						
'Dwarf Green Curled' (syn. 'Half Tall')	Dwarf habit, with tightly-curled leaves	April—May	July	Compact habit	Very hardy	Boil for about 10 minutes, adding salt to taste, and chop after cooking
'Frosty'	Produces a large quantity of curled and crinkled leaves, carried clear of the soil despite dwarf habit	April—May	July	Withstands frost particularly well	Very dwarf — growing only about 30cm (1ft)	As 'Dwarf Green Curled'
'Half Tall' see 'Dwarf Green Curled'						
Broccoli						
'Purple Sprouting'	Produces small sprigs of miniature 'cauliflowers' in spring	April	May—June	Particularly hardy	Early and late forms are available, to extend the cropping programme	A useful vegetable for Feb.—April
'White Sprouting'	Similar to 'Purple Sprouting', but with white 'cauliflowers'	April	May—June	Very good quality	As 'Purple Sprouting'	As 'Purple Sprouting'
Brussels Sprouts						
'Citadel'	A maincrop cultivar with medium-sized dark green sprouts tightly packed on the stems	March—April	May—June	Very heavy yield of uniform buttons	An F1 hybrid. Ready from Dec. onwards. Remains in good condition for a long period	Quality sprouts. Suitable for freezing
'Fasolt' see 'Zid'						
'Peer Gynt'	Fairly dwarf plant with uniform, medium-sized dark green buttons along the length of the stem	March—April	May—June	Superb flavour. Firm sprouts, easy to pick	An F1 hybrid. Matures in Oct. and crops until Dec.	Excellent quality. Good for freezing
'Perfect Line'	A mid-season cultivar producing medium-sized, solid buttons	March—April	May—June	Useful to follow 'Peer Gynt'. Very high yield	An F1 hybrid. Matures in Dec. and Jan.	Reasonable flavour
'Zid' (previously known as 'Fasolt')	An excellent cultivar, producing dark green, medium-sized sprouts that are smooth and solid	March—April	May—June	An excellent late cultivar to produce a late crop for continuity	An F1 hybrid of fairly tall growth. Crops well into Feb.	Good flavour. Suitable for freezing

Below: runner bean *'Scarlet Emperor'*. *Below right:* cabbage *'January King'*. *Far below right:* beetroot *'Boltardy'*

Name	Description	Sow	Plant	Special merits	Remarks	Culinary notes
Cabbages (spring cutting)						
'April'	Compact with neat, pointed hearts. Few outer leaves	July–Aug.	Sept.–Oct.	Very early	Ready for use as early as April	Good quality
'Offenham — Flower of Spring'	Compact, solid, pointed hearts. Short stems	July–Aug.	Sept.–Oct.	Very hardy. Good flavour	One of the most reliable spring cabbages	Very good flavour
'Wheeler's Imperial'	Dark green leaves. Matures early	July–Aug.	Sept.–Oct.	A dependable cultivar of medium-early maturity	Can also be sown in spring	Good quality
Cabbages (summer and autumn cutting)						
'Derby Day'	Dark green, ball-head cultivar	March–April	May–June	Resistant to bolting	Quick growing	Good flavour
'Golden Acre' (syn. 'Primo')	Round heads of rock-like firmness and medium size. Compact plants	March–April	May–June	An outstanding cultivar for a quick crop and good flavour	Can be harvested in about twelve weeks from an *in situ* sowing	Very good flavour
'Greyhound'	An early-maturing pointed cabbage of compact habit	March–April	May–June	One of the best pointed cultivars for early crops	It is also useful for an autumn sowing	Good flavour
'Hispi'	A pointed cabbage, maturing very early	March–April (also see Remarks)	May–June (also see Remarks)	Its compact habit makes close spacing possible	An F1 hybrid. Ideal for successional sowing under glass from late Jan., for planting out in the spring	Sweet flavour
Primo see 'Golden Acre'						
'Stonehead'	Compact, but with a solid round head of good size	March–April	May–June	Useful where space is limited	An F1 hybrid. Will stand for several months	Reasonable flavour
'Winnigstadt'	A compact cabbage with a well shaped pointed heart	March–April	May–June	An ideal cabbage for spring sowing	A good exhibition cultivar	Good flavour
Cabbages (winter cutting)						
'Celtic'	Round, solid heads with rather savoy-like leaves. It will stand through to Jan. and Feb.	May	June–July	Extremely hardy. Ready for cutting in Dec.	An F1 hybrid. Remains in good condition for a long time before splitting.	Reasonable flavour
'Christmas Drumhead'	A dwarf, compact round cabbage with a solid heart	May	June–July	Useful to provide heads in Nov.	An old cultivar, but still useful	Reasonable flavour
'Hidena'	Slightly oval, very hard heads of a large size	May	June–July	Very good culinary qualities	An F1 hybrid. Heads not required for immediate use should be lifted and stored, with root attached, in a cellar or shed	Very good flavour. Useful to shred for eating raw
Cabbages (savoy)						
'Best of All'	Large heads with solid hearts. Dark green in colour	April–May	July	Good exhibition cultivar	Produces solid hearts in Oct. and Nov.	Moderate flavour
'January King'	A distinctive cabbage with rather coarse outer leaves, some heart leaves taking on a purplish colour as they mature	April–May	July	An invaluable vegetable during severe winters	Matures in early Dec., but will stand until April	Good flavour
'Winter King'	Large heads on short-stemmed plants. Attractive dark green leaves	April–May	July	One of the most frost resistant of all cabbages	Matures from Nov. onwards	Reasonable flavour
Cabbage (Chinese)						
'Sampan'	A distinctive shape, making a large conical heart	See Remarks	—	Easier than most other Chinese cabbage cultivars to grow, being less inclined to bolt	Unlike most other cultivars, can be sown in spring as well as July	Excellent when cooked like cabbage or eaten raw in a salad
Calabrese						
'Corvet'	Compact plants of about 60cm (2ft), with an abundance of smaller shoots following the central head	April–May	June	Useful for limited space	An F1 hybrid. Ready in about 60 days after transplanting	Cut the spears when about 15cm (6in) long and peel the stem before cooking and serving like asparagus. Suitable for freezing
'Green Comet'	Produces medium-sized, deep green heads, and few lateral shoots	April–May	June	Exceptionally early. A heavy cropper	An F1 hybrid. Very uniform, and can be ready in as little as 40 days after transplanting	Good flavour. Freezes well
Capsicums						
'Ace'	Heavy crops of large fruit	March	May–June	Ideal for greenhouse cropping	An F1 hybrid. Suitable for forcing	Suitable for freezing
'Canape'	Deep green fruits, turning to bright red on maturity	March	May–June	One of the best to try outdoors in a suitable area	An F1 hybrid. Matures early	Suitable for freezing

Vegetables

Name	Description	Sow	Plant	Special merits	Remarks	Culinary notes
Carrots						
'Amsterdam Forcing'	A small, stump-rooted cultivar not much larger than a finger	March	—	One of the best for early forcing, in frames or under cloches	Sow at fortnightly intervals under cloches, from Feb.	Good quality, with almost no core. Good for freezing
'Autumn King'	Long, heavy, stump-rooted, orange flesh	April–July	—	Produces a heavy yield. Good keeping qualities	Recommended as one of the best for maincrop sowing	Fine flavour
'Early Nantes' see 'Nantes'						
'Nantes' (syn. 'Early Nantes')	Cylindrical, stump-rooted. Does not grow large	March	—	A good cultivar for growing under cloches	Useful for pulling young	Very little core, sweet flavour. Freezes well
'Chantenay Red Cored'	Stump-rooted, intermediate length	April–July	—	An early maincrop, but also stores well	Useful for sowing in late summer	Small core, similar colour to the flesh
'Early French Frame' previously known as 'Parisian Rondo'	Round roots, about 5cm (2in) in diameter when mature	March	—	Very early. Good for forcing	Suitable for successional sowing outdoors	Good flavour
'Parisian Rondo' see 'Early French Frame'						
'Pioneer'	Cylindrical roots up to 20cm (8in) long; very even	April–July	—	Heavy yield, and very good quality	An F1 hybrid. Medium early	Tender, sweet roots. Freezes well
'St Valery'	Long, tapering roots, beloved by exhibitors	April–July	—	Good exhibition cultivar	Good colour, and tender. Maincrop	Tender
Cauliflowers (summer and autumn cultivars)						
'All The Year Round'	Compact heads with good curds surrounded by dark green leaves	Jan.–Feb. indoors April–May outdoors	March–June	Useful where one cultivar is required for successional sowings to mature over a long period	An old cultivar, but still worthy of a place in the vegetable garden	Good table quality. Suitable for freezing
'Dominant'	A robust cauliflower with firm, quality, pure-white heads, well protected by inside leaves	Feb.–March indoors April–May outdoors	March–June	Produces first-class heads	Suitable for spring or autumn sowing	Very good quality. Good for freezing
'Kangaroo'	Firm white heads of good size	April–May	June–July	Heads at the end of Sept. and into Oct.	Very good for exhibition	Excellent eating qualities
'Mechelse Classic'	Extremely dwarf, producing fine white curds	Feb.–March indoors April–May outdoors	March–June	Very early, producing heads in June	Useful because it matures at a time when most fresh vegetables are still scarce	Curds of considerable culinary merit
'Snowball — Early Snowball'	Close, white heads of medium to small size	Jan.–Feb. indoors April–May outdoors	March–June	Ideal for forcing, or early crops outdoors	Can be sown as early as January, and is also useful for autumn sowing	Good quality
Cauliflowers (winter and spring cultivars)						
'English Winter–Late Queen'	Can be cut during May and June. First-rate heads of good quality	May–June	June–July	Very hardy	A really reliable cultivar for garden use	Suitable for freezing
'English Winter–St. George'	Very large heads, which can be cut in April	May–June	June–July	The heads are exceptionally tight	Solid, pure-white heads	Suitable for freezing
'Angers No. 2'	A winter-maturing cultivar with heads of good depth	May	June	Ready Feb.–April	Very hardy	Good quality. Suitable for freezing
Celeriac						
'Alabaster'	White flesh and skin, with the flavour of celery	April–May	May–June	Turnip-shaped roots	Can be damaged by severe frost, so lift in Nov. and store in sand	Can be grated raw in salads
'Marble Ball'	Large, solid and globular-shaped roots	April–May	May–June	Excellent for storing	As 'Alabaster'	As 'Alabaster'
Celery						
'Giant Pink'	An excellent pink cultivar	March–April	May–June	Good for exhibition purposes	A cultivar that blanches easily and quickly	Crisp and flavoursome
'Giant White'	Solid, crisp, white stems with an outstandingly pleasant flavour	March–April	May–June	Good for the table	Protect the stems during blanching	Very crisp stems
'Solid White'	A popular crisp, white cultivar	March–April	May–June	Ideal for exhibition purposes	Protect the stems during blanching	Superb in salads
Celery (self-blanching)						
'Golden Self-blanching'	Tender, crisp, creamy sticks, ready in Oct.	March–April	May–June	One of the best self-blanching cultivars	Compact, and free from 'strings'	Crisp and nutty
'Lathon Self-blanching'	Very crisp stems; a strong-growing cultivar	March–April	May–June	Resistant to bolting	The compact, solid, yellow sticks are free from 'strings'	Excellent flavour

Name	Description	Sow	Plant	Special merits	Remarks	Culinary notes
Chicory						
'Normato'	The white chicons remain compact without a covering of soil	June–July	—	Superb for forcing	A new cultivar which is much easier to grow than many traditional ones	Good flavour
'Witloof'	Produces large chicons of fine flavour	June–July	—	Excellent for forcing	A very hardy cultivar	An easily-grown winter salad cultivar
Cucumbers (frame cultivars)						
'Butcher's Disease Resisting'	An old and well-established cultivar with a strong constitution	Feb.–April indoors May in frame	—	Resistant to several diseases	Produces a heavy crop	Excellent flavour
'Telegraph'	A well-known cultivar; good-sized fruits with smooth skins	Feb.–April indoors May in frame	—	A really reliable cropper	Combines quality with a good crop	Pleasant flavour
Cucumbers (ridge)						
'Burpee Hybrid'	Straight, well-formed fruits, with smooth, dark green skins	April–May	June	A superb outdoor cultivar	An F1 hybrid, producing fruits with exactly the same appearance	Good quality
'Burpless Tasty Green'	The fruits are not bitter, and can reach 25–30cm (10–12in) long	April–May	June	Uniform fruits	An F1 hybrid, with tender skin. Peeling is not necessary	Good flavour, Can be eaten like celery
Kohl rabi						
'Green Vienna' see 'White Vienna'						
'Purple Vienna'	Apple-like 'bulbs', with a purplish colour. The flesh is white	April–July	—	One of the earliest cultivars to mature	Very short topped	Superb flavour. Grate for use in salads, or cook as turnips
'White Vienna' (syn. 'Green Vienna')	Pure white flesh. The swollen stems are like pale green turnips	April–July	—	One of the earliest cultivars to mature	Very short topped	As 'Purple Vienna'
Leeks						
'Giant Winter–Catalina'	Long, thick and fleshy stems, with a non-bulbous root end	March–April	June	Superb quality for winter use	Remains in good condition for a long time	Mild flavour
'Lyon'	Tender, solid white stems — one of the best cultivars	March–April	June	Very resistant to damage from frost	Free from coarseness	Good flavour
'Musselburgh'	A famous Scottish leek, producing long and succulent thick stems	March–April	June	Ideal for home and exhibition use	Very hardy. Stands well in hard weather	Excellent flavour

Below: leek *'Musselburgh'*. *Below right:* marrow *'Long Green Bush'*

Vegetables

Name	Description	Sow	Plant	Special merits	Remarks	Culinary notes
Lettuces (butterhead types)						
'All The Year Round'	A hardy and very compact cultivar	March–July	April–Aug.	Slow to run to seed	Equally good for spring or autumn sowing	Very crisp, and extremely well flavoured
'Avondefiance'	Solid, tender hearts. Dark green	March–July	April–Aug.	Resistant to mildew	Good for sowing in June	Good flavour
'Buttercrunch'	Small, dark green heads. Crisp and succulent, with a central heart of creamy-yellow leaves	March–July	April–Aug.	'Stands' extremely well	Even the older plants remain crisp and fresh	Excellent in salads — it is crisp and fresh
'Fortune' see 'Hilde II'						
'Hilde II' (syn. 'Fortune')	Large, tight heads	Jan.–July	March–Aug.	Recommended for sowing under glass in Jan. or Feb. for transplanting outside	Useful for early-maturing outdoor crop if sown under glass	Good flavour
'Sigmadeep'	Dark leaved cultivar producing crisp, fleshy heads	March–July	April–Aug.	Shows good resistance to tipburn	Compact, upright habit	Crisp
Lettuces (crisphead types)						
'Avoncrisp'	Crisp and brittle hearts — a little smaller than 'Great Lakes'	March–July	April–Aug.	Has some resistance to downy mildew, tip burn and grey mould	An ideal garden lettuce, which succeeds even in hot, dry spells. It is remarkably slow to bolt	Crisp
'Great Lakes'	Very large hearts, which are crisp and solid	March–July	April–Aug.	Slow to bolt in dry weather	Excellent for hot and dry soils	Very crisp
'New York' see 'Webb's Wonderful'						
'Tom Thumb'	A small cultivar, bearing very crisp, solid and sweet hearts	March–July	April–Aug.	Good for small gardens and frames	Can be planted close together	Good for individual salads — the heads are often the size of a tennis ball
'Webb's Wonderful' (syn. 'New York')	A very robust and large cultivar. Very crisp and sweet	March–July	April–Aug.	Survives hot and dry weather	The tightly-folded heads are blanched white	Pleasantly crisp
Lettuces (cos types)						
'Little Gem'	Perhaps the sweetest and best flavoured of all lettuces. Deep green hearts	March–July	April–Aug.	A lettuce with little waste	A cultivar with few rivals	Fresh and crisp
'Lobjoit's Green'	A dark green cultivar, with medium to large, firm heads	March–July	April–Aug.	An old and established cultivar — very trustworthy	The heads are well folded	Crisp
'Winter Density'	Dark green heads, and looks slightly like a cabbage type	March–July	April–Aug.	A very adaptable cultivar to most conditions	For use in winter or summer	Crisp, sweet heads
Lettuces (winter-maturing)						
'Dandie'	A good forcing cultivar, with a 'butterhead' leaf formation	Aug.–Nov.	—	Good for heated or frost-free greenhouses	Very high yielding and early	Crisp
'Kwiek'	A Nov.–Dec. cropping lettuce, with floppy leaves not forming the traditional heart	Aug.–Sept.	—	Superb for winter use	Suitable for a cold greenhouse	Good quality
'Valdor'	A large winter lettuce, with deep green, crisp, solid hearts	Aug.–Sept.	—	Resistant to cold and wet conditions	Not suitable for spring or summer sowing	Delightfully crisp
Lettuces (loose-leaf type)						
'Salad Bowl'	Beautifully curled, fresh green leaves, somewhat resembling endive	March–July	—	Does not bolt	Excellent for dry areas	The individual leaves can be picked as required
Marrows (trailing type)						
'Long Green Trailing'	The fruits are cylindrical, long and thickening at the blossom end. The fruits are green, with lighter stripes	April–May	June	Good for exhibition purposes	Require a rich, moist soil	A very adaptable vegetable — may be served in many different ways
'Long White Trailing'	A very free-cropping variety, bearing large, white fruits	April–May	June	Good for exhibition purposes	Require a rich, moist soil	As 'Long Green Trailing'
'Vegetable Spaghetti'	Medium-size fruit, about 20cm (8in) long, and borne on trailing stems	April–May	June	Very easily grown in a corner of the garden	An interesting vegetable, both to grow and eat	The fruit is boiled, and the inside removed and eaten like spaghetti — very tasty
Marrows (bush type)						
'Green Bush' see 'Long Green Bush'						
'Long Green Bush' (syn. 'Green Bush')	Matures early. Prolific in its production of dark green marrows with paler stripes	April–May	June	Good for both exhibition and the table	A neat and compact habit	Very tender

Name	Description	Sow	Plant	Special merits	Remarks	Culinary notes
'Long White Bush' (syn. 'White Bush')	Creamy-white fruits of medium size	April–May	June	Good for both exhibition and the table	A neat and compact habit	Tender
'White Bush' see 'Long White Bush'						
'Zucchini'	An early and very heavy cropper. The fruits are long, and a very deep emerald green	April–May	June	Can be used as 'courgettes' when 15–20cm (6–8in) long	Very attractive fruits	Superb flavour

Onions

Name	Description	Sow	Plant	Special merits	Remarks	Culinary notes
'Ailsa Craig'	One of the most well-known and popular of all onions. The globe-shaped onions have a rich, golden straw covering	March–April (see Remarks)	—	Good for both exhibition and the table	Suitable for both spring and autumn sowing. For large bulbs, can also be sown in heat in Jan.	Has a mild flavour
'Bedfordshire Champion'	A heavy cropping cultivar, producing large, globe-shaped, straw-coloured bulbs	March–April	—	Keeps well	Excellent for general garden use	Pleasant flavour, neither too strong nor too mild
'Rijnsburger'	An exceptionally heavy and reliable cropper. The bulbs are straw-coloured, firm, with white flesh	—	Plant sets in March–April	A good keeping onion — until Feb. or March	Matures early. Usually available as 'sets'	Has a mild flavour
'Rijnsburger — Conquest'	Round bulbs of good size	Feb.–March	—	Good keeper	Fine shape and colour	Excellent flavour
'White Lisbon'	Silvery-white in colour. A very popular cultivar	See Remarks	—	Very quick growing	Can be sown at practically any time of the year, using cloches if necessary	Generally used for pulling young as 'spring' onions. Has a mild flavour

Onions (Japanese)

Name	Description	Sow	Plant	Special merits	Remarks	Culinary notes
'Express Yellow'	A flattish onion with dark yellow skin	Aug.	—	Very early crop	A very high yielding F1 hybrid	Useful for a very early crop when onions are often expensive
'Senshyu Semi-Globe Yellow'	Flattish in shape, with deep yellow skin	Aug.	—	Very early crop	Overwinters very well	As 'Express Yellow'

Parsnips

Name	Description	Sow	Plant	Special merits	Remarks	Culinary notes
'Avonresister'	Small and conical roots, free from blemishes	Feb.–April	—	Resistant to canker	The roots are more uniform in size and shape than most other cultivars	Attractive roots for cooking whole for the table
'Improved Hollow Crown'	Long, smooth tapering roots, symmetrical in shape	Feb.–April	—	Good for the table and exhibition purposes	Needs a deep, well-cultivated soil	The clear-grained roots have an excellent flavour
'Tender and True'	An excellent cultivar with long, tapering roots. Good quality, with a smooth, white skin	Feb.–April	—	Excellent for both exhibition and culinary purposes	Useful for small gardens	Very tender and sweet

Peas (first early)

Name	Description	Sow	Plant	Special merits	Remarks	Culinary notes
'Feltham First'	Big, well-filled pods, on plants which are quite hardy. Round-seeded cultivar. Dwarf	Oct.–Nov., March, or June	—	Superb for early garden use	Suitable for autumn sowing	Sweetly flavoured, and very tender
'Hurst Beagle'	Blunt, well-filled pods, often maturing earlier than 'Feltham First'. Dwarf	Oct.–Nov. March, or June	—	A very good early cropper	The earliest wrinkled seed cultivar	Excellent flavour. A good freezer
'Kelvedon Wonder'	A very popular wrinkled-seeded cultivar. Dark green, pointed pods, about 7.5cm (3in) long. Dwarf	March or June	—	Good crop on sturdy plants	Not suitable for autumn sowing	Very sweet-tasting peas. Suitable for freezing
'Little Marvel'	Stump-ended pods, hanging in pairs. The peas are tightly packed in the pods. Dwarf	Oct.–Nov. March, or June	—	A heavy-yielding cultivar	Ideal for garden use	Sweet flavour. Suitable for freezing

Peas (second early)

Name	Description	Sow	Plant	Special merits	Remarks	Culinary notes
'Early Onward'	Blunt, dark green pods, well filled with peas, and often reaching 9cm (3½in) in length. Dwarf	March–April	—	Heavy cropping early cultivar	Excellent garden cultivar	Fine flavour. Good for freezing
'Hurst Green Shaft'	Slightly earlier than 'Early Onward', with pods containing nine or ten peas. Medium height	March–April	—	Resistant to downy mildew and fusarium wilt	A highly recommended cultivar for garden use	Excellent flavour. Freezes well
'Kelvedon Monarch' (syn. 'Victory Freezer')	Straight, blunt-nosed pods, often 7.5cm (3in) long. Dwarf	March–April	—	Very good cropper	Good garden cultivar	Sweet. Suitable for freezing
'Victory Freezer' see 'Kelvedon Monarch'						

Vegetables

Name	Description	Sow	Plant	Special merits	Remarks	Culinary notes
Peas (maincrop)						
'Dwarf Defiance' (syn. 'Rentpayer')	Long, straight pods containing up to nine peas	April–May	—	One of the dwarfest late cultivars, at 60cm (2ft)	Dark green, pointed pods	Good flavour but not as suitable as 'Onward' for freezing
'Onward'	A first-class maincrop pea. Dark green, blunt-nosed pods, borne in pairs. Medium height	April–May	—	Resistant to fusarium wilt	Very heavy cropper	Fine flavour. Suitable for freezing
'Rentpayer' see 'Dwarf Defiance'						
Potatoes						
'Desiree'	A good cropper and very flavoursome. A red-skinned cultivar with kidney-shaped tubers	—	April	Superior quality	A high-yielding cultivar	The pale-lemon flesh rarely discolours during cooking. A good cultivar from which to make chips
'Maris Peer'	A high quality, oval, white-skinned cultivar	—	April	Remains in good condition until Jan.	Exceptionally heavy yield	Cooks well
'Maris Piper'	A maincrop cultivar, which is fast replacing 'Majestic'. The oval tubers have white flesh	—	April	Resistant to one type of eelworm	Yields very well	A really good flavour
'Pentland Javelin'	Displays a smooth, white flesh. A vigorous and heavy cropper	—	March	Resistent to eelworm attack	This cultivar has superseded the old 'Arran Pilot'	Has a good flavour, and cooks well
Radishes						
'Cherry Belle'	Brilliant red, round, smooth globes like cherries	March–July	—	A good early radish	A white-fleshed cultivar	Remains crisp for a long time
'French Breakfast'	A well-known cultivar, with cylindrical, scarlet roots. Their tips are white	March–July	—	A reliable cultivar	Quickly matures	A tasty and mild flavour
'Scarlet Globe'	Brilliant red, with white flesh	March–July	—	Remains crisp and fresh	A good garden cultivar	Delicate flavour
'Sparkler'	Globe-shaped, bright scarlet, and distinctively tipped with white	March–July	—	Very uniform in size	Ready in about 20 days after sowing	Crisp and sweet
Radishes (winter)						
'Black Spanish Round'	Black, round and with succulent white flesh. Much larger than a normal radish	July–Aug.	—	Stores well in sand	Often 10cm (4in) across	Served sliced or grated in a salad. They are not served whole
'China Rose'	Oval roots, deep rose with a white tip	July–Aug.	—	Stores well in sand	Often 13–15cm (5–6in) long and 5cm (2in) in diameter	As 'Black Spanish Round'
Salsify						
'Sandwich Island'	Brownish-white roots, resembling a slender parsnip	March–April	—	Well worth trying as a winter vegetable with a difference	Very nutritious, with an oyster-like flavour	Sweet flavour — a much esteemed vegetable
Scorzonera						
'Russian Giant'	Similar to salsify, but with black-skinned roots.	March–April	—	An easily-grown yet unusual vegetable	Lift the roots as required	Scald the roots, then scrape them and leave in water with a few drops of lemon for one hour. Then boil until tender
Shallots						
'Giant Red'	Large bulbs with a pronounced red skin	—	Feb.–March	Perhaps the best flavoured shallot cultivar	Keeps well	Mild, spicy yet sweet
'Giant Yellow'	Similar large bulbs to 'Giant Red', but with normal colouring	—	Feb.–March	Keeps exceptionally well	Very easy to grow	Mild, agreeable flavour
'Hative de Niort'	Very large, yellow-skinned bulbs	—	Feb.–March	A superb exhibition cultivar	Does not keep well	Perhaps a little large for some culinary purposes
Spinach						
'Broad Leaved Prickly'	Thick and fleshy, dark-green leaves	Aug.–Sept.	—	Very hardy	Ready for use from November	Succulent leaves
'Greenmarket'	Large, dark green leaves	Sept. or March–April	—	Extremely heavy yield. Slow to run to seed	Shows resistance to mosaic virus	Good flavour
'Longstanding Round'	Dark green leaves	Feb.–July	—	A quick-growing cultivar	Pick continuously for the best yield	Freezes well
Spinach (New Zealand)						
New Zealand Spinach	Mild flavoured, unlike ordinary spinach. Soft thick, fleshy leaves with a crystalline appearance	May	—	Will crop over a long period without running to seed in dry weather	Soak the seeds to assist germination	Delightful flavour

Name	Description	Sow	Plant	Special merits	Remarks	Culinary notes
Swedes 'Best of All'	A yellow-fleshed globe, with small neck and purple skin	May–June	—	Particularly hardy	Will stand all winter	Sweet flavour
Sweet corn 'Earliking'	Large cobs of first-class quality. Heads well protected by the green leaves	April indoors May outdoors	May–June	Very early	An F1 hybrid	Sweet flavour
'Kelvedon Glory'	First-rate cobs of very high quality. The cobs are pale yellow, and packed with corn	April indoors May outdoors	May–June	Reliable	Yields very well. An F1 hybrid	Delicious flavour
Tomatoes 'Alicante'	Smooth, red fruits, free from greenback	March–April	June	Early to mature	Reliable under glass and in the open	Sweet and juicy
'Golden Sunrise'	Golden-yellow, medium-sized fruits	March–April	June	Very reliable cropper	Can be grown either in a cold greenhouse or outdoors	Distinctive flavour
'Harbinger'	Early maturing, producing quality fruits	March–April	June	Heavy cropper	Does well in the open and under glass	Excellent eating qualities
'Outdoor Girl'	Large trusses, bearing many medium-sized fruits. Has a good red colour	March–April	June	Specially developed for growing in the open	Very sturdy plants	Excellent flavour
'Sigmabush'	A bush cultivar bearing outstandingly good fruit	March–April	June	Ripens evenly, even under bad conditions	An F1 hybrid, superb for even and early fruits outdoors	Quality fruits
Turnips 'Golden Ball'	A dwarf and compact, round and yellow-balled cultivar, with tender, yellow flesh	March–May		Keeps very well in store	A really hardy turnip that can be left in the ground for a long time. Excellent for exhibition purposes	Tender
'Green Globe' see 'Imperial Green Globe'						
'Imperial Green Globe' (syn. 'Green Globe')	Round roots, half green and half white skin with pure white flesh	July–Aug.	—	Ideal for turnip tops in the winter and spring	A maincrop turnip	Good flavour
'Snowball'	Well formed, round and white roots	March–May	—	Good for table and exhibition purposes	A quick-growing cultivar	Mild flavour
'White Milan'	Flat roots, of medium size and very smooth	March–May	—	Dwarf and compact	Ideal for small gardens, frames and cloches	Very tasty

Below: salsify 'Sandwich Island'. Below right: turnip 'Imperial Green Globe'

Herbs

Although the term herb covers a wide range of plants, including medicinal plants, those listed in the following table are primarily grown for their culinary merits. Anyone particularly interested in using a wide variety of herbs in their cookery can find many more with which to experiment, but those listed here form the basis of any collection of kitchen herbs.

Because many different types of plant — from annuals to shrubs — can be used as herbs, they naturally have very different habits. In the days when large gardens were more common and herbs were grown in special areas, often in symmetrical beds, this did not matter much. But in a small, modern garden it may be necessary to grow herbs for the kitchen in a variety of sites around the plot. Parsley, for instance, can be grown in pots indoors, in a window-box outside, or in the open garden as an attractive edging to flower borders or vegetable beds; sweet bay can be grown as an untrained bush in the shrub border, or as a clipped specimen in a tub by the front door. Rosemary and sage are perfectly at home at the front of a shrub border, where they are decorative as well as useful. Chives can be grown in pots indoors to extend the season, but outdoors they are equally at home in the vegetable plot or at the front of an herbaceous border, where their mauve-purple flowers can be most decorative. There is no excuse for being without fresh herbs, no matter how small the garden.

The amount of a particular herb required for a dish is often small, and a few plants of each kind will usually be adequate for most families, with enough left to dry and preserve.

The best time to cut for drying is when the plant is in full growth, just before flowering. Harvest on a dry day, and spread out indoors to dry. Some form of fine netting is preferable to newspaper to dry them on, as it allows the air to circulate more freely. They can be left in a shed or warm, dry but well ventilated cupboard for a few days, but keep in the dark, as light will affect the natural oils. Alternatively they can be made into small bunches and hung upside down from a shelf in a cupboard.

As soon as the leaves have become dry and brittle, rub them from their stalks (pick off individually if large, like sweet bay) and store them in airtight jars. Don't forget to label them, as plants that look completely distinctive when growing can look surprisingly similar as dried leaves in a jar.

It may be worth freezing a little surplus parsley. It can be frozen in small bunches, and the sprigs rubbed in the bag between the fingers before use and while still frozen. This will cause the leaves to crumble and saves chopping; use while still frozen.

Name	Description	Height/spread	Treat as	Propagation	Remarks	Harvesting and use
Angelica Angelica archangelica	A handsome plant grown as a biennial, with large fern-like leaves and umbrella-type heads of tiny white flowers	H: 1.5–2.1m (5–7ft) S: 90cm (3ft)	Biennial	Sow in a prepared seed-bed in Aug.	In spring transplant seedlings to a shady position, spacing 90cm (3ft) apart. Keep well watered	Cut off flowering and leaf stalks while still green and tender, in May or June. Handy to use to decorate cakes and desserts
Balm, lemon Melissa officinalis	A low bushy plant with almost circular wrinkled leaves, softly hairy and intensely lemon-scented. Tiny purple-pink flowers are produced in July	H: 75cm (2½ft) S: 45cm (1½ft)	Perennial	Is easily raised from seed sown in open soil in May	Cut back foliage to crown in autumn	Young leaves can be picked from early spring until autumn. Use them to flavour summer drinks, rice puddings, custards and fruit salads
Basil, sweet Ocimum basilicum	A half-hardy annual with fleshy stems and thick leaves 7.5cm (3in) long, and with a strong smell of cloves	H: 60cm (2ft) S: 30cm (1ft)	Annual	Sow seed in a heated greenhouse in March, harden-off and plant out in late May	Can be grown successfully in 15cm (6in) pots, or in troughs	When the plants are in flower, cut down to soil level and store for winter use. Fresh leaves can be used throughout summer. Use sparingly in curries, or with tomatoes, mushrooms, eggs or cheese
Bay, sweet Laurus nobilis	A bushy evergreen tree for sheltered areas. Strongly aromatic leaves and clusters of small yellow flowers in May. Size can be contained by growing in a tub or clipping to shape	H: 4.5m (15ft) S: 4.5m (15ft)	Perennial	Take cuttings 10cm (4in) long, with a heel, in Aug. or Sept. Insert in equal parts peat and sand and supply bottom heat	Plant in March or April in a sunny position, or in a large tub. Plants in tubs can be trained to shape in early autumn	Cut off young leaves as required. Use to flavour casseroles or soup, or with fish
Borage Borago officinalis	A plant with bristly and hairy leaves and beautiful bright blue star-like flowers in clusters. In mild districts it may flower until Dec.	H: 15–60cm (1–1½ft) S: 23–30cm (9–12in)	Annual	Sow seed from March to May	Set the plants 30–45cm (1–1½ft) apart each way	Cut off leaves as required. The cucumber-flavoured leaves are used in summer fruit cups and salads. The flowers can be candied
Caraway Carum carvi	Frond-like leaves and a long tap root are characteristics of this plant. Tiny white flowers appear in May and June	H: 60cm (2ft) S: 30cm (1ft)	Biennial	Sow seed outdoors during late spring, in well-drained soil on a sunny site	Thin seedlings to about 20–30cm (10–12in) apart each way. Flowers are produced the following year	The narrow black seeds are ready for harvesting in July or Aug. Use them in cakes, bread, biscuits, or cheese dishes
Chamomile Chamomilla recutita (syn. Matricaria recutita, M. chamomilla)	The finely divided fern-like leaves are grey-green in colour, about 2.5cm (1in) long and strongly aromatic. Flowers are daisy-like and appear in June, but may last until Sept.	H: 38cm (15in) S: 20cm (8in)	Annual	Sow seed in spring, or early autumn, where they are to grow	Thin to 23cm (9in) apart, and grow in a sandy soil in full sun. Do not allow the soil to dry out	The flowers can be used fresh or dried, as an infusion to make chamomile tea. It is an aid to digestion

Name	Description	Height/spread	Treat as	Propagation	Remarks	Harvesting and use
Chives Allium schoenoprasum	A plant with grass-like foliage that dies down in autumn. A useful herb for containers or tubs	H:15–25cm (6–10in) S:23cm (9in)	Perennial	Mature plants can be divided and replanted. Seed can be sown in open soil in April	Pick off flower heads as they form. Divide and replant every three years. Placing a cloche over the plants in autumn extends the season	Pick the leaves as required. They have a mild onion flavour and are used in salads, soups, sandwiches and rice dishes
Clary Salvia sclarea	A biennial grown for its coloured 'leaves' on the flowering stems — blue, rose, purple, white — as well as for flavouring	H:60cm (2ft) S:30cm (1ft)	Biennial	Sow seed outdoors in spring, thinning to 30cm (1ft) apart	Any good soil suits this herb, ideally in full sun	The leaves are normally used fresh, but can be dried. Use them to flavour soups and casseroles
Fennel Foeniculum vulgare	A tall plant with feathery leaves, branching stems and umbrella-like clusters of tiny yellow flowers in mid to late summer	H:1.5m (5ft) S:45cm (1½ft)	Perennial	Sow seed outdoors in spring, thinning to 60cm (2ft) apart	Fennel prefers a moist soil in sun or light shade. Support with twiggy sticks may be necessary	The leaves can be used fresh, or collected and dried. They are chopped for use in fish dishes and fish sauces
Garlic Allium sativum	The cloves of this bulbous plant have a strong and distinctive flavour. The top growth resembles onions. It is a useful herb to grow in containers such as pots or boxes	H:45cm (1½ft) S:23cm (9in)	Replant annually	Plant the cloves in late Oct. or in Feb., 20cm (8in) apart and at twice their own depth	A rich soil in full sun is best. Remove flowering stems as they appear	Harvest the cloves when the leaves begin to yellow. Use sparingly in meat dishes, salads and omelettes
Marjoram, sweet Origanum majorana	A low, bushy plant with small grey-green leaves, and white flowers in July. These first appear as greenish knobs. It can easily be grown in small pots	H:20cm (8in) S:30cm (1ft)	Half-hardy annual or hardy perennial	Sow seed under glass in warmth in Feb. or March, or outdoors in late May. Take cuttings in April or May	Space 23cm (9in) apart, and keep moist	Leaves can be picked separately, or the whole plant lifted after flowering and hung up to dry. Use the leaves to flavour sausages and beef dishes
Mint Mentha spp.	The common 'mint sauce' species is the one most frequently grown, but there are many others, with flavours such as peppermint, spearmint, pineapple, apple, and ginger	H:20–60cm (8–24in) S:30cm (1ft)	Perennial	Divide plants in spring or autumn, or take cuttings during early summer (use a sandy soil and keep moist)	Keep the plants free of weeds. To restrict root growth and unwanted spread, plant in an old bucket sunk in the soil	Use fresh leaves as required, to flavour dishes and drinks
Parsley Petroselinum crispum	A biennial often treated as an annual, with the well-known curled and divided leaves much used as decoration. A good herb to grow in containers	H:15cm (6in) S:23cm (9in)	Annual	Sow outdoors in mid spring. Can also be sown in early July for use, with protection, until the next season's crop	Remove flowering stems unless seed is required. Normally parsley germinates readily from fresh seed	Pick fresh leaves as required. Use for sauces or as a garnish
Rosemary Rosmarinus officinalis	A Mediterranean ever-grey shrub, not completely hardy in the British Isles. It produces spikes of blue flowers in May	H:1.5m (5ft) S:1.5m (5ft)	Perennial	Take cuttings (15cm/6in long) in May. Remove lower leaves and insert in a sandy soil	Provide a sunny position in light soil	Cut off whole sprigs and hang up to dry. The strongly aromatic leaves are used sparingly with lamb, pork, veal, chicken, bread and cakes
Sage Salvia officinalis	An evergreen low-growing shrub with grey-green wrinkled and woolly leaves, which have a slightly bitter flavour	H:60cm (2ft) S:30cm (1ft)	Perennial	Take cuttings in spring or early summer. Stems may root if the plants are earthed up at the base: sever and transplant when rooted	Plant in a sheltered position in a light soil. Renew the plants about every four years	Pull off leafy shoots and bunch together to dry. This can be done just before or during flowering, although the flowers are not gathered. Use to flavour pork, duck, veal, fish, and cheese
Sorrel, French Rumex scutatus	A sprawling plant that dies down in autumn. The leaves, shaped rather like a round shield, are fleshy and grey-green	H:30cm (1ft) S:15cm (6in)	Perennial	Sow seed outdoors in spring, thinning to 30cm (1ft) apart. Large clumps can be divided in spring	A moist soil is required, in sun or shade. Do not let the plants flower	Cut off leaves as required. They can be used to flavour soups or as a salad vegetable
Tarragon, French Artemisia dracunculus	A bushy plant that dies down in autumn, although it may be evergreen in mild areas	H:60–90cm (2–3ft) S:30cm (1ft)	Perennial	Divide roots in spring	It is essential to plant in well-drained soil, in a sunny position. Space 45cm (1½ft) apart each way. In cold areas the crown may need winter protection	Cut the leaves as required and use fresh. Use sparingly in casseroles, chicken and egg dishes, or for tarragon vinegar
Thyme Thymus vulgaris	A small evergreen shrub, and a herb that does well in containers	H:23cm (9in) S:30cm (1ft)	Perennial	Layer plants every few years, and replant the bed with them spaced 30cm (1ft) apart	Plant in a light soil in full sun	Cut the foliage during July and Aug., and hang up in bundles to dry. The tiny pungent leaves are used to flavour stuffings, beef, veal, chicken, cheese and pasta

The gardener's year
January

Flowers

Little outdoor work can be done in the garden this month. If new areas are to be planted with shrubs or other plants, or sown with seed in the spring, plan these on paper now and order your plants, seeds, or bulbs from nurserymen and seedsmen.

Protect with cloches the flowers of Christmas roses (*Helleborus niger*) to prevent weather or bird damage (see also December).

Water plants in containers sheltered from the weather, such as windowboxes, hanging baskets and pots on patios.

Take root cuttings of herbaceous perennials, such as anchusa, gaillardia, romneya, oriental poppy (*Papaver orientale*), and verbascum. Place them in boxes of a cuttings compost in a cold-frame or in a sheltered corner of the garden under cloches.

Fruit

If weather and soil conditions are suitable, plant fruit trees and bushes.

Complete the pruning of established fruits and spray them all, except strawberries, with a tar-oil winter-wash to kill insect pest eggs.

Inspect fruits in store and remove any that are diseased.

Vegetables

Order seeds, seed potatoes and plants this month. Store them in a cool, frost-free and rodent-free place until required.

In warm and sheltered gardens, the first sowings of certain cultivars of peas and broad beans can be made if the soil is friable and not too wet or cold. Also plant the first batch of shallots.

Where necessary, apply lime to the soil — if not already done. Do not mix lime and animal manures.

Lift parsnips and leeks as required.

Inspect root vegetables in store and remove any that show signs of disease.

Trees, shrubs and climbers

If the weather is suitable and the soil well prepared and in a friable condition, plant trees, shrubs and climbers. During inclement weather, store the plants in hessian or straw in a cool, frost-free place, or unwrap them and heel them into a trench in a sheltered part of the garden.

Prevent branches being broken by the weight of snow, removing it by hand. Ensure that small or tender plants have adequate protection.

Check all plant supports and ties to ensure they are firm and in good condition.

Under glass

Order seeds and new plants now for sowing and planting during the next two months.

Ventilate and water existing plants carefully to keep them in good health.

Remove dead flower heads and leaves to prevent infection and if necessary spray against pests or diseases.

Make the first sowing of greenhouse tomato seeds in boxes or pots in heat.

In the home, water houseplants given as Christmas presents, according to their requirements, and give them the temperature and amount of light they need (see pages 174–181).

As forced bulbs, particularly hyacinths, tulips and narcissi, in bowls reach the correct stage of growth, bring them from the cold into the home. Water them as necessary.

Plant hippeastrums (amaryllis) to flower next month.

Check that all seed sowing and potting equipment is in good condition.

. . . and don't forget

Clear away all leaves and debris by raking or brushing them into heaps and placing them on the compost heap.

Prepare the ground for new lawns by digging the area whenever soil conditions permit. Check that the drainage is all right. Leave the soil surface roughly dug to enable the frost to produce a fine tilth.

Tread and firm the soil around plants recently set in position, especially if it has been loosened by frost or the plants rocked by wind.

Check all machinery and tools to ensure they are in good working order for the coming season.

Make a note of paved or concrete areas that collect moisture which ices up, and correct the levels when time and weather permit. Also, keep drainage areas free of debris.

Keep an area open in ice on the garden pool, to allow fish to breathe.

The gardener's year
February

Flowers

Cut down herbaceous plants not previously pruned in November or December. Compost or burn the dead foliage. Hoe or lightly fork the soil, incorporating a general-purpose fertilizer. Remove all weeds.

In warm gardens, plant gladioli and anemone corms, also ranunculus tubers. Lift and thin out clumps of snowdrops (galanthus) after flowering and replant immediately.

Mulch lily-of-the-valley (convallaria) with well-rotted compost or peat.

If areas are free of plants and the soil workable, fork now for setting out summer bedding plants, such as dahlias and chrysanthemums, later. Also, fork and prepare the ground for new herbaceous perennials.

Complete the flower seed order or buy direct from shops or garden centres before stocks are sold out.

Water outdoor plants set in containers in sheltered areas.

Fruit

Complete the planting of fruit trees and bushes, and stake them securely.

Finish pruning and winter spraying.

Spray peaches against leaf-curl disease. Pollinate early-flowering fruits such as apricots, peaches, nectarines and plums, using a paintbrush or piece of cotton-wool on a stick. Also, protect these fruits from frost damage by covering them at night with a light material or polythene sheeting.

Cover some strawberry plants with cloches for earlier than normal fruiting.

Remove the flowers from strawberries planted this month to prevent them fruiting in the first year.

Apply a general-purpose fertilizer to the soil around all fruit trees and bushes. Lightly hoe it in, and add a layer of mulching material.

Vegetables

Protect rhubarb, to force early stems.

Prepare the ground for sowings of several vegetables next month.

Continue to sow broad beans and peas, and plant shallots. Also plant early potatoes, onion sets and Jerusalem artichokes.

Protect broccoli from frost damage by bending the leaves over the heads.

Sow hardy annual herbs at the end of this month.

Start sprouting maincrop seed potatoes in a light, frost-proof place.

Trees, shrubs and climbers

Continue to plant trees, shrubs and climbers or heel them in if planting is not possible.

Cut out dead, diseased and damaged wood and burn it. Prune large-flowered clematis, wisteria, honeysuckle (lonicera) and ornamental grape vines (vitis).

Prepare, by double digging, new sites for hedges and evergreen trees and shrubs to be planted next month.

Under glass

Begin sowing seeds of half-hardy flowering annuals and summer bedding plants in heat — 10–15°C (50–60°F). Also, sow greenhouse display plants such as primulas, tuberous begonias, winter cherry (*Solanum capsicastrum*) and gloxinias (sinningias).

Start into growth chrysanthemums, dahlias, fuchsias and pelargoniums, and take cuttings when growths are long enough.

Sow seeds of lettuces, broad beans, Brussels sprouts, cabbages, cauliflowers, leeks, carrots, beetroot, cucumbers, melons, sweetcorn, onions, mustard and cress and a further batch of tomatoes for greenhouse cropping. Thin out the seedlings when large enough to be handled.

Syringe greenhouse grape vines with water to induce new growth. Pollinate greenhouse peaches, almonds, apricots and nectarines.

Water and ventilate the greenhouse to ensure correct humidity, temperature and freedom from draughts.

Keep plants free of pests and diseases.

Bring indoors the last of the forced bulbs grown in bowls. Gradually harden off those bulbs that have finished flowering and water with a liquid fertilizer to replenish food stocks.

. . . and don't forget

Tread and firm soil around recently planted trees and shrubs which have been raised by the action of frost.

Check existing lawns for waterlogged areas and spike or fork to improve the drainage. Rake and give the first mowing when the grass is 5–7.5cm (2–3in) high. Brush off debris, leaves and wormcasts and apply a wormkiller.

Continue to prepare new lawn sites.

Keep an air hole in the ice on garden pools.

The gardener's year
March

Flowers

Prepare the ground for sowings of hardy annuals by forking the soil and adding a general-purpose fertilizer. In sheltered and warm gardens, the first sowings may be made at the end of this month.

Remove dead heads of spring-flowering bulbs to conserve the strength of the bulbs.

Plant gladioli corms, lily bulbs and ranunculus tubers, also hardy herbaceous perennials. Divide large clumps of perennial plants and replant the younger outer growths.

Hoe, feed and mulch herbaceous borders.

Plant out unsprouted dahlia tubers and cover them with a mulch to protect against frost.

Water outdoor plants in containers in sheltered areas.

Fruit

If not done last month, hoe in a general-purpose fertilizer round the root areas of all fruits and apply a layer of mulching material. Remove all weeds.

Tie in new shoots of cane fruits to their supports.

Continue to pollinate and protect from frost fruits such as apricots, peaches, nectarines and plums.

Place cloches over strawberries to obtain early fruits.

Spray apples and pears with a fungicide to prevent scab disease.

Remove low-growing or damaged stems from bush fruits such as gooseberries and currants.

Continue to plant strawberries, but don't let them fruit in the first year — remove the blossoms.

Vegetables

Dig up any swedes, parsnips and leeks that are still in the soil and prepare the ground for new crops.

As soon as the weather is suitable and the soil friable, start successional sowings of green vegetable crops, including lettuces and radishes, either where they are to mature or in seed-beds. Continue planting potatoes, shallots and onion sets.

Thin out sowings of broad beans and peas made last month. Insert stakes or supports.

Give spring cabbages a nitrogenous fertilizer to encourage growth.

Trees, shrubs and climbers

Complete the planting of new trees, shrubs and climbers — both deciduous and evergreen — by the end of the month. Top-dress them with manure, compost or peat.

Set out hedging plants in ground prepared last month.

Prune bush hybrid tea and floribunda roses, and shorten tips of lateral growths on climbing roses to encourage more blooms.

Cut back the hard and old wood from shrubs that bear flowers on new growth, such as the butterfly bush (*Buddleia davidii*), caryopteris, deciduous ceanothus, tree hollyhock (hibiscus), and tamarisk (*Tamarix pentandra*).

Remove dead wood and very old wood from winter-flowering shrubs, such as chimonanthus and viburnums.

Hoe carefully to remove weeds and work in a general-purpose fertilizer over the root areas of trees, shrubs and climbers. Give these plants a good mulch.

Under glass

Complete the sowing of half-hardy and summer-flowering bedding plants. Prick out seedlings of those sown last month into boxes for hardening off next month.

Continue to sow or plant greenhouse flowering plants, and thin the seedlings of those sown last month.

Discard winter-flowering pot plants, such as cinerarias and calceolarias. Remove the dead flowers from azaleas and cyclamen, and fruits from solanums, if the plants are to be kept for next year.

Take cuttings of chrysanthemums, dahlias, fuchsias and pelargoniums, also perpetual-flowering carnations.

Start into growth tuberous begonias and gloxinias (sinningias).

Continue to spray grape vines daily with water. Grape vines and stone fruits, such as peaches and almonds, need sufficient water to keep the root area moist.

Sow melons, cucumbers, aubergines, sweetcorn, peppers and celery.

As forced bulbs complete their flowering, move them to a cool place. Feed with a liquid fertilizer.

. . . and don't forget

Tread and firm soil loosened by frost, and re-firm plants rocked by wind.

Continue to treat lawns in the manner recommended last month.

Finish preparing the site for new lawns which are to be created from seed or turf next month.

Check that all plant supports are secure.

Start spraying against insect pests as soon as they are noticed.

The gardener's year
April

Flowers

Sow hardy annual seeds where they are to flower, in previously prepared ground, either in a border of their own or as fillers among other plants.

Remove the dead heads from flowering bulbs. Apply a foliar feed to the leaves and bulbs to encourage them to flower the following year.

Plant out forced bulbs in bowls when they have finished flowering and been hardened off. These will add to the garden display next spring.

Plant out dahlia tubers as soon as the ground is workable.

Continue to plant gladioli corms and lily bulbs, also other bulbous plants such as ranunculus, anemones, montbretias and nerines.

At the end of this month, plant out hardened-off chrysanthemum cuttings. Lift and divide hardy chrysanthemums which have wintered outdoors — replant young healthy pieces immediately and discard old and central pieces.

Continue to water outdoor plants in containers in sheltered areas.

Fruit

Spray all fruits with insecticides and fungicides to control pests and diseases when the flowers are not fully open — spray before bud-burst or after petal-fall.

Lightly prune newly-planted plums and established figs, and disbud at intervals the sideshoots of fan-trained peaches and nectarines. Thin the fruits of peaches and nectarines when marble-sized to allow the remainder to develop fully.

Remove the flowers from newly-planted fruit trees and bushes to prevent them fruiting this year. This helps build up their strength for the following year.

Water container grown plants and weed the borders.

Vegetables

Continue successional sowings of most vegetable crops, including lettuces, radishes, chicory, endive and parsley, either where they are to mature or in seed-beds. Start sowings of root crops such as carrots, beetroot, parsnips, swedes and turnips.

Thin out or transplant seedlings of vegetables sown last month.

Stake peas and beans.

Earth-up early potatoes and plant maincrop cultivars.

Plant out vegetables raised earlier under glass and which have been well hardened.

Sow seeds of annual and perennial herbs.

Spray against pests and diseases as soon as they are noticed.

Trees, shrubs and climbers

If the pruning of roses, winter-flowering shrubs, and those which flower on this year's growth, was not completed last month, finish it as quickly as possible.

Plant out pot-grown clematis and prune back.

All climbers and wall shrubs should have new growths tied in as they appear.

Hoe carefully round root areas, remove weeds, and mulch. Shallow-rooting plants, such as magnolias and rhododendrons, are best not hoed but given a deep layer of mulch over the roots — use acid peat for rhododendrons.

Under glass

Thin out seedlings of half-hardy plants sown last month, and gradually harden them by moving them to cold-frames.

Rooted cuttings of chrysanthemums, dahlias, fuchsias and pelargoniums should also be hardened off in frames for planting out next month.

Pot-on greenhouse plants such as chrysanthemums, tuberous begonias and gloxinias, also new cyclamen. Older cyclamen that have finished flowering should be rested.

Plant greenhouse tomatoes into a soil-bed, pots, growing-bags or rings (if grown by the ring-culture method).

Sow hardy tomato cultivars for planting outdoors in summer.

Thin out seedlings of greenhouse cucumbers, melons, peppers and aubergines. Also, thin and start to harden off sweetcorn and celery for planting out next month.

Thin the fruits of greenhouse grapes.

Ventilate the greenhouse more freely, lower the temperature (except if frosts are expected) and water the plants regularly to prevent drying out.

Spray or fumigate the plants against pests and diseases.

Most houseplants will now start to require more water and liquid feeding.

. . . and don't forget

Mow lawns, apply weed and moss-killers if necessary, and give the first spring dressing of a lawn fertilizer.

Sow or turf new lawns, but take more care when cutting the grass and do not over-use the mower during the first summer.

This is a good month to create a water garden. Therefore, place orders for plants needed next month.

The gardener's year
May

Flowers

Remove spring bedding plants that have finished flowering. Discard those plants such as wallflowers (cheiranthus) and forget-me-nots (myosotis), but heel-in bulbs and polyanthuses in a spare part of the garden where they may complete their growth and be ready for planting again in autumn.

Fork over the ground after lifting the plants, work in a general-purpose fertilizer and tread the soil firm. Rake it to produce a good tilth.

Towards the middle or end of the month, set out summer bedding plants that have been hardened off.

Also, change spring bedding plants in containers for summer bedding plants, and continue to water regularly those containers in sheltered places.

Plant out hardened-off rooted cuttings of chrysanthemums, dahlias, pelargoniums and fuchsias.

Many half-hardy annuals can be sown where they are to flower.

Thin hardy annuals sown *in situ*.

Sow seeds of hardy perennials and biennials in a seed-bed for flowering next year.

Continue to plant gladioli for a succession of bloom.

Give taller-growing flowering plants stakes or short pea sticks to support them as they grow. Where necessary, tie in the new growth.

Hoe shallowly to remove weeds and incorporate a general-purpose fertilizer. Follow this with a mulch when the soil is wet.

Fruit

Summer prune fruit trees, especially pyramids and cordons.

Spray all fruits against pests and diseases, before flowers are fully open, or when they are over.

Start to thin peach and nectarine fruits if not ready last month.

Protect strawberry flowers from late frosts by covering them with cloches. Remove runners, unless wanted for propagation.

Vegetables

Thin vegetable seedlings sown last month, or transplant them from the seed-bed to their cropping positions.

Remove cloches from all except the most tender vegetable crops.

Plant out sweetcorn and celery that have been hardened off after being sown in the greenhouse. Both these vegetables may be sown outdoors now.

Sow sprouting broccoli, outdoor cucumbers, kale, marrows and swedes.

Continue sowing suitable cultivars of green vegetables and salad crops for successional cropping.

Give liquid feeds to all outdoor vegetables and water the soil during dry periods.

Hoe the soil regularly and mulch whenever possible.

Tie in peas and beans to supports.

Spray the plants regularly against pests and diseases.

Trees, shrubs and climbers

Prune or trim hedging plants as necessary.

Tie in new growths of climbers or wall shrubs.

Remove the dead flowers from rhododendrons.

Cut out weak, dead or unwanted shoots from evergreen trees and shrubs. Any overgrown ones can be cut hard back to produce fresh shoots from the base.

If roses have produced several shoots from the points above the pruning point, now is the time to cut out the unwanted shoots.

Container-grown plants, which can be planted at any time of year, can be set out now to give summer colour.

Under glass

Put into frames any plants that need hardening off before being planted in the open at the beginning of next month. Also place in frames, greenhouse plants not required for summer decoration and which can rest in a protected position, such as hippeastrums and cyclamen.

Stand pots of half-hardy chrysanthemums in the open for the summer; stake, water and feed them.

Pot-on earlier sowings and cuttings of greenhouse plants, such as fuchsias and geraniums (pelargoniums).

Make sowings of spring-flowering greenhouse primulas, cinerarias and calceolarias, and prick them out as soon as possible.

Plant melons and cucumbers where they are to grow in the greenhouse, and provide the necessary supports.

Cut out sideshoots of tomatoes, and as soon as the first flowers appear water and feed them regularly. Tie the sideshoots to supports.

Water all the plants regularly, and ventilate and shade the greenhouse.

Apply pesticides regularly.

Water and feed indoor plants.

. . . and don't forget

Mow lawns regularly and water them during dry periods, especially if newly sown or turfed. Apply weedkillers to established lawns, if required.

If frost threatens, protect young plants just set out by covering them with cloches or hessian.

Set water plants in position in the pool.

The gardener's year
June

Flowers

Make sure that the remains of spring bedding plants have been cleared away. Replace these plants with permanent ones or summer bedding subjects which have been thoroughly hardened off.

Thin *in situ* sowings of hardy and half-hardy annuals.

Continue to support tall-growing flowers, tying new growth to stakes.

Water and mulch bulbous plants such as gladioli and lilies.

Continue to sow hardy biennials and perennials in a seed-bed.

Plant out chrysanthemums, dahlias, fuchsias and pelargoniums. Nip out the main growth buds to form bushy plants.

If naturalized bulbs are overcrowded, they can be lifted after the leaves have yellowed. Dry and clean them, and store in a cool and airy place until replanting time in autumn.

Weed and water all plants.

Apply insecticides, fungicides and fertilizers.

Fruit

Protect strawberries from slugs and birds by putting polythene sheeting or straw round the plants and covering them with netting. Continue to remove runners, or lift rooted ones and plant them elsewhere.

If too many fruits have formed on plums, apples and pears, thin the clusters after the natural June drop that normally occurs this month and early July.

Tie in the shoots of cane fruits to their supports. Thin out the canes if too many have been formed.

Lightly prune gooseberries and both red and white currants.

Continue thinning peach and nectarine fruits. Lightly prune bush peach trees.

Spray all fruit trees and bushes with insecticides and fungicides, according to the manufacturer's instructions.

Water, weed and mulch the plants.

Vegetables

Earth-up maincrop potatoes and start lifting early cultivars.

Plant out hardened-off celery and leek plants.

Continue sowings of green vegetables to supply late crops.

Thin out previous sowings or transplant the young plants from the seed-bed to their permanent quarters.

Make small sowings of salad crops among other vegetables to give continuity of supplies. Sow swedes and chicory for winter use.

Plant out hardened-off tomatoes, covering them with cloches. If necessary, support the individual plants with stakes.

Support peas and beans. Also, pinch out the tops of broad beans.

Water and feed vegetables regularly.

Plant out early herb sowings. Sow perennial herbs in a seed-bed for transferring to their final quarters in autumn.

Thin out marrows and cucumbers sown last month to allow plenty of space to grow.

Trees, shrubs and climbers

Continue to trim or cut hedges.

Tie in the shoots of climbers or wall shrubs.

Prune early-flowering clematis species and shorten growths of flowering quince (chaenomeles). Also, cut back old flowering shoots, and

dead unwanted branches of shrubs, that have flowered earlier, such as the flowering currant (ribes), broom (cytisus) and rock roses (helianthemum).

Disbud hybrid tea roses.

Under glass

Place azaleas, cinerarias, primulas, calceolarias, winter cherry (solanum) and cyclamen in a cold-frame for the summer before returning them to the greenhouse in autumn for winter and spring flowers. Keep the plants well watered, and shade them from hot sun.

Feed and water tomato plants regularly and start picking fruits. Continue to tie them to supports and remove the sideshoots.

Thin grape bunches by about one-third.

Stop cucumber plants at the desired height. Tie into supports young shoots, and remove male flowers (those without embryo fruits behind). Also, remove all growths beyond two leaves after the fruits.

Fertilize melons by removing the male flowers and dusting the pollen on to the female flowers.

Water all greenhouse plants as required. Damp down the floor to increase humidity, and ventilate and shade according to requirements.

Continue to water and feed plants in pots in the home.

. . . and don't forget

Mow your lawns regularly. Use a rake to lift weeds and creeping stems so that the mower cuts them off. Give summer dressings of fertilizers and weedkillers.

Start making plans for any new areas of the garden which are to be redesigned.

The gardener's year
July

Flowers

Place supports — stakes or short pea sticks — for border plants and tie in new growths.

Dead-head flowering plants regularly to ensure further blooms.

Start picking everlasting flowers for drying for winter flower arrangements.

Layer stems of border carnations for new plants.

Keep gladioli and lilies well watered.

Chrysanthemums in pots outdoors for the summer should be staked for support, and the stakes tied to a straining wire to prevent the pots blowing over. Water and feed the plants regularly.

Tulips heeled in from spring bedding schemes should have completed growth by now. Lift, clean and store bulbs in a dark cool, airy place until planted again in autumn.

Start planting autumn-flowering bulbs such as colchicums (autumn crocus), nerines and sternbergias in rough grass areas, under trees, or among shrubs.

Early-flowering irises can be lifted and the rhizomes divided. Replant only the healthy outer portions.

Water and feed all flowering plants regularly and spray with pesticides as necessary. Remove weeds from the borders.

Fruit

Protect bush and cane fruits from birds by spreading nets over them. Start picking the fruits when they are ripe. Prune these bushes and canes after all the fruits have been picked.

Take tip cuttings of black currants, and layer blackberries and loganberries, if new plants are required.

Summer-prune trained plum, apple and pear trees and complete the thinning of fruit if not done last month.

When strawberry picking is completed, remove the polythene or burn the straw round the plants. If not burnt, cut the leaves back with shears.

Spray with insecticides and fungicides, as required, and ensure that all the fruits are thoroughly watered.

Vegetables

Harvest vegetables as they mature.

Pull up and destroy the remains of early peas, beans, cabbages and other vegetables that have finished cropping, and use the ground for other crops.

Sow seed of suitable cultivars of spring cabbages, turnips, carrots, lettuces, pickling onions, winter radishes, beet, parsley, peas and winter spinach.

Water and feed outdoor tomatoes, marrows and cucumbers and remove the male flowers from the latter. Stop the main shoots when they have covered the required growth area.

Hoe the soil regularly to remove weeds, and if possible add a mulch.

Thin herb seedlings from last month's sowings.

Lift shallots and put them in a sunny place to ripen.

Trees, shrubs and climbers

Continue to trim and prune hedges.

Prune shrubs that have finished flowering by cutting back old and unwanted shoots, and trimming back shoots that have flowered to fresh young growths. Prune species clematis.

Remove dead flower heads from roses, except hip-bearing shrub and species roses.

Tie in the new growths of climbers and wall shrubs.

Water, feed and mulch plants regularly and, in particular, do not let hydrangeas and rhododendrons suffer from drought.

Remove weeds, and use pesticides when required.

Under glass

Continue to feed and water tomato plants regularly. Pick fruits as they ripen, remove sideshoots, also the tips of the main shoots when the plants reach the desired height. Keep tied to supports.

Top-dress the root areas of cucumbers with animal manure or well-rotted compost with a general fertilizer mixed in. Continue to remove male flowers, and nip off the shoots at two leaves beyond each fruit. Syringe the plants daily with water and shade them from hot sun. Pick the cucumbers as they ripen.

Cut back sideshoots to two leaves beyond each melon fruit and support the developing fruits with nets hung from the roof wires. Allow plenty of sun to reach the fruit, removing some leaves, and syringe daily with water.

Shade flowering plants in the greenhouse and cut off flowers as they fade.

Propagate pot plants such as *Begonia rex*, saintpaulias, busy Lizzies (impatiens), ivies (hedera), *Hoya carnosa* and hydrangeas.

Make further sowings of cinerarias, calceolarias, gloxinias and primulas for spring flowering and prick them out as soon as possible.

Repot last year's cyclamen and start them into growth.

Ventilate, water and damp-down the greenhouse daily, and if necessary shade the plants.

Make a note of any greenhouse or frame repairs to be carried out now or next month.

Feed and water indoor plants.

. . . and don't forget

Treat lawns in the same way as recommended last month. Keep the lawn edges tidy by cutting or trimming them.

The gardener's year
August

Flowers

Stake tall dahlias and chrysanthemums and tie in the stems. For larger flowers, remove the side flower buds of dahlias and weak side stems of chrysanthemums.

Pick sweet peas (*Lathyrus odoratus*) regularly to ensure continuity of flowers.

Continue to dead-head flowers to encourage further blooms.

Cut down by half herbaceous plants that have finished flowering.

Increase pansies and violas by rooting cuttings in boxes.

Sow *in situ* hardy annuals such as godetia, sweet sultans, alyssum, larkspur, calendulas, cornflowers, agrostemma and candytuft, for early flowering next summer.

Remove all weeds, and mulch and water as necessary. If you are going away on holiday, water the plants thoroughly before leaving, and then add an additional layer of mulching material.

At the end of the month, make the first plantings of narcissus and daffodil bulbs outdoors. Also, plant bulbs of snowflake (leucojum), belladonna lily (*Amaryllis belladonna*) and crown imperial (*Fritillaria imperialis*).

Start planting the first batches of forced bulbs in bowls for flowering indoors in winter. Keep them in a cool and dark place.

Water half-hardy chrysanthemums in pots standing outdoors.

Spray with insecticides and fungicides, as necessary.

Fruit

Pick the first of the early apple and pear fruits and use them immediately.

Set out strawberry plants — either new ones bought in or healthy rooted runners from existing stock.

Continue picking bush and cane fruits. Prune them when all of the fruits have been picked.

If plum trees are heavily laden with fruit, support the branches with timber.

Vegetables

Harvest all vegetables as they mature. If you are going on holiday, ask neighbours or friends to continue cropping the plants.

Lift onions and shallots if not taken up last month. Use immediately any that are soft, but ripen others in a sunny position for storage and use later.

Lift and store beetroot.

Plant into their final positions vegetables such as Brussels sprouts, winter cabbages and purple-sprouting broccoli. Firm them in well and water each plant thoroughly.

Sow suitable cultivars of spring cabbages, onions and spinach for winter use. Also, make the last outdoor sowings of salad crops. Thin out seedlings of crops that were sown last month.

Pinch out the tips of outdoor tomato plants to encourage the fruits to ripen.

Cut and dry herbs in readiness for winter use.

Weed, water, mulch and use insecticides and pesticides before going on holiday.

Trees, shrubs and climbers

Continue to trim and prune hedges.

Trim lavender bushes lightly with shears, after first picking the dried flower heads.

Prune climbing and rambler roses that have finished flowering. Give all roses a dressing of potash to help ripen the stems. Remove rose sucker growths by cutting them off just below ground level.

Take half-ripe cuttings of heathers buddleia, berberis, cotoneaster, lavender and santolina. Keep them well watered.

Under glass

Continue to treat tomato plants as recommended for last month.

Pick cucumbers as they mature and continue syringeing them daily with water. Also use a liquid feed.

Grapes should be ripe for picking now. When all the branches have been cut, spray daily with water to deter red spider mite.

Shade all flowering plants, and remove dead blooms.

Sow seed of cyclamen for flowering 12-15 months later.

Take cuttings of fuchsias, pelargoniums and heliotrope.

Plant winter and spring flowering plants such as lachenalias, freesias and arum lilies.

Pot on young specimens of winter and spring flowering plants raised from seed sown previously, and start giving weekly feeds of liquid fertilizer.

Water all the plants thoroughly and ventilate and shade the greenhouse as necessary.

If going on holiday and automatic watering equipment is not installed, make arrangements with friends or neighbours to look after the greenhouse.

To prevent pot plants drying out in the home while away, sink the pots into bowls of moist peat or use a proprietary wick watering system. The glass fibre wicks feed water from a reservoir into individual pots.

. . . and don't forget

Mow the lawns regularly. If going away, leave the grass cuttings on the lawn's surface to help preserve soil moisture.

This is a good time to plan new patios and paths.

The gardener's year
September

Flowers

Remove dead flower heads and stems from herbaceous perennials that have finished blooming.

Tie in the taller and later-flowering plants to their supports.

Towards the end of this month, pull up the remains of annuals and bedding plants from borders and containers, and add them to the compost heap. Fork over the soil, adding bonemeal fertilizer, and firm it in preparation for setting out spring bedding plants or sowings of annuals at the end of this month or the beginning of next.

Carefully lift gladioli corms and dahlia tubers. Remove the dead foliage and soil, and store them in a cool and frost-free place for the winter.

Prepare sites for herbaceous plants and plant subjects such as paeonies, various forms of irises, and hardy carnations and pinks.

Cut and dry seed-heads of flowers such as poppies, Chinese lanterns (physalis) and honesty (lunaria) for winter flower arrangements.

Plant outdoor bulbs such as daffodils, hyacinths, scillas, winter aconites, snowdrops, crocuses and muscari in positions where they are to bloom. Plant *Iris unguicularis* for flowering from November to February.

Plant more bowls of forced bulbs for flowering indoors during winter and spring. Keep them in a cool and dark place, and water if necessary.

Prepare sites for the majority of hardy herbaceous perennials to be planted next month.

Fruit

Pick apples and pears as they ripen and store healthy fruits.

Harvest plums when they are ripe and prune the trees afterwards.

Finish picking autumn-fruiting raspberries, loganberries and blackberries and prune back the old canes to soil-level.

Prepare the ground thoroughly for any new fruit trees and bushes to be planted this autumn or early winter.

Pick autumn-fruiting strawberries and cover the plants with cloches to protect them against weather and birds.

Vegetables

Lift and store maincrop potatoes and carrots.

Continue to cut and use marrows.

Pull up old pea and bean haulms. Clean and keep the supports for next year.

Lift chicory roots, and store for forcing indoors to provide winter chicons.

Plant out winter and spring cabbages, kale and savoys.

Pick all fruits from tomato plants and ripen them indoors. Pull up and discard the plants.

Compost or discard any finished vegetables before they start rotting.

Plan next year's cropping rotation of vegetables.

Dig thoroughly all spare ground, enriching it with animal manure or well-rotted compost (but do not lime at the same time). Leave it rough dug.

Trees, shrubs and climbers

Most hedges can have their last trimming or pruning at the end of this month.

All sites for hedges and new trees and shrubs to be planted later in the year or early next year, should be prepared now. Prepare the ground thoroughly, by double digging and manuring the sub-soil.

Continue to dead-head roses. Finish pruning ramblers and climbers, and tie in new replacement shoots.

Tie in new growths of climbers and shrubs trained against supports.

Under glass

Pick all tomato fruits at the end of the month and ripen green ones in the home. Pull up the plants and compost them, after removing the strings or supports. Fork over the soil, and sterilize it if infected by diseases or pests.

Pick all cucumbers and compost the plants.

Finish harvesting melons and remove the plants.

Remove all shading, give plants less water and ventilate according to weather. It may be necessary to start heating the greenhouse at the end of this month.

Prick out cyclamen sown last month.

Winter and spring flowering plants should be brought in from cold-frames. Water and feed them as required. Continue to water and feed the other greenhouse plants started into growth last month.

Sow suitable cultivars of lettuces, radishes and carrots under cloches or in cold-frames for winter use.

Indoor houseplants can now be fed and watered less frequently. Remove them from window areas at night in case there are cold draughts.

. . . and don't forget

Lessen the frequency of lawn mowing. Spike or fork the lawn if compacted. Apply an autumn lawn fertilizer. Sow new lawns and prepare the site for turfing next month.

Continue to remove weeds regularly and spray against pests and diseases.

The gardener's year
October

Flowers

Lift all annuals and half-hardy bedding plants, including dahlias and gladioli for storing. Prepare the ground or containers for spring bedding plants and bulbs. After flowering, lift chrysanthemums, cut back their top growth, and store in a cool frost-free place for winter. Pelargoniums should be tipped back to remove any flowering shoots.

Finish setting out all spring-flowering bedding plants such as wallflowers (cheiranthus) polyanthuses and forget-me-nots (myosotis).

Complete the planting of bulbs, including tulips, where they are to flower, either in naturalized areas or as formal bedding.

Cut down herbaceous perennials as they finish flowering. Lightly hoe or fork the soil to remove foot-marks and work in well-rotted compost and some bonemeal.

If herbaceous plants are old or overgrown, lift and divide them. Replant the newer outside pieces of the clumps in prepared and fertilized soil. Discard the old, central parts.

Plant new herbaceous plants in ground prepared for them last month.

Remove all stakes and supports, cleaning and storing them for use next year.

Make a final planting of forced bulbs in bowls for late winter and spring flowering in the home. Store them in a cool, dark frost-free place.

Lift half-hardy summer-flowering bulbs such as ixias and sparaxis, and store in a cool, frost-free place.

Fruit

Continue to pick and store apples and pears.

Tie in new canes of fruits to their supports, and remove old canes that have fruited.

Continue to pick strawberries, and after fruiting remove the protective cloches. Complete the setting out of new plants.

Plant in prepared sites any new fruit trees, bushes or canes received at the end of this month.

Clear the soil of weeds around established fruits, and generally tidy the areas. Ensure all supports are in good condition to withstand winter gales.

Spray with fungicides or insecticides, where necessary.

Vegetables

Finish lifting and storing maincrop potatoes.

Cut any marrows remaining and store them for later use. Remove and compost the plants.

Set out the last of winter and spring cropping Brussels sprouts, cabbages, kale and broccoli.

Bend the top leaves over cauliflower heads to prevent damage from frost and rain.

Finish planning a vegetable crop rotation scheme for next year and dig over all spare areas. Leave the soil rough dug.

Trees, shrubs and climbers

In a good growing season, hedges may require a further trimming or pruning this month. Clip back deciduous hedges planted in spring to encourage a bushy base.

Thoroughly prepare the ground for new trees, shrubs and climbers if not done previously. Set out new plants received this month. Evergreens are best planted this month or in March or April, but deciduous types can be set out whenever soil and weather permit, from October to April.

Remove the dead heads from roses that continue flowering well into early winter.

Prepare the ground for new roses by digging it deeply and manuring the sub-soil.

Hoe in mulches round established trees, shrubs and climbers, and remove weeds. Bonemeal fertilizer can be worked in at the same time.

Under glass

Bring in pots of half-hardy chrysanthemums that have been standing outdoors during the summer. Disbud to get large flowers, and water and feed the plants regularly.

Plants may now need some heat to protect them from frosts. Water the plants more sparingly, except those making full growth, and ventilate them carefully to prevent draughts.

Gloxinias and tuberous begonias that have finished flowering should be rested now.

If perennial bedding plants, such as fuchsias, chrysanthemums, pelargoniums (geraniums) and heliotropes are stored in the greenhouse, water them lightly occasionally to prevent them drying out. Cuttings may be taken now.

Plants in cold-frames should be watered as required, and the frames covered at nights when frost is likely. Thin salad crops sown last month.

Reduce the frequency of watering and feeding houseplants, and keep away from draughty positions.

. . . and don't forget

Lawn mowing generally ceases this month in all except mildest areas. Bumps and hollows in the lawn can be corrected at this time of year.

Lay new turves, firming and watering.

Brush or rake up leaves, adding them to the compost heap.

The gardener's year
November

Flowers

Complete the forking of herbaceous borders. Cut back herbaceous plants that have finished flowering.

Set out new herbaceous plants if the soil and weather are suitable. If not, heel in the plants in a shallow trench, sheltered from wind, until conditions improve.

Also, plant out hardy border carnations and pinks, preferably in a slightly alkaline soil — add hydrated lime, if necessary.

Spring bedding plants, such as wallflowers (cheiranthus), polyanthuses and forget-me-nots (myosotis) not used in bedding schemes can be planted in other parts of the garden to give spring colour.

Plant lily bulbs if the soil is not too wet. Otherwise store them overwinter in a cool place in boxes of slightly damp peat.

Continue to prepare borders for new plants by digging and incorporating manure or well-rotted compost.

Check that forced bulbs planted in pots are adequately moist. Bulbs showing more than 2.5cm (1in) of growth should be moved to a cool and shady place in the home or greenhouse.

Fruit

Inspect stored fruits and discard any that are diseased. Pears may be ripened by bringing them into the warmth indoors.

Prepare sites for new plants by double digging and working manure or well-rotted compost into the sub-soil.

Let the ground settle — or tread it firm — before planting.

Plant new fruit trees, bushes and canes, and ensure they are firmly fixed to supports. Prune immediately after planting. If the weather is very dry, water the plants and keep the soil in the root area moist. If the weather and soil conditions are unfavourable for planting, heel in the new stock or store in a cool, frost-free place.

Clean the soil of weeds and fallen leaves.

Vegetables

In warm areas, broad beans can be sown under cloches.

Stake Brussels sprouts in exposed positions or draw up soil round the stems to prevent the plants being blown over in gales.

Lift celery as required.

Hoe in a dressing of sulphate of potash among spring cabbages, kale and broccoli.

Set out new rhubarb plants.

Trees, shrubs and climbers

Plant out any new trees, shrubs, climbers or roses in ground prepared last month. Ensure they are firmly planted.

If the ground has not been prepared, or soil or weather is unsuitable for planting, store the new plants in a cool, frost-free place with hessian or straw around their roots. Alternatively, heel them into a sheltered area of soil outdoors.

Protect slightly tender young or newly-planted shrubs with a straw covering or with hessian to make a windbreak.

Check that all supports and ties are secure enough to withstand winter gales.

Under glass

Keep the temperature to the minimum required, and ventilate on fine days but avoid draughts, and do not overwater. Protect the plants in cold-frames from night frosts by covering the lights.

Put chicory plants in pots of soil and cover to keep them in the dark to produce blanched chicons for winter use. This can be done at intervals to ensure successional cropping.

Check stored and resting plants to ensure they have sufficient moisture to prevent shrivelling.

Keep winter and spring flowering plants watered.

Spray, dust or fumigate to keep the greenhouse free from pests and diseases.

Reduce the watering of foliage houseplants, but give those plants in flower the amount needed to keep the soil moist. Protect all houseplants from draughts.

Gradually, increase light and warmth for forced bulbs in bowls that have been brought into the home for early flowering.

. . . and don't forget

Complete the laying of lawn turves. Renovate worn patches on existing lawns.

Continue to rake and brush up leaves and debris.

The gardener's year
December

Flowers

Prepare the beds or borders for sowing or planting in the spring, digging the soil thoroughly and adding compost or manure. Leave the soil rough dug to allow winter frosts and weather to break it down.

Slightly tender herbaceous perennial plants are best covered with straw or bracken to protect them from frost.

Protect Christmas roses (*Helleborus niger*) from weather damage by putting dry peat round the plants and covering them with cloches.

Apply slug pellets among herbaceous plants.

If lily bulbs are received, either plant them if the ground is workable or store them, as recommended last month.

In mild weather, hoe among spring bedding plants and herbaceous perennials to remove any weeds.

Take in further bowls of forced bulbs as the growth reaches about 2.5cm (1in).

Fruit

Check all stored fruits and continue to ripen pears indoors.

Prune established and new fruit trees and bushes. Remove rotten fruits left hanging on the branches and burn them to prevent the spread of disease.

Spray with tar-oil winter-wash to kill winter eggs of pests.

If soil and weather permit, continue to plant new fruit trees and bushes as they are received. If not, heel in or store them in a cool, frost-free place.

Give a dressing of sulphate of ammonia to fruit trees growing in grass.

Vegetables

Harvest vegetables as required.

Check vegetables in store and remove any that are diseased or rotten.

Continue to lift chicory and rhubarb for forcing.

Clear up the vegetable garden of finished plants and fork over all vacant soil in preparation for next year's crops.

Prepare your seed orders.

Trees, shrubs and climbers

Continue planting trees, shrubs, climbers and roses. If weather and soil conditions are unsuitable, heel-in or store the plants in a frost-free place — as previously recommended.

Prune back about half the growth of hybrid tea and floribunda roses to prevent gale damage (final pruning is best done in March).

Complete the forking or hoeing round existing plants.

Protect with straw, or screens of hessian or polythene, those subjects that are not fully hardy and could be damaged by cold winds and frosts.

Tread and firm soil raised by frosts in the root area of recently set out plants to avoid pockets in the soil.

Under glass

Keep the greenhouse temperature at the minimum required level, ventilate carefully, and water the plants according to their needs.

Check resting plants and do not let them dry out.

Cover the lights of cold-frames during frosty weather to prevent damage to plants.

Dust, spray or fumigate the greenhouse to prevent pest and disease attacks.

Take into the home plants in flower, such as primulas, winter cherries (*Solanum capsicastrum*) and azaleas.

Forced bulbs which flower earliest, such as hyacinths and narcissi, can also be taken into the home; continue to take in other bowls of bulbs as they reach the correct stage of growth.

With all flowering plants at this time of year, water sparingly to keep the soil just moist. Lightly spray the leaves daily with water if the atmosphere is very dry, and remove dead flower heads.

Pot-grown chrysanthemums in the greenhouse which have finished flowering can be cut down. Remove them from their pots, and put in boxes. Water them occasionally, and store until brought into growth in spring.

Continue to bring into the home or greenhouse chicory for forcing.

Prune greenhouse grape vines and, if not detrimental to other plants, paint with tar-oil winter-wash.

Sow cauliflower seed for early cropping next year.

Sow mustard-and-cress seed and mung beans at regular intervals to give salad material.

. . . and don't forget

Repair broken lawn edges by turning the damaged edges inwards.

Continue to rake up leaves and debris.

Prepare orders for plants, bulbs and seeds for next year, and plan on paper any new ideas for the garden layout.

Glossary

Acid As soil classification, indicates pH reading below 7, although 6.5 is often considered neutral for horticultural purposes. Normally implies lack of lime, but can also be induced by an excess of organic matter in the soil.

Activator Chemical product (normally a powder or granules) to speed decay of material on compost heap.

Adventitious Plant organ (bud or root, for instance) that appears other than in normal place.

Aerial root One that arises anywhere above ground (for instance, an adventitious root from a stem).

Aggregate Usually, sand and gravel mixture for concrete mixes. Also used to indicate material used to retain moisture on greenhouse benches or as a growing medium in ring culture and hydroponics.

Air layering Propagation technique, layering the plant in air instead of soil. The cut stem is usually tightly packed round the wound with damp moss until roots show.

Algae Microscopic plants (normally green) that thrive in still water and damp surfaces.

Alkaline Converse of acid: a soil with a pH reading above 7. Usually indicates a limy soil.

Alpine In everyday terms, small plants for a rock garden; strictly, those that grow in mountainous regions.

Alternate Leaf arrangement on stem, arising singly on alternate sides.

Anaerobic Able to live without air or oxygen (usually refers to bacteria). *Cf* Aerobic.

Annual Seed-grown plant that flowers, sets seed and dies in one growing season. Term also loosely applied to some perennials that flower and seed in first year.

Anther Pollen-bearing male plant organ, normally part of stamen (*qv*).

Aphids Rapid-breeding sap-sucking pests which also carry virus diseases. Greenfly and blackfly are the commonest in Britain.

Aquatic Strictly, a plant that lives entirely in water, but also applied to floaters and marginals whose roots alone are permanently or mainly submerged.

Asexual Non-sexual; propagation either vegetatively or through division of a plant cell.

Auxins Plant components (chemical, hormone) affecting speed and form of growth.

Axil Upper angle of junction between leaf and stem.

Axillary Bud that grows from axil; usually removed from tomatoes and chrysanthemums.

Bark ringing Cutting or removing section of bark to restrict growth and encourage fruiting.

Basal Generally, referring to the lower leaves. Basal rot is a fungal disease affecting bulbs.

Bastard trenching Old term for double digging (*qv*), the soil being dug to two spade depths.

Beard Tuft of hair on lower petals (particularly irises).

Bedding Plants (or planting scheme) offering temporary — usually spring or summer — display of flowers that have been raised elsewhere.

Biennial A plant that makes its initial growth in first year from seed, flowers in the second and then dies.

Big bud Swelling caused by mites infecting dormant buds of currants.

Bi-generic Hybrids between species of two different genera.

Black-spot Fungus disease, particularly of roses, that disfigures and finally destroys the leaves.

Blanching Method of excluding light from vegetable stalks (especially celery) to whiten the plant and improve flavour.

Blind Failure of growing point of a plant to develop properly; often applied where flowers do not bloom.

Bog plant One that thrives in perpetually damp conditions.

Bole Technically, trunk of a tree; loosely used as referring to the base.

Bolting Premature flowering and running to seed by vegetables.

Botrytis (grey mould) Fungus disease prevalent in damp conditions and badly ventilated greenhouses.

Bonsai Trees and shrubs artificially miniaturized by confining the roots and training young shoots to the required shape by tying in with wire.

Bordeaux mixture Copper sulphate and lime, used mainly as a fungicide.

Bottom heat Warmed soil or compost to give cuttings and seedlings an easier start. Mainly applied by buried electric wiring; formerly by placing in a manure heap (see Hotbed).

Bract Flower 'substitute': modified leaf, often brightly coloured, as in poinsettia.

Brassica Wide range of vegetables of Cruciferae family, including Brussels sprouts, cabbages and cauliflowers.

Break Branch or fork produced by pinching out growing tip to induce earlier and better flowering. See Disbudding, Pinching-out.

Budding Propagation method (notably with fruit and roses) whereby a bud is inserted into a T-cut made in bark of host plant and securely bound.

Bulb Underground stem, usually of fleshy scales, storing food for embryo plant. The term is sometimes used to cover corms, rhizomes and tubers.

Bulbil Miniature bulb on stem of mother plant, usually in a leaf axil.

Calcifuge Generally refers to lime-hating plants (calcicole plants are those that thrive in lime).

Callus Corky tissue forming over a wound in the bark, or thickened tissue that forms over a wound on a cutting.

Calyx Sepals, outer ring of flower parts. See Perianth.

Cambium Tissue or layer immediately beneath the bark, the region of active growth.

Capillary Syphoning action, raising water to the plant from an absorbent surface such as sand or a flannel-type cloth. Lamp wicks can also be used to transfer water from a container to plants situated at a higher level.

Capsule Dry pod of a plant which splits to discharge seed.

Carpel Female flower unit: ovary, stigma and style.

Catch crop Quick-maturing crop raised between others ripening later.

Catkin Spike of flowers or bracts, normally unisexual and pendulous.

Cheshunt compound Copper sulphate and ammonium carbonate spray, used to combat fungus diseases, notably damping off (*qv*).

Chlorophyll Green factor in leaves which absorbs light and converts it to energy.

Chlorosis Yellowing of leaves. Caused by disease, chlorophyll failure, or iron or manganese deficiency.

Chromosome Vital hereditary factor. Chromosomes, minute elements in each cell, contain the genes (*qv*). Plants with the normal count for the species are diploids (*qv*); those with 1½ times are triploids (*qv*) and those with double are tetraploids (*qv*). Modern breeding techniques can deliberately affect the chromosome count in an attempt to produce better plants.

Cloche Originally, a portable bell-shaped glass cover to encourage seed germination and protect early growth; now mainly of tent or tunnel shape and made of plastic.

Clone Collective term for plants propagated vegetatively down the line from one parent. *Cf* Strain.

Columnar Tall or tapering growth.

Compost 1. Growing medium (mainly peat, loam, sand and fertilizers) in which plants are raised. 2. Recycling technique whereby decaying vegetable matter plus activating chemical makes humus-containing substitute for animal manure.

Compositae The daisy family, largest among flowering plants, with approximately 15,000 members, ranging from chrysanthemums and dahlias to dandelions and lettuces.

Conifer Strictly, a cone-bearing tree, but used also to include yew and *Ginkgo biloba*.

Contact poison Chemical (usually a spray) causing quick death of weed or pest at which it is directed.

Container-grown Plant grown in a pot or other container (as opposed to one lifted from the field for transplanting). Container-grown plants can be planted at almost any season as the roots are less disturbed.

Coral spot Fungal disease of fruit, especially red currants, distinguished by red 'cushion' spots on dead tissue.

Cordate Heart-like leaf shape.

Cordon Method of training fruit tree, as single stem. There are also double and triple cordons, with two and three main stems respectively.

Corm Form of bulb, but made up of swollen stem, not leaves, and therefore lacking the onion-type layers.

Corona Crown, or part of flower growth on the corolla or perianth (*qv*).

Corymb Cluster of flowers, flat-topped in shape.

Cotyledon Seed leaf (*qv*).

Cristate Crested; a leaf form mainly of ferns and cacti.

Crock Drainage material placed in bottom of flower pot.

Cross Generally, a hybrid: offspring of parents of different cultivars.

Crown Point from which shoots grow; also applied loosely to a complete root, notably rhubarb.

Crown bud One that appears after a plant has been 'stopped' (*qv*).

Cruciferous (cruciform) Plant belonging to the family whose leaves form a cross-like shape, such as wallflowers and cabbages.

Cultivar A variety raised in cultivation.

Cutting Method of vegetative propagation, using a severed piece of stem or leaf from parent plant.

Damping down A method of increasing humidity by wetting floor and staging of a greenhouse.

Damping off Disease normally caused by overcrowding and too-moist conditions in a greenhouse. Fungi attack stem base, causing collapse of the plant.

Deciduous Plants that lose leaves at end of season. *Cf* Evergreen.

Dentate Toothed edge to leaf.

Dibber Blunt-pointed tool for making planting holes.

Dibble Act of using a dibber.

Dicotyledon Plant that produces its seed leaves in pairs.

Dieback Progressive death of shoot or branch from tip back to stem.

Digitate Finger-like leaf shape.

Diploid With normal chromosome count (*qv*).

Disbudding Removal of surplus buds or shoots to encourage one flower of exhibition size.

Disk Centre mass of florets forming a circular shape, as in daisies.

Diurnal Flowers that open by day and close at night.

Division Propagation by dividing roots into two or more parts.

Dormancy Resting period of seed or plant.

Dot plant One, usually taller than neighbours, used to provide contrast in height, shape or colour in a bedding scheme.

Double digging See Bastard trenching.

Downy mildew Fungal disease, notably affecting cabbages, lettuces and onions, resulting from damp, cool conditions.

Drawn Elongated thin and weak plants grown in dark or too-crowded conditions.

Drill Groove made in seed bed for sowing in a line.

Dutch light Small frame with one top light (pane of glass) used for hardening-off plants.

Earthing-up Drawing soil round stem of plant to keep out light, or to support against wind.

Elliptic Oval-shaped leaves.

Epiphyte A plant growing on another but not taking nourishment from it.

Ericaceous Plants of the heather family.

Espalier Fruit training system whereby branches are spread out horizontally, usually trained along wires.

Etiolated Blanched, the result of plants being grown in poor light.

Evergreen Slight misnomer: the plant gradually moults rather than shedding all its leaves together. *Cf* Deciduous.

Everlasting Another misnomer: reference is to long-lasting ability of some flowers to retain shape and some colour when dried.

Eye 1. Growth bud of a tuber (such as potato). 2. Different-coloured centre of a flower.

F₁ First filial generation: the cross between two pure-bred parents. Crossing, done by hand, results in bigger, better and stronger plants, seed from which does not come true.

F₂ Second generation from crossing of F₁ hybrids.

Falls Outer petals of irises, particularly those hanging vertically.

Fan-trained Fruit trees pruned and shaped so that branches radiate like a fan.

Fasciated Freak harmless condition whereby stem or flower is flattened or two or more are fused together.

Fastigiate Erect, upright form of growth, branches close together.

Fertilize 1. Sexual union of two plants, male pollen transferred either naturally or by hand. 2. Encouragement of plant growth by feeding with manure or chemical stimulant.

Fibrous Thin fibre-like mass of roots: *cf* tap-root, tuber.

Filament Stalk of a stamen (*qv*), bearing the anther (*qv*).

Fillis Soft string, usually green, used for tying.

Fimbriated Fringed, usually flower or petal.

Flocculated Clay soil improved by adding lime to provide a coarse and more porous structure.

Florets Small flowers making up the whole flower head.

Foliar feed A fertilizer to encourage growth, that can be absorbed by the leaves.

Form Variant, or different strain from the normal plant.

Frame Low-built structure with removable glass to protect seedlings and other plants against cold; the intermediate stage for greenhouse-raised plants before planting out: hardening-off. Frames can be 'cold' or 'heated' (with bottom heat (*qv*) or heating cables around sides).

Friable Soil that is light, crumbly and moist.

Frond Leaf, specifically of a fern.

Fungicide Chemical sprayed on plants to combat effects of fungus diseases, such as mildew and black-spot.

Fungus Plants lacking chlorophyll which must therefore feed on live, decaying or dead matter because they cannot manufacture their own food. Many are microscopic and disease-carrying, so harmful; some are beneficial through breaking down tissue and releasing useful bacteria; still others (such as mushrooms) are edible.

Gall Abnormal swelling, frequently ball-shaped, caused by insects, bacteria or fungi.

Genes Molecular material determining genetic make-up and heredity. See also Chromosomes.

Genus A group of plants with similar characteristics, considered as a closely related family. A genus usually contains many species, but can contain only one.

Germination Emergence of root and shoot from seed.

Glaucous With a bluish bloom.

Graft Union of two plants by merging cambium tissue (*qv*) with the aim of affecting shape or yield. There are several methods, widely used in producing roses and fruit trees.

Graft union Point (usually slight swelling on stem) where graft has been made.

Green manuring Growing and digging in quick-growing leafy crop, such as lupins or mustard to improve soil.

Ground-cover Very low-growing plants able to form a compact mat, useful in preventing emergence of weeds.

Half-hardy Plant that needs protection from frost but can withstand a fairly low temperature.

Hardening-off Gradually acclimatizing protected plants to outside conditions.

Hardwood cutting One taken, usually in autumn, from shrub or tree when wood is fully ripe.

Hardy Plant able to withstand most weather conditions without protection.

Haulm Top-growth of vegetables, notably peas and potatoes.

Heel Strip of bark and stem torn off with a sideshoot pulled away as a cutting.

Heeling-in Temporary planting to prevent drying out while awaiting transfer to permanent quarters.

Herbaceous Plant with non-woody stem that dies away at end of growing season.

Herbicide Chemical formulation to kill plants — usually used as a weedkiller.

Hermaphrodite Bi-sexual: both male and female organs on same flower.

Honey fungus Armillaria root rot: deadly 'bootlace' fungus that attacks privet and other shrubs. Usually betrayed by presence of honey-coloured toadstools.

Hormone Growth-regulating substance occurring naturally; some synthetic versions stimulate desired root growth, others kill weeds by over-stimulating development.

Hose-in-hose Unusual flower formation giving appearance of one inside another.

Hotbed Manure heap providing bottom heat (*qv*) as it warms up for plants growing on the top.

Humus Dark brown decayed vegetable matter.

Hybrid Offspring from parents of different species or genera. An F_1 hybrid may be between cultivars of the same species.

Hybridization Art of crossing one or more generations to improve growth and yield, often to produce new varieties.

Hydroponics Soilless cultivation. Plant roots grow in a sterile base of sand, vermiculite or baked clay, and draw food from special nutrients.

Incurved Inward-curving petals, forming a ball-like flower. *Cf.* Recurved, Reflexed.

Inflorescence Flower cluster of a plant.

Inorganic Inanimate: usually applied to chemical fertilizers not containing carbon.

Insecticide Insect-killing chemical.

Internode Stem portion between two joints or nodes.

Joint Junction point between stem and leaf or leaf stalk. Also known as a node.

Juvenile leaves Leaves that differ in appearance from mature growth in some plants, notably conifers.

Keel Boat-shaped central ridge or petal, as with pea flowers.

King fruit Dominating fruit in a cluster.

Knot garden One laid out to strict geometrical design, with low-cut box edging. Also known as parterre.

Lanceolate Spear-shaped leaf, broader in middle and tapering to both ends.

Laciniate Leaves or petals shaped to form irregular fringe.

Lateral Normally, fruit-producing sideshoot or branch of a fruit tree. See Leader and Sideshoot.

Layering Propagation method whereby a shoot, held in contact with soil while still attached to plant, forms roots.

Leaching Draining away of nutrients from soil.

Leader Terminal (end) shoot or branch which, left unpruned, will extend in same direction from trunk. Laterals and sideshoots (*qv*) grow out from leaders.

Leafmould Valuable composting ingredient or mulch; partially decayed leaves.

Leguminous Refers to a member of the pea family, producing a legume, or pod.

Lime Alkaline substance used for countering acidity in soil. Some soils have a predominant lime content. See pH.

Linear Long narrow leaf shape.

Loam Well-balanced soil with even mixture of clay and sand, with good organic matter (humus) content.

Maiden First-year tree (usually fruit) after grafting or budding.

Maincrop Crop (following early cultivars) of vegetables allowed to run to maturity. Usually applied to roots (such as potatoes and carrots) capable of being stored.

Meristem Plant tissue area, usually apical or cambium (*qv*), where cells can divide and multiply. Because of the vast amount of material available, meristem culture is a means of rapid propagation of a number of plants. Meristem culture is also used to raise disease-free stock.

Microclimate The immediate climate, in a very restricted area, closely surrounding a plant.

Mildew Range of fungus diseases in two main types: Powdery mildew mainly affects fruit, roses, and chrysanthemums, while downy mildew chiefly affects lettuces and onions. Both prevail in damp, cool conditions.

Mist unit Automatic device in greenhouses for fine-spraying plants when humidity drops, thus preventing dehydration.

Monocarpic Plants that die after fruiting once, but unlike an annual may take many years to flower.

Monoecious A subject which has separate male and female flowers on the same plant.

Moraine See Scree.

Mulch Top-dressing, usually of a bulky organic substance such as peat, compost or leafmould, used to conserve moisture and keep down weeds. Black polythene is also used.

Mutation Loosely, a 'sport', or change in a plant's inherited characteristics.

Naturalize To plant for permanancy in a natural setting; specifically refers to bulbs planted in large numbers.

Neutral Reference to soil with pH factor between 6.5 and 7.0, neither too acid nor too alkaline. See pH.

Node Joint in stem from which leaf or another stem branches. See Joint.

Nodule Swelling in leguminous roots caused by presence of nitrogen-fixing bacteria.

NPK The formula expressing percentages of nitrogen, phosphate and potash in compound fertilizers.

Oblanceolate Lance-shaped leaf, narrower at base.

Oblong Leaf shape; longer than broad.

Obovate Egg-shaped leaf, broadest at top. *Cf* Ovate.

Offset Bulb or offshoot growing from parent.

Organic Usually refers to fertilizers: 1. Chemical compound containing carbon; 2. Natural manure or compost.

Ovate Egg-shaped leaf, broadest at stem. *Cf* Obovate.

Ovoid Oval-shaped leaf.

Palmate Hand-shaped leaf. See Digitate.

Pan Compacted soil layer, impervious to air and water.

Panicle Branching cluster of flowers.

Parterre See Knot garden.

Parthenocarpic Producing fruits without pollination.

Pathogen Disease-causing organism.

Peat Partly-decayed vegetation, richly acid, widely used in growing composts and, with nutrients, in peat bags and blocks. Available in various forms.

Pelleted Individual seed coated with inert material, often containing nutrient, to aid sowing and germination.

Perennial In general terms, an herbaceous plant that flowers annually for at least two years.

Pesticide Chemical compound for killing insects, mites or fungi.

Petiole Leaf stalk.

Photosynthesis Process by which chlorophyll in leaf converts water and carbon dioxide into sugar, a vital step in plant growth.

pH Stands for Potential Hydrogen. Scale indicating acid or alkaline content of soil, rising from 0 (pure acid) to 14 (pure alkaline). Below 7 is acid; above, alkaline. The range 6.5–7.0 is regarded as neutral for plants and is therefore the best because it will grow the widest range of popular plants.

Picotee With different coloured band round edge of petal.

Pinching-out Removal of tip or growing shoot, or terminal bud, to encourage branching. See Disbudding, Break.

Pinnate Feathery-type leaf.

Piping Cutting (usually of pinks) taken by pulling off a young shoot at a joint.

Pistil Female flower organ, comprising ovary, style, and stigma.

Plunge Bed in which potted plants can be sunk to their rims to remain cool and moist. Bulbs for indoors can also be plunged to encourage a good root system.

Pollard Removal of tree boughs back to the trunk.

Pollen Male fertilizing agent.

Pollination Transfer of pollen from anther to stigma (*qv*).

Pollinator Generally, an apple tree of different cultivar from those around it, pollen from which will enable them to produce a better crop.

Pompon Small ball-shaped flower.

Pot Plant container; traditionally of clay but now also largely of plastic. Usually cone-shaped but also square.

All have drainage holes in the bottom and some have holes in the sides for ventilation.

Potting-on Transplanting a plant that has outgrown a pot into a larger one, the next stage beyond potting-up.

Potting-up Transplanting a young plant to a larger container, the next stage beyond pricking out.

Predator Usually refers to beneficial insects that attack harmful ones (ladybirds kill aphids for instance).

Pricking-out Transferring small seedlings that have recently germinated into pots or boxes — allowing them more space to develop.

Propagation Raising new plants, by seed or vegetatively (*qv*).

Prostrate Low or flat growth.

Pruning Cutting back unwanted parts of woody plants to let in air and light, improve growth and fruiting, and reduce risk of disease.

Pseudo-bulb Thickened stem near surface, resembling a bulb (seen in orchids).

Raceme Cluster of single flowers along the flower head.

Radicle First root of a seedling.

Recurved petals Curving downward or backward. *Cf* Incurved.

Reflexed Recurved, more sharply.

Remontant Recurrent, flowering more than once in a season.

Reversion 1. Condition by which variegated leaves become green or the strongest element in a graft or hybrid takes over. 2. Effect of big bud on black currants, resulting in tiny fruits as in the wild.

Rhizome Tuberous sprouting root.

Ridging Digging technique whereby soil is piled into a peak along an entire strip, thus exposing a larger surface area to weather.

Ring culture Method of growing tomatoes in a bottomless pot, stood on bed of aggregate (moist peat or gravel). Feeding roots remain in the pot, the water roots penetrate the aggregate.

Rogue Plant that does not conform to normal characteristics; a sport.

Root Underground part of plants, drawing food and water from soil or compost. Tap-roots have one main stem; fibrous roots are a spreading mat of fine 'fibres'.

Rooting compound Chemical preparation in which cuttings are dipped to encourage formation of roots. See also Hormone.

Rootstock 1. Plant on to which scion (*qv*) of tree is grafted. 2. Crown of an herbaceous plant.

Rosette Ring of petals close together, or overlapping, on a short stem.

Rotation Succession plan for a vegetable plot, ideally split into three parts, so that no crop is grown in the

same place two years running.

Runner Shoot growing along the ground, rooting at intervals to form new plants. Applies especially to strawberries. See also Stolon.

Sagittate Leaf shape, resembling an arrow-head.

Sap Plant's 'bloodstream': the fluid that flows through it, translocating nutrients and the products of photosynthesis.

Sapling Young tree before formation of crown.

Saprophytic Plant that lives on decaying organic matter.

Scale Thin membranous tissue on surface of stem or leaf.

Scion Shoot or bud grafted on to a rootstock (*qv*).

Scree Bed of grit or small stones to give coarse drainage for alpine plants. Also known as a moraine.

Seed leaf First leaf (sometimes a pair) appearing after germination.

Self-fertile Plant (usually a fruit tree) capable of fertilization by its own pollen.

Self-sterile Incapable of self-fertilization; needing pollen from another cultivar.

Sepal Separate leaf of a calyx (*qv*).

Sequestrene A chemical compound (usually iron or magnesium) enabling certain plants to assimilate minerals normally locked in the soil in an unavailable form. Also known as chelates.

Serrate With saw-tooth leaf shape.

Set 1. Fertilization of flowers and formation of fruit. 2. Certain bulbs (such as onions and shallots) at a stage for planting.

Shard Drainage crock at bottom of a flower pot.

Sheath Tubular leaf protecting a plant organ.

Shrub Woody plant growing out from base and with no trunk.

Sideshoot One growing out from a main stem. See Lateral.

Slip Heel cutting.

Snag Rough edge left by inefficient pruning, providing entry for insects or disease spores.

Softwood cutting One taken as a green shoot from new non-woody growth.

Soil block Compressed and shaped mass of compost (usually peat and soil) in which seeds are sown and remain when planted out, thus reducing risk of setback.

Soilless compost Normally peat and sand but can also include vermiculite or other inorganic matter.

Spadix Flower form consisting of a thick fleshy spike surrounded by a sheath or spathe (*qv*).

Spathe Bract enclosing flower structure. See Spadix.

Spatulate Leaf or flower shape: blunt end, narrow at base, like a spatula.

Species Plants of the same specific kind. Several related species may belong to the same genus (*qv*).

Spike Flower head in which individual flowers are almost stalkless.

Spit Spade's depth of soil; about 30cm (1ft)

Spores Speck-like reproductive (self-fertile) bodies of flowerless plants or organisms.

Sport Accidental genetic change in make-up of a plant, causing unexpected shape, size or colour.

Spur Short branch of fruit tree.

Stalk Stem of plant organs. See Stem.

Stamen Male, pollen-bearing flower organ. See Anther, Filament.

Standard 1. Single-stemmed tall young tree. 2. Upper petals of some flowers (such as irises).

Stem Main stalk of a plant.

Sterile 1. Purified sowing or potting mixture, or ingredient thereof. 2. Infertile plant.

Sterilization Means of cleansing soil of weed seeds, fungi and bacteria, usually by heat.

Stigma Female flower organ: part where pollen is received.

Stipule Leaf-like sheath at base of flower or leaf stalk.

Stock Root-providing part of a grafted plant, receiving the scion (*qv*).

Stolon A runner (*qv*).

Stomata Minute pores, usually in leaves, that enable plant to breathe.

Stool 1. Base of bushy plant producing shoots at ground level. 2. Plant cut to ground level to provide new shoots for propagation.

Stop Removing growing tip to encourage branching or flowering.

Strain Seed-produced plants from a common ancestor. *Cf* Clone.

Stratify Method of helping germination of hard seeds by storing in wet sand at low temperature.

Striated Striped.

Strig Cluster of currants.

Strike To root a cutting.

Style Female flower organ, linking ovary and stigma.

Subsoil Soil below digging depth, normally lacking humus.

Succulent A plant with thick, fleshy leaves or modified stems that serve as leaves; usually able to store water.

Sucker Basal shoot, frequently from a grafted woody plant.

Synonym Usual reference is to an old or alternative name for a particular plant. Usually abbreviated syn.

Systemic Chemical that penetrates all the plant's tissues, attacking pests or diseases.

Tap-root Long, strong primary root of certain plants, stretching down into soil. *Cf* Fibrous root.

Tender Plant that is susceptible to damage at low temperatures.

Tendril Thread-like feeler by which many climbing plants cling to a wall or other support.

Terminal Usually refers to bud at end of a stem, kept when others are pinched out to improve size for showing.

Tetraploid Plant that has four sets of chromosomes (*qv*) instead of the normal two.

Thinning Removal of surplus plants from bed or seed-box to enable remainder to flourish without undue disturbance.

Thong Root cutting, especially of seakale.

Thorn Another term for spine (*qv*).

Tilth Soil broken down into small crumbs, as for seed-bed.

Tine Prong of fork or rake.

Tip-bearing Fruit tree producing flowers and fruit buds at end of shoots ('Worcester Pearmain' apple is a notable example).

Tomentose Hairy or woolly-leaved.

Top-dress 1. To spread and lightly rake in fertilizer on soil. 2. To remove and replace top layer of soil or compost in a pot.

Topiary Art of shaping dense leaved shrubs (such as box and yew) into patterns or forms.

Top-soil Fertile top layer in which most plants root; normally approximately one spade's depth.

Trace elements Natural substances required by plants in minute doses, among them iron, manganese, boron and copper.

Transpiration Loss of moisture from leaves.

Transplant Removal of plant from one place to another, usually where it is to mature.

Tree Woody plant branching from the upper part of a single trunk. *Cf* Shrub.

Trenching Deep digging, to approximately 90cm (3ft) depth and width, to provide a rich layer of manure or compost for certain crops such as sweet peas and celery, but not advisable on heavy water-holding soils.

Trifoliate Three-leaved.

Triploid Plant with three sets of chromosomes (*qv*) instead of normal two.

True leaves Normal adult foliage appearing after the seed leaves (*qv*).

Truncate Flat-ended leaf shape, as though cut across the middle.

Truss Cluster of flowers or fruit.

Tuber Food-storing root or stem, usually underground.

Turgid Erect and fresh-looking as after watering — opposite of wilted.

Type Basic original form, as distinct from subsequent varieties or cultivars.

Umbel Umbrella-shaped flower head, with all flower stalks branching from one point.

Variegated Two or more colours in leaves or petals; generally refers to white or cream markings on foliage.

Variety Variant from original species or hybrid. Some occur naturally; those induced by cultivation are now called cultivars.

Vegetative Propagation other than from seed: dividing, layering, grafting or taking cuttings.

Venation Arrangement of veins in a leaf.

Vernalization Means of forcing, speeding development of seeds, bulbs, and so on, usually by keeping at very low temperatures for some weeks, after which they move rapidly through the growth stages.

Virus Highly infectious disease-causing micro-organism carried through the sap and frequently transmitted by sap-sucking insects.

Viscid Sticky, viscous.

Ward(ian) case Glass container for growing plants, nowadays usually a carboy or similar, housing a 'bottle garden'.

Watershoot Useless sappy quick-growing shoot arising from bud on old branch of fruit tree.

Weeping Said of tree or variety whose branches droop vertically.

Whorled With three or more flowers or leaves in a ring at one stem joint.

Windbreak Hedge or fence provided to protect tender plants from prevailing wind.

Xerophyte Term applied to cacti and other succulents with special water storage system to counter arid conditions of natural habitat.

Zygomorphic Flowers with petals that are symmetrical yet with different shapes and sizes.

Index

Text references are indicated by numbers in roman type, while illustrations are shown in italic numerals.
The glossary of terms has not been indexed as the various gardening operations and terms that are explained are already in alphabetical order.

A

Acacia, false see *Robinia pseudoacacia*
Acanthus mollis 91
A. spinosus 150
Acer grosseri hersii 85, 124
A. negundo 'Elegantissimum' see *Acer negundo* 'Elegans'
A. n. 'Elegans' 124
A. palmatum 91
A. pensylvanicum 85
A. pseudoplatanus 85
Achillea 150
Achillea millefolium 41, 43
Achimenes 174
Aconitum × *cammarum* 150
Acorus calamus 'Variegatus' 172
Adam's needle see *Yucca filamentosa*
Adiantum capillus-veneris 174, 176
Aechmea rhodocyanea 174
Aegopodium podagraria 40, 42
Aesculus hippocastanum 85
Aethionema 'Warley Rose' 168
African corn lily see *Ixia*
African daisy see *Dimorphotheca*
African harlequin flower see Sparaxis
African lily see *Agapanthus campanulatus*
African marigold see *Tagetes erecta*
African violet see *Saintpaulia ionantha*
Agapanthus 150
Agapanthus campanulatus 61
A. 'Headbourne Hybrids' 91
Ageratum 141
Aglaonema 174
Agropyron repens 41, 42
Agrostis tenuis 65
Alchemilla mollis 150
Alder see Alnus
Alkanet see *Anchusa azurea*
Allium aflatunense 160
A. flavum 160
A. giganteum 160
A. moly 160
A. oreophilum 160
Alnus 84
Aloe variegata 174
Alstroemeria 'Ligtu Hybrids' 151
Althaea rosea 71
Alum root see Heuchera
Aluminium plant see *Pilea cadierei*
Alyssum maritimum see *Lobularia maritima*
A. saxatile 70, 168
Amaryllis belladona 160, 207

Amelanchier canadensis 124
American gooseberry mildew 51
Ampelopsis veitchii see *Parthenocissus tricuspidata* 'Veitchii'
Anaphalis triplinervis 151
Anchusa azurea 151
A. capensis 141
Androsace carnea 168
Anemone, De Caen see *Anemone coronaria*
    St. Brigid see *Anemone coronaria*
Anemone coronaria 160
A. × *hybrida* 71, 151
A. nemorosa 78, 168
Angelica 198
Angel's tears see *Narcissus triandus*
Annual chrysanthemum see *Chrysanthemum carinatum*
Annuals 70, 73
Anthemis tinctoria 151
Antirrhinum 141
Anthurium andreanum 99
A. scherzerianum 174
Ants 46
Aphelandra squarrosa 99
Aphids 45, 46, 46
Aponogeton distachyus 172
Aporocactus flagelliformis 174
Apple canker 49
    cordons 115
    'Cox' Orange Pippin' 116
    cultivars 182—183
    cultivation 116
    'Ellison's Orange' 114
    rootstocks 114
    scab 51
Apricot 183
April, gardening in 203
Aquilegia 71
Aquilegia 'Dragonfly' 151
A. 'Long-spurred Hybrids' 153
Arabis albida see *Arabis caucasia*
A. caucasia 168
Araucaria araucana 124
Arbours 29
Arbutus unedo 124
Arches 32
Armeria maritima 60, 168
Armillaria mellea 48, 49
Arrowhead see *Sagittaria sagittifolia*
Artemisia lactiflora 151
Artichoke 188
    cultivars 188
    Jerusalem 108
Artillery plant see *Pilea muscosa*
Aruncus dioicus 151
A. sylvester see *Aruncus dioicus*
Arundinaria japonica see *Pseudosasa japonica*
A. nitida see *Sinoarundinaria nitida*
Asclepias curassavica 175
Asparagus (vegetable) 188
    'fern' 175
Asparagus densiflorus 175
A. plumosus see *Asparagus setaceus*
A. setaceus 175
A. sprengeri see *Asparagus densiflorus*
Aspect 14
Aspidistra elatior 175
Asplenium bulbiferum 55
Aster, dwarf see *Callistephus chinensis*

Aster novi-belgii 151
Astilbe × *arendsii* 151
Astrantia maxima 152
Astrophytum myriostigma 175
Aubrieta 168
Aucuba japonica 124
August, gardening in 207
Autumn crocus see *Colchicum autumnale*
Autumn gentian see *Gentiana sino-ornata*
Azalea 91, 125
Azalea indica 99, 101
A. 'Roshomon' 15

B

Baby's breath see *Gypsophila repens*
Baby's tears see *Soleirolia soleirolii*
Bacterial diseases 49
Balloon flower see *Platycodon grandiflorus*
Balm, lemon 198
Bamboo see *Sinoarundinaria nitida* and *Pseudosasa japonica*
Barbecues 35
Barberry see Berberis
Barrel cactus see *Echinocactus grusonii*
Barrenwort see *Epimedium grandiflorum*
Basic slag 39
Basil, sweet 198
Bay, sweet 198
Bean, broad 108
    cultivars 188
Bean, French 108
    cultivars 189
Bean, runner 108
    cultivars 189
    'Prizewinner' 108
    'Scarlet Emperor' 190
Bear grass see *Camassia leichtlinii*
Bear's breeches see *Acanthus mollis* and *Acanthus spinosus*
Bedding plants 63
    schemes 71
Beds 17
Beech see *Fagus sylvatica*
    hedge of 15
Beet, seakale 109
    cultivars 189
Beet, spinach 109
    cultivars 189
Beetle, violet ground 44
Beetroot 108
    'Boltardy' 190
    cultivars 189
    golden 108
Begonia boweri 175
B. manicata 175
B. masoniana 175
B. rex 54, 175, 206
B. semperflorens 37, 63, 141
Bell heather see *Erica cinerea*
Belladonna lily see *Amaryllis belladonna*
Bellflower see *Campanula lactiflora*

Bellis perennis 41, 42, 73, 141
Beloperone guttata 175
Beneficial insects 44
Berberis darwinii 125
B. × *stenophylla* 15, 62, 125
B. thunbergii 125
Bergamot see *Monarda didyma*
Bergenia cordifolia 152
Betula 84
Betula pendula 125
B. p. 'Fastigiata' 86
B. p. 'Youngii' 86
Biennials 73
Billbergia nutans 175
Bindweed see *Calystegia sepium*
Birch see Betula
Birds 82, 82
    bullfinch 82
    robin 82
Bishop's cap cactus see *Astrophytum myriostigma*
Bitter root see Lewisia
Black medick see *Medicago lupulina*
Blackberries 118
    cultivars 183
Blackcurrants 118
    'Boskoop Giant' 184
    cultivars 183
Black-eyed Susan see *Thunbergia alata*
Blackfly 45, 46, 46
Black-spot 48, 51
Blanket flower see Gaillardia
Bleeding heart see *Dicentra spectabilis*
Blood flower see *Asclepias curassavica*
Bluebell see *Scilla non-scripta*
Bocconia cordata see *Macleaya cordata*
Bonemeal 39
Borage 198
Borders 17
Borecole 109
    cultivars 190
Boronia megastigma 99
Boston ivy see *Parthenocissus tricuspidata* 'Veitchii'
Botrytis 51
Bougainvillea × *buttiana* 175
    'Kiltie Campbell' 176
Box see *Buxus sempervirens*
Boysenberry 185
Broccoli 190
Brodiaea laxa see *Triteleia laxa*
B. uniflora see *Ipheion uniflorum*
Broom see *Cytisus scoparius*
Broom, pineapple see *Cytisus battandieri*
Broom, Warminster see *Cytisus* × *praecox*
Brown top bent see *Agrostis tenuis*
Brussels sprout 109
    cultivars 190
Buddleia davidii 56, 83, 125, 202
Bugbane see *Cimicifuga racemosa*
Bulbs 72
Bullfinch 82
Bumblebee 44
Busy Lizzie see *Impatiens wallerana*
Butomus umbellatus 172
Buttercup, creeping see *Ranunculus repens*
Butterfly bush see *Buddleia davidii*

217

Acknowledgments

The publishers would like to thank the following individuals and organisations for their kind permission to reproduce the pictures in this book:

The A–Z Collection 12, 29 above right, 75, 131 left, 133 left, 186 right; Bernard Alfieri 73 below, 85 centre right, 117, 118 above, 129 left, 133 right, 143 right; Heather Angel/Biofotos 76 above, 80 below, 83 centre, 84, 147, 176 above right; Pat Brindley 10, 11, 13 below, 14, 15 above and below, 35 below, 58–59, 60 above, 63 left, 71 top right, 74 above and below, 76 below, 78, 79 above, 80 above, 81 above and below, 85 above right, 86, 87 above right and below right, 88 above, 89 below, 95 below left, 98 below left and right, 99 above and below, 106, 108 below, 109–115, 126, 129 above right, 139 left, 143 left, 144 left and right, 148 left and right, 153 left, 162–164, 170 left, 176 left, 178 left and right, 183 left and below right, 190–193; R. J. Corbin 16, 17, 22, 23, 38, 39, 57, 65, 116 below; John K. B. Cowley 122–123; V. Finnis 71 above left, 72 below right, 157, 170 right; Brian Furner 131 right; Susan Griggs Agency (M. Boys) 92, 93 below right; Melvin Grey 105 above right; David Hosking 82 above; David Hoy Publications 43, 63 right, 66, 67, 90 above; George Hyde 44 – 48; Paul Kemp 105 below; Marshall Cavendish Picture Library 104 below; Bill McLaughlin 34 above, 93 above left and right; Owen Newman 83 above; N.H.P.A. (M. Savonius) 36 below, (James) 82 below, (Dalton) 83 below; Harry Smith Horticultural Photographic Collection endpapers; 8– 9, 13 above, 24 below left and right, 25, 26 above and below, 29 left, 32– 33, 37 below, 49 above and below, 50 above and below, 51, 57 above, 60 below, 62 above and below, 64– 65, 68, 69 above and below, 70, 71 centre and below, 72 left and above right, 73 above, 85 below right, 87 left, 88 below, 89 above, 91, 95 above and below right, 98 above left, 120 above and below, 166 left and right; Spectrum 1, 50 below right, 90 below, 153 right; Stapley Water Gardens 35 above; Michael Warren 6– 7, 20, 29 below right, 37 above, 79 below, 94, 108 above, 115 above and below right, 116 above, 118 below, 119, 129 below right, 139 right, 140, 144 centre, 155, 176 below right, 183 above right, 186 left, 197; Elizabeth Whiting and Associates 102, 103, 104 above, 105 above left; Paul Williams 2– 3, 21, 100– 101; George Wright 24 above, 36 above, 96; Zefa (G. Seider) 85 left.

Illustrations by:
Ed Stuart 97
Paul Buckle and Terri Lawlor, all other illustrations
Case: Chelsea Physic Garden/Vivien Fifield.

PDO 80-296